C000125633

MAS

The Modern Architecture Symposia, 1962–1966
A Critical Edition

Edited by Rosemarie Haag Bletter and Joan Ockman,
with Nancy Eklund Later

THE TEMPLE HOYNE BUELL CENTER
FOR THE STUDY OF AMERICAN ARCHITECTURE
COLUMBIA UNIVERSITY IN THE CITY OF NEW YORK

DISTRIBUTED BY
YALE UNIVERSITY PRESS
NEW HAVEN AND LONDON

The Modern Architecture Symposia,
1962–1966: A Critical Edition

Published by:
The Temple Hoyne
Buell Center
for the Study of
American Architecture

Generously supported by:
Elise Jaffe + Jeffrey Brown,
the Graham Foundation for
Advanced Studies in the Fine Arts,
and the Architectural History
Foundation

Designed by Thumb/Luke Bulman
with Camille Sacha Salvador

Typeset in Dolly and Helvetica

Printed in Hong Kong
by Regal Printing

Distributed by Yale University Press
302 Temple Street
P.O. Box 209040
New Haven, CT 06520-9040
yalebooks.com/art

ISBN 978-0-300-20995-2
Library of Congress Control
Number: 2014942185

A catalogue record for this book is
available from the British Library.
This paper meets the requirements
of ANSI/NISO Z 39.48-1992
(Permanence of Paper).

10 9 8 7 6 5 4 3 2 1

CONTENTS

Preface

MAS. This is the acronym by which this document has become known amongst the many individuals who have worked on it for more than a decade at Columbia University's Temple Hoyne Buell Center for the Study of American Architecture, and beyond. The acronym refers to the Modern Architecture Symposia, a series of three gatherings convened by the noted architectural historians Henry-Russell Hitchcock and George Collins at Columbia in 1962, 1964, and 1966, in close collaboration with Columbia's Avery librarian Adolf Placzek and the architect Philip Johnson. Each symposium focused on a decade excerpted from what was by then considered modern architecture's "heroic" period. The three events focused on the 1920s, the 1930s, and the 1910s, in that order. Assembled largely by Hitchcock and Collins, the list of participants reads like a veritable who's who of North American architectural scholarship and criticism, then and now: Stanford Anderson, H. Allen Brooks, William H. Jordy, Edgar Kaufmann, Jr., Sibyl Moholy-Nagy, Vincent J. Scully, Jr., Robert A. M. Stern, Rudolf Wittkower, and Catherine Bauer Wurster, among others.

The complete proceedings are collected here for the first time, introduced by Rosemarie Haag Bletter and with an essay by former Buell Center director Joan Ockman, who co-edited the volume, and to both of whose initiative and insight it owes its existence. In the early stages, they were assisted by Inderbir Singh Riar. In its final form, the volume benefited from the keen editorial eye of Nancy Eklund Later, who stitched everything together. Of the three symposia, only the proceedings from the second, from 1964, have been published previously, in a special issue of the *Journal of the Society of Architectural Historians*. The proceedings from the 1962 meeting were circulated to a very small number of readers in mimeograph form, and those from 1966 were never circulated at all. Although some of the participants later published versions of their papers, the great majority never did, adding to the uniqueness and historical interest of the document. The overall volume has been fastidiously assembled from heterogeneous sources: the 1962 mimeograph, the 1964 publication, and, for 1966, an annotated transcript and tape recordings held in the Avery Architectural Archives. Where possible, illustrations selected by the protagonists for the 1964 publication have been reproduced; to these have been added period illustrations of key buildings referred to in the proceedings.

The present volume therefore includes the two introductory essays, the transcripts of the papers presented, with illustrations, as well as — importantly — the often-lively exchanges among the participants and related background material from the archives. The archival material, which offered a solid foundation on which to build, was given to Avery Library in the early 1990s by Christiane Crasemann Collins. In addition, when possible, participants were contacted to address ambiguities or gaps in the record, as were relevant published sources.

We hope these efforts will result in at least two things, of equal value: First, a one-of-a-kind record of a crucial period in the history, and the historiography, of modern architecture in the North American academy; and second, a thought-provoking stimulus for similar, studied reflection in other areas, up to and including the present. For in the end, you have in your hands the record of many voices, many debates, and many arguments that have mainly been heard behind closed doors up until now. Intriguingly, the insularity that has left its mark on every word is also what has allowed those voices to speak at their fullest, unguardedly, and often at their highest pitch. More than fifty years after the words recorded on these pages were uttered, we are pleased to be able to open the doors and invite you to listen in.

—Reinhold Martin
  Director, The Temple Hoyne Buell Center
  for the Study of American Architecture
  September 2014

Acknowledgments

This book has been in the making at the Buell Center for more than a dozen years. It was initiated under the directorship of Joan Ockman, and many people have contributed to bringing it to fruition over the years. At the Buell Center, we are especially grateful to Alissa Anderson, Allison Carafa, Peter Eisenman, Salomon Frausto, Sara Goldsmith, Anthony Graham, James Graham, Anna Kenoff, Diana Martinez, Jacob Moore, Stephanie Salomon, and Inderbir Singh Riar; and at Yale University Press, our gratitude goes to Patricia Fidler, Madeline Kloss, and former editor Michelle Komie. In addition to their role as hosts, the staff at the Avery Architectural and Fine Arts Library has backed the project's documentation and dissemination since the beginning. Former Avery Director Gerald Beasley, current Director Carole Ann Fabian, and Curator of Drawings and Archives Janet Parks merit special recognition in this respect.

Finally, without the erudition and insight of Joan Ockman and Rosemarie Haag Bletter; the enthusiasm and perspective of Robert A. M. Stern; the indispensable advice of Mary McLeod and Martin Filler; the critical eye of Nancy Eklund Later; the support of Elise Jaffe + Jeffrey Brown, the Graham Foundation for Advanced Studies in the Fine Arts, and the Architectural History Foundation; and the valuable collaboration of Christiane Crasemann Collins, this important record would have never come into being.

Editors' Note

The original organizers of the Modern Architecture Symposia worked directly with participants to revise the transcripts of the 1962 and 1964 proceedings. In editing the unpublished 1966 proceedings, we have followed their lead, filling in details regarding architects, buildings, publications, and events we thought obscure while retaining the idiosyncrasies of language that lend these documents a flavor of their time. Our clarifications, as well as those of the previous editors, appear in brackets throughout the volume, as do summaries of symposium dialogue removed due to publishing constraints. Within the notes, our insertions are attributed to "Ed." Cross-references to the proceedings are cited by participant's name and symposium year, followed by page number within the current volume.

Together with the unabridged transcripts of each symposium, correspondence and other documents relating to the MAS are preserved in the George Collins Papers, which are held in the Department of Drawings & Archives of Avery Architectural and Fine Arts Library at Columbia University. Items from the Modern Architecture Symposium series are identified here by author, title, and date but without reference to specific box and file numbers, as cataloguing is still in process at the time of this writing. Additional information may be found at http://clio.columbia.edu/catalog/10820511.

During the proceedings, some MAS participants projected slides to illustrate the buildings they discussed. Slide lists are preserved in the MAS archives for some presentations but not for all. In illustrating this volume, we decided to feature a cross-section of buildings named in the proceedings. Some are canonical works long associated with the modern movement. Others are buildings nominated by the organizers or participants as significant works of their time. A small selection are works less familiar today that were mentioned during the symposia. Curated by James Graham, a current doctoral candidate in Architecture and the director of publications at Columbia's Graduate School of Architecture, Planning, and Preservation, the image gallery is designed to cast interesting light on the historiography of modern architecture as documented in the MAS proceedings.

Introduction

Rosemarie Haag Bletter

On May 5, 1962, Henry-Russell Hitchcock and Philip Johnson came together with a group of colleagues and their students to debate the significance of modern architecture of the 1920s. They had, of course, done something similar in 1932, when, at the behest of their friend the museum director Alfred H. Barr, Jr., they mounted the *Modern Architecture: International Exhibition* at the Museum of Modern Art (MoMA) in New York. There, and in a book, *The International Style: Architecture Since 1922*, which served as a companion volume, Hitchcock and Johnson had forged a conception of modern architecture against which all buildings of the twentieth century would subsequently be judged. Thirty years later, at the symposium they convened at Columbia University, it became clear that the two elder statesmen of modern architecture were no longer united, however, by a singular conception of the movement.

Hitchcock, the historian, had come to regard the period of the 1920s as a "creative (if not the most productive)" time for modern architecture, in some ways comparable to the High Renaissance. But he had also come to view the modern movement as a "closed historical period"—one that was "positively traditional" and "no longer part of anyone's present." For Hitchcock, the modern movement had become "modernism."[1] Johnson, a practicing architect more attuned to current attitudes, had, on the contrary, come to see the 1920s period as only part of an ongoing and continually unfolding movement. For him, the International Style had diminished in significance compared to other developments: it was so eclipsed by other moments, in fact, that it had become a "dirty word."[2]

Once a foregone conclusion, the supposed "victory" of the early modern movement had again become the subject of critical debate.[3] The conflicting opinions that would surface during the Modern Architecture Symposium (MAS) in 1962, and would be explored in greater depth during subsequent symposia held in 1964 and 1966, exposed the widening fault lines dividing architects and historians, critics and curators, in the 1960s. Among those lending voice to these opinions were William Jordy, Vincent Scully, Catherine Bauer Wurster, James Marston Fitch, David Gebhard, H. Allen Brooks, Eduard Sekler, Henry Millon, Peter Collins, Sibyl Moholy-Nagy, Colin Rowe, and Edgar Kaufmann, Jr.—scholars who, like Hitchcock and Johnson, would exert a lasting impact on the historiography of modern architecture.

The MAS were co-sponsored by Columbia University's Avery Architectural and Fine Arts Library and Department of Art History and Archaeology. Hitchcock was appointed chairman, with Johnson taking part in their planning and financing.[4] The primary catalysts and organizers of the MAS, however, were George Collins, a professor of modern architecture in the Department of Art History and Archaeology and at the School of Architecture, and Adolf Placzek, the director of Avery Library. They no doubt chose to bring Hitchcock into the project in light of his preeminence in the field of architectural history. Although technically not involved in the planning process, he exerted great influence on all three conferences through the framing of their subject matter and through his masterful control over the flow of informal discussion. Less directly involved was Rudolf Wittkower, the distinguished Renaissance art historian who was then chair of Columbia's art history department. On leave at the time of the first symposium, he attended only the 1964 and 1966 sessions, and then only as a guest rather than a speaker.

Precedents

A number of conferences held prior to 1962 help put the debates that took place at the MAS in historical context. The most immediate inspiration for the gatherings was the XXth International Congress of the History of Art, also held at Columbia, in 1961. Hitchcock chaired a session on Frank Lloyd Wright and the architecture of 1900, which was followed by lively discussion by Columbia faculty members, among them George Collins.[5]

Another conference, held at Columbia's School of Architecture in 1961, most likely also inspired the first MAS. Charged with improving the public image of the school, Charles Colbert, dean of the School of Architecture from 1960 to 1963, organized "Four Great Makers of Modern Architecture: Gropius, Le Corbusier, Mies van der Rohe, Wright."[6] Held at a time when the fervor of the early modern movement had dissipated and contemporary architects, perhaps predictably, were searching for guidance, the conference talks celebrated the achievements of the "masters." Le Corbusier and Walter Gropius delivered their own presentations and received honorary degrees. Mies, unable to attend for health reasons, was represented in an interview conducted for the occasion by Peter Blake and read aloud at the conference.[7] Wright, the oldest of the four, was present only in memory, having died two years earlier. Although thought-provoking contributions by Collins and Wittkower, as well as by James Marston Fitch, Serge Chermayeff, Ernesto Rogers, José Luis Sert, and Gerhard Kallmann, suggested new directions for the history of modern architecture, the thrust of the program remained the sanctification of the masters. This point was not lost on conference-goers: historian and critic Sibyl Moholy-Nagy (the second wife of László Moholy-Nagy) forcefully objected, from the conference floor, to the anointing of these figures as the great founders of modern architecture.

An opening salvo against a canonical modernism had actually been launched at an earlier conference, which took place at MoMA in 1948. The gathering convened to address the question raised in a session titled "What is Happening to Modern Architecture?" and had been organized in response to comments Lewis Mumford made in a *New Yorker* column the previous year.[8] There the critic denounced the technocentricity of much modern architecture and called for greater emphasis on human functions and feelings.[9] As a model, he held up the San Francisco Bay Area style, with its natural materials and environmental adaptation. Implicit in Mumford's shift away from the International Style was a critique of Hitchcock and Johnson's 1932 exhibition, which made MoMA a somewhat surprising host for the event, and Mumford an equally surprising choice as moderator. The conference, however, was "carefully orchestrated" by Johnson to feature the critic's adversaries, together with a few supporters.[10]

Mumford, Johnson's "old bête noire,"[11] faced nineteen highly opinionated colleagues at the gathering: among the speakers were Hitchcock, Johnson, Barr, Gropius, Blake, and Kallmann, along with Kaufmann, Marcel Breuer, and

George Nelson. Barr was particularly defensive, repeating the claim he had made in his foreword to the 1932 volume that the International Style held in check the "chaos" of "modernistic" buildings such as the Chrysler and Empire State. He lumped the recent architecture of Britain, Sweden, and Switzerland together with that of the Bay Area, which he dismissively dubbed the "International Cottage Style."[12] Always less overtly polemical than Barr or Johnson, Hitchcock identified a cottage architecture of sorts in the rubble walls of Le Corbusier's early 1930s work, and while he conceded that Mumford's Bay Area style might provide a useful model for designing the detached villa, he maintained that it lacked relevance for other, larger building types. Mirroring Barr's, and MoMA's, long-standing prejudice against the more populist, exuberant art deco style, he condemned the Chrysler and Empire State buildings as inadequate expressions of commercial life.

The 1948 conference at MoMA constituted an important prelude to the MAS. Its transcripts document an early shift in the general climate of opinion surrounding modern architecture, along with the emergence of internal tensions among historians and critics of the movement. They also highlight specific points of controversy that would reappear, still unresolved, in the 1960s. The skyscraper typology would become a topic for further discussion on Columbia's campus, as would the Bay Area and other regional styles, as the struggle to reposition works inside and outside the modernist canon intensified. Indeed, Scully, present as an observer at the 1948 conference, would use arguments posited there as the basis for his critique of modern architecture and urbanism in his 1964 MAS talk, "Doldrums in the Suburbs."

The Modern Architecture Symposia

Although Hitchcock was the designated chairman for all three symposia, Placzek and especially Collins did most of the preparatory work for the events. Collins and Hitchcock corresponded frequently, occasionally including Placzek. Letters flew back and forth between New York and Northampton, Massachusetts, where Hitchcock was teaching at Smith College, with quite a few crossing in the mail. (The telephone was used only to resolve urgent problems.) Although there are not many letters by Johnson, there is clear indication that Hitchcock often consulted him; indeed, some of the general organizational meetings took place at Johnson's Glass House in New Canaan, Connecticut.[13]

The correspondence suggests that the symposia were planned as biennial events from an early date.[14] All three conferences were closed to the public. The four organizers selected the panelists, and each panelist invited two guests. Many of the initial attendees returned for subsequent symposia, and new ones were added each year. The conferences were organized as working sessions, with speakers projecting slides on a screen and passing books and other visual materials around the seminar table. The intention was to keep the meetings fairly small and informal, with ample time for discussion and socializing built into the schedule.

During the 1962 symposium, the speakers made only brief statements, leaving most of the two-day event for open discourse. The format of the later symposia became somewhat more structured, with an official meeting on Saturday and informal discussion sessions on Sunday. In 1962 the Saturday meeting took place in an art history classroom in Schermerhorn Hall; during subsequent symposia, it was held in a larger lecture hall at the Law School. The more informal discussion sessions on Sunday took place in Avery Library. For the 1962 and 1964 conferences Placzek also organized an accompanying exhibition of books relevant to the period covered by the talks.

The first Modern Architecture Symposium, subtitled Architecture 1918–28: From the Novembergruppe to the CIAM, covered the core years of the modern movement. It was clearly centered on European events, which, however, were discussed largely from an American perspective. In the 1964 session dealing with the 1929–39 period and the 1966 symposium covering the years 1907–17, the organizers attempted to strike more of a balance between European and American developments.[15]

When Collins, Placzek, and Hitchcock began planning the MAS in the fall of 1961, they approached as speakers some of the best-known historians of the modern movement: Mumford and Blake, along with Sigfried Giedion, Reyner Banham, Leonardo Benevolo, Nikolaus Pevsner, J. M. Richards, and Bruno Zevi. None of them was able to attend. Some perhaps declined because there were no funds available to bring them from Europe; others (such as Banham, for example) cited previous commitments.[16] But in the end the organizers assembled a group of well-respected scholars to take stock of important developments within the historiography of modern architecture and even set some new directions.

Modern Architecture Symposium 1962: 1918–1928

In advance of the May 1962 event, Hitchcock sent to all prospective participants a Statement of Purpose. There he acknowledged that many of the early histories of the modern movement were polemical in nature and called instead for a more objective analysis.[17] He noted that certain architects and movements dismissed previously had acquired more relevance by the 1960s. Two such movements — functionalism and expressionism — would be the major focus of the 1962 discussions.[18] Of the two, functionalism had gained wider acceptance among historians as a pervasive concept of the period in question. Expressionism, which flourished briefly before and then after World War I, had been largely discredited as episodic and inconsequential, but in light of Collins's personal interest in the movement, it received equal billing on the program.[19]

Historians of the modern movement associated functionalism with the architectural developments of the 1920s early on. In *The International Style: Architecture Since 1922*, Hitchcock and Johnson laid out their argument for an aesthetic, formal style positioned in opposition to functionalism, which they perceived as mechanistic and thus lacking in artistic concerns. But by 1962, rival definitions of the term had begun to surface, which posed a challenge to this simple opposition.[20] At the symposium, participants would sift through evidence supporting functionalism as a complex and multivalent concept at work in early twentieth-century architecture.

Peter Collins began the session by identifying two distinct manifestations of functionalism — a mechanistic tradition and an organic one. He stressed that the two were not mutually exclusive and that architects often addressed them simultaneously. Moholy-Nagy enhanced this notion by adding economic, social, and aesthetic functions to the mix, while Péter Serényi stressed the ethical considerations associated with functionalism, tracing its utopian strain back to Jean-Jacques Rousseau, Henri de Saint-Simon, and Jean-Baptiste Fourier. Other MAS participants examined functionalism's origins in England and Germany. The English adaptation of the house to its climate was recast as a kind of functionalism of the environment, a move that clearly reflected the interests of the 1960s more than it did architectural thinking of the 1920s.

The attendees of the 1962 MAS were not the first to acknowledge the problematic nature of functionalism: Mumford had criticized the excessive reliance on a technocentric reading of function and expressed his deep misapprehension of "form follows function" in his essay "Function and Expression in Architecture," published some ten years prior to the conference.[21] Nor would the MAS participants be the last to question functionalism's usefulness, both as a guiding value in creating architecture and as an expository term used to categorize it. Hitchcock commented during the proceedings that functionalism tended to be "expressed as an aspiration more than a reality."[22] Taking this thought one step further, Stanford Anderson, a guest at the 1964 proceedings and a speaker at the 1966 event, would later dismiss functionalism altogether as an irrelevant rhetorical device.[23]

The discussion of expressionism during the afternoon session comprised an even more significant attempt to redefine the received history of the modern movement. By the time Pevsner and Giedion had written their influential histories, expressionism had been long abandoned by most of its erstwhile practitioners, making the historians' amnesia somewhat understandable. The first historians of the modern movement saw expressionism as a brief and irrational interruption of otherwise uniform progress toward a better, more rational future. During the Nazi period, the avant-garde was attacked in general, but those working in the expressionist mode were singled out for opprobrium. After World War II ended, it was more comfortable to resurrect a cohesive avant-garde than attempt to deal with the more difficult or critical dimensions of modern architecture. What undoubtedly stimulated a reexamination of expressionist architecture was the turn by some architects to a kind of neo-expressionism during the 1950s and early 1960s, which (along with new brutalism) represented an implicit rejection of the progressivist convictions of the earlier generation. The shift away from seemingly rationalist forms in the buildings of contemporary architects stimulated historians to take another look at expressionist trends in early modern architecture.[24]

The MAS discussion centered on the historical definition of expressionism and its sources of inspiration, first narrowly and then broadly constructed. Its very character or nature was debated: Was it primarily subjective and emotional (that is, about *self*-expression), or did it speak to something more—a kind of "symbolic expression"? Did functionalism, with its subjugation of artistic expression to other, "functional" concerns, constitute its antithesis? Expressionist projects, although relying heavily on the architect's imagination, frequently aspired to improving external, or social, conditions. This utopian strain, and the mystical or spiritual underpinnings that often attended it, suggested an engagement of expressionist architects with culture beyond the merely personal, even when the works existed only on paper. The contributions of Paul Scheerbart, Bruno Taut, Hermann Finsterlin, and the members of the De Stijl movement and the Amsterdam School were all discussed within this context.[25]

Whom to include and whom to exclude under the expressionist banner became a recurring theme of the session. Collins's broad interpretation, which went well beyond a single visual "style," bolstered the case for including a wide range of works; it opened the door for Kaufmann to propose an American form of expressionism in the art deco–inspired skyscraper. Others suggested the works of Hugh Ferriss, Barry Byrne, and Bruce Goff. How wide to cast the net remained, to Hitchcock's way of thinking, an open question, but just as several modernisms were emerging from the dual-themed symposium, so too were several expressionisms.

Whether the neo-expressionist architecture of the 1950s was indeed a revival of a post–World War I moment or whether it constituted something totally new and different would also remain unresolved. What seems clear, however, is that this interest in the earlier movement, which centered not only on its formal tendencies but also on its visionary and utopian leanings, reflected the deep resonance of the work among architects and historians of the post–World War II era.[26] Like the session on functionalism, the one on expressionism can be seen as an effort to expose the diversity of modern architecture and to reintegrate work excluded previously from historical consideration in light of a shifting set of contemporary criteria.

Modern Architecture Symposium 1964: 1929–1939

The planning for the May 1964 symposium began informally in the summer of 1962, when Collins and Placzek spoke by phone with Johnson, who shared their enthusiasm for hosting another conference.[27] Collins wrote to Hitchcock in November of 1963 to ask whether he would be willing to serve again as chairman and moderator, assuring him, "As usual we will handle all paperwork and 'arrangements' from this end." Collins suggested a thematic approach, with "Modulars and Theories of Proportion in the Twentieth Century" as a possible subject.[28] Hitchcock responded with a rather testy two-page, single-spaced letter in which he asserted his preference for a chronologically circumscribed period: this, he maintained, had provided the "real give and take" at the International Congress of the History of Art that inspired the MAS. He added that, while he was not averse to a nonchronological framing, should one be adopted he would then not be able to serve as chair (in light of too many other commitments) and might come only as a guest. He suggested that Collins could chair the event instead.[29] Collins quickly replied:

> Our symposium is *you*, insofar as such an event can be described in terms of one person.... The state of high excitement that prevailed during the entire day of May 5, 1962 was owing almost entirely to your neat packaging of our miscellaneous suggestions and the amusing and almost tyrannical way in which you managed your cast of characters.[30]

Collins agreed to focus the symposium on the period from 1929 to 1939, and Hitchcock relented.

In the same letter, Collins relayed that some audience members had complained after the 1962 symposium that not all panelists "were sufficiently prepared."[31] As a remedy, he suggested that participants should submit preliminary statements in advance of the symposium.[32] The 1964 MAS was, as a result, more formally organized, with full-fledged papers delivered by speakers on Saturday, followed by a discussion session moderated by Hitchcock on Sunday.

Most of the participants of the previous symposium were invited to attend. Additional panelists and guests included Stanford Anderson, Percival Goodman, William Jordy, Elizabeth Mock Kassler, Paul F. Norton, Christian Otto, Colin Rowe, Eduard Sekler, Colin St. John Wilson, Rudolf Wittkower, and Catherine Bauer Wurster. The Hungarian national and former Bauhaus student Andrew (Andor) Weininger (he played the clown in several of Oskar Schlemmer's theater pieces) also attended as a guest, providing a direct personal connection to the Bauhaus. Robert A. M. Stern served as Hitchcock's assistant.[33]

In his introduction to the symposium (once again circulated prior to the conference), Hitchcock stressed the spread and transformation during the 1930s of the modern movement—a movement that had become somewhat different at the periphery than at its center. He juxtaposed modernism's earlier internationalism with the subsequent flourishing of regional styles, the emergence of nationalistic tendencies, and the gravitation toward neoclassicism in areas dominated by totalitarian regimes. He also noted the shift in modern architecture's center stage from Europe to the United States, due only in part to the emigration of several major figures from Nazi Germany.[34] All of these developments would be explored further during the 1964 conference.

Collins had originally proposed that the panelists should choose the topics of their papers themselves, but documents suggest that the organizers asked some speakers to present talks on specific subjects.[35] Hitchcock's chronological framing proved more relevant to some topics than to others: Some speakers preferred to take 1927 as the start date for the period rather than 1929, in light of the 1927 Weissenhof exhibition and the competition for the Palace of the League of Nations of the same year, and to extend the time period under discussion into the 1940s. Interestingly, not all of the panelists zeroed in on 1929 as a crucial divide for architecture; only those who dealt explicitly with social issues, such as housing, tended to acknowledge the significant impact that the stock market crash and the Great Depression had on architecture.

Several papers focused on American architecture. Catherine Bauer Wurster, a housing specialist who was by then a professor at the University of California, Berkeley, looked at Bay Area architecture of the 1930s, which she defended against earlier criticism as "only 'regional' in the sense that it suited the climate and the way of life."[36] Edgar Kaufmann spoke on Wright's slim but "idealistic" work of 1925 to 1935, and Carroll Meeks, on Yale University's architecture and the Ivy League tradition.

Hand in hand with these explorations of American developments went a reevaluation of the International Style and its legacy in the 1930s. William Jordy began his presentation with a critique of Hitchcock and Johnson's "brisk summary" of 1932 as somewhat formalist in nature and suggested that if one applied only the narrow criteria developed there to buildings done after 1932, few outstanding examples could be found.[37] From his examination of European and American buildings he concluded that, more than any other decade, the 1930s saw the erosion of the Beaux-Arts aesthetic by the International Style, resulting in a hybridity evident in works such as Rockefeller Center.[38]

Mock Kassler (formerly the director of MoMA's Department of Architecture and Bauer Wurster's sister) expanded on Jordy's critique further, to deliver one of the symposium's harshest diatribes against the International Style.[39] "I am convinced," she remarked, "that the International Style, as the dominant movement of the 1930s, produced no buildings of intrinsic value in this country. And I also now begin to question whether it really was very important in the development of our architecture [today].... The International Style has contributed very little."[40]

In his talk "Doldrums in the Suburbs," Scully took aim at American architectural developments during the 1930s within an urban context. He criticized both the "organic" architecture of the Bay Area and the "inorganic" houses by Gropius and Breuer as, in different ways, suburban, small-scale, pictorial, and urbanistically destructive. He called instead for a redefinition of the city along monumental lines, holding up as models the "muscular," "heroic" work of Le Corbusier and the "[s]trong, big, masculine, and powerful" forms of Alvar Aalto and Louis Kahn of the postwar period.[41] Challenges to this call for urban monumentality as a counter to suburban sprawl would arise during the Sunday session, and would continue for decades to follow.[42]

In some of the most inflammatory language of the conference, Moholy-Nagy asserted in her talk on the diaspora that "America looked the other way when Gropius and Breuer built those ugly little houses, leading up to that permanent diner, the Harvard Graduate School of Design."[43] She maintained that architects such as Erich Mendelsohn, after leaving their homeland, never quite adapted to their new surroundings and became party to the "slow death" of American architecture and urbanism in the 1930s. The "halo of greatness" around the former Bauhaus teachers had become questionable in her eyes, as it had for others, with the difference that Moholy-Nagy was fearless in her criticism of postwar architecture and its sacred cows.

If old spheres of influence seemed to have dwindled, new ones had emerged. Several talks openly addressed the effect of political regimes on building between 1929 and 1938: Henry Millon spoke on Fascist Italy; Eduard Sekler, on the reaction to Hitler in Austria; Christian Otto, on National-Socialist Germany; and George Collins, on Franco's Spain.[44] All of them explored the varied accommodations made by architects working in restrictive totalitarian settings. The observed shared reliance on neoclassical vocabulary seemed to beg the question, Is there an automatic link between politics and formal expression? But perhaps more surprising than the answer (Hitchcock and others responded unequivocally in the negative) was the fact that totalitarian architecture — the "architecture of bureaucracy," as Hitchcock branded it[45] — was discussed at all. It was an adventurous undertaking for the period, especially among a group of historians more typically intent on studying the avant-garde. By delving into the topic, these scholars may have been telegraphing the political activism of the 1960s. On the whole, however, this architecture, with its distasteful associations with World War II, was still too charged to be examined by many attendees.[46] Histories of Nazi and Fascist architecture would begin to appear slightly later, when a generation of scholars who had not suffered directly at the hand of these oppressive regimes could more comfortably assess their architectural output.[47]

The symposium concluded on Sunday with a discussion of the presentations and their general methodology. The English architect Colin St. John Wilson, a visiting critic at Yale University at the time, initiated this debate when he harshly condemned the entire proceedings as "so much talk purely at the level of forms," detached from the problems of society.[48] Fellow Englishman Colin

Rowe added that the cataloging of modernism's various regional character-istics somewhat resembled "taking the inventory of a deceased's estate,"[49] a point on which Moholy-Nagy and others agreed. Surely, those talks informed by political considerations challenged this assertion. Still, American architectural history of the period hewed closely to the stylistic-formalist mode.[50]

European architecture, Wilson maintained, always sprang from a polemical body of ideas, whereas American criticism was anti-intellectual: "In America there is no public forum for the exchange of ideas."[51] In a very real sense, however, the MAS themselves belied Wilson's criticism. While not "public forums" per se, they did provide a setting for intellectual discourse (as had their progenitors at Columbia and MoMA). There was certainly no lack of debate in the United States, even if that debate did not conform to the British model. The issue of the appropriate historical methodology for modern architecture would not be resolved at the 1964 meeting, however. Instead it was picked up again two years later, when yet another group of scholars assembled to exchange ideas and discuss issues at the third MAS.

Modern Architecture Symposium 1966: 1907–1917

The same committee organized the 1966 symposium as the previous ones, with Hitchcock as chairman and moderator, and Collins and Placzek as planners. Otto took Stern's place as Hitchcock's assistant.[52] In the fall of 1965, Hitchcock wrote Collins and Placzek that he had just met with Johnson, who was "not only pleased with our ideas but ready again to make a generous contribution."[53] In response to Johnson's request that more "new faces" be added, the committee asked a group of younger architectural historians to participate. Some of the speakers from previous symposia came as guests, and Leonard Eaton, Winston Weisman, and David Gebhard joined the event as speakers.[54] Banham was again asked but could not attend.[55]

The third MAS focused on the decade prior to the one covered in the 1962 conference: the period of 1907 to 1917. Some attendees, like Moholy-Nagy, saw the work of these years, with its neoclassicism and its emphasis on the detached villa, as belonging to a previous era. Hitchcock acknowledged as much in his prefatory statement but maintained that, although not commonly recognized for its role in the modern movement, the period did include the founding of the Deutscher Werkbund and the emergence of De Stijl, and was thus worthy of study.

The symposium opened with a reception on Friday evening, held on the fourth floor of Avery Hall, where a special exhibition had been installed. Collins had asked Johnson and Stern to mount a photographic exhibit featuring what each considered the ten most significant buildings of the period in discussion. During the reception, the two provided brief rationales for their respective selections.[56] Their lists overlapped only in one instance: Wright's Robie House. Both included buildings by Gropius, Adolf Loos, and Behrens. Johnson additionally chose to feature work by Le Corbusier, Mies, Antonio Sant'Elia, Antoni Gaudí, and Josef Hoffmann, while Stern alone highlighted works by Warren & Wetmore, Charles Rennie Mackintosh, Michel de Klerk, Hans Poelzig, and Edwin Lutyens, along with a second building by Wright. Although most of the selections were not surprising given the established historiography of this period, what stands out are the classicizing works by Behrens, Mies, Warren & Wetmore, and Lutyens, which could be interpreted as signaling a wider acceptance of such forms (as well as Johnson's own developing preferences) in the 1960s.

The conference commenced on Saturday morning with a series of talks on American architecture: Edgar Kaufmann, Jr., spoke on Wright; H. Allen Brooks, on the Midwest and the Prairie School; David Gebhard, on West Coast developments; and Winston Weisman, on the skyscraper. Each presentation expanded the range of acceptable subject matter and explored new historiographical methods. Kaufmann addressed Wright with a level of biographical detail and psychological depth uncharacteristic of mainstream architectural history at the time. Brooks examined the influence of the Prairie School beyond Wright and the Midwest. Gebhard highlighted the proliferation of styles on the West Coast (Craftsman, Mission, Spanish Colonial, and more) and situated the avant-garde within the context of popular trends. Weisman grounded his talk in the then startling assertion that "the prime motivating factor [of skyscraper construction] was economic, not aesthetic or social"—a significant reworking of the traditional narrative.[57]

Presentations on European architecture focused on national and regional variations and individual architects or buildings not traditionally included as part of modernism's history at the time. Leonard Eaton's discussion of Scandinavian architecture noted several simultaneous trends, such as national romanticism, neoclassicism, and "Americanism." Theodore Brown's talk on Holland brought to light the moralizing aspects and mystical beliefs behind both the Amsterdam School and De Stijl, neither of which had been widely discussed previously. Once again delivering the most polemical presentation of the conference, Moholy-Nagy identified the Deutscher Werkbund as the only original architectural contribution made by Germany in a thousand years, and Bruno Taut as its most gifted and influential teacher.[58] Several other participants agreed that Taut had been too long neglected.

In contrast to Taut, Peter Behrens had long been recognized as an important figure in the canonical histories of modern architecture. In his talk, Stanford Anderson began to erode the traditional perception of Behrens as an innovator, and recast him instead as more of a redefiner of earlier cultural traditions. Similarly, David Mackay, an English architect working in Barcelona, allowed historians to judge the departure of Gaudí's work from the regional norm in a more meaningful way by positioning it against the backdrop of the Catalan "Renaissance" and the production of his Catalan contemporaries. In his presentation Colin Rowe identified Le Corbusier's previously ignored, prewar Villa Schwob, with its neoclassical features and mannerist details, as the most important protomodern building of the decade and a critical link to the architect's postwar designs.[59]

It was during the Sunday session that the issues surrounding historical methodology that had been debated but left unresolved in 1964 came once again to the surface. Moholy-Nagy delivered an impassioned if somewhat dismissive critique of conventional architectural history as she viewed it, saying, "I spent a very sleepless night after yesterday…because I felt we spent so much time on all these totally irrelevant little villas, and little churches, and little this and little that." [60] Ever the polemicist, she asserted that it was more important to mine the past for its relevant lessons in regard to current societal "problems." In response, Wittkower stated that he himself preferred the more "objective" approach to architectural history: although it was perhaps easier to do history by "hindsight," he found it more important to engage in a broad study of history. "I personally, for instance, am not terribly interested in all the little houses in the western United States," he conceded, "but I think they belong to the panorama. We have to discuss them." Then, in something of an about-face, Wittkower ended his remarks by giving indirect praise to his former student Rowe's use of history to portray broader notions of meaning and order.[61] Clearly, by 1966 the methodological landscape had grown increasingly complex.

The conference concluded with a call for input on topics for a future symposium. A range of subjects was proposed, from urban planning to the theory of modern architecture.[62] In a telling move, one guest suggested devoting two distinct sessions to the two conflicting approaches to history—the "history of things" versus the "history of ideas": James Grady, a professor at Georgia Institute of Technology, wrote to Placzek after the conference, "After Moholy-Nagy's expression of dissatisfaction I wondered if it might be possible in a future meeting to discuss ideas in one session and accomplished works in another."[63] Placzek replied, "Sibyl's expressions of dissatisfaction have by now become a regular feature of the Symposia, but this time she made even me (who is fond of her) a bit hot under the collar."[64] If the range of methodologies employed in examining the history of modern architecture had multiplied, the choice of one approach over another had grown, if not contentious, then certainly impassioned.

A fourth MAS would never be convened. The sheer effort required to organize such gatherings may have hastened the symposia's end. But perhaps more likely, the student demonstrations and political protests against the Vietnam War that engulfed Columbia and other college campuses around the country in 1968 (the projected year of the event) may have created an inhospitable climate.[65] Six years later, in October of 1974, Collins and Placzek would have the opportunity to chair another conference together; this time, at Fairleigh Dickinson University in Hackensack, New Jersey. As its title, "Art and Ideology: Architecture—Can Buildings Reform Society?" implies, the talks reflected the politics of their time.[66] Collins's concern for embedding the discussion of architecture in its political context would reverberate there and in the research of his students, who would publish their work in the 1970s and 1980s. Events such as this, coupled with those of other institutions, including the Institute for Architecture and Urban Studies, founded in 1967, would surely help counter the criticism voiced by Colin St. John Wilson in the 1964 session that architectural ideas were absent from the American scene.

The hosting of the final MAS in 1966 coincided with the publication of Robert Venturi's *Complexity and Contradiction in Architecture*—a book long credited with having propelled architectural discourse toward what, by the late 1970s, came to be called postmodernism.[67] The MAS proceedings show, however, that tendencies toward a critical reevaluation of the modern movement had been gathering speed for some time and in multiple camps. Historians had already begun to investigate modern architecture outside the boundaries prescribed by its earliest chroniclers. They were motivated to do so, at least in part, by their encounters with the experiments of architects who were themselves wrestling with modernism's legacy. Those experiments had resulted in work quite unlike the staid, corporate modernism that drew the fire of postmodernists. The three symposia held at Columbia in the 1960s brought into focus the many modernisms that took place in different contexts and at different times throughout the twentieth century. The talks and discussions enriched the contemporary understanding of the modern movement in its aesthetic, cultural, psychological, symbolic, regional, national, political, ethical, economic, and chronological dimensions. They showed the modern movement to be far less monolithic than either earlier historians or postmodern polemicists would have it be. In their loosening of ties with the canon of modern architecture, these conferences signaled a postmodern attitude in advance of the postmodern movement, that is, before critics such as Charles Jencks could enshrine the modern movement in a new set of misunderstandings.

Notes

1. Henry-Russell Hitchcock, "Chairman's Memorandum," Jan. 1962. MAS 1962, rpt. 88.

2. Philip Johnson, MAS 1962, 123. The full quotation reads, "Well, International Style is a dirty word now. There is a great renewal of interest in things from early Poelzig through work in Hamburg and in Amsterdam. Gaudí to De Klerk have more importance now for eclectics than the International Style of the 1920s."

3. In his preface to *Built in USA: Post-war Architecture* (ed. Henry-Russell Hitchcock and Arthur Drexler [New York: MoMA and Simon & Schuster, 1952]), Johnson wrote, "The battle of modern architecture has long been won." [8]

4. Johnson donated shares of his Aluminum Limited capital stock in support of the first symposium. He also provided funds, through more conventional means, for the second and third events. MAS 1962, 1964, and 1966. The symposia's costs were also underwritten by the Graduate Faculties of Columbia University.

5. George R. Collins and Adolf K. Placzek, "Statement by the Organizers," MAS 1962, 94. See also Hitchcock, "Chairman's Memorandum." According to Christiane Crasemann Collins, the idea for the first MAS symposium was originally her husband's: George Collins then discussed it with Placzek. Crasemann Collins, interview with the author, 14 Aug. 2006.

6. See Richard Oliver, "History VI: 1959–1968," in *The Making of an Architect, 1881–1981*, ed. Richard Oliver (New York: Rizzoli, 1981), 170–2. For transcripts of lectures delivered at the conference, see *Four Great Makers of Modern Architecture: Gropius, Le Corbusier, Mies van der Rohe, Wright* (New York: Columbia University, 1963; rpt. New York: da Capo, 1970). Although School of Architecture faculty members James Marston Fitch and Percival Goodman and Dean Kenneth A. Smith would participate in various MAS proceedings, the School of Architecture did not play an official role in the symposia.

7. One wonders why Mies was not also offered an honorary degree. Mies was extremely competitive with Gropius, whom he considered an architect inferior to himself, but his absence was most likely due to reasons of health; in the last decade of his life he suffered from arthritis, which confined him to a wheelchair much of the time. See Franz Schulze, *Mies van der Rohe: A Critical Biography* (Chicago: University of Chicago Press: 1985), 284.

8. "What is Happening to Modern Architecture?" *The Museum of Modern Art Bulletin* XV, no. 3 (Spring 1948): 1–21. Lewis Mumford, "Sky Line," *The New Yorker*, 11 Oct. 1947.

9. Mumford makes a similar argument in his book *Technics and Civilization* (1934; rpt. New York: Harcourt, 1963, with a new introduction).

10. Franz Schulze, *Philip Johnson: Life and Work* (New York: Alfred A. Knopf, 1994), 182. Although Mumford had been responsible for the housing section of MoMA's *Modern Architecture: International Exhibition*, his emphasis on social issues indicated that he was by no means aligned with Hitchcock and Johnson's aestheticized formulation of modern architecture.

11. Ibid.

12. "What is Happening to Modern Architecture?" 5–8. Barr's critical comments about art deco architecture appeared in the foreword to Henry-Russell Hitchcock and Philip Johnson, *The International Style: Architecture Since 1922* (1932; rpt. New York: Norton, 1966).

13. Collins to Hitchcock, Placzek, and Johnson, 27 Dec. 1963.

14. See Hitchcock to Collins, 17 Nov. 1963.

15. Throughout the symposia, these date ranges were referred to as "decades," even though, as Collins pointed out, each was actually a period of eleven years. Collins, MAS 1966, 237.

16. For correspondence with potential attendees, see the Collins archive. MAS organizers continued to pursue Banham and Zevi for later sessions, but schedules could never be synchronized. Among others who were approached but did not attend were Arthur Drexler, director of the Department of Architecture and Design at MoMA; architecture critic Ada Louise Huxtable; architectural historian Helen Searing, who was then working on her dissertation at Yale University; and Barcelona architect Oriol Bohigas. Cedric Price was expected to attend the 1966 session but never came.

17. The highly ideological *The International Style: Architecture Since 1922* (New York: Norton, 1932), co-authored by Hitchcock and Johnson, had been an exception to Hitchcock's usual approach, which tended to be more academic and expository. Hitchcock's earlier history, *Modern Architecture: Romanticism and Reintegration* (New York: Payson & Clarke, 1929), had in fact taken a broader view of the period, juxtaposing the avant-garde (or "new pioneers") with a second group (the "new tradition") whose architecture incorporated the vestiges of traditional form. Many historians consider this multilayered understanding of modern architecture more representative of Hitchcock's approach, and also more fruitful than the either-or approach of *The International Style*.

18. The themes were most likely Collins's suggestion, since letters exchanged

between Hitchcock and Collins regarding the organization of subsequent symposia establish that Hitchcock was not interested in thematic approaches. Crasemann Collins stated that her husband was intent on dealing with subjects that were, at the time, outside the standard discourse of the 1920s. Crasemann Collins, interview with the author.

19. Giedeon's *Space, Time and Architecture: The Growth of a New Tradition* (Cambridge, Mass.: Harvard University Press, 1941) barely mentions (but nevertheless criticizes) major expressionist figures Erich Mendelsohn and Bruno Taut, even in its later editions; see for example, the fifth (revised and enlarged) edition of 1967. Pevsner's *The Pioneers of the Modern Movement* (New York: Harper and Row, 1936) is mute on the topic. Collins and his wife, on the other hand, had just finished translating, editing, and expanding Ulrich Conrads and Hans Sperlich's *The Architecture of Fantasy: Utopian Building and Planning in Modern Times* (1960; rpt. New York: Praeger, 1962). The volume contained many expressionist designs and seminal texts, some of which were read aloud at the 1962 conference.

20. Hitchcock and Johnson, *The International Style*, 35; Hitchcock, MAS 1962, 98. See also Henry-Russell Hitchcock, "The International Style Twenty Years After," *Architectural Record* 110 (Aug. 1951): 89–97, in which Hitchcock claimed that what he and Johnson wrote in 1932 was still basically true for early modernism but that their book had not been intended to present a closed system, nor had it been meant to be about all modern architecture.

21. See Lewis Mumford, "Function and Expression in Architecture," *Architectural Record* 110 (Nov. 1951): 106–12. Here he writes: "Actually, functionalism is subject to two main modifications. The first is that we must not take function solely in a mechanical sense, as applying only to the physical functions of the building. Certainly new technical facilities and mechanical functions required new forms; But so, likewise, did new social purposes and new psychological insights." [110] Although not so different from his attitudes of the 1930s, Mumford's inflected voice was a great exception in 1951 and remained so, to a certain extent, in 1962.

22. Hitchcock, MAS 1962, 98.

23. See Stanford Anderson, "The Fiction of Function," *Assemblage* 2 (Feb. 1987), in which he identifies functionalism as a "weak concept, inadequate for the characterization or analysis of any architecture." [21]

24. Walter Creese cited the many parallels between expressionism and the architecture of the late 1950s. Creese, MAS 1962, 117. Architectural historians began publishing on expressionism at about the same time; see, for example, Reyner Banham, "The Glass Paradise," *Architectural Review* 125 (Feb. 1959): 87–9; and Vittorio Gregotti, "L'Architettura dell'Espressionismo," *Casabella* 254 (Aug. 1961): 24–50. Full-fledged histories of expressionist architecture began appearing in the mid-1960s; see Dennis Sharp, *Modern Architecture and Expressionism* (New York: Braziller, 1966); F. Borsi and G. K. König, *Architettura dell'Espressionismo* (Genoa: Vitali & Ghianda, 1967). Wolfgang Pehnt's *Expressionist Architecture* (New York: Praeger, 1973) presented an overly broad view of expressionism, which extended to such movements as Italian futurism.

25. During the conference, Hitchcock admitted that Taut had been too much taken for granted. Later editions of his *Architecture: Nineteenth and Twentieth Centuries* (first published in 1958), however, do not include mention of Taut, Vladimir Tatlin, or El Lissitzky. See Henry-Russell Hitchcock, *Architecture: Nineteenth and Twentieth Centuries*, fourth ed. (Harmondsworth: Penguin, 1977). These omissions might also reflect Hitchcock's general bias against unbuilt works.

26. MoMA's 1960 exhibition *Visionary Architecture*, although not dealing with expressionism per se, featured architectural projects that were experimental in the extreme, indicating a renewed interest in freer conceptual explorations among a younger generation of architects.

27. Johnson would again agree to contribute funds to defray the cost of the conference.

28. Collins added that Wittkower was back at Columbia that year and "would be an invaluable asset on the panel." Collins to Hitchcock, 11 Nov. 1963.

29. Hitchcock to Collins, 17 Nov. 1963.

30. Collins to Hitchcock, 21 Nov. 1963. Significantly, Collins also wrote that if Hitchcock were not willing to be chair in 1964, then he would favor "making the event a triennial" by waiting until 1965.

31. Ibid. See also Collins to Hitchcock, Johnson, and Placzek, 27 Dec. 1963, in which he mentions the "laxness of preparation in the past."

32. This apparently happened: during the planning stage Hitchcock wrote to Collins, "There has been a telephone call from Colin [Rowe] and I believe he will turn up probably as a guest. As you are aware, it is very unlikely that he would commit himself to anything that requires even a brief written statement in advance!" Hitchcock to Collins, 20 Feb. 1964. Rowe did indeed attend the 1964 conference as a guest. He would subsequently manage to produce a half-page preliminary statement in advance of his participation in the 1966 session.

33. Henry Millon, who had served as Hitchcock's assistant for the 1962 symposium, had been asked to play this role again but responded late, after the job had been offered to Stern. See Collins to Hitchcock, 24 Apr. 1964.

34. Hitchcock, MAS 1864, 130.

35. In a letter to Hitchcock, Collins complained that Scully was "playing hard to get and fretting about the subject we saddled him with. I have written telling him to choose his own." Collins to Hitchcock, 31 Mar. 1964. Other letters from Collins to Hitchcock suggest that Collins also asked Moholy-Nagy to speak about the "diaspora," which she agreed to do.

36. Catherine Bauer Wurster, MAS 1964, 201.

37. William H. Jordy, MAS 1964, 142. On the use of the term "International Style" in the United States and Europe during the 1930s, see *Progressive Architecture* 62, no. 2 (Feb. 1982), published on the occasion of the fiftieth anniversary of the MoMA exhibition and the publication of the book *The International Style*. The opinions expressed in these essays, by historians such as Richard Guy Wilson, Robert A. M. Stern, and Helen Searing, are far less negative than those expressed by Jordy and Mock Kassler at the 1964 MAS; for Mock Kassler's comments see below.

38. Jordy, MAS 1964, 145.

39. Mock Kassler's comments are made even more interesting by her past association with MoMA. She assumed an important position at the museum in the late 1930s, when Johnson left for Nazi Germany and John McAndrew, who had replaced him, joined the military. Her publications and exhibitions especially during the war years moved away from the aesthetic concerns of Johnson and took a populist and pragmatic direction that included housing—a direction McAndrew had initiated. In 1942 Mock Kassler became the director of the museum's Department of Architecture, but she left MoMA in 1946 when the men came back after the war. See Schulze, *Philip Johnson*, 173–4. She would later maintain that Philip Goodwin and Wallace K. Harrison, both trustees and architects, had supported her tenure there and that Johnson did not force her out upon his return. The official history of MoMA, however, does not even mention her. See Sam Hunter, *The Museum of Modern Art, New York* (New York: H. N. Abrams, in association with MoMA, New York, 1984), introduction.

40. Elizabeth Mock Kassler, MAS 1964, 215.

41. Vincent Scully, MAS 1964, 172.

42. Scully's presentation was subsequently republished and widely read as part of the sizable literature on American urbanism. For publication details, see Scully, MAS 1964, 219–61.

43. Sibyl Moholy-Nagy, MAS 1964, 154.

44. Largely absent from the discussion was the Soviet Union. The inaccessibility of Soviet archives, the limited contact during the Cold War, and the difficulty of the language delayed the appearance of full-fledged studies of Soviet architecture until the end of the 1960s. Among the first historiographic efforts, Camilla Gray's *The Great Experiment: Russian Art, 1863–1922* (London: Thames and Hudson, 1962) focused on art. Anatole Kopp's *Town and Revolution*, originally published in French in 1967 and translated by Thomas E. Burton for George Braziller in 1970, dealt with architecture. Kenneth Frampton's essay, "The Work and Influence of El Lissitzky" [*Architects' Yearbook* XII (1968): 253–68], was one of the earliest contributions by an architectural historian.

45. Hitchcock, MAS 1964, 212.

46. When organizing the event, Collins encountered clear resistance in getting anyone to "bite off the Totalitarian problem." Collins to Hitchcock, 21 Nov. 1963. He asked Johnson to talk about "The Totalitarian Reaction," but Johnson refused, explaining that he did not want to give a talk on totalitarian architecture at all. Johnson to Collins, 16 Jan. 1964, Box 5, Folder 18. (Johnson added, "Personally I think the Nazis were better than Roosevelt, but I haven't time to dig up the proof…. I will have to ask you to ask someone else for 'The Totalitarian Reaction.'" This previously unpublished comment seems to answer the question, which was still unresolved at the time of Johnson's death in 2005, as to whether he had changed his thinking about the Nazis in the postwar years.) After he had been turned down by Johnson, Collins turned to his student Otto, who had "recently done a bang-up job on Nazi planning theory," to prepare the talk instead. Collins to Hitchcock, 29 Apr. 1964.

47. One of the first was Barbara Miller Lane's *Architecture and Politics in Germany, 1918–1945* (Cambridge: Harvard University Press), which first appeared in 1968. The book, which addresses both the 1920s and 1930s, examined various approaches—neoclassical, vernacular, and a modern industrial mode, depending upon the building type—all within the officially sanctioned Nazi context. Anna Teut's *Architektur im Dritten Reich* (Berlin: Ullstein Bauwelt Fundamente), which appeared a year before Lane's book, reprinted a significant number of documents affecting architecture during this period. Robert R. Taylor's *The Word in Stone: The Role of Architecture in the National Socialist Ideology* (Berkeley: University of California Press) would not appear until 1974.

48. Colin St. John Wilson, MAS 1964, 186.

49. Colin Rowe, MAS 1964, 209.

50. For more on the methodological divide separating architectural historians in America from those in other countries during this period, see Joan Ockman's essay, esp. 21–8.

51. See the slightly different versions of this essay which appeared in *Program*, a publication of the Columbia School of Architecture, and *Architectural Design*, referenced in Wilson, MAS 1964, 222n94.

52. Stern had become a problematic presence for Collins. In a letter to Hitchcock, Collins complained, "[T]his time we certainly do not want him on the panel again; his antics last time caused us more headaches than all the other contributors combined. He is a good guy, but not really of prima donna status yet, and if I am to get the Symposium off the ground again I simply must be able to count on cooperation rather than roadblocks from the panelists, and in particular from your assistant (who gets an honorarium for the purpose)." Collins to Hitchcock, 29 Nov. 1965.

Collins had become annoyed with Stern while preparing the 1964 conference papers for publication in the *Journal of the Society of Architectural Historians*. Stern was late in providing footnotes for his own essay and in returning Scully's "Doldrums in the Suburbs" manuscript, which he had borrowed for publication in *Perspecta*. In an undated and apparently unsent letter to Stern, held in the Avery archive, Collins wrote, "I have no intention of having what is on the whole a solid performance reunied [*sic*, ruined] by a young smarty-pants like yourself."

53. Hitchcock to Collins and Placzek, 29 Nov. 1965.

54. Technically speaking, Gebhard appears to have invited himself to speak at the conference. See Hitchcock to Collins, 27 Feb. 1966, and Placzek to Hitchcock, 1 Mar. 1966. In another change, the talks of the 1966 symposium were shortened to twenty minutes to leave more room for discussion than had been available in the previous sessions. Collins to Hitchcock, 29 Nov. 1965.

55. The organizers did not have funds to cover Banham's travel expenses but were hoping he would be in the United States at the time of the symposium; this turned out not to be the case. Collins to Hitchcock, 29 Nov. 1965; Placzek to Hitchcock, 8 Jan. 1966.

56. For notes from Johnson's and Stern's presentations, see 234–6.

57. Winston Weisman, Preliminary Statement, MAS 1966.

58. Moholy-Nagy, MAS 1966, 280–4.

59. Rowe's talk was a reprise in a much briefer version of his essay "Mannerism and Modern Architecture," published in the *Architectural Review* in 1950 and reprinted later in Rowe's *Mathematics of the Ideal Villa and Other Essays* (Cambridge, Mass.: MIT, 1976), 30–57.

60. Moholy-Nagy, MAS 1966, 304.

61. Rudolf Wittkower, MAS 1966, 310–1.

62. Collins solicited ideas directly from scholars after the symposium adjourned. Alvin Boyarsky, the American director of the Architectural Association in London, wrote, "It might be well to concentrate on the development of the theory of architecture."

63. Grady to Placzek, 20 May 1966.

64. Placzek to Grady, 27 May 1966.

65. Crasemann Collins, interview with the author. George and especially Christiane Crasemann Collins were involved in a demonstration against the construction of a university gymnasium on public parkland (Morningside Park) between the Columbia campus and Harlem, which played a large role in precipitating the events on campus somewhat later.

66. The proceedings were subsequently published as "Symposium on Politics and Architecture," in *Via* 4 (1986): 154–71.

67. Robert Venturi, *Complexity and Contradiction in Architecture* (Cambridge, Mass.: MIT Press, 1966). An excerpt of the book also appeared in *Perspecta* in 1965.

Looking Back at the 1960s Looking Back:
History and Historiography
at the Modern Architecture Symposia

Joan Ockman

Between the world of "current events" and the world of "history" there is ever an
indeterminate limbo; nor does the world of history, of that which is well and truly past,
follow the world of the present at an even distance and a regular pace.

—Henry-Russell Hitchcock, Modern Architecture Symposium, 1962

The Modern Architecture Symposia (MAS) brought together at Columbia University a highly distinguished group of architectural historians, their invited guests, and students. Only the 1964 proceedings were widely disseminated, published in March 1965 as a special issue of the *Journal of the Society of Architectural Historians*. The 1962 proceedings were distributed to a relatively small number of scholars as an edited transcript, and the 1966 proceedings, while conserved in the archives of Avery Architectural and Fine Arts Library as a transcript, with hand-written emendations by George Collins, were never published.[1] Most scholars have therefore known the MAS only secondhand, and the conferences have failed to receive the attention they deserve as documents of an important moment of ferment in both the reception of modern architecture and the evolution of American architectural scholarship. Collectively, they attest to the conceptual and methodological evolution in professional architectural-historical scholarship that took place over the course of the twentieth century. This essay examines the historiographic and ideological debates that surrounded the three symposia.

The purpose of the MAS was to take stock of the present state of architectural research and publication in both Europe and the United States, to highlight scholarly differences and lacunae, and to exchange new findings. As Henry-Russell Hitchcock, who presided over all three events, reminded the participants in a memorandum preceding the 1966 symposium:

> [T]he purpose of these gatherings has never been to arrive at conclusions,
> even tentative, but rather to revive historical and critical interest in topics
> that have long been taken too much for granted—to revive interest and to
> throw light on half-forgotten divergences in theory and in form that have
> often proved to be almost as lively matters for discussion today as they were
> in the periods reviewed.[2]

Yet while the stated objective was straightforward enough—namely, to broaden architectural knowledge of the first half of the twentieth century—and while the atmosphere was collegial and not atypical of other elite academic gatherings, the symposia also served to expose cultural shifts and generational rifts that were occurring in the 1960s—in the field of architectural scholarship as in virtually all other aspects of American society. Indeed, while the 1966 meeting concluded with a general consensus that many more topics remained to be considered, an intended fourth symposium, to take place in 1968, never occurred, not only because of the increasingly volatile political climate on Columbia's campus at the time but also because of a tacit recognition that some kind of watershed had been crossed.

At the time of the MAS, Collins, one of the two chief organizers, held a joint appointment at Columbia in the Department of Art History and Archaeology and the School of Architecture, and was engaged in writing on city planning, Spanish architecture, and the architecture of fantasy. Adolf Placzek, the other main organizer, was an émigré scholar who had studied medicine and architectural history in Vienna before fleeing Nazism for London. Subsequently moving to New York, he took up library science at Columbia and became the head librarian of Avery Library. To each of the conferences, Placzek contributed a review of the "literature of the decade," and in 1962 and 1964 he curated an accompanying exhibition of books and journals.[3] Collins and Placzek together with Philip Johnson persuaded Hitchcock to serve as chairman of the three symposia, and Johnson also provided funding for them.

In the early 1960s, Hitchcock was in between appointments at Smith College and the Institute of Fine Arts at New York University. Having published his first important book, *Modern Architecture: Romanticism and Reintegration*, in 1929, not long after completing his education at Harvard University, he was the acknowledged *éminence grise* of nineteenth- and twentieth-century American architectural historiography. The stamp of his formidable intellect and wide-ranging knowledge would be evident throughout the proceedings.

The participants of the MAS ranged in age from those, like Hitchcock and Johnson, born shortly after the turn of the century, to a middle generation born in the 1910s and 1920s, to a handful of recently minted Ph.D.s born during the Great Depression and years prior to World War II. The last group largely comprised students of one or more of the older professors. In addition to this academic succession, there was also an assorted representation of nonacademics—architectural practitioners, museum curators, and critics. About one quarter of the participants were either born or educated outside the United States. The attendees also varied considerably in their training. Many, including the organizers themselves, did not hold doctoral degrees, reflecting both the interruption of their studies by World War II and the fluidity still existing among disciplines and career paths in that era—a situation that would change in coming decades with increasing professionalization and greater demand for specialization.

Despite the international purview of the subject matter and the varied background of the participants, however, the complexion and agenda of the symposia were decidedly American.[4] Indeed, much as Hitchcock and Johnson's International Style exhibition at the Museum of Modern Art (MoMA) in 1932 had recast the progressive architectural developments in Europe in an image more acceptable to the American public, so the three conferences, by enlarging the historical panorama of modern architecture to give developments in the United States greater attention, may be seen as a bid to increase the prestige of American architectural scholarship within post–World War II culture.

Problems of Historical Distance, Cultural Difference, and Periodization

The topics the MAS addressed were relatively new as scholarly matters: as of 1962, thirty years after the International Style exhibition, only one doctoral dissertation had yet been written in the United States on European modern architecture.[5] Glaring gaps in scholarly knowledge existed, which became a repeated refrain at the symposia and a special preoccupation of Hitchcock. Little or nothing existed in English, for example, on developments in the Soviet Union and Eastern Europe, despite the important contributions of those regions to modern architecture during the various decades under consideration; this was, of course, not entirely surprising in the Cold War context.[6] Yet work on the American skyscraper was equally spotty. This deficiency, to which Winston Weisman called attention at the 1966 meeting, reflected a modernist bias against the eclecticism exhibited by that building type during the early decades of its development and, indeed, raised a fundamental question of nomenclature: did "modern architecture" designate a specific ideological conception and formation, or did the term simply denote a chronological period?

This was a loaded question, tied to the very meaning and autonomy of the discipline. Hitchcock and the organizers had chosen a decade structure for each meeting: the 1962 symposium focused on the years 1918 to 1928; the 1964 meeting, on the period from 1929 to 1939; and the 1966 meeting, on the years 1907 to 1917. As various participants had occasion to comment during the successive symposia, this framing device imposed artificial breaks on a continuously unfolding narrative and served to expose the nonsynchronicity of architectural history, both in its respective cultural contexts and in relation to the history of modernity in general. While global events, such as the two world wars and the Great Depression, could perhaps be taken as universal demarcation points, their impact on different architectural developments varied, and the chronological bracketing also underscored the differences between, say, the new architecture of Weimar Germany and that in the United States during the same years. Placzek reported:

> [I]t is rather significant how much trouble we had to agree on a take-off date. Mr. [Robert A. M.] Stern argued that architecturally 1927 was far more decisive than 1929. This brings up a point of methodology. How should art historians properly date — in decades, or even centuries? Should we follow historical events of sometimes cataclysmic importance? These are rarely immediately followed by equally dramatic breaks in style. Undoubtedly the collapse of the German and the American economies in 1929 was such an event. Naturally, nothing equally drastic happened in architecture.... This, of course, is a problem which extends to all history writing or history arranging.[7]

That historiography was a matter of "arranging" as much as "writing" was a key insight.

A related problem for historians of modern architecture in the 1960s looking back at the first half of the century was how to gain an objective view of relatively recent developments. This task could be especially fraught for those who had witnessed or even participated in the events of the decades under consideration. For example, for Sibyl Moholy-Nagy — whose father had been a prominent architect in Dresden, Germany, during the early years of the century and whose husband, László Moholy-Nagy, had been one of modern architecture's protagonists—it was difficult not to take a polemical stance. Despite the questioning to which modern architecture had been subjected in the 1950s by an important group of postwar architects and critics (a subject to which we shall return), the achievement of its basic values and aims remained an unfinished project for many, bound up with the radical and traumatic experiences of twentieth-century modernity. As Eduard Sekler, a boy in Vienna in the 1930s when his family was forced to leave Austria, acknowledged in 1964:

> I was...reminded forcefully that there is a tremendous difference between "personal time" and "historic time," and that it was impossible for me to achieve the kind of dispassionate judgment in the handling of material for this period which we all at least *aim* for when handling historical evidence. I was at the same time too close and too personally involved.... "Personal time" is something very non-homogeneous; some events assume enormous importance and others seem to have faded out; personal judgment prevails and significance may be apportioned in a very different fashion from the way in which it is distributed by later historians. I think this distinction, which I had to rediscover for myself here, though I knew about it in theory from my methodological training, is something which is rather important to keep in mind.[8]

On the other hand, for historians who had come of age in the United States, the recent past was less psychologically and emotionally charged. In his 1955 essay "Three Decades of Art History in the United States: Impressions of a Transplanted European," Erwin Panofsky suggested that geographic and cultural distance could have a similar kind of effect on scholars to historical distance:

> The European scholars either unconsciously yielded to, or unconsciously struggled against, deep-rooted emotions which were traditionally attached to such questions as whether the cubiform capital was invented in Germany, France, or Italy.... Seen from the other side of the Atlantic, the whole of Europe from Spain to the Eastern Mediterranean merged into one panorama the planes of which appeared at proper intervals and in equally sharp focus.... In the United States such men as Alfred Barr and Henry-Russell Hitchcock, to name only two of the pioneers in this field, could look upon the contemporary scene with the same mixture of enthusiasm and detachment, and write about it with the same respect for historical method and concern for meticulous documentation, as are required of a study on fourteenth-century ivories or fifteenth-century prints. "Historical distance" (we normally require from sixty to eighty years) proved to be replaceable by cultural and geographical distance.[9]

If detachment and empiricism tended to be characteristic of earlier American scholars, however, the wave of intellectuals propelled by the European events onto university campuses in the United States from the mid-1930s onward introduced new ideas and attitudes. These would be organically absorbed by the upcoming generation of American architectural historians. Panofsky was not among those in attendance at the MAS, but as a preeminent émigré intellectual (based first at New York University's Institute of Fine Arts and then at Princeton University's Institute for Advanced Study) he would inflect American scholarship in the direction of principles of symbolic meaning. The convergence of

Continental thought with native American values resulted in a "positivistic *Kunstwissenschaft*," hailed by many in the 1950s as a "providential synchronism" and one of the triumphs of postwar liberalism.[10]

Not all American scholars initially found this convergence sympathetic, however. William Jordy, for one, a student of Panofsky's at the Institute of Fine Arts in the early 1940s and an attendee at the 1964 and 1966 MAS, found the Germanic orientation too rigid for his liking. He eventually chose to complete his doctoral studies in Yale University's newly established American Studies program.[11] Two decades later, however, in his most ambitious and widely acclaimed essay, "The Symbolic Essence of Modern European Architecture of the Twenties and Its Continuing Influence," of 1963, Jordy would coin the concept of "symbolic objectivity" to characterize what he saw as radically new about the architecture of the 1920s. In seeking to reconcile modern architecture's idealist foundations with its factual, scientific side, Jordy could hardly have arrived at a more compact synthesis of European and American thought.[12]

A Native Preference for Facts and Forms, and Its Critique

By the 1980s, "theory" would become so dominant in architectural discourse that the term came to designate an autonomous field of specialization. Yet in the early 1960s the pursuit of theoretical speculation was relatively rare and even suspect for American architectural historians. During World War II, the word had acquired ideological and illiberal connotations, as in "race theory," for example. The antipathy to theoretical discourse may also be traced to an earlier period. In the 1920s, when historians in the visual arts undertook to modernize the field by shedding the provincialism of genteel taste, hagiography, and Ruskinian moral sentiment that had variously marked historiography in the United States to that point, they embraced the ideal of "fastidious scholarship."[13] This meant eschewing dogmatic approaches and a priori assumptions in favor of empirically derived evidence, direct perceptual experience, and a close focus on the formal and material qualities of the object of study.[14] Unlike architectural critics and journalists, from whose engagement with the practices and issues of the day they studiously took their distance, they placed paramount value on expert technique and careful philology, and they also chose to apply their tools of stylistic connoisseurship and formal analysis to circumscribed topics, inclining to neglected or undervalued areas of study. This was in part out of a sense of being Johnny-come-latelies with respect to their European forerunners and in part out of a sort of democratic pluralism.

This American attitude became ingrained, and it would prevail for several decades, notwithstanding the influence of the émigré scholars. As James Ackerman stated at the end of the 1950s, a time when the social sciences reached the apex of their prestige in American academia:

> The typical American art historian is, like his fellow scientist and businessman, distinguished for his know-how. He has developed sensitive techniques for dealing with historical data, and is singularly free of national or parochial biases. He does not twist facts to fit a theory, because for him facts are sacrosanct. He publishes only when he has new information to offer, and seldom writes vague

and subjective books for sale at Christmas. Sparing no pains to thoroughly investigate his subject, he is characteristically reliable.[15]

Such, indeed, may be said to have been the intellectual predisposition of Hitchcock, who, in a reminiscence written in 1949, unapologetically attributed his preference for a nonpartisan, inclusivist approach—what he described as a "liberal attitude"—to his training at Harvard in the 1920s.[16] Striving to balance "an informed interest in the present and a perpetual awareness of the past," he was not unmindful, as Helen Searing and others have emphasized, of the social, cultural, and material contexts surrounding the architecture about which he wrote. But he was "not very interested in architectural theory," as Searing puts it,[17] and he was constitutionally averse to ideological argumentation. At the 1966 symposium Hitchcock stated:

> The early histories of modern architecture were inevitably works of propaganda, whether they were written by architects or by critics. At some point (it is hard to say exactly when) we suddenly realized that this propaganda had produced myths, and we began to desire to investigate what lay behind these myths and to dissolve them.... [W]e are no longer merely concerned with what, at the beginning, were thought to have been the few constituent elements. It is very hard for us to say now what is constituent until we have the broader type of examination that we have tried to carry through here.[18]

Hitchcock's reference to modern architecture's "constituent elements" was an unmistakable rebuke of Sigfried Giedion's *Space, Time and Architecture*, published in 1941, which had explicitly aimed—in both its effort to identify the "constituent facts" of modern architecture and its Hegelian unfolding—to program architecture's future direction.

Of course, Hitchcock himself had indisputably played a promotional role in bringing modern architecture to triumph in the United States as co-curator of the International Style exhibition in 1932. He later sought, however, to blunt the polemical thrust of that event.[19] In the post–World War II period he continued to produce architectural criticism, writing with genuine appreciation and insight about the buildings of his own time, from the work of Skidmore, Owings & Merrill to new architecture in Latin America. At the same time, his "catholicity of judgment" and penchant for "multiplying possible points of view," as Colin Rowe would put it, increasingly made his scholarly publications into thickets of factual information.[20] Rowe, in an astute review of Hitchcock's *Architecture: Nineteenth and Twentieth Centuries*, wrote admiringly of the American historian's encyclopedic erudition and especially applauded Hitchcock for having refused to buy into the teleological claims of modern architecture: "The disappearance of the idea that Modern architecture is going to redeem the world is what most strikingly differentiates Hitchcock's book from earlier treatments of the same period. Obviously Modern architecture is not going to redeem the world." [21] But Rowe was nonetheless forced to conclude that *Architecture: Nineteenth and Twentieth Centuries* was "a book without a climax." [22] While a lack of tendentiousness might be appropriate in writing about the Anglo-American architectural tradition, Rowe reflected, Hitchcock's "superb account of stylistic manifestations, running on as it does without reference to ideas" was inadequate for purposes of assessing so ideologically charged and intellectually poignant a body of work as that of, say, Le Corbusier.[23]

Ironically, Hitchcock's ostensibly value-free objectivity had the potential to be not entirely innocent of ideology itself. As Rowe would recognize later, when reconsidering the impact of MoMA's International Style show, the curators' effort to divest the European work of its original social and political under-pinnings — their recasting of modern architecture as primarily a formal and stylistic manifestation — had had its own radical aftereffects, whether or not these were consciously contemplated at the time: namely, of making modern architecture "safe for capitalism."[24] (Catherine Bauer had actually said much the same thing in 1932; the exhibition, she wrote in a letter to Lewis Mumford, had made modern architecture "safe for millionaires."[25]) The triumph of liberalism, it turned out, did not spell the end of ideology, as its apologists claimed in the 1950s, but rather amounted to another ideology, with an implicit value system of its own.

Rowe, one of the most original architectural thinkers of his generation, attended both the 1964 and 1966 symposia, where he could only have felt himself awkwardly suspended between his two former mentors: Hitchcock and Rudolf Wittkower. Having written a doctoral dissertation on Inigo Jones under Wittkower at the Warburg Institute in the late 1940s, Rowe had come to Yale in 1952 in order to do postgraduate work under Hitchcock — a conscious decision to temper the effects of the Germanic ambiance in which he had been immersed in London with an American perspective. Like Hitchcock, Rowe had become strongly disaffected with modern architecture's utopian afflatus and, by the mid-1950s, fusing Wittkower's strong history of ideas with Hitchcock's connoisseurial historiography, had arrived at his own personal synthesis of their discrepant approaches. In the meantime, Wittkower had become chair of Columbia's art history department.[26] Rowe's intervention in the discussion session at the 1964 symposium attests to his continuing difficulty in reconciling his own proclivity for intellectual engagement with Hitchcock's "cultural agnosticism":

> I did feel yesterday that I was rather being an observer of a number of people per-haps taking the inventory of a deceased's estate. And I also felt there were a great many people, let's say, not seeing the wood for the trees. I thought that all the exotic trees in a forest were being itemized; but I felt, to some extent, the animat-ing principle of the forest was not being discriminated, not being observed.... What I am really trying to do, Mr. Hitchcock, is inject into your territory a method which Mr. Wittkower used for the Renaissance. He produced the idea of the Renaissance as the projection of the Platonic cosmos, and one is convinced that the 1920s and the 1930s, to be really alive, have to be treated in some way or other like this.[27]

How, Rowe asked, could one make sense of the architectural developments of the 1920s and 1930s without reference to the atmosphere of "millennial pol-itics" and committed socialism that surrounded them? Rowe's own politics, it should be noted, were more right than left; his intellectual pantheon included figures such as Edmund Burke, Benjamin Disraeli, and Karl Popper. Yet while Marxism was "in bad odor" in the late 1950s — "It is extremely difficult and unpleasant to deal with this sort of matter," Rowe acknowledged — it was, in his opinion, the "vital principle" that characterized the earlier period of history, and the historian had perforce to engage it in order to bring its architecture and ideas to life.[28]

More generally, transplanted historians such as Rowe were unafraid to take on large ideas. In contrast to the edifying, politely appreciative, and democratic but parochial and fact-oriented Americans,[29] they were prepared to go out on a limb without fear of dilettantism. In this regard, Rowe acknowledged at the 1964 symposium that he felt closest kinship, at least temperamentally, to Colin St. John Wilson and Moholy-Nagy. Wilson, a practicing architect from England on the faculty of the School of Architecture at Cambridge University and also a visiting professor at Yale at this date, had begun his career in the London County Council Architects' Office in the early 1950s, a time when Corbusian ideas heavily influenced Britain's leading architects. In his brief talk at the symposium, entitled "The Committed Architect," Wilson stated that architecture was always the carrier of "a body of ideas" made manifest in "the body of a building." Noting that he was speaking "as a sort of foreigner in your midst," he continued:

> I am truly surprised to hear so much talk purely at the level of forms, and all I can say now is that to have called the International Style the "International Style" in 1932 was indeed to point out that it had died. To mention the battle which started within CIAM and which is still perhaps being waged now by the young Angries and the Brutalists, or whatever you would like to call them — the younger generation which feels this architecture of ideas has been betrayed in some way — is to raise a note which has been absent here today.[30]

European Commitment Versus American Agnosticism

Wilson's invocation of the battle within CIAM and the "young Brutalists" was, of course, a reference to the ideas and stance of the British architects Alison and Peter Smithson and their continental colleagues in Team 10. These self-appointed representatives of the new generation of European architecture had mounted an aggressive attack against the International Congresses of Modern Architecture, since the late 1920s the institutional standard-bearer of modern architecture, condemning the organization's functionalist orthodoxy and offering a vision of modern architecture and urbanism more attuned to the specificities of inhabitation and everyday life. The conflict between Team 10 and CIAM, whose general secretary, elder statesman, and historian was Giedion, lasted through the 1950s and culminated in CIAM's dissolution in 1959. In 1962, the year of the first Columbia symposium, the *Team 10 Primer*, a set of position statements by the group's various members, appeared in the British journal *Architectural Design*.[31] Yet Wilson's comments were the only allusion at the three MAS meetings to these important developments, whose implications extended not just to contemporary architectural practice but also to the historical debate on the modern movement.

Likewise absent from the three symposia was an architectural historian who was deeply engaged in the European rethinking of modern architecture, Reyner Banham. A friend of both Rowe and Wilson, Banham had not only been the initial chronicler of the new brutalist phenomenon in Britain but was the author of a revisionist history of modern architecture that was published in 1960, *Theory and Design in the First Machine Age* (to which we shall return). Although twice invited to take part in the MAS, Banham declined, citing other commitments. Another architect who was part of Team 10's circle in the 1960s, the Italian Giancarlo de Carlo, and who was in the United States as a guest teacher at Yale, was expected to speak at the 1966 symposium but did not appear. A decade earlier, De Carlo had been a member of the editorial board of the Italian journal *Casabella-Continuità*, which, under the editorship of Ernesto Rogers, was one of the most tendentious and influential architectural journals in the world. Yet the searching philosophical and historical reassessments of modern architecture that were carried out within the folds of CIAM and in the pages of the leading European journals in the 1950s largely remained outside the purview of American architectural historians until later.[32] Rather, the rethinking of "modernism," as modern architecture was increasingly known in the United States, continued to center on matters of form and style.

The other speaker whom Rowe credited at the MAS for being willing to indulge in theoretical speculation, Moholy-Nagy, was even more outspoken than he in challenging American habits of mind. A feisty personality who belonged to the same generation as Hitchcock and Johnson, she was the author of a book on vernacular architecture and an admirer of the expressionist aesthetic of Bruno Taut, Erich Mendelsohn, and Hans Scharoun over the functionalist line of Walter Gropius, Marcel Breuer, and their American disciples.[33] She also harbored an animus toward Mies van der Rohe, not just for his classicizing architecture but also for his willingness to work under the Third Reich. In her intervention at the MAS in 1964, she asserted, "I am more interested in the general mood of [the 1930s] and the psychological basis of it. I know this is an un-American activity."[34] This remark and especially her comments at the 1966 symposium became flashpoints exposing the ideological differences among the participants.

In 1966, the "controversy" (as it became known) came to a head on the second day, after a student of Edgar Kaufmann, Jr., was invited by Hitchcock to present some evidence she had uncovered concerning the birth date of Frank Lloyd Wright. Much ballyhooed by Kaufmann in his own presentation on Wright the previous day, the evidence showed that Wright's birth date was 1867 rather than 1869, as hitherto accepted. Moholy-Nagy hazarded the observation that she did not see what difference this biographical detail made since Wright was a genius in any case. Placzek countered that "utmost precision" was the sine qua non of historical scholarship. Moholy-Nagy then proceeded to preface her own presentation, on Italian futurism, by stating:

> I must say that I spent a very sleepless night after yesterday. I left the very nice party very unhappy, because I felt we had spent so much time on all these totally irrelevant little villas, little churches, little this and little that. It was a bit of rustication here, a bit of new material there. All this so totally defeated my personal idea of architectural history.... [P]araphrasing Francis Bacon: History is a computation backward from our own time. If this is so, then I think it is our duty to find out what it actually was in the past that created our current concept of architecture, or at least our current problems of architecture.[35]

To this accusation Placzek replied:

> In defense of some of yesterday's proceedings, I would like to take up for things which constitute history per se or history *an sich* — things which have no direct

application to what we are doing now but which are interesting as historical phenomena, in Ranke's words, "as it actually happened." As for [Francis] Bacon's "computation backward," I think architectural students whom we are trying to fill with a little bit of knowledge of historical forms, historical shapes, historical phenomena, will always be glassy-eyed as soon as they think what they are learning cannot be applied to Harrison and Abramovitz.... Do we really only want to see history applied? Or do we want history per se?[36]

Wittkower, who was then called upon to give his views on "the purpose of symposia in the history of architecture," began by diplomatically crediting Moholy-Nagy as a "prophet, a propagandist, a great critic" and affirming that it was necessary for historians to engage in speculation.[37] But he also took the opportunity to demur from Rowe's interpretation of Le Corbusier's Villa Schwob the day before, suggesting that his former student had perhaps been a little fanciful in reaching for Renaissance precedents for this early building in the Swiss architect's career while ignoring the more immediate inspiration of Auguste Perret. He then went on:

It is relatively easy to have hindsight and say we only want to concern ourselves with what has turned out to be important, but this is never the way history works.... I think we are bound to point out within the decades we're choosing for consideration the entire panorama of what happened. I personally, for instance, am not terribly interested in all the little houses in the western United States, but.... So I feel very distinctly, if I may also speak for the future of these symposia, that we should carry on, plow on, in a proper historical fashion. We should discuss all the evidence and bring it to bear upon the whole area, the broad panorama, with which we are concerned — to try to re-create, as Dolf Placzek has said, the entire picture of the past, meanwhile never forgetting what is important for the present situation.[38]

It is noteworthy that in 1949 Wittkower had concluded his seminal book *Architectural Principles in the Age of Humanism* with just such a presentist view, stating that he hoped his historical research might have some topicality for architects of his own time. The theory of proportions, he wrote, was "again very much alive in the minds of young architects to-day, and they may well evolve new and unexpected solutions to this ancient problem."[39] In fact, the book's appearance at a moment when Le Corbusier's Modulor system was arousing great interest among architects in Britain and elsewhere led to the coining of a new, short-lived "ism" in England—New Palladianism. Yet in response to Hitchcock's question about the purpose of symposia in the history of architecture, Wittkower cautioned against selectively discounting any historical subject matter:

When I grew up in the 1920s, we wanted to do away with the art nouveau.... [W]e felt that it was absolutely senseless to do scholarly work on it. I was a student then: now that forty years have gone by, my judgment has settled down and I tend to be more objective.... [H]istorical negatives...in the period with which we are concerned appear to us now as historical positives. That is, of course, one of the reasons why it would be a mistake to limit ourselves only to ideas which seem to us important at this particular moment. Thirty years from now we may have another symposium, and some of us may be here, and we may have the minutes of this symposium before us. I wonder to what extent the values will have changed.[40]

The demand for a "relevant" architectural history—an adjective that would become a buzzword in the 1960s, above all signifying social relevance—was not limited to international panelists and guests, but also came from other, more American quarters at the MAS. The desire to read history through the lens of the present was to some extent associated with a position that Lewis Mumford had put forward since the 1920s. Not too surprisingly, Mumford himself did not attend the symposia. A self-taught critic who had left college before graduating, Mumford had no formal training in art history. His wide-ranging knowledge of architecture—as well as of other disciplines, from literature and philosophy to technology and sociology—was part of his search for what he called a "usable past," one that could be put in service of the unprecedented social and environmental challenges of the day.[41] At the International Style exhibition in 1932, his humanistic view of modern architecture had put him at odds with Hitchcock and Johnson, who marginalized his contribution to the show's housing section. Over the years, his disenchantment with a modern architecture defined primarily in formal and stylistic terms deepened, and in April 1962, a few weeks before the first MAS, a diatribe by him, "The Case against Modern Architecture," appeared in *Architectural Record*. It was a broad-scale condemnation of modernism not just for its failure to deliver on its social promises but for its superficiality and degradation of the human environment.[42] Yet while Mumford would undoubtedly have been a Cassandra-like presence in the context of the decorous academic conversations at the Columbia symposia, his position had a representative in Catherine Bauer Wurster, who took part in the 1964 meeting.[43]

Mumford's protégée in the 1930s and his collaborator on the housing section at the MoMA exhibition, Bauer Wurster was married to the architect William Wurster, whose houses in the San Francisco Bay area Mumford had praised after World War II as an example of a more humanistic and regionally sensitive modernism. Active over the years as a leading urban reformer, she had visited Europe in the 1930s and documented its new architecture firsthand, publishing an important volume comparing modern housing in Europe to that in the United States.[44] In her contribution to the 1964 symposium, titled "The Social Front of Modern Architecture in the 1930s," she criticized the modern movement for its "prima donna dogmas" and for later devolving into empty formalism:

> [T]he three original leaders who went on to become the most famous and influential world leaders in architecture—Le Corbusier, Mies, and Gropius—contributed, I think, nothing further to the rational solution of social or functional problems, or even to technological progress. The same can be said of most of their direct disciples. I need not explain here the various directions they took, but the differences have been wholly in terms of aesthetic expression. They have been equally unconcerned with the advancement of practical solutions for the urban and regional environment.[45]

It is worth noting that Bauer Wurster began her talk with a passing reference to Jane Jacobs's groundbreaking book *The Death and Life of Great American Cities*, which had appeared three years earlier. Otherwise, Jacobs's impassioned defense of American cities against the top-down urban theories of modernist planners and critics (including Mumford) and the urban renewal policies that had unraveled the social fabric of neighborhoods across the United States went unmentioned during the MAS proceedings.

Close to Bauer Wurster's point of view was that of James Marston Fitch. Like Mumford, Fitch had no professional training as a historian. After leaving Tulane University's architecture school without a degree, he worked for a time as a draftsman in Nashville, Tennessee, before apprenticing with the architect and planner Henry Wright, then served briefly in the low-cost housing division of the Federal Housing Authority in Washington, D.C. Prior to joining Columbia's architecture faculty in 1954, he was an editor and journalist at *Architectural Record* and then *House Beautiful*. His first book, *American Building: The Forces That Shape It*, published in 1947, addressed the general reader rather than the specialist. Although coming out of an entirely different context from Rowe, Moholy-Nagy, and Wilson, Fitch likewise challenged his fellow historians on their aversion to theoretical argumentation. At the 1964 gathering he observed:

> [I]t is my own impression that speculative literature — the very technique and habit of speculative thought — has disappeared from the scene. I consider this a loss. One of the great virtues of the decade we have discussed was its absorbing interest in theory, especially utopian theory....
>
> The most we can claim today is that we have taken the constituent elements of the earlier decades, 1918–28 and 1929–39, and put them into common circulation. We have smoothed off some of the rough edges of earlier stylistic invention; we have managed to synthesize the idioms of powerful innovators like Walter Gropius, Mies Van der Rohe, and Le Corbusier into some kind of common language of form. But I feel very strongly that we have done little else. Of course, many of us here, who lived and worked through that decade, are in a very ambivalent position. This must be especially true of Russell Hitchcock: he is involved in architectural history at so many levels right now that he must often wonder whether he is the object of historical investigation, or the subject of it, or the agent of it.[46]

This remark concerning the contradictions of Hitchcock's role was astute. Yet Fitch's own position was, in fact, not without ambiguity. He had recently published a monograph in the George Braziller series Masters of World Architecture on another figure absent from the symposia, Walter Gropius. Gropius's aura, like Giedion's and Mumford's, hovered about the proceedings somewhat uneasily.

Since arriving in the United States in 1937 to chair the architecture department of Harvard's Graduate School of Design, Gropius had been the exponent of an architectural education based on practical training, coordinated teamwork, and humanistic professionalism. His hostility toward both academic and "great man" conceptions of architecture — "Forget the battle of the styles and get to work on the development of architecture for better living," he admonished his design students — led him to rule out the teaching of history within the architecture school curriculum, at least for beginning students.[47] This notorious proscription served to reinforce the chasm at Harvard between Robinson Hall (then the home of the architecture department) and the Fogg Art Museum with its finely honed philological practices, and, by virtue of

Gropius's enormous prestige as an architect and educator, to widen the breach between architectural history and practice in postwar America in general.

The one major exception to Gropius's downplaying of history at Harvard was, of course, Sigfried Giedion, whom Gropius had succeeded in bringing to the university in 1938–9, officially as the Charles Eliot Norton chair in poetry. In this capacity Giedion had delivered his missionary lectures on the history of modern architecture. He wrote to Gropius six months before his arrival at Harvard, stating:

> I want to simplify things as far as I am capable and for once to try actually to obtain a total overview. In this manner the students should get the awareness and above all the reassurance that they truly stand in a tradition and that it is their task, now finally, to arrive at…a synthesis…. The overcoming of specialization and the preparation for a universalism, which solves even individual problems with consideration of the whole, surely is the altogether essential point concerning us today. I.e., culture or disintegration.[48]

Giedion's lectures would be published two years later as *Space, Time and Architecture: The Growth of a New Tradition*. In 1962, however, in a new introduction entitled "Architecture in the 1960s: Hopes and Fears," written for the fourth, enlarged edition of the book, the historian had to acknowledge that his *Zeitgeschichte* had reached "a kind of pause, even a kind of exhaustion."[49] Commenting on a symposium held at the Metropolitan Museum in New York in the spring of 1961 that addressed the question "Modern Architecture: Death or Metamorphosis?" he lamented that architecture in the early 1960s was beset by confusion, fatigue, escapism, and superficiality. Even if the epithet "International Style" had never really been embraced in Europe, modern architecture, under the worldwide sway of American influence, had been hijacked by a "harmful" emphasis on style: "The moment we fence architecture within a notion of 'style,' we open the door to a formalistic approach." "Playboy-architecture," he wrote (in a barely disguised reference to Johnson) was in vogue, "an architecture treated as playboys treat life, jumping from one sensation to another and quickly bored with everything." Insisting that the task of contemporary architecture remained "the interpretation of a way of life equivalent to our period," he pointed to a few developments that continued to give reason for cautious optimism: regional developments in Finland, Brazil, and, most recently, Japan; the late work of Le Corbusier; the further evolution of lightweight steel and concrete structures; and a new sculptural and mural sensibility in architecture.[50] Five years later, in 1967, in the fifth and last edition of *Space, Time and Architecture*, which appeared two years after Le Corbusier's death and a year before his own, Giedion stalwartly continued to update the book, adding substantial new material on a "third generation" of modern architects, exemplified by the Danish architect Jørn Utzon, while denouncing unnamed younger architects proposing fanciful and technology-obsessed schemes for underground cities and airborne megastructures.[51]

By the second half of the 1960s, the changing of the guard of modern architecture was clearly at hand. Mies and Gropius would both die in 1969. But even more emblematic than the passing of the great men was the evidence of late modern architecture itself. In between the first and second MAS, held on McKim, Mead & White's Columbia campus in uptown Manhattan, the Beaux-Arts monument of Pennsylvania Station, a masterwork by the same firm, was demolished in midtown, making way for the construction of Madison Square Garden and the banal new station below it. At the same time, a dozen blocks away, adjacent to the city's other great rail station, Grand Central, the behemoth Pan Am Building—designed by Gropius in collaboration with Pietro Belluschi, then dean of Massachusetts Institute of Technology's school of architecture—was topped off. This double blow to the urban fabric of New York City probably did as much as any other conjunction of historical events in the postwar period to "shatter the modernist dream," as one historian has put it.[52] If Gropius at this date could in all good conscience justify the demolition of Penn Station (and the threat posed to Grand Central by his own building) on the grounds that the Beaux-Arts was no more than a "pseudo-tradition"—as he continued to maintain in 1964[53]—then the enormous gap between his built practice and his rhetoric was grotesquely evident to almost everyone else.

Fitch, for his part, had written about Gropius admiringly in his 1960 monograph and continued to characterize Gropius's contributions to architectural education, design, and criticism as heroic and prophetic in his next book, *Architecture and the Esthetics of Plenty*, published in 1961. In 1963, however, he joined the last-ditch effort to save Penn Station and, while never publicly criticizing Gropius, in the years that followed became a leading figure in the American preservation movement.[54] Meanwhile, these nearby realities of late modern architecture entered the informed exchanges at the three Columbia symposia only obliquely. Just one speaker briefly raised the issue of historic preservation and modern architecture's place in the contemporary city; this was Thomas Howarth, a Scottish émigré to Canada teaching at the University of Toronto and a specialist on Charles Rennie Mackintosh, who made an impromptu appearance at the 1966 MAS.

The University Context and the Resurgence of Politics

Even though American art-historical scholarship started to shed its emphasis on connoisseurship and stylistic attribution in the 1950s and concern itself more with iconographic issues, its practitioners still had little overarching philosophical or theoretical ambition. For the most part, the profession remained an agglomeration of individual interests and expertise ensconced in a burgeoning university system in which enrollments were expanding, research funding was ever more available, and professors' salaries and status were rapidly rising. "It was pleasant," one chronicler of the period wrote, "for men whose wives had typed out their dissertations on the kitchen table to become directors of research institutes."[55]

The price for this privileged academic status was ideological compliance. With the transformation of the liberal university into a full-scale bureaucracy, what was expected of American scholars was, simply put, a maximum of competence with a minimum of dissent. James Ackerman was among the first in his profession to warn against this state of affairs as signaling an impending crisis. In an address delivered at the College Art Association in 1958 titled "On American Scholarship in the Arts," he observed that his colleagues had become docile cogs in a system that required one to "[slice] the pie of history into large or small helpings of period and area and then...[eat] it chronologically." Denouncing the preference for "cold fact" over "hot ideas" in a thinly veiled allusion to the Cold War context, he deplored that "we have been bullied by our materialistic surroundings into a suspicion of theory, into an unwillingness to examine the principles and values by which we work." He concluded by urging his colleagues to don the mantle of the public intellectual. It was essential to communicate with lay audiences as well as specialized ones, he argued, and to reconstitute the discipline as an ethical alternative to "the race toward the destruction of civilization."[56]

Eight years later, the situation had apparently not changed much. A 1966 study for the College Art Association funded by the Ford Foundation confirmed Ackerman's diagnosis, attributing the malaise in American art history departments to the bureaucratization, conformism, and narrowness that the American university system had fostered since the war:

> With few exceptions, the triumphs of American art history scholarship have been won through careful workmanship and method, rather than through fresh discovery or the formulation of new ideas.... The preoccupation with soundness, the over-emphasis on method, the caution and conservatism of American art history are qualities which are university-bred. They are academic qualities. Like the eclectic campus architecture which surrounds him, the American student and scholar in the humanities is profoundly conditioned by the economics of the academic marketplace and the bureaucratic patterns of university administration.[57]

Meanwhile, outside the ivory tower, the destructive tendencies noted by Ackerman were in full evidence. Although the first three years of the 1960s were more or less continuous with the previous decade, characterized by an optimistic mood in keeping with the "Camelot" presidency of John F. Kennedy and an ongoing economic expansion, Kennedy's assassination, mounting racial strife in American cities, and a sharp escalation of hostilities in Vietnam (accompanied by increasing call-ups in the draft) dramatically darkened the national atmosphere. The conformist climate and consensus of the 1950s gave way to protest and counterculture, with increasingly politicized students and teachers on campuses across the country condemning the university as complicit in a hegemonic military-industrial-academic complex.

This is a familiar enough story. Yet it bears repeating here for the sake of reflecting on whether, or to what degree, the national turbulence and anti-establishment mood crept into the discussions of modern architecture at Columbia in 1962, 1964, and 1966.[58] Was the pervasive distrust of power structures and the disillusionment with institutions sublimated in demands for a new kind of historiography at the MAS? Certainly for unreconstructed members of the older generation such as Hitchcock, politics continued to be a kind of indiscretion or distraction in relation to the study of aesthetic phenomena. As he stated at the 1964 symposium:

> My own conclusion is that it is rather pointless to look for automatic connections between political movements and architecture. There is the amusing cartoon by Osbert Lancaster of two identical facades, identical, that is, except that one has Nazi eagles and the other has the hammer and sickle. He says one is Soviet architecture and the other is Nazi architecture. But he could perfectly well have put in a third sketch of what was then the new State Department in Washington, with the American eagle on it, and said that that was the architecture of "free enterprise," or capitalism, or whatever you like. In other words, my

simple suggestion would be merely to say that it is all the monumental architecture of bureaucracy; it doesn't make much difference what the politics of the builders are, the results are much the same.[59]

For other scholars, however, the complicity of both architecture and historiography with repressive regimes raised more troubling questions, going well beyond superficial resemblances between monuments.[60] Notable from this point of view is a 1964 talk by Henry Millon on the role historians of art and architecture played in Mussolini's Italy, in which he carefully detailed how official intellectuals served the interests of the Fascist state by legitimizing its nationalist and expansionist policies.

The Turn to Theory in Architecture

In addition to everything else they famously were, the 1960s were also the decade of modern architecture's rewriting. The worldwide triumph of "modernism" in the 1950s had taken place amid rising doubts about its fundamental values. At the same time, the expansion of the historical canon to admit "anti-rationalist" movements, such as art nouveau and German expressionism;[61] the emergence of heterodox approaches to form-making among erstwhile modern architects, from neoliberty in Italy to the eclecticism of Johnson, Edward Durell Stone, Minoro Yamasaki, Eero Saarinen, and others in the United States; and, not least, the sense that World War II had ushered in a dramatically new phase of history all contributed to a belief that the architecture of the first half of the century needed to be rehistoricized. Increasingly, scholars ceased to regard modern architecture as an absolute break with the past, as the avant-garde had proclaimed in the 1920s, but rather saw it as part of an evolutionary development ongoing from the nineteenth century. At the same time, depending on one's point of view, it appeared either to have arrived at a point of stability and permanence in the last third of the century — a kind of modern classicism — or else to be fast approaching a state of exhaustion and closure.[62]

While these various *prises de position* did not rise to the level of a theoretical discourse in the 1950s, by the 1960s the demand for a comprehensive theory that could clarify modern architecture's significance with respect to both the present and future intensified, even in the nontheoretically inclined United States. The turn to theory at a moment of historical upheaval coincided with the resurgence of politics in society at large, as already suggested, and exposed the need for different criteria of architectural judgment as well as new institutional and disciplinary foundations. Although a full-blown account of the evolution of architectural theory in the postwar period is beyond the scope of this essay, a brief examination of some salient Anglo-American and Italian contributions during the 1960s toward that development is germane. They help to place the methodological and philosophical debates that surfaced at the MAS into a broader context, even as they blur the line between theories of architectural history and of architectural design.

One of the earliest attempts to come up with a synthetic theoretical-historical explanation of modern architecture within the postwar context was John Summerson's 1957 address to the Royal Institute of British Architects (RIBA), "The Case for a Theory of Modern Architecture." Summerson's aim was to find a unique and definitive principle by which to distinguish modern architecture from all its predecessors:

> Ever since the modern movement got onto its feet, questions have been asked about what it stands on. An association of some kind between what is vaguely called "theory" and what is vaguely called "modern architecture" continues, I believe, to be a topic frequently debated, and I am told that teachers in some of the schools feel a practical need for some sort of theoretical formula as a means of introducing students to the principles of modern design. Hence this paper, which offers nothing new but is simply an investigation — an attempt to discover whether there does exist any basis of principle applicable to modern architecture, different from the bases applicable to any other architecture.[63]

After sorting through various postulations by the protagonists of the earlier period, in particular Le Corbusier's *Vers une architecture* and László Moholy-Nagy's *The New Vision*, Summerson arrived at the concept of "program" as modern architecture's unifying theoretical principle. He defined program as "the spatial dimensions, spatial relationships, and other physical conditions required for the convenient performance of specific functions."[64] If this seems more or less to amount to a restatement of functionalist doctrine, it is not surprising as Summerson, who was trained in the 1920s as an architect and not a historian, had been an active participant in the 1930s in the Modern Architecture Research Group (MARS), the British wing of CIAM. Two years after his RIBA address, he reaffirmed his theory in the introduction to a book assessing the achievements of modern architecture in Britain, asserting that the ideals of the interwar decades had now largely been attained and that modern architecture had reached maturity: "We are no longer," he declared, "in the period of 'towards an architecture.'" The tenets of modernism, he believed, would henceforth spread ever more widely in architecture's built realizations.[65]

Published three years after Summerson's RIBA address, Reyner Banham's *Theory and Design in the First Machine Age* was a more challenging and ambitious contribution to the rethinking of modern architecture. Based on his doctoral dissertation written under Nikolaus Pevsner at the Courtauld Institute, the book was a rejection of his teacher's canonical interpretation of the *Zeitgeist* of modern architecture in *Pioneers of the Modern Movement, from William Morris to Walter Gropius*, originally published in 1936. Pevsner, in any case, had retreated after the war into a revindication of the English picturesque.[66] In contrast, Banham, who had studied aeronautical engineering before turning to architectural history, focused on the changing role of the architect in an age of mechanized technology and consumer culture. In *Theory and Design in the First Machine Age* — a rereading of the architecture ushered in by the Industrial Revolution from the standpoint of his own time, the "second machine age" — he noted that "we yet lack a body of theory proper to our own Machine Age [and] are still free-wheeling along with the ideas and aesthetics left over from the first."[67]

Criticizing the superficiality of modern architecture's technological claims, he sought to demonstrate its continuity with Beaux-Arts tradition. The "International Stylists," he wrote, had "only looked at problems of modifications of the surface of end-products, which end-products were inherently sub-functions of a technically obsolete world."[68] Yet out of this demythologizing narrative Banham spun a new myth of technological evolution, with

Buckminster Fuller emerging at the end of the book as hero figure, literally deus ex machina, and Italian futurism serving as a foundation for his theoretical edifice. Banham's book would fodder the ideas of a new avant-garde in the 1960s, especially those of the British group Archigram, whose members looked to him as a father figure. At the same time, his colleague Alan Colquhoun would criticize his argument for its failure to acknowledge sufficiently technology's symbolic and aesthetic aspects.[69]

An entirely different rewriting of modern architecture's history, no less theoretically ambitious, came from an author who took part in the 1962 MAS. Peter Collins completed the manuscript for his *Changing Ideals in Modern Architecture, 1750–1960* in 1963, and the book was published in 1965. Like Banham, the British-born Collins took his distance from Giedion, Pevsner, and the first generation of historians of modern architecture. Yet as the dates in his title suggest, he located the origins of modern architecture not in the technological transformations brought on by the Industrial Revolution but in the philosophical thought of the Enlightenment and the inception of the modern discipline of history itself. Modern architecture had arisen, in Collins's view, precisely in the breach between architectural theory—specifically the classical theory of architecture—and architectural history:

> [T]he theory of architecture is concerned with everything pertaining to the way people actually build in the present, whereas the history of architecture is concerned with the way people used to build in the past.... The history of the changing attitudes towards architectural theory during the last two centuries is of unusual interest. Before 1750, as we have seen, there was no possibility of a conflict between architectural theory and architectural history, since architectural history did not properly speaking exist, the virtues of Classicism were unquestioned, and every study of an antique or early renaissance monument was thus related to the theory of current design. The first awareness of any conflict between the two notions seems to occur in Leroy's study of the Athenian antiquities (1758).... Within a century the history of architecture had almost entirely supplanted the theory of architecture.[70]

In pinpointing this epistemological break as modern architecture's foundational moment, Collins explicitly sought to go beyond the historiographies produced by Hitchcock and Giedion, both of whom had concerned themselves, in his view, "essentially with the evolution of forms, rather than with the changes in those ideals which produced them." He aspired instead to write what he called, following César Daly, "a philosophical history of architecture," setting out to study the values and aspirations that had enabled the architect over the past two centuries to translate into built practice "what we may call his theory of architecture."[71]

Like Summerson's and Banham's, Collins's reading of history, and in particular his view of structural rationalism as key to the thought of architectural modernism, reflected his own formation and career. After training as an architect in the 1930s and serving in the British army during the war, he worked in the office of Denis Honegger, a Swiss follower of Auguste Perret. Returning to England in the early 1950s, he wrote his master's thesis on Jacques-François Blondel while teaching architecture at Manchester University. In 1955 he left England for an appointment at Yale's School of Architecture, teaching history there for two semesters before ending up at McGill University in Montreal,

Canada, where he continued to teach both history and design until his death in 1981. *Changing Ideals* appeared in his career midway between two other books, *Concrete: The Vision of a New Architecture* (1959) and *Architectural Judgment* (1971). Collins's veneration of Perret and his appreciation of the postwar work of Skidmore, Owings & Merrill were matched by his hostility toward all forms of avant-gardism. Conservative in disposition, he preferred "law-givers" over "form-givers,"[72] and "obedience to principles" over "architectural novelty for its own sake."[73] In this sense, *Changing Ideals*—which explicitly subscribes to Summerson's notion of program as the distinctive principle of twentieth-century architecture and opens with a triumphalist preface by John Bland hailing "the commencement of the classic age of modern architecture"—was the antithesis of Banham's future-oriented *Theory and Design in the First Machine Age*.

At the same time, Collins's insistence on a more complex relationship between modern architecture and historical precedents bears comparison to the most radical and influential theoretical statement of the decade, at least in the English language: Robert Venturi's *Complexity and Contradiction in Architecture*. Written in 1962, it was published in Yale's journal *Perspecta* in 1965 and republished in book form by MoMA the following year. Johnson had heretically proselytized a historicist eclecticism since the mid-1950s, and Rowe had even earlier "indiscreetly" (but with more analytical rigor) juxtaposed modern and premodern architecture, advocating cultivated visual ambiguities and "inverted spatial effects" as an antidote to the monotonous formal repetitions of postwar modernism.[74] But it was Venturi's "gentle manifesto" proclaiming "less is a bore" that dealt a deathblow to the lingering positivist and purist pieties harbored within late modern architecture culture.

Complexity and Contradiction was the product of an architectural practitioner who was immersed in architectural history.[75] In the book's acknowledgments, Venturi expresses gratitude not only to colleagues, such as Vincent Scully, Robert A. M. Stern, and his future wife and partner Denise Scott Brown, but also, in the second edition, to the art historian Richard Krautheimer, whose insights into the Roman baroque had inspired Venturi's appreciation of that style during a fellowship at the American Academy in Rome in the mid-1950s. In turn, Scully, in his introduction to Venturi's book, compared it in epochal import to Le Corbusier's *Vers une architecture*, while also lauding it as "a very American book, rigorously pluralistic and phenomenological in its method."[76]

Complexity and Contradiction is also permeated with references to the New Criticism, the dominant Anglo-American school of literary criticism during the postwar period, which Venturi initially encountered as an undergraduate at Princeton. Characterized by a methodology of "close reading," the New Criticism bears similarities to the formalist theory that the art critic Clement Greenberg was advancing at the same time in relation to modernist painting. Venturi's text is replete with references to T. S. Eliot, Cleanth Brooks, and William Empson, the last of whom had argued in his seminal *Seven Types of Ambiguity*—first published in 1930 but widely disseminated in the United States in the late 1940s and 1950s—that imprecision of meaning was not necessarily a deficiency in literary texts but rather could be deliberately mobilized by gifted authors to give expression to intrinsic tensions, conflicts, and paradoxes. Such "contradictions," Venturi felt intuitively, were characteristic of late modern culture in general and gave the architecture of his day greater aesthetic affinity with periods such as mannerism and the baroque than with the High Renaissance and its philosophical certainties and sense of equilibrium.

Fundamentally, *Complexity and Contradiction* was a theory of architectural form. In a review of the book published in 1967, Peter Collins allowed that Venturi's revalorization of the qualities set forth in the book's title was a useful corrective to the reductive abstractions of modernism. But he went on to criticize the author for his lack of attention to questions of program and construction, suggesting that Venturi's presentation of favorite historical images would have been "more suitable for accompanying the mechanical projection of a touristic sequence of 35-mm slides" than for "elucidating why complexity and contradiction are essential components of any architectural problem." [77] Venturi himself would subsequently acknowledge this criticism, stating in a note to the book's second edition, of 1977:

> I now wish the title had been *Complexity and Contradiction in Architectural Form*, as suggested by Donald Drew Egbert. In the early '60s, however, form was king in architectural thought, and most architectural theory focused without question on aspects of form. Architects seldom thought of symbolism in architecture then, and social issues came to dominate only in the second half of that decade. [78]

Thus, while Venturi's polemic of "both-and" broke the stranglehold of a puritanical modernism and reflected a new kind of use of both theory and history, it also remained well within the bounds of the American formalist tradition. In his next book, *Learning from Las Vegas* (1972), written with Scott Brown and Steven Izenour and later subtitled *The Forgotten Symbolism of Architectural Form*, Venturi would enlarge his perspective from strictly aesthetic considerations to symbolic and iconographic ones, reading the urban imagery of Las Vegas as a system of signs. Yet both books remained at arm's length with respect to the more radical politics of their day, endorsing the populist and commercial values of Main Street and the Las Vegas Strip.

A book that would have as profound an effect in Europe as *Complexity and Contradiction* would have in America and that, together with Venturi's manifesto, would be credited with the historical shift that came to be called "postmodernism" was Aldo Rossi's exactly contemporary *L'architettura della città* (*The Architecture of the City*). Like Venturi's book, Rossi's appeared in 1966, but its argument had been elaborated over the course of the previous several years, and it too emerged from a young architect's desire to put historical knowledge in the service of his own designs. For Rossi, however, who emerged from the intellectual circle around Rogers at *Casabella*, and who stubbornly joined the Communist Party in Italy at a moment when many of his compatriots were leaving it in the wake of revelations of Stalin's brutalities, the aim was not to authorize ambiguity or license rule-breaking but rather the opposite: to discover the "fixed laws" of architectural typology, to overcome individual subjectivity by grounding form-making in precepts that could be established in a contemporary equivalent of a classical architectural treatise:

> Around 1960 I wrote *The Architecture of the City*, a successful book. At that time, I was not yet thirty years old, and as I have said, I wanted to write a definitive work: it seemed to me that everything, once clarified, could be defined. I believed that the Renaissance treatise had to become an apparatus which could be translated into objects. I scorned memories, and at the same time, I made use of urban impressions: behind feelings I searched for the fixed laws of a timeless typology. I saw courts and galleries, the elements of urban morphology, distributed in the

city with the purity of mineralogy. I read books on urban geography, topography, and history, like a general who wishes to know every possible battlefield—the high grounds, the passages, the woods. I walked the cities of Europe to understand their plans and classify them according to types. Like a lover sustained by my egotism, I often ignored the secret feelings I had for those cities; it was enough to know the system that governed them. Perhaps I simply wanted to free myself of the city. Actually, I was discovering my own architecture.[79]

As this retrospective confession—which comes from Rossi's *A Scientific Autobiography*, published a decade and a half later, when he was fully immersed in postmodernist poetics—makes clear, his earlier book had unconsciously been a turning point in his thought. Contemporary with broader European intellectual shifts, Rossi's attempt to sustain an Enlightenment belief in an architecture based on a universal logic was already compromised and colored by a more complex and subjective vision of urban experience. Rather than the scientific work of theory and history that he initially intended it to be, *The Architecture of the City* was in effect a "project"—an "architectural project," as he would state in his introduction to the German edition of the book.[80]

The fundamental originality of Rossi's treatise was not just to transfer the focus of theoretical discourse from architecture to the city, but to the city considered as an agglomeration of architectural form. His critique of modern architecture's "naive functionalism"—its ingenuous claims to be rational—had already been made by others. What was new in Rossi's "neorationalism" was his interpretation of architectural-urban form as an "ultimate verifiable fact," a material and geographic concretion of collective human experience.[81] The notion of autonomy famously associated with his thinking was above all an effort to grasp the effect architecture (as opposed to all other kinds of forces) had on the city through a precise study of the functioning of its actual monuments and building types, and to mobilize this effect for purposes of design. As Rossi observed, historians had neglected to investigate architecture's material impact on urban reality:

> Artistic investigations have diminished while philological studies on this or that historical period, reconstructions of facts, and punctilious studies of events multiply. I do not deny the importance of the latter contributions, but they cannot be decisive for a theory of design. This becomes clear when one confronts the legacy of the Modern Movement, which is often either taken as dogma (even though it is not well understood) or relegated to a historiographical event.... Ultimately, *the history of architecture is the material of architecture*.[82]

In this sense, Rossi's "historical materialism," if we may use this term very literally, must also be understood as a rejection of late modernist theories of urbanism. While the latter were giving rise in the 1960s to megastructure proposals, cybernetic cities, utopian-dystopian schemes predicated on a "new urban dimension," and the like, Rossi's book was an explicit rejection of such thinking.[83]

These observations on Rossi lead us back to the previously discussed differences between American and European architecture culture at this time, in particular to Hitchcock's antipathy to theoretical speculation, and to one other book by an Italian historian. Published in 1968, Manfredo Tafuri's *Teorie e storia dell'architettura* (*Theories and History of Architecture*) appeared the same year its author took over as director of the Department of Architectural History at the Istituto Universitario di Architettura in Venice. Less a history of modern architecture than a methodological prolegomenon to one, *Teorie e storia* should be read not only in relation to Rossi's "tract" but also as Tafuri's commentary on contemporary architectural historiography. He not only reflects critically on the architectural historians closest to him—Bruno Zevi, Giulio Carlo Argan, and Leonardo Benevolo, among others—but he also demonstrates his attentive reading of the British and American historians and theorists: Hitchcock, Giedion, Pevsner, Summerson, Banham, Peter Collins, and Venturi.

The main thrust of Tafuri's criticism is aimed against what he calls "operative history," and it is especially, although by no means exclusively, directed against Zevi and Giedion, whom he accuses of a "mythical deformation of historical reality," motivated by the desire to bring about a particular architectural tendency:

> Instead of making history one makes *ideology*: which, besides betraying the task of history, conceals the real possibilities of transforming reality.... Books like Giedion's *Space, Time and Architecture* and Zevi's *Storia dell'architettura moderna* are, at once, both historiographical contributions and true architectural *projects*.... The exceptional importance of Giedion's history is in its being one of the first attempts at relinking modern architecture to the past, as a pointer for future developments. In this sense, the past is continually used as a confirmation of the present: history legitimizes what is already there, has a tranquillizing function.... This objective limitation, clear in Giedion's work, is typical of most present historiography and criticism.... Operative criticism is, then, an ideological criticism (we always use the term ideological in its Marxian sense): it substitutes ready-made judgments of value (prepared for immediate use) for analytical rigor.[84]

This definition, which adheres strictly to the Marxist conception of ideology as false consciousness, is indebted to Argan, whose essay "Architecture and Ideology" had appeared in 1957 (coincidentally the same year as Summerson's "Case for a Theory of Modern Architecture"). Argan had argued that "rationalism" was largely an "illusion" and an "anxious aspiration" on the part of modern architects; it was not a principle that could be educed from a rigorous historical analysis of modern architecture itself but was rather an ideological construct that reflected the crisis in bourgeois values brought on by capitalist modernity.[85] The task of the architectural historian, therefore, was nothing more nor less than a critique of this compensatory formation.

Tafuri would propound the same argument more stridently in his next book, *Progetto e utopia (Architecture and Utopia)*, of 1973, an expansion of an essay that had appeared in *Contropiano* four years earlier. But Tafuri's critique of operative history would lead him into a methodological cul-de-sac from which he found it hard to escape. In *Progetto e utopia* he insisted that at the present stage of history there could be no "hopes in design," no possibility of creating an architecture for a "liberated society." [86] Despite vague references (like the one in the passage above) to "the real possibilities of transforming reality," Tafuri's argument precluded both the historian and the architect from hazarding any ideas about those possibilities. If this refusal amounted to a kind of negative operativity—inasmuch as it polemically prescribed what practicing architects could not do—it also left the architectural historian with little to go on beyond "analytical rigor" and "more careful philology." [87]

In the face of this impasse, Tafuri would largely abandon modern architecture as a focus of his writing by the mid-1980s, turning back to the Renaissance in his subsequent books and insisting on the necessity of bringing the "multiple perspectives of history itself," its "dishomogeneity" and "radical fragmentation," to bear.[88] Thus, in a case of very strange bedfellows, Tafuri and Hitchcock, whose work the former aptly characterized in *Theories and History* as "agnostic exegesis,"[89] would both end up endorsing a "non-operative" practice of history underpinned by an encyclopedic command of historical knowledge.

In actuality, the neoliberal agnosticism of Hitchcock and the post–Marxian critique of Tafuri, just like the respective approaches of Venturi and Rossi, were no more akin than the word "contradiction" in the title of Venturi's book was a reference to Marxist dialectics. Arguably, however, Rossi's reading of the city in terms of architectural form and Tafuri's insistence on a history without tendency facilitated the acceptance and absorption of their "foreign" ways of thinking into the American context. One of the platforms for this assimilation was the Institute for Architecture and Urban Studies (IAUS), an architectural think tank that would shortly be established in New York. It is perhaps no accident that Peter Eisenman, named its first director in 1967 and a protégé of Colin Rowe, was in the audience at the 1966 symposium at Columbia, as was Kenneth Frampton, who, together with Eisenman, would become a founding editor of the institute's influential journal *Oppositions*. Over the next decade, the IAUS would be instrumental in overcoming the innate anti-intellectual bias in American architecture culture, and *Oppositions* would raise architectural theory to the same disciplinary status as architectural history, transmitting ideas from the Venice School and other European sources to the next generation of American architects and scholars.

Paradoxically, what the discussions at the MAS reveal is that the advent of theory in the American architectural context in the 1960s was both a reversal of the long-standing hostility to intellectual speculation in American visual culture and at the same time a continuation of the preexisting American inclination toward formalism. It is not surprising, therefore, that the new disposition to theory would flourish in architecture schools in the United States over the next couple decades. Postmodernism—in its "historicist" as well as "deconstructivist" variants—was in many respects a new name for an old way of thinking: namely, a formalistic approach to architecture. Inasmuch as both American architectural historiography and American architectural practice had accorded priority to form since at least the time of MoMA's International Style exhibition, each served, for much of the twentieth century, to reinforce the other.

Notes

1. The transcript of the 1962 proceedings was made available for purchase in mimeographed form through the Avery Library after Bruno Zevi, editor-in-chief of *L'Architettura*, canceled plans to publish it in the Italian magazine owing to a lack of suitable photographs. See Zevi to Collins, 10 Dec. 1963. Edited versions of the 1964 presentations constituted the entire March 1965 volume of the *Journal of the Society of Architectural Historians*. Robert Branner, a medieval scholar on Columbia University's art history faculty, was serving as editor of the journal at the time, so publication implicitly became an interdepartmental matter. Tapes of the 1966 event were transcribed, and Collins partially corrected the transcript, with some assistance from the participants themselves. The organizers felt ambivalent, however, about how best to publish it; although a second offset edition or *Journal* volume were explored, in the end the 1966 session was never published. Several of the MAS presentations derived from previously published works or were published subsequent to their delivery at Columbia; for the publication history of specific essays see the editors' notes to the proceedings.

2. Henry-Russell Hitchcock, MAS 1966, 229.

3. The images contained in this volume were culled in large part from the books and journals that Placzek incorporated in his 1962 and 1964 exhibitions and discussed in his review of the literature for each period under consideration. Exhibition lists are held in the George Collins archive, Avery Library, Columbia University, New York.

4. I follow the conventional shorthand throughout this essay of using "American" to indicate "of the United States of America."

5. This situation would change over the next decade, with a dozen more dissertations appearing by 1972. Barbara Miller Lane's dissertation, *Architecture and Politics in Germany, 1918–1945*, written at Harvard University and published as a book by Harvard University Press in 1968, was the first. For a list of all dissertations, see Peter Kaufman and Paula Gabbard, "American Doctoral Dissertations in Architectural and Planning History, 1898–1972," in *The Architectural Historian in America: A Symposium in Celebration of the Fiftieth Anniversary of the Founding of the Society of Architectural Historians*, ed. Elisabeth Blair MacDougall (Washington, D.C.: National Gallery of Art, 1990), 288–304.

6. See Rosemarie Haag Bletter, Introduction, 14n44.

7. Placzek, MAS 1964, 213.

8. Eduard Sekler, MAS 1964, 188. Italics in original.

9. Erwin Panofsky, "Three Decades of Art History in the United States: Impressions of a Transplanted European," in *Meaning in the Visual Arts* (Chicago: University of Chicago Press, 1955), 328–9.

10. Ibid., 332; 329–30. See also Irving Lavin, "Theory in My Time," *Art Bulletin* 78 (1996): 14.

11. See Mardges Bacon, Introduction to William Jordy, *"Symbolic Essence" and Other Writings on Modern Architecture and American Culture* (New Haven: Yale University Press, 2005), 4, 6.

12. Ibid., 20ff.

13. Panofsky, "Three Decades of Art History," 326.

14. For an illuminating discussion of the relationship between scientific empiricism and formalism in American aesthetic scholarship, specifically in relation to Hitchcock's writing, see Marie Frank, "Hitchcock and Harvard: The Historical Context of Formalist Aesthetics," in *Summerson and Hitchcock: Centenary Essays on Architectural Historiography*, ed. Frank Salmon, *Studies in British Art* 16 (New Haven: Yale University Press, 2006), 221–42.

15. James Ackerman, "On American Architectural Scholarship in the Arts," *Art Journal* 17 (1958): 359.

16. Hitchcock's reminiscence appeared in the *Harvard Class Notes*; cited in Helen Searing, "Henry-Russell Hitchcock: The Architectural Historian as Critic and Connoisseur," in MacDougall, ed., *The Architectural Historian in America*, 251.

17. Ibid., 258.

18. Hitchcock, MAS 1966, 307.

19. See Henry-Russell Hitchcock, "The International Style Twenty Years After," *Architectural Record*, Aug. 1951, 89–97.

20. Colin Rowe, BBC script, 1958; published as "Review: *Architecture: Nineteenth and Twentieth Centuries* by Henry-Russell Hitchcock," in *Texas, Pre-Texas, Cambridge*, vol. 1 of *As I Was Saying*, ed. Alexander Caragonne (Cambridge, Mass.: MIT Press, 1996), 183.

21. Ibid., 184. See also in the same volume, Rowe's essay "Henry-Russell Hitchcock," 11–23.

22. Ibid., 183.

23. Ibid.

24. Colin Rowe, Introduction to *Five Architects* (New York: Wittenborn, 1972), 4.

25. Catherine Bauer to Lewis Mumford, 29 Jan. 1932, Mumford Papers, University of Pennsylvania, Philadelphia, Pa.; cited in Terence Riley, *The International Style: Exhibition 15 and the Museum of Modern Art* (New York: Rizzoli and Columbia Books of Architecture, 1992), 85.

26. On the faculty of the Warburg Institute from 1934 through 1956, Wittkower held a visiting professorship at Harvard in the 1950s before arriving at Columbia as chair of the art history department in 1956. He advised Rowe also to go to Harvard, to work with Giedion, but Rowe felt Hitchcock was the superior historian. See "Henry-Russell Hitchcock," *As I Was Saying*, 21.

27. Colin Rowe, MAS 1964, 209. The term "cultural agnosticism" is Hitchcock's own; see Searing, "Henry-Russell Hitchcock," 251.

28. Rowe, MAS 1964, 209.

29. This characterization is a paraphrase of the art historian Colin Eisler; see his *"Kunstgeschichte* American Style," in *The Intellectual Migration: Europe and America, 1930-1960*, vol. 2 of *Perspectives in American History*, ed. Donald Fleming and Bernard Bailyn (Cambridge, Mass.: Charles Warren Center for Studies in American History, Harvard University, 1968), 613.

30. Colin St. John Wilson, MAS 1964, 186.

31. "Team 10 Primer, 1953–62," *Architectural Design* 12 (Dec. 1962): [entire issue].

32. Another Italian invitee to the MAS who did not attend was the architect and historian Bruno Zevi. Zevi was likewise no stranger to architectural polemics or to the American scene. He had spent the years of World War II studying architecture at Harvard and, as a proponent of a new direction for post-Fascist Italy, was a champion of the "architecture of democracy" of Frank Lloyd Wright. Though very different personalities, both he and Banham were strongly attracted to American culture, sharing a belief in its ideals of openness and freedom.

33. Moholy-Nagy published *Native Genius in Anonymous Architecture* (New York: Horizon Press) in 1957, seven years before the opening of Bernard Rudofsky's more famous *Architecture without Architects* exhibition at MoMA.

34. Sibyl Moholy-Nagy, MAS 1964, 203.

35. Moholy-Nagy, MAS 1966, 304.

36. Placzek, MAS 1966, 307.

37. Rudolf Wittkower, MAS 1966, 310–1.

38. Ibid.

39. Rudolf Wittkower, *Architectural Principles in the Age of Humanism* (London: Alec Tiranti, 1952), 135.

40. Wittkower, MAS 1966, 317–8.

41. The phrase "usable past," originally coined by the literary critic Van Wyck Brooks in 1918, was adopted by Mumford in relation to architecture. See Robert Wojtowicz, "Lewis Mumford: The Architectural Critic as Historian," in MacDougall, ed., *The Architectural Historian in America*, 237–49.

42. The essay was republished by Mumford the following year in his collection *The Highway and the City* (New York: Harcourt Brace, 1963), 150–64.

43. This was the only symposium Bauer Wurster attended; she died in a hiking accident the same year.

44. Catherine Bauer, *Modern Housing* (Boston and New York: Houghton Mifflin, 1934).

45. Catherine Bauer Wurster, MAS 1964, 174–5.

46. James Marston Fitch, MAS 1964, 196–9.

47. Walter Gropius, "Eight Steps toward a Solid Architecture," *Architectural Forum*, Feb. 1954; rev. and rpt. as "Architect—Servant or Leader?" in Walter Gropius, *Scope of Total Architecture* (New York: Harper & Brothers, 1955), 91; see also his "Blueprint of an Architect's Education," 47–8 in the same volume. For more on Gropius and architectural education, see Anthony Alofsin, *The Struggle for Modernism: Architecture, Landscape Architecture, and City Planning at Harvard* (New York: W. W. Norton, 2002); Jill Pearlman, *Inventing American Modernism: Joseph Hudnut, Walter Gropius, and the Bauhaus Legacy at Harvard* (Charlottesville: University of Virginia Press, 2007); and Winfried Nerdinger, "From Bauhaus to Harvard: Walter Gropius and the Use of History," in Gwendolyn Wright and Janet Parks, eds., *The History of History in American Schools of Architecture* (New York: Buell Center for the Study of American Architecture and Princeton Architectural Press, 1996), 89–98.

48. Sigfried Giedion, quoted in Eduard Sekler, "Sigfried Giedion at Harvard University," in MacDougall, ed., *The Architectural Historian in America*, 268.

49. Sigfried Giedion, *Space, Time and Architecture: The Growth of a New Tradition*, fourth ed., enlarged (Cambridge, Mass.: Harvard University Press, 1962), xxvi.

50. Ibid., xxvi–xxvii.

51. Sigfried Giedion, *Space, Time and Architecture: The Growth of a New Tradition*, fifth ed., revised and enlarged (Cambridge, Mass.: Harvard University Press, 196), 861–2.

52. Meredith Clausen, *The Pan Am Building and the Shattering of the Modernist Dream* (Cambridge, Mass.: MIT Press, 2006).

53. Walter Gropius, "Tradition and Continuity in Architecture," *Architectural Record*, July 1964, 152; cited in Nerdinger, "From Bauhaus to Harvard: Walter Gropius and the Use of History," 96, and Clausen, *The Pan Am Building*, 328.

54. Fitch would establish the historic preservation program at Columbia, the first such program in an American university, in 1967.

55. Godfrey Hodgson, *America in Our Time* (New York: Doubleday, 1976), 96.

56. James Ackerman, "On American Scholarship in the Arts," *College Art Journal* XVII, no. 4 (1958): 360–2.

57. Andrew C. Ritchie, ed., with Lorenz Eitner, Norman L. Rice, and Jules D. Prown, *The Visual Arts in Higher Education* (New Haven: College Art Association of America, 1966), 57; cited in part in Eisler, "*Kunstgeschichte* American Style," 615.

58. For an attempt to interconnect different levels of social praxis in the 1960s, see Fredric Jameson, "Periodizing the 60s," in *The Ideologies of Theory: Essays, 1971–1986*, vol. 2 of *Syntax of History* (Minneapolis: University of Minnesota Press, 1988), 178–9.

59. Hitchcock, MAS 1964, 211–2.

60. Hitchcock's reference here to the "monumental architecture of bureaucracy" actually contradicts the positive comments he had made earlier concerning the architecture of bureaucracy. See "The Architecture of Bureaucracy and the Architecture of Genius," *Architectural Review* 101 (Jan. 1947): 6, in which he explicitly uses the term *bureaucracy* "without the pejorative connotation" to characterize the well-executed large-scale work of a firm such as Albert Kahn Associates.

61. Cf. Nikolaus Pevsner and J. M. Richards, eds., *The Anti-Rationalists: Art Nouveau Architecture and Design* (New York: Harper & Row, 1973), a collection of essays mostly published in *Architectural Review* between 1959 and 1968; see esp. Pevsner's Introduction, in which he undertakes a self-criticism of his 1936 *Pioneers of the Modern Movement, from William Morris to Walter Gropius*.

62. The debate over "continuity or crisis" was articulated most succinctly by Ernesto Rogers in the Italian context; see his editorial "Continuità o crisi," *Casabella* 215 (Apr.–May 1957): 2–4.

63. John Summerson, "The Case for a Theory of Modern Architecture," *RIBA Journal*, June 1957, 307.

64. Ibid., 309.

65. Sir John Summerson, Introduction to Trevor Dannatt, *Modern Architecture in Britain* (London: Batsford, 1959), 11–2, 28. Three decades later, in the aftermath of the experiences of the 1970s and 1980s, Summerson would disavow his thesis of 1957 as having been overly optimistic, acknowledging that it was out of touch historically with the cultural shifts that were already taking place. John Summerson, *The Unromantic Castle and Other Essays* (London: Thames and Hudson, 1990), 7–8.

66. Pevsner's turnabout had culminated in his Reith Lectures of 1955, published as *The Englishness of English Art* (London: Architectural Press, 1956), in which he presented the picturesque as an ongoing expression of the British national character. In 1960 Pevsner would issue a new edition of *Pioneers of Modern Design* (originally published as *Pioneers of the Modern Movement*), acknowledging Banham's influence on additions and alterations to the book, although these largely had to do with admitting previously neglected figures such as Gaudí and Sant'Elia to the canon.

67. Reyner Banham, *Theory and Design in the First Machine Age* (London: Architectural Press, 1960), 1.

68. Banham, quoting from a 1955 letter sent by Buckminster Fuller to John McHale, ibid., 326.

69. See Alan Colquhoun, "The Modern Movement in Architecture," *British Journal of Aesthetics* 2, no. 1 (Jan. 1962): 59–65; rpt. in his *Essays in Architectural Criticism: Modern Architecture and Historical Change* (Cambridge, Mass.: MIT Press, 1981), 21–5. See also his "Symbolic and Literal Aspects of Technology," *Architectural Design* 32 (Nov. 1962): 508–9; rpt. in the same collection, 26–30. Colquhoun's criticism was not entirely dissimilar to the dialectical argument Jordy put forward a year later in his previously discussed essay "The Symbolic Essence of Modern Architecture of the Twenties and Its Continuing Influence." Another early commentator on Banham's book was Sibyl Moholy-Nagy, who, while generally reviewing it positively, took Banham to task for giving too much credence to the effects of academic and avant-garde theories on the practical evolution of architecture; see her "An Overestimation of Theory," *Progressive Architecture*, Apr. 1961, 200.

70. Peter Collins, *Changing Ideals in Modern Architecture: 1750–1950*, second ed. (Montreal: McGill-Queen's University Press, 1998), 141.

71. Ibid., 16.

72. See Peter Collins, "The Form-Givers," *Perspecta* 7 (1961): 91–6.

73. P. Collins, *Changing Ideals*, 299.

74. The words in quote marks are from Rowe's essay "Mannerism and Modern Architecture" (1950), rpt. in *Mathematics of the Ideal Villa and Other Essays* (Cambridge, Mass.: MIT Press, 1976), 51.

75. Venturi received his architectural education at Princeton, where, under the Beaux-Arts master Jean Labatut, there was a closer relationship between historical research and architectural design than at most other schools. One of Venturi's most important mentors at Princeton was Donald Drew Egbert, a social historian of American architecture and modern intellectual thought. Egbert, who had written a lukewarm review of Hitchcock's *Modern Architecture: Romanticism and Reintegration* in 1930 and was critical of the International Style show over the

years, was not invited to the MAS.

76. Vincent Scully, Introduction to Robert Venturi, *Complexity and Contradiction in Architecture* (New York: MoMA, 1966), 11.

77. Peter Collins, "Order in Complexity: *Complexity and Contradiction in Architecture* (Robert Venturi)," *Landscape*, Autumn 1967, 37.

78. Robert Venturi, *Complexity and Contradiction in Architecture*, second ed. (New York: MoMA, 1977), 14.

79. Aldo Rossi, *A Scientific Autobiography* (Cambridge, Mass.: MIT Press, 1981), 15–6.

80. Aldo Rossi, Comment on the German Edition (1973), in *The Architecture of the City* (Cambridge, Mass.: MIT Press, 1982), 179.

81. Ibid., 29.

82. Aldo Rossi, Introduction to the Portuguese Edition (1971), in ibid., 169–70. The italics are Rossi's.

83. See Pier Vittorio Aureli, *The Project of Autonomy: Politics and Poetics within and against Capitalism* (New York: Princeton Architectural Press, 2008).

84. Manfredo Tafuri, *Theories and History of Architecture* (New York: Icon Editions, 1979), 151–3. The italics are Tafuri's. Translation slightly modified.

85. Giulio Carlo Argan, "Architettura e ideologia," *Zodiac* 1 (1957): 47–82, Engl. tr. in *Architecture Culture, 1943–1968: A Documentary Anthology*, ed. Joan Ockman (New York: Rizzoli, 1993), 253–9.

86. Manfredo Tafuri, *Architecture and Utopia: Design and Capitalist Development* (Cambridge, Mass.: MIT Press, 1976), 179, 182.

87. See Tafuri, *Theories and History of Architecture*, 152–3. Cf. another disquisition on method by Tafuri, titled "The Historical 'Project,'" published as the introduction to *The Sphere and the Labyrinth: Avant-Gardes and Architecture from Piranesi to the 1970s*, tr. Pellegrino D'Acierno and Robert Connally (Cambridge, Mass.: MIT Press, 1987). As the scare quotes around the word "project" suggest, Tafuri continued to rethink his critical methodology over the years, and the scientific-Marxist conception of ideology and history defended in his earlier books would subsequently be inflected by poststructuralism and other critical theories. I have tried to address the evolution in Tafuri's thought in my essay "Venice and New York," *Casabella* 619/20 (Jan.–Feb. 1995): 56–71.

88. Manfredo Tafuri, "The Historical 'Project,'" 2, 8.

89. Tafuri, *Theories and History of Architecture*, 135.

MAS 1962 session, Columbia University. Participants shown include: Henry-Russell Hitchcock (seated, second from left); Henry Millon (seated, third from left); Mary Patricia May Sekler (seated in audience, center); and Adolf K. Placzek (standing in audience, leaning).

MAS 1964 session, Columbia University. Participants shown include: Henry-Russell Hitchcock (seated at table, far left); Colin Rowe (seated in back, center); and George R. Collins (seated at table, center).

MAS Participants

Stanford Anderson (b. 1934; MAS 1964, 1966) began a Ph.D. at Columbia University in 1962. In 1968 he successfully defended his dissertation on Peter Behrens before a committee composed of fellow MAS participants Henry-Russell Hitchcock, George Collins, Edgar Kaufmann, and Robert Rosenblum. Anderson published numerous articles on Behrens, in *Architectural Design*, *Oppositions*, and *Perspecta*; his definitive monograph *Peter Behrens and a New Architecture for the Twentieth Century* appeared in 2000. He began teaching at MIT in 1963 and in 1974 co-founded (with Henry Millon and others) its Ph.D. Program in History, Theory, and Criticism of Architecture, Art, and Urban Form.

Alfred H. Barr, Jr. (1902–1981; MAS 1964, 1966), a founder and figurehead of New York's modern art and architecture scene, fulfilled the role of elder states-man at the MAS. As a doctoral candidate at Harvard, Barr curated the Fogg Art Museum's first-ever exhibit on modern art and was subsequently asked to serve as director of the newly founded Museum of Modern Art (MoMA) in New York. Shortly after taking up the post in 1929, he invited Henry-Russell Hitchcock and Philip Johnson to accompany him throughout Europe, where they visited the Bauhaus and gathered material for what would become the museum's seminal *Modern Architecture: International Exhibition* (1932). Following his removal as director in 1942, Barr remained at the MoMA in various roles including director of museum collections, a position he held from 1947 to 1967.

Catherine Bauer Wurster (1905–1964; MAS 1964) graduated from Vassar College in 1926. A self-identified "houser," she traveled frequently to Europe in the 1930s to study housing reform. She curated the housing section of MoMA's 1932 *Modern Architecture: International Exhibition* and organized its 1936 exhibition *Architecture in Government Housing*. Her now-classic volume *Modern Housing* appeared in 1934. An influential social welfare advocate, she co-authored the U.S. Housing Act of 1937 and served in numerous posts, including executive secretary of the Regional Planning Association of America and the Housing Committee of the American Federation of Labor. When (shortly before her death) she attended the 1964 MAS, she was a professor of city and regional planning at the University of California.

Elizabeth Bauer Kassler (1911–1998; MAS 1964, 1966), the younger sister of Catherine Bauer Wurster, joined the curatorial staff of the Museum of Modern Art in 1937, where she collaborated with John McAndrew on the traveling exhibition *What is Modern Architecture?* (1938) and organized the better-known *Built in USA* (1944). She served as head of the Department of Architecture during World War II and contributed to the volumes *Tomorrow's Small House: Models and Plans* (1945), *If You Want to Build A House* (1946), and *The Architecture of Bridges* (1949). An important document of modern landscape design, Kassler's *Modern Gardens and the Landscape* appeared in 1964.

H. Allen Brooks (1925–2010; MAS 1962, 1964, 1966) is best known for his in-depth scholarly work on Frank Lloyd Wright and Le Corbusier. After serving in World War II, he earned his master's from Yale in 1955 and his Ph.D. from Northwestern in 1957. His book *Prairie School: Frank Lloyd Wright and His Midwest Contemporaries*, an elaboration of his dissertation, appeared in 1972. Brooks edited and oversaw the publication of the epic thirty-two volume *Le Corbusier Archive* (1982–4) for the Fondation Le Corbusier and subsequently wrote *Le Corbusier's Formative Years: Charles-Edouard Jeanneret at La Chaux-de-Fonds* (1997).

Theodore M. Brown (life dates unknown; MAS 1962, 1964, 1966), a historian of Dutch architecture and the De Stijl movement, received his training at Harvard University. At the time of the MAS, he was teaching art history at the University of Louisville; he later moved to Cornell. Among other volumes, he authored *The Work of G. Rietveld, Architect* (1958), the first scholarly monograph on this important architectural figure.

George R. Collins (1917–1993; MAS 1962, 1964, 1966) was the principal organizer of the MAS, acting as both host and liaison between his fellow organizers Hitchcock, Johnson, and Placzek. He joined the faculty of Columbia's Department of Art History and Archaeology in 1946, after earning his bachelor of arts (1939) and master of fine arts (1942) degrees from Princeton University and serving with the American Field Service (1942–5). He wrote extensively on Antoni Gaudí, publishing the first English-language monograph on the Spanish architect in 1960. His seminal volume *Camillo Sitte and the Birth of Modern City Planning*, co-authored with his wife, Christiane Crasemann Collins, appeared in 1965. Collins spent his long and productive academic career at Columbia, retiring in 1986; the transcripts and other materials relating to the MAS are preserved in the George Collins Papers, held in the archives of the university's Avery Architectural and Fine Arts Library.

Peter Collins (1920–1981; MAS 1962) trained as an architect at the Leeds College of Art from 1936 to 1939. After World War II he worked in the Swiss office of Denis Honegger and the Paris office of Pierre-Édouard Lambert. He received his master's degree from the Manchester University School of Architecture with a thesis on Jacques-François Blondel and began teaching at McGill University in 1956; he remained on the faculty there until his death in 1981. Known for his great wit and love of minutia, Collins authored several influential volumes, including *Concrete: The Vision of a New Architecture* (1959) and *Changing Ideals in Modern Architecture* (1965). In 1971 Collins obtained a law degree from Queen's University; his final contribution, *Architectural Judgment* (1972), brought legal reasoning and methods to bear on the critical assessment of architecture.

Walter Creese (1919–2002; MAS 1962), a noted scholar of American architecture and planning, received his doctorate in art history from Harvard University in 1950. He taught at numerous institutions before settling at the University of Illinois in 1968, where he taught until his retirement in 1987. Creese served as president of the Society of Architectural Historians (1958–60), having previously edited its journal (1950–3). His published work includes the *Art Bulletin* essay "Fowler and the Domestic Octagon" (1946) and the books *The Search for Environment* (1966), *The Crowning of the American Landscape* (1986), and *TVA's Public Planning: The Vision, The Reality* (1990).

Leonard K. Eaton (1922–2014; MAS 1966) received his Ph.D. in American civilization from Harvard University in 1951 and taught architectural history at the University of Michigan from 1950 to 1988. Eaton's books on modern subjects include *Landscape Artist in America: The Life and Work of Jens Jensen* (1964), *Two Chicago Architects and Their Clients: Frank Lloyd Wright and Howard Van Doren Shaw* (1969), and *American Architecture Comes of Age: European Reaction to H. H. Richardson and Louis Sullivan* (1972).

James Marston Fitch (1909–2000; MAS 1962, 1964, 1966) began engineering studies at the University of Alabama at the age of fifteen. After two years, he left to work in an architect's office and later enrolled at the School of Architecture at Tulane; he was awarded an honorary doctorate there in 1997. In 1936 he moved to New York to become an editor at *Architectural Record* and subsequently also worked at *Architectural Forum* and *House Beautiful*. Fitch's first book, *American Building: The Forces that Shape It*, appeared in 1948; his monograph on Walter Gropius, in 1960, just prior to the start of the MAS. A teacher at Columbia, he helped establish a certificate program in historic preservation there in 1967 and in 1972 the country's first master's in historic preservation.

David Gebhard (1927–1996; MAS 1966), a noted expert on West Coast architecture, received his doctorate from the University of Minnesota in 1957 with a dissertation on Purcell and Elmslie. In 1962 he began to teach at the University of California, Santa Barbara, and serve as director of the University Art Museum, where a year later he founded the Architectural Drawings Collection. His *Guide to Architecture in Southern California* (co-authored with Robert Winter) was published just prior to his appearance at the 1966 MAS. Subsequent publications include his monograph on Rudolf Schindler (1972) and a book on Frank Lloyd Wright's California work.

Henry-Russell Hitchcock (1903–1987; MAS 1962, 1964, 1966) served as chairman for all three MAS. As the senior historian of the modern movement, his role was pivotal in identifying topics for discussions, framing the chronological boundaries of each working session, inviting participants, introducing the proceedings, and steering the actual symposium discussion. Hitchcock had received his master's from Harvard University in 1927. At the behest of Alfred Barr, Jr., he traveled throughout Europe with Philip Johnson in 1930–1 to gather material for an exhibit held at the fledgling Museum of Modern Art in New York in 1932. Their seminal *Modern Architecture: International Exhibition* and book *International Style: Architecture Since 1922* were largely responsible for introducing European modern architecture to the United States. An extremely prolific scholar, Hitchcock authored a myriad of equally notable volumes prior to organizing the MAS: *Modern Architecture: Romanticism and Reintegration* (1929), *In the Nature of Materials, 1877–1941: The Buildings of Frank Lloyd Wright* (1942), *Architecture: Nineteenth and Twentieth Centuries* (1958), and *The Architecture of H. H. Richardson and His Time* (1961). He taught art history at a number of prestigious institutions and was on the faculty of Smith College at the time of the Columbia symposia.

John M. Jacobus (b. 1927; MAS 1962, 1964) received his Ph.D. from Yale University in 1956 with a dissertation on the architecture of Viollet-le-Duc. He has taught at several institutions including the University of California,

Indiana University, and Dartmouth, where he is currently professor emeritus. An architectural critic, Jacobus wrote essays for the *Architectural Review* in the mid-1960s, notably on James Stirling's Engineering Building at Leicester University and Eero Saarinen's John Deere office building in Moline, Illinois. His book-length writings on modern architecture include *Philip Johnson* (1962) and *Twentieth-Century Architecture: The Middle Years, 1940–1965* (1966).

Philip C. Johnson (1906–2005; MAS 1962, 1964, 1966) was a chief organizer and financial backer of the MAS. Known in the 1960s as an architect and figurehead of the New York design community, he began his professional career in 1932 as the first curator of the Museum of Modern Art's new Department of Architecture. Together with Henry-Russell Hitchcock, he mounted the influential *Modern Architecture: International Exhibition* that same year. After a brief dalliance with fascist politics followed by U.S. military service in World War II, he completed an architecture degree at Harvard. Johnson built a variety of notable works, including his own home, the Glass House (1949), and the MoMA Sculpture Garden (1952), and he collaborated with Mies van der Rohe on the Seagram Building (1958). Other significant works followed, earning him the AIA Gold Medal (1978) and the inaugural Pritzker Prize (1979).

William H. Jordy (1917–1997; MAS 1964, 1966) studied under Erwin Panofsky at the Institute of Fine Arts at New York University (1939–41). After completing his military service, he received his Ph.D. from Yale University in 1947. He taught at Brown University from 1955 until 1985, in the departments of art and architectural history as well as American civilization. He also served intermittently as director of the Society of Architectural Historians (1960–3, 1965–8, 1978–80). Jordy wrote extensively on modern and contemporary architecture. His seminal "The Symbolic Essence of Modern European Architecture of the Twenties and Its Continuing Influence" appeared in *American Society of Architectural Historians Journal* in October 1963. His book-length works include *The Aftermath of the Bauhaus in America: Gropius, Mies, and Breuer* (1968), *Progressive and Academic Ideals at the Turn of the Twentieth Century* (1972), and *The Impact of Modernism in the Mid-Twentieth Century* (1972).

Edgar Kaufmann, Jr. (1910–1989; MAS 1962, 1964, 1966) born into a wealthy family, taught himself the history of art and architecture during study trips in Vienna, London, and Florence. He moved to New York in the early 1930s to become a painter and in 1934 entered Frank Lloyd Wright's studio as an apprentice. During his one-year stay at Taliesin, Kaufmann convinced his father to commission Wright to build what would become Fallingwater. In 1938 the MoMA organized an exhibition on the celebrated house at Bear Run, and the museum's director, Alfred Barr, Jr., offered Kaufmann a position as his personal assistant. In 1963 Kaufmann was appointed professor of art history at Columbia University, a position he held until 1980.

David Mackay (b. 1933; MAS 1966) received his diploma in architecture from Northern Polytechnic in London in 1958. A year later he moved to Barcelona to conduct an extensive study of Spanish architecture, for which he received RIBA's Andrew N. Prentice Prize in 1960. In 1962 he began a (still-active) partnership with architects Josep Martorell and Oriol Bohigas, and in 1966 received the title of architect from the Escola Tècnica Superior d'Arquitectura in

Barcelona. He is the author of *Contradictions in Living Environment: An Analysis of 22 Spanish Houses* (1971) and *Modern Architecture in Barcelona, 1854–1939* (1985).

Carroll L. V. Meeks (1907–1966; MAS 1962, 1964) taught the history of art and architecture at Yale University. A devoted member of the Society of Architectural Historians, Meeks served as secretary-treasurer (1942), vice-president (1944–8), president (1949 and 1957), and director (1950–6, 1958–6). His diverse published works include the *Bibliography of Architectural Criticism in America, 1864–1929* (1934), "Books and Buildings, 1449–1949: One Hundred Great Architectural Books Most Influential in Shaping the Architecture of the Western World," published in conjunction with an exhibition at Yale (1949), *Railroad Station: An Architectural History* (1956), and *Italian Architecture, 1750–1914* (1966).

Henry Millon (b. 1927; MAS 1962, 1964) earned his master's in architecture from Tulane and Ph.D. in art history from Harvard University. His dissertation on Guarino Guarini (1964) was supervised by Rudolf Wittkower. He taught at MIT and published extensively on Renaissance and Baroque architecture. In 1974, Millon co-founded with Stanford Anderson and others the Ph.D. Program in History, Theory, and Criticism of Architecture, Art, and Urban Form at MIT. In 1979 he become the first dean to head the Center for Advanced Studies in the Visual Arts at the National Gallery of Art, a position he held until 2000.

Dorothea Maria Pauline Alice Sybille ("Sibyl") Pietzsch Moholy-Nagy (1903–1971; MAS 1962, 1964, 1966), the daughter of an architect, studied art, history, and philosophy at the universities of Leipzig and Frankfurt. She moved to Berlin in 1925 to pursue an acting career. She met László Moholy-Nagy in 1930 and collaborated with him on a motion picture. The couple married two years later and in 1936 fled Germany together, going first to London and then the United States, where László directed the New Bauhaus and later the Institute of Design in Chicago. After her husband's death in 1946, Sibyl began her career as an architectural historian and critic. Through her teaching at the Pratt Institute (1951–69) and frequent contributions to *Architectural Forum* and *Progressive Architecture*, she became legendary for her outspoken nature and acerbic wit. Her books include *Native Genius in Anonymous Architecture* (1957) and *Matrix of Man: An Illustrated History of Urban Environment* (1968).

Paul F. Norton (1917–2007; MAS 1964, 1966) received his Ph.D. from Princeton University in 1952. He was hired in 1958 to form and lead a new department of art history at the University of Massachusetts, Amherst, where he subsequently spent much of his teaching career. A frequent contributor to the *Journal of the Society of Architectural Historians*, he published numerous book reviews and scholarly essays on American and European topics. Norton also co-authored *The Arts in America: The Nineteenth Century* (1969; he was personally responsible for the section on architecture) and wrote *Amherst: A Guide to Its Architecture* (1975).

Christian F. Otto (1940–2013; MAS 1964, 1966) was a master's candidate at Columbia University when the MAS were held, working with symposia organizer George Collins on his thesis "German Architecture and the November Revolution" (1966). Otto also earned a Ph.D. in art history from Columbia, in

1971, with a dissertation on Balthasar Neumann's church architecture. In 1970 he began teaching at Cornell, where he remained for more than forty years. He published many works on Neumann as well as other subjects; in 1991 he co-authored *Weissenhof 1927 and the Modern Movement in Architecture*.

Mark L. Peisch (b. 1921; MAS 1962, 1964, 1966) received his bachelor's in art history from Dartmouth College in 1944. After completing his military service in 1947 and teaching briefly at Dartmouth, Peisch enrolled as a graduate student at Columbia University, where he was mentored by such noted scholars as Talbot Hamlin, Adolf Placzek, Jacques Barzun, Meyer Schapiro, and Rudolph Wittkower. Peisch received his Ph.D. in 1959; his dissertation was published in 1964 under the title *The Chicago School of Architecture: Early Followers of Sullivan and Wright*. While continuing to study and write on the Prairie School, Peisch held positions in academic administration at Columbia.

Adolf K. Placzek (1913–2000; MAS 1962, 1964, 1966) was one of the chief organizers of the MAS. He contributed historiographical exhibitions or annotated bibliographies to each event. Having begun doctoral studies in architectural history at the University of Vienna in 1934, he was prevented from earning his degree by the Nazi invasion of Austria. (The university awarded him a Ph.D. with honors in 1998.) After immigrating to the United States, Placzek received his library science degree from Columbia. During his long tenure as librarian of the university's Avery Architectural and Fine Arts Library (1948–80), he considerably expanded its holdings and oversaw the publication of the multi-volume *Catalog of the Avery Memorial Architectural Library* and *Avery Index to Architectural Periodicals*. Placzek also edited the four-volume *Macmillan Encyclopedia of Architects* (1982) and, in 1993, launched the Society of Architectural Historians' *Buildings of the United States* book series.

Helen Rosenau (1900–1984; MAS 1966) studied art history at the universities of Munich, Halle, Berlin, Bonn, and Hamburg, working under the direction of Heinrich Wölfflin and Erwin Panofsky, among others. She graduated in 1930 from Hamburg and immigrated in 1933 to Zurich and then England to escape the Nazi regime. She received her doctorate in 1940 from the Courtauld Institute and taught at several British institutions (including the University of Manchester, at the time of the MAS). Rosenau is especially known for her work on eighteenth-century French architecture, Boullée in particular.

Robert Rosenblum (1927–2006; MAS 1962, 1964), an art historian, received his master's from Yale University (1950) and Ph.D. from the Institute of Fine Arts (1956). At the time he attended the MAS, he was teaching at Princeton. In 1966 he took a position at the Institute of Fine Arts, where he remained until his death. From 1996 he also served as curator of twentieth-century art at the Guggenheim Museum. A prolific scholar with far-ranging interests, Rosenblum published broadly. His contributions include the groundbreaking *Transformations in Late 18th-Century Art* (1967) and (with H. W. Janson) *Art of the Nineteenth Century* (1984), as well as monographs on subjects as diverse as Ingres and Andy Warhol.

Colin Rowe (1920–1999; MAS 1964, 1966) had already published two of his most canonical essays by the time he attended the 1964 MAS: "The Mathematics of the Ideal Villa: Palladio and Le Corbusier Compared" (1947) and Part One of the two-part "Transparency, Literal and Phenomenal" (1963), which he co-authored with Robert Slutzky. He graduated from the Liverpool School of Architecture in 1946 after serving in the British army during World War II and then studied at the Warburg Institute in London, where he completed a thesis on the theoretical drawings of Inigo Jones under Rudolf Wittkower. After studying briefly at Yale University with Henry-Russell Hitchcock, he held teaching positions at the University of Texas, Austin, and Cambridge University before finally settling in at Cornell in 1962. He retired in 1990 and in 1995 was awarded the RIBA Royal Gold Medal.

Eugene Santomasso (1938–1993; MAS 1966) was a doctoral candidate at Columbia University during the 1966 MAS. He completed his Ph.D. in 1973 with a thesis entitled "Origins and Aims of German Expressionist Architecture: An Essay into the Expressionist Frame of Mind in Germany, Especially as Typified in the Work of Rudolf Steiner." He taught art history at Columbia beginning in 1967, also receiving appointments at Brooklyn College and at the Graduate Center of the City University of New York.

Vincent J. Scully, Jr. (b. 1920; MAS 1962, 1964) entered Yale University as an undergraduate in 1936 and studied English, his interest in art history emerging only in his final semester. Following military service in the Army Air Corps, he returned to Yale in 1946 to study art history and architecture at the graduate level. He completed his Ph.D. in 1949 with a thesis entitled "The Cottage Style: An Organic Development in Later 19th-Century Wooden Domestic Architecture in the Eastern United States." His advisor was Henry-Russell Hitchcock. Scully is perhaps best known as the teacher of generations of architects: he became a professor of art history at Yale in 1949, where he taught, among other courses, his famed "Introduction to the History of Art" until 2009. His broad architectural interests are emblematic of a period in which the subject matter of scholarly research grew increasingly eclectic: his enthusiastic endorsement of Robert Venturi's *Complexity and Contradiction in Architecture* (1966) provides evidence of this. In addition to monographs on Frank Lloyd Wright and Mies van der Rohe, his major books include *The Shingle Style: Architectural Theory and Design from Richardson to the Origins of Wright* (1955) and *Modern Architecture: The Architecture of Democracy* (1961).

Eduard F. Sekler (b. 1920; MAS 1964, 1966) received his degree at the Technical University in Vienna. After working briefly there as an architect, he moved to London and studied at the Warburg Institute under Rudolf Wittkower. He received his Ph.D. from the University of London in 1948. In 1955 he was invited by José Luis Sert to teach architectural history at the Harvard Graduate School of Design. In 1962 he was appointed coordinator of studies at the newly founded Carpenter Center for the Visual Arts and from 1966 to 1976 served as its first director. He co-founded the university's Visual and Environmental Studies Department in 1968. His important monograph on Josef Hoffmann appeared in 1982. Sekler retired from Harvard in 2004.

Mary Patricia May Sekler (b. 1932; MAS 1964, 1966) received her Ph.D. in fine arts from Harvard University in 1973 with her dissertation, "The Early Drawings of Charles-Edouard Jeanneret (Le Corbusier), 1902–1908." In 1974 she co-curated an exhibit on Le Corbusier's teacher, Charles L'Eplattenier, at the Musée des Beaux-Arts of La Chaux-de-Fonds and edited a related catalogue. The bulk of her scholarly research and writing, however, remained focused on Le Corbusier himself. She is married to Eduard Sekler.

Péter Serényi (1931–2012; MAS 1962, 1964) completed his master's in history at Yale (1958) and his Ph.D. in art history at Washington University (1968) with the dissertation "Le Corbusier's Art and Thought, 1918–1935." He was an instructor at Amherst College at the time of the 1962 conference. Serényi later taught in the Department of Art and Architecture at Northeastern University, which he chaired from 1983 to 1996. In 1975 Serényi edited the volume *Le Corbusier in Perspective*, which included essays by Reyner Banham, Alan Colquhoun, Peter Collins, Rudolf Wittkower, and Kenneth Frampton, as well Colin Rowe's seminal "The Mathematics of the Ideal Villa" of 1947.

Colin St. John Wilson (1922–2007; MAS 1964, 1966) began his studies in architecture at Cambridge and, after serving in World War II, earned his degree from University College in London in 1949. A practicing architect from 1956 on, he was responsible for the new British Library in London. This controversial project, originally proposed for a site in London's historic Bloomsbury district in 1962, was delayed by protests, budget cuts, and political wrangling, and was completed only three decades later. Wilson taught at Cambridge, where he chaired the School of Architecture from 1975 to 1989. Late in his career he authored *Architectural Reflections: Studies in the Philosophy and Practice of Architecture* (1992) and *The Other Tradition of Modern Architecture* (1995).

Robert A. M. Stern (b. 1939; MAS 1964, 1966) received his master's in architecture from Yale University in 1965. After working as a designer in the office of Richard Meier and practicing in partnership with John S. Hagmann, he founded his own firm in 1977. Stern served as program director (1965–6) and president (1973–7) of the Architectural League of New York. He began teaching at Columbia University in 1969, where he also served as director of the Historic Preservation Program and as the first director of the Temple Hoyne Buell Center for the Study of American Architecture (1984–8). He later became a professor of architecture at Yale University, where he was appointed dean in 1998. Stern has built an array of private residences and institutional buildings and writes extensively on modern and contemporary architecture.

Winston Weisman (1909–1997; MAS 1966) received his master's in art history from at the Institute of Fine Arts (1936) and his Ph.D. in art history and studio art from Ohio State University (1939) with a dissertation on Rockefeller Center. His interest in the skyscraper typology would lead him to author numerous essays, including "Who Designed Rockefeller Center?" (1951), "New York and the Problem of the First Skyscraper" (1953), and "Philadelphia Functionalism and Sullivan" (1961). Weisman taught at Pennsylvania State University. In 1970, he began documenting the cast-iron architecture of New York south of Houston Street: this research formed the basis for the Landmarks Commission's 1973 designation of SoHo as a landmark district.

Rudolf Wittkower (1901–1971; MAS 1964, 1966), best known as the author of *Architectural Principles in the Age of Humanism* (1949), received his doctorate in art history from the Berlin University in 1923 and studied in Rome as a research fellow at the Biblioteca Hertziana until 1933. He taught at the Warburg Institute and the University of London before moving to the United States and to Columbia University in 1956. After retiring in 1969, he held positions at the National Gallery of Art in Washington, D.C., Cambridge University, and the Institute for Advanced Study at Princeton. An extremely prolific scholar, Wittkower wrote on an immense range of Renaissance and baroque figures, including Alberti, Bernini, Inigo Jones, Michelangelo, Palladio, Piranesi, Poussin, and Raphael.

SELECTED BUILDINGS

1. Martin Nyrop
Copenhagen City Hall, Copenhagen, 1892–1905

2. Adolf Loos
Kärntner (or American) Bar, Vienna, 1907
Selected as an important building of 1907–17
by Philip Johnson

3. Hans Poelzig
Werdermühle, Breslau, Germany
(now Wroclaw, Poland), 1906–7
Selected as an important building of 1907–17
by Robert A. M. Stern

4. Starrett & Van Vleck
Everett Building, New York, 1908

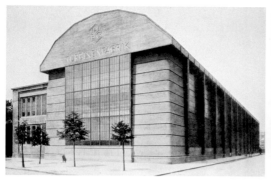

5. Peter Behrens
AEG Turbine Factory, Berlin, 1908–9
Selected as an important building of 1907–17
by Philip Johnson

6. Hunt, Eager, & Burns
Bent House, Los Angeles, 1909

8. Frank Lloyd Wright
Robie House, Chicago, 1909
Selected as an important building of 1907–17
by Philip Johnson and Robert A. M. Stern

7. Charles Rennie Mackintosh
School of Art, Glasgow, 1897–1909, west wing
Selected as an important building of 1907–17
by Robert A. M. Stern

9. Peter Behrens
AEG High Tension Factory, Berlin, 1910
Selected as an important building of 1907–17
by Robert A. M. Stern

10. Gesellius, Lindgren and Saarinen
Helsinki National Museum, Helsinki, 1910

11. Holabird & Roche
Brooks Building, Chicago, 1909–10

13. Greene & Greene
Culbertson House, Pasadena, California, 1911

12. Adolf Loos
Steiner House, Vienna, 1910
Selected as an important building of 1907–17
by Robert A. M. Stern

14. Josef Hoffmann
Stoclet Palace, Brussels, Belgium, 1905–11
Selected as an important building of 1907–17
by Philip Johnson

15. McKim Mead & White
Pennsylvania Station, New York, 1911

16. Hans Poelzig
Water Tower, Posen, Germany (now Poznán, Poland), 1911

17. Purcell and Elmslie
Bradley Bungalow, Woods Hole, Massachusetts, 1911

18. Frank Lloyd Wright
Avery Coonley Playhouse, Riverside, Illinois, 1911
Selected as an important building of 1907–17
by Robert A. M. Stern

19. Peter Behrens
German Embassy, St. Petersburg, 1911–2
Selected as an important building of 1907–17
by Philip Johnson

20. Irving Gill
Miltimore House, South Pasadena, California, 1911–2

21. Walter Gropius and Adolf Meyer
Fagus Shoe-Last Factory, Alfeld-an-der Leine,
Germany, 1911–2
Selected as an important building of 1907–17
by Philip Johnson

22. Cass Gilbert
Woolworth Building, New York, 1911–3

23. Ludwig Mies van der Rohe
Kröller–Müller House
Wassenaar, the Netherlands, 1912–3
Selected as an important building of 1907–17
by Philip Johnson

24. Reed & Stem and Warren & Wetmore
Grand Central Station, New York, 1903–13
Selected as an important building of 1907–17
by Robert A. M. Stern

25. Hendrik Berlage
Holland House, London, 1914

26. Antoni Gaudí
Crypt of the Colonia Güell Chapel, Barcelona, 1898–1914
Selected as an important building of 1907–17
by Philip Johnson

27. Walter Gropius and Adolf Meyer
Werkbund Model Factory, Cologne, 1914
Selected as an important building of 1907–17
by Robert A. M. Stern

28. Josef Hoffmann
Austrian Pavilion courtyard, Werkbund Exhibition,
Cologne, 1914

29. Eliel Saarinen
Helsinki Railway Station, Helsinki, 1906–14

30. Antonio Sant'Elia
Città Nuova (project), 1914
Selected as an important building of 1907–17
by Philip Johnson

32. Percy Dwight Bentley
Emil Mueller House, La Crosse, Wisconsin, 1915

31. Bruno Taut
Glass House, Deutscher Werkbund Exhibition
Cologne, 1914

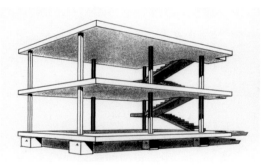

33. Le Corbusier
Maison Dom-Ino (prototype), 1915
Selected as an important building of 1907–17
by Philip Johnson

34. Bertram Goodhue and Carlton Winslow
Panama–California Exposition, San Diego, 1915

35. Le Corbusier
Villa Schwob, La Chaux-de-Fonds, Switzerland, 1916

36. Marinus Jan Granpré Molière
Tuindorp Vreewijk, Rotterdam, 1916

37. Robert van 't Hoff
Huis ter Heide, near Utrecht, 1915–6

38. Willis Polk
Hallidie Building, San Francisco, 1917

39. Michel de Klerk
Eigen Haard Housing Block and Post Office,
Amsterdam, 1913–20
Selected as an important building of 1907–17
by Robert A. M. Stern

40. Vladimir Tatlin
Monument to the Third International (project), 1919–20

41. Robert Wiene
The Cabinet of Dr. Caligari, movie still, 1920

42. Gino Coppedé
Quartiere Coppedé, Rome, 1921

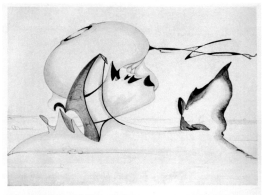

43. Hermann Finsterlin
Casa Nova–Zunkunftsarchitektur (project), 1921

44. Erich Mendelsohn
Einstein Tower, Potsdam, Germany, 1921

46. Hans Poelzig
Salzburg Festival Theater, Salzburg, Austria, 1919–21

47. Frank Lloyd Wright
Barnsdall (Hollyhock) House, Los Angeles, 1921

45. Ludwig Mies van der Rohe
Friedrichstrasse Skyscraper, Berlin, 1921

48. Le Corbusier
Maison Citrohan (prototype), 1920–2

49. Leendert Cornelis van der Vlugt
Gewerbeschule (Trade School), Groningen,
the Netherlands, 1922

50. P. V. Jensen-Klint
Grundtvig Church, Copenhagen, 1922

51. Walter Gropius
Monument to the Fallen, Berlin, 1923

52. Georg Muche
Haus am Horn, Weimar, Germany, 1923

53. Rudolph Schindler
Pueblo Ribera, La Jolla, California, 1923

54. Frank Lloyd Wright
Millard House, Pasadena, California, 1923

55. Fritz Höger
Chilehaus, Hamburg, Germany, 1923–4

56. Le Corbusier
Pavillon de l'Esprit Nouveau, Paris, 1925

57. Walter Gropius
Bauhaus Building, Dessau, Germany, 1923–5

58. El Lissitzky
Cloud Hangers, Moscow, 1925

59. J. J. P. Oud
Café de Unie, Rotterdam, 1925

60. Gerrit Rietveld
Schroeder House, Utrecht, 1924–5

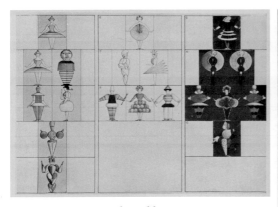

61. Oskar Schlemmer
Bauhaus stage design, 1924–5

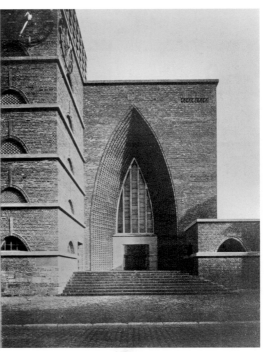

62. Dominikus Böhm
Siedlungkirche, Mainz–Bischofsheim, Germany, 1926

63. Brinkman & Van der Vlugt
Van Nelle Factory, Rotterdam, 1926

64. Francis Barry Byrne
Church of Christ the King, Tulsa, Oklahoma, 1925–6

65. Walter Gropius
Siedlung, Dessau–Törten, Germany, 1926

66. Walter Gropius
Bauhaus Master's House, Dessau, Germany, 1926

67. Hugo Häring
Farm, Gut Garkau, Germany, 1922–6

68. Ernst May
Siedlung Römerstadt, Frankfurt-am-Main, 1926

69. Rudolph Schindler
Lovell Beach House, Newport Beach, California, 1926

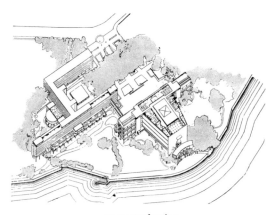

70. Le Corbusier
League of Nations competition entry, Geneva, 1927

71. Buckminster Fuller
Dymaxion House (project), 1927

72. Ludwig Mies van der Rohe
Weissenhofsiedlung, Stuttgart, 1927

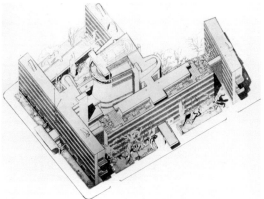

73. Le Corbusier
Centrosoyus, Moscow, 1928

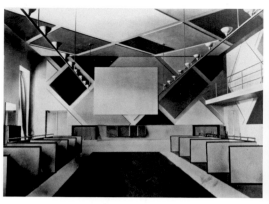

74. Theo van Doesburg
Cafe Aubette, Strasbourg, France, 1928

75. Richard Neutra
Lovell Health House, Los Angeles, 1928

77. Alvar Aalto
Turun Sanomat, Turku, Finland, 1929

76. Rudolf Steiner
Goetheanum, Dornach, Switzerland, 1928

78 b. Le Corbusier and Pierre Jeanneret
Villa Savoye, Poissy, France, ca. 1956

78 a. Le Corbusier and Pierre Jeanneret
Villa Savoye, Poissy, France, 1929

79. Hugh Ferriss
Metropolis of Tomorrow (project), 1929

81. Ludwig Mies van der Rohe
German Pavilion, Barcelona, 1929

80. Hood & Howells
Daily News Building, New York, 1929–30

82. Clarence S. Stein and Henry Wright
Radburn, New Jersey, 1929

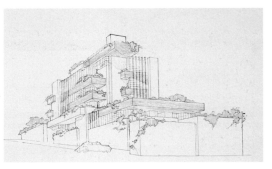

83. Frank Lloyd Wright
Noble Apartments (project), Los Angeles, 1929

85. Sir Edwin Lutyens
Palace of the Viceroy and Capitol Complex,
New Delhi, 1911–31
Selected as an important building of 1907–17
by Robert A. M. Stern

84. Le Corbusier
Villa de Mandrot, Le Pradet, France, 1931

86. Marcel Breuer
Harnischmacher House, Wiesbaden, Germany, 1932
Nominated as an important building of 1929–39
by Henry-Russell Hitchcock

88. Frank Lloyd Wright
Broadacre City (project), 1932

87. Howe and Lescaze
Philadelphia Savings Fund Society (PSFS) Building,
Philadelphia, 1932
Nominated as an important building of 1929–39
by Henry-Russell Hitchcock

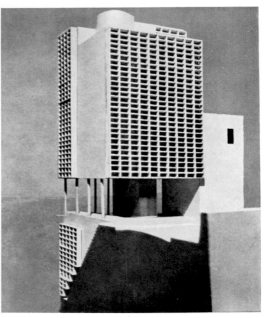

89. Eugène Beaudouin and Marcel Lods
Cité de la Muette, Drancy, Paris, 1933
Nominated as an important building of 1929–39
by Henry-Russell Hitchcock

90. Le Corbusier
Project for an Apartment, Algiers, 1933
Nominated as an important building of 1929–39
by Péter Serényi

91. Oscar Stonorov and Alfred Kastner
Carl Mackley Houses, Philadelphia, 1934
Nominated as an important building of 1929–39
by George Collins

92. Brinkman & Van der Vlugt
Bergpolder Apartments, Rotterdam, 1934
Nominated as an important building of 1929–39
by Henry-Russell Hitchcock

93. Alfred and Emil Roth and Marcel Breuer
Dolderthal Apartments, Zurich, 1934
Nominated as an important building of 1929–39
by Henry-Russell Hitchcock

94. Carlos Arniches, Martin Dominguez
and Eduardo Torroja
Zarzuela Hippodrome, Madrid, 1935
Nominated as an important building of 1929–39
by George Collins

95. Eugène Beaudouin and Marcel Lods
Open-Air School, Suresnes, France, 1935
Nominated as an important building of 1929–39
by Henry-Russell Hitchcock

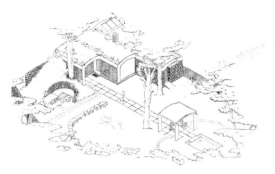

96. Le Corbusier and Pierre Jeanneret
Maison de week-end, La Celle-Saint-Cloud, France, 1935

97. Richard Neutra
Bell (Corona Avenue) School, Los Angeles, 1935
Nominated as an important building of 1929–39
by Henry-Russell Hitchcock

98. Erich Mendelsohn
Chaim Weizmann House, Rehobeth, Israel, 1935–6

99. Richard Neutra
John Nicholas Brown House, Fishers Island,
New York, 1936
Nominated as an important building of 1929–39
by Henry-Russell Hitchcock

100. Giuseppe Terragni
Casa del Fascio (now Popolo), Como, Italy, 1932–6
Nominated as an important building of 1929–39
by Adolf Placzek

101. C. Howard Crane
Earls Court, London, 1937
Nominated as an important building of 1929–39
by Kenneth Smith

102. Ignazio Gardella
Tuberculosis Clinic, Alessandria, Italy, 1936–8

103. José Luis Sert and Luis Lacasa
Spanish Pavilion, World's Fair, Paris, 1937

104. Grosser and Schürmann
City of 20,000 Inhabitants (project), 1938

106. Walter Gropius and Marcel Breuer
Gropius House, Lincoln, Massachusettes, 1938

105. Raymond Hood and others
Rockefeller Center, New York, 1931–7
Nominated as an important building of 1929–39
by William Jordy

108. Albert Kahn
Dodge Truck Plant, Warren, Michigan, 1938
Nominated as an important building of 1929–39
by Henry-Russell Hitchcock

107. William Crabtree and others
Peter Jones Department Store, London, 1938
Nominated as an important building of 1929–39
by Henry-Russell Hitchcock

109. Tecton Group
Finsbury Health Centre, London, 1938
Nominated as an important building of 1929–39
by Kenneth Smith

110. Frank Lloyd Wright
Taliesin West, Scottsdale, Arizona, 1938
Nominated as an important building of 1929–39
by Elizabeth Mock Kassler

111. Alvar Aalto
Sulphate pulp mill, Sunila, Finland, 1936–9
Nominated as an important building of 1929–39
by William Jordy

112. Alvar Aalto
Villa Mairea, Noormarkku, Finland, 1938–9
Nominated as an important building of 1929–39
by George Collins

113. Cesare Cattaneo
Apartment House, Cernobbio, Italy, 1938–9
Nominated as an important building of 1929–39
by Colin Rowe

114. Philip Goodwin and Edward Durell Stone
Museum of Modern Art, New York, 1939
Nominated as an important building of 1929–39
by Henry-Russell Hitchcock

115. Albert Kahn and Norman Bel Geddes
General Motors Pavilion, New York World's Fair,
Flushing Meadows, New York, 1939

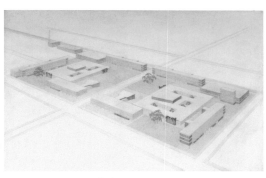

117. Gunnar Asplund
Woodland Crematorium, Stockholm, 1935–40
Nominated as an important building of 1929–39
by Eduard Sekler

116. Ludwig Mies van der Rohe
Illinois Institute of Technology (IIT), campus plan
Chicago, 1939

118. Pier Luigi Nervi
Military Hangers, Orbetello, Italy, 1938–42
Nominated as an important building of 1929–39
by Henry-Russell Hitchcock

Illustration Credits

1. Photograph from *Architectural Record*, October 1905. Photographer unknown
2. Photograph from the Architectural Press Archive/RIBA Library Photographs Collection. Work of Adolf Loos © 2014 Artists Rights Society (ARS), New York/Bildrecht, Vienna
3. Photograph from Foto Marburg/Art Resource, N.Y.
4. Photograph from the Museum of the City of New York. Photograph by the Wurts Bros. (New York, N.Y.)
5. Photograph from Foto Marburg/Art Resource, N.Y.
6. Photograph from *Western Architect*, April 1910. Photographer unknown
7. Photograph courtesy of the Hunterian, University of Glasgow. Photograph by Annan, Glasgow
8. Photograph courtesy of the Frank Lloyd Wright Foundation and the Frank Lloyd Wright Foundation Archives (Museum of Modern Art/Avery Architectural & Fine Arts Library, Columbia University, New York). Work of Frank Lloyd Wright © 2014 Frank Lloyd Wright Foundation, Scottsdale, Ariz./Artists Rights Society (ARS), N.Y.
9. Photograph from Foto Marburg/Art Resource, N.Y.
10. Photograph from the National Board of Antiquities. Photograph by Heikki Havas
11. Photograph from the Chicago History Museum, HB-38581-P. Photograph by Bill Engdahl, Hedrich-Blessing
12. Photograph from the Albertina, Vienna. Work of Adolf Loos © 2014 Artists Rights Society (ARS), New York/Bildrecht, Vienna
13. Photograph courtesy of Mary and Howard Durham
14. Photograph © WOKA LAMPS VIENNA
15. Photograph by Peter Moore © Barbara Moore/VAGA, N.Y., from *The Destruction of Penn Station* (D.A.P., 2000)
16. Photograph from Foto Marburg/Art Resource, N.Y.
17. Photograph © Wayne Andrews/Esto
18. Photograph courtesy of the Frank Lloyd Wright Foundation and the Frank Lloyd Wright Foundation Archives (Museum of Modern Art/Avery Architectural & Fine Arts Library, Columbia University, New York). Work of Frank Lloyd Wright © 2014 Frank Lloyd Wright Foundation, Scottsdale, Ariz./Artists Rights Society (ARS), N.Y.
19. Photograph from Foto Marburg/Art Resource, N.Y.
20. Photograph © Tim Street-Porter
21. Photograph courtesy of the Harvard Art Museums/Busch-Reisinger Museum. Photographer unknown. Work of Walter Gropius © 2014 Artists Rights Society (ARS), New York/VG Bild-Kunst, Bonn
22. Photograph from the Collection of the New-York Historical Society
23. Digital image © Museum of Modern Art/Licensed by SCALA/Art Resource, N.Y. Work of Ludwig Mies van der Rohe © 2014 Artists Rights Society (ARS), New York/VG Bild-Kunst, Bonn
24. Photograph from W. Middleton, *Grand Central* (Golden West Books, 1977). Photograph by David V. Hyde/Penn Central Company
25. Photograph from the Architectural Press Archive/RIBA Library Photographs Collection
26. Photograph "Cripta Güell2o" by Canaan. Licensed under Creative Commons BY-SA 3.0
27. Photograph courtesy of the Harvard Art Museums/Busch-Reisinger Museum. Photographer unknown. Work of Walter Gropius © 2014 Artists Rights Society (ARS), New York/VG Bild-Kunst, Bonn
28. Photograph © IMAGNO/Austrian Archives
29. Photograph from the Museum of Finnish Architecture. Photograph by Apollo
30. Photograph from the RIBA Library Books & Periodicals Collection
31. Photograph from Foto Marburg/Art Resource, N.Y.
32. Photograph © 1972 Prairie School Press. Used by permission along with that of Mrs. Kenneth Dahl, who supplied the original
33. Work of Le Corbusier © F.L.C./ADAGP, Paris/Artists Rights Society (ARS), New York, 2014
34. Photograph courtesy of the Division of Rare and Manuscript Collections, Cornell University Library
35. Work of Le Corbusier © F.L.C./ADAGP, Paris/Artists Rights Society (ARS), New York, 2014
36. Photograph from the Collection Het Nieuwe Instituut, Archive (code): TENT, Inv. Nr.: n12
37. Photograph from the Collection Het Nieuwe Instituut, Archive (code): HOFF, Inv. Nr.: p8
38. Photograph courtesy of the Library of Congress, Call No. HABS CAL,38-SANFRA,149–1
39. Photograph courtesy of the Library of Congress, Call No. LC-USF34-003306-HG-Z-C [P&P]
40. Photograph from bpk, Berlin/Art Resource, N.Y.
41. Film still from Deutsche Kinemathek
42. Photograph © and courtesy of Judith Testa
43. Image from *Wendingen* 3, 1924. Work of Hermann Finsterlin © 2014 Artists Rights Society (ARS), New York/VG Bild-Kunst, Bonn
44. Photograph from SLUB Dresden/Deutsche Fotothek
45. Image from Bauhaus-Archiv Berlin. Work of Ludwig Mies van der Rohe © 2014 Artists Rights Society (ARS), New York/VG Bild-Kunst, Bonn
46. Photograph from Foto Marburg/Art Resource, N.Y.
47. Photograph courtesy of the Frank Lloyd Wright Foundation and the Frank Lloyd Wright Foundation Archives (Museum of Modern Art/Avery Architectural & Fine Arts Library, Columbia University, New York). Work of Frank Lloyd Wright © 2014 Frank Lloyd Wright Foundation, Scottsdale, Ariz./Artists Rights Society (ARS), N.Y.
48. Work of Le Corbusier © F.L.C./ADAGP, Paris/Artists Rights Society (ARS), New York, 2014
49. Photograph from the Collection Het Nieuwe Instituut, Archive (code): TENT, Inv.Nr.: 0308
50. Photograph from the Royal Library, Denmark
51. Photograph courtesy of the Harvard Art Museums/Busch-Reisinger Museum. Photographer unknown. Work of Walter Gropius © 2014 Artists Rights Society (ARS), New York/VG Bild-Kunst, Bonn
52. Photograph from bpk, Berlin/Art Resource, N.Y. Work of Georg Muche © Bauhaus-Archiv Berlin
53. Photograph from the R. M. Schindler papers, Architecture and Design Collection, Art Design & Architecture Museum, UC Santa Barbara © UC Regents
54. Photograph courtesy of the Frank Lloyd Wright Foundation and the Frank Lloyd Wright Foundation Archives (Museum of Modern Art/Avery Architectural & Fine Arts Library, Columbia University, New York). Work of Frank Lloyd Wright © 2014 Frank Lloyd Wright Foundation, Scottsdale, Ariz./Artists Rights Society (ARS), N.Y.
55. Photograph from SLUB Dresden/Deutsche Fotothek
56. Work of Le Corbusier © F.L.C./ADAGP, Paris/Artists Rights Society (ARS), New York 2014
57. Photograph courtesy of the Harvard Art Museums/Busch-Reisinger Museum. Photographer unknown. Work of Walter Gropius © 2014 Artists Rights Society (ARS), New York/VG Bild-Kunst, Bonn
58. Photograph from the Getty Research Institute, Los Angeles (950076). Work of El Lissitzky © 2014 Artists Rights Society (ARS), New York
59. Photograph from the Collection Het Nieuwe Instituut, Archive (code): OUDJ, Inv. Nr.: ph255. Work of J. J. P. Oud © 2014 Artists Rights Society (ARS), New York/c/o Pictoright Amsterdam
60. Photograph from Foto Marburg/Art Resource, N.Y. Work of Gerrit Rietveld © 2014 Artists Rights Society (ARS), New York/c/o Pictoright Amsterdam
61. Image from *Bauhaus, 1919–1928*, eds. Herbert Bayer, Walter Gropius, Ise Gropius (Museum of Modern Art, 1938)
62. Photograph © Rheinisches Bildarchiv Köln
63. Photograph courtesy of Broekbakema

Architects Rotterdam

64. Photograph from the Chicago History Museum, ICHi-68780

65. Photograph from Bauhaus-Archiv Berlin. Work of Walter Gropius © 2014 Artists Rights Society (ARS), New York/VG Bild-Kunst, Bonn

66. Photograph courtesy of the Harvard Art Museums/Busch-Reisinger Museum. Photographer unknown. Work of Walter Gropius © 2014 Artists Rights Society (ARS), New York/VG Bild-Kunst, Bonn

67. Photograph © and courtesy of Peter Blundell Jones. Work of Hugo Häring © 2014 Artists Rights Society (ARS), New York/VG Bild-Kunst, Bonn

68. Photograph from Foto Marburg/Art Resource, N.Y.

69. Photograph from the R. M. Schindler papers, Architecture and Design Collection, Art Design & Architecture Museum, UC Santa Barbara © UC Regents

70. Work of Le Corbusier © F.L.C./ADAGP, Paris/Artists Rights Society (ARS), New York 2014

71. Photograph courtesy of the Estate of R. Buckminster Fuller

72. Photograph from ullstein bild/Granger Collection, New York. Work of Ludwig Mies van der Rohe © 2014 Artists Rights Society (ARS), New York/VG Bild-Kunst, Bonn

73. Work of Le Corbusier © F.L.C./ADAGP, Paris/Artists Rights Society (ARS), New York 2014

74. Photograph courtesy of the Musées de Strasbourg

75. Photograph from the Julius Shulman Photography Archive, Research Library at the Getty Research Institute (2004.R.10) © J. Paul Getty Trust. Used with permission.

76. Photograph from Rudolf Steiner, *Ways to a New Style in Architecture* (Anthroposophical Pub. Co., 1927). Used with permission of the Rudolf Steiner Archive

77. Photograph © Alvar Aalto Museum. Photograph by Gustaf Welin. Work of Alvar Aalto © 2014 Artists Rights Society (ARS), New York/KUVASTO, Helsinki

78a. Digital image © Museum of Modern Art/Licensed by SCALA/Art Resource, N.Y. Work of Le Corbusier © F.L.C./ADAGP, Paris/Artists Rights Society (ARS), New York 2014

78b. Photograph from the Architectural Association Photo Library

79. Image courtesy of the Avery Architectural & Fine Arts Library, Columbia University, New York

80. Digital image © Museum of Modern Art/Licensed by SCALA/Art Resource, N.Y. Photograph by Berenice Abbott © Berenice Abbott/Getty Images

81. Digital image © Museum of Modern Art/Licensed by SCALA/Art Resource, N.Y. Work of Ludwig Mies van der Rohe © 2014 Artists Rights Society (ARS), New York/VG

Bild-Kunst, Bonn

82. Image from the Clarence S. Stein papers, #3600. Courtesy of the Division of Rare and Manuscript Collections, Cornell University Library

83. Image courtesy of the Frank Lloyd Wright Foundation and the Frank Lloyd Wright Foundation Archives (Museum of Modern Art/Avery Architectural & Fine Arts Library, Columbia University, New York). Work of Frank Lloyd Wright © 2014 Frank Lloyd Wright Foundation, Scottsdale, Ariz./Artists Rights Society (ARS), N.Y.

84. Work of Le Corbusier © F.L.C./ADAGP, Paris/Artists Rights Society (ARS), New York 2014

85. Photograph © *Country Life*

86. Photograph from the Marcel Breuer papers, Archives of American Art, Smithsonian Institution. Photograph by Wolf and Lotte Schede-Foto.

87. Photograph from the Library Company of Philadelphia

88. Photograph courtesy of the Frank Lloyd Wright Foundation and the Frank Lloyd Wright Foundation Archives (Museum of Modern Art/Avery Architectural & Fine Arts Library, Columbia University, New York). Work of Frank Lloyd Wright © 2014 Frank Lloyd Wright Foundation, Scottsdale, Ariz./Artists Rights Society (ARS), N.Y.

89. Photograph from the Académie d'architecture/Cité de l'architecture et du patrimoine/Archives d'architecture du XXe siècle © Fonds Lods. Work of Eugène Beaudouin © 2014 Artists Rights Society (ARS), New York/ADAGP, Paris

90. Work of Le Corbusier © F.L.C./ADAGP, Paris/Artists Rights Society (ARS), New York 2014

91. Photograph from the Philadelphia Record Photograph Morgue (DAMS #10855, page 3), Historical Society of Pennsylvania

92. Photograph courtesy of Broekbakema Architects Rotterdam

93. Photograph from the Marcel Breuer papers, Archives of American Art, Smithsonian Institution. Photographer unknown

94. Photograph from The Concrete Society

95. Photograph from the Académie d'architecture/Cité de l'architecture et du patrimoine/Archives d'architecture du XXe siècle © Fonds Lods. Work of Eugène Beaudouin © 2014 Artists Rights Society (ARS), New York/ADAGP, Paris

96. Work of Le Corbusier © F.L.C./ADAGP, Paris/Artists Rights Society (ARS), New York 2014

97. Photograph from the Historic Architecture and Landscape Image Collection (Digital File # 46870.jpg), Ryerson and Burnham Archives, Art Institute of Chicago

98. Photograph from bpk, Berlin/Kunstbibliothek, Staatliche Museen, Berlin/Art Resource, N.Y.

99. Photograph from the Richard and Dion Neutra papers, UCLA Library Special Collections

100. Photograph from the RIBA Library Photographs Collection

101. Photograph from the Architectural Press Archive/RIBA Library Photographs Collection

102. Photograph from the RIBA Library Photographs Collection

103. Photograph © Ministère de la Culture/Médiathèque du Patrimoine, Dist. RMN-Grand Palais/Art Resource, N.Y.

104. Image from Gottfried Feder, *Die Neue Stadt* (J. Springer, 1939)

105. Photograph courtesy of the Library of Congress, Call No. LC-G612- 20950

106. Photograph courtesy of the Library of Congress, Call No. HABS MASS,9-LIN,16—20. Work of Walter Gropius © 2014 Artists Rights Society (ARS), New York/VG Bild-Kunst, Bonn

107. Photograph from the RIBA Library Photographs Collection

108. Photograph from the Chicago History Museum, HB-04803-I2. Photograph by Ken Hedrich, Hedrich-Blessing

109. Photograph from the Architectural Press Archive/RIBA Library Photographs Collection

110. Photograph courtesy of the Frank Lloyd Wright Foundation and the Frank Lloyd Wright Foundation Archives (Museum of Modern Art/Avery Architectural & Fine Arts Library, Columbia University, New York). Work of Frank Lloyd Wright © 2014 Frank Lloyd Wright Foundation, Scottsdale, Ariz./Artists Rights Society (ARS), N.Y.

111. Photograph © Alvar Aalto Museum. Photograph by Heikki Havas. Work of Alvar Aalto © 2014 Artists Rights Society (ARS), New York/KUVASTO, Helsinki

112. Photograph © Alvar Aalto Museum. Photograph by Gustaf Welin. Work of Alvar Aalto © 2014 Artists Rights Society (ARS), New York/KUVASTO, Helsinki

113. Photograph © and courtesy of Foto Vasconi–Cernobbio

114. Photograph from the Museum of Modern Art Archives, New York. Digital image © Museum of Modern Art/Licensed by SCALA/Art Resource, N.Y.

115. Photograph © General Motors 2014

116. Digital image © Museum of Modern Art/Licensed by SCALA/Art Resource, N.Y. Work of Ludwig Mies van der Rohe © 2014 Artists Rights Society (ARS), New York/VG Bild-Kunst, Bonn

117. Photograph from the Swedish Centre for Architecture and Design, ARKM.1985-109-351. Photograph by C. G. Rosenberg

118. Photograph © Alessandro Vasari

MAS 1962

THE DECADE
1918-1928

Chairman's Memorandum

....

Henry-Russell Hitchcock
January, 1962 *

The decade following World War I, in international retrospect, seems to
have been the most creative (as distinguished from productive) period of
twentieth-century architecture. What came before, despite the individual
importance of Frank Lloyd Wright's Prairie period, has seemed to many critics
but preparation and, until quite lately, what followed has been in very large
part only realization of what the 1920s had adumbrated. Thus, with all due
allowance for the dangers of argument by historical analogy, the 1920s have a
certain similarity with the 1510s when the Renaissance reached, in concepts at
least, its apogee, or with the 1630s and the 1770s.

Whatever else we may think today about the period of the 1920s (and visits
today to its key monuments can be very, very disappointing), we are forced in
1962 to realize that it is no longer part of anyone's present—not even of those
architects such as Ludwig Mies van der Rohe, Le Corbusier, or Walter Gropius,
who were among its great international leaders. Insofar as they gave the
twentieth century certain new forms, those forms are not new any longer but
positively traditional by now. Yet until very lately the polemics and the achievements of the years 1918–28 have been treated by writers on modern architecture
as if they were still actual, a part of our living present rather than our immediate heritage.

Between the world of "current events" and the world of "history" there
is ever an indeterminate limbo; nor does the world of history, of that which is
well and truly past, follow the world of the present at an even distance and a
regular pace. There is no mystical value in the passage of a generation—in this
case actually some forty years—since both old and young sense the world in
chronological (i.e., period) blocks, and sense those blocks differently in every
field from politics to popular music. Architecture is perhaps slower moving
in this respect—that is, recognition of the arrival and of the ending of specific
periods is less clear and less rapid—than certain of the other arts. This is
partly because the full realization of the recurrent aspirations of architects
requires wider social support than in the case, say, of painting, or of poetry,
and partly because architecture is, in Talbot Hamlin's terms, in some real
sense "an art for all men" and not merely for those most closely in touch
with it.

However that may be, several books and many articles of the last few years
have made evident that the 1920s are coming to be recognized as a closed historical epoch. Nikolaus Pevsner, exaggeratedly, has even seen the danger of a
new sort of historicism based on the actual revival of aspects of the architecture of the twenties: physiognomically, indeed, there is much to justify such a
critical conclusion, and even perhaps psychologically. Yet of conscious revivalism there has surely been very little, and that chiefly in Italy, where the period
nominally revived has been an earlier stage of twentieth-century architecture.

The charge that the historical study of a period of the past will necessarily lead to imitation of its forms, a recurrent criticism of historical study in the arts not unsupported by what happened in the eighteenth and nineteenth centuries, is by now generally exploded, however strongly the generation of architects now over seventy—the new architects, in fact, of the 1920s!—may have reacted earlier in this century against the presumptive dangers of historical studies in architectural training. The study of the further past is surely no longer considered corrupting; the study of the nearer past should be even less harmful, at least as regards architecture.

The study of the history of modern architecture, however, was for a long time highly tendentious, and several of the most widely read books in the field consist frankly of special pleading in support of certain a priori critical positions rather than objective reports of what actually happened. But now we have moved far beyond the 1920s, and the time has certainly come to reexamine all that took place in that critical period—not to speak of the artistic and social context in which the new architecture of the period was formed—carefully and with cool objectivity. As regards the period in which some of us, at least, grew up and concerning which others who are younger have taken their attitudes from their elders—architects, teachers, and critics—the time has come to reexamine the inherited legends, reassess the goals, and reconsider the extent to which those goals were—or even perhaps could have been—achieved.

Since the field of action in the 1920s was international, although doubtless focused in Western Europe, new studies of single architects' careers and even of single countries, however badly needed, cannot alone serve the basic demand. Yet as with any historical problem of wide ambiance, various different aspects are complex enough to require detailed special investigation before a new and more accurate general synthesis can safely be hazarded. Even to determine which are, internationally, the more significant aspects and to apprehend their relationships one to another requires contacts and interchanges of opinion and of unpublished information among scholars.

The discussion session held in connection with one of the sections of the XXth International Congress of the History of Art in September 1961 at Columbia University, which centered on the architecture of the early years of the twentieth century, suggested to several participants, including representatives of the Columbia Department of the History of Art and of the Avery Library, that similar discussion sessions might profitably be organized around the problems of the period 1918–28. If such sessions are to be effective, however, it is important that out of the nearly endless possible aspects of a study of the architecture of those years a few topics should be chosen in advance which would offer opportunities for comment from a considerable number of scholars, and topics which are intrinsically important rather than peripheral. In the latter respect it will undoubtedly be found that certain currents and certain architects' lines of development that were too frequently dismissed around 1930 as aberrant have very much more interest today in the light of developments of the last fifteen years. As regards the former consideration, the best way to find out which problems interest more than one or two scholars will be to have each participant send in several suggestions. From these individual suggestions—many of which presumably will be identical or closely related—a limited agenda can be prepared and circulated. Thus, when the discussions take place, the participants will already know what aspects of the overall subject will be specifically dealt with and can be ready to make their individual contributions in developing them.

Such a conference—for it will be that, rather than a conventional panel discussion before an audience—is necessarily an experiment, although not without precedent in other fields of study. If it proves profitable as a whole, and also to the individual participants, it might well be repeated annually, either for further exploration of the same period of architectural history or for some other earlier, or even perhaps later, subject.

* Circulated to prospective participants in advance of the symposium

Topics for Consideration at the Morning and Afternoon Working Sessions

Organizing Committee
April 24, 1962 *

Saturday Morning Session: Functionalism

1. Validity of the term: broad or narrow definition
2. Immediate origins and dissemination of ideals
3. Relation to new visual ideals: cubism, futurism, purism, De Stijl, constructivism, engineering works, etc.
4. Relation to new building materials and methods: economic ambiguity
5. Social and political relations †
6. Degree of realization by 1930

Saturday Afternoon Session: Expressionism

1. Definition: narrow or broad; German or international; theoretical bases
2. Approximate dates of beginnings, peak, and decline
3. Relations to late historicism: romanticism vs. classicism
4. Relation to International Style: countercurrent or passing phase
5. Revaluation of individuals
6. Relative historical importance

* Circulated to participants in advance of the symposium
† Items five and six slated but not formally discussed

Modern Architecture Symposium 1962 Proceedings
May 5, 1962

....

Roster of Participants

Henry–Russell Hitchcock, Smith College
Chairman
Henry Millon, Massachusetts Institute of Technology
Assistant to the Chairman

H. Allen Brooks, University of Toronto
Theodore M. Brown, University of Louisville
George R. Collins, Columbia University
Peter Collins, McGill University
Walter Creese, University of Illinois
James Marston Fitch, Columbia University
John M. Jacobus, University of California
Philip C. Johnson, New York City
Edgar Kaufmann, Jr., New York City
Carroll L. V. Meeks, Yale University
Sibyl Moholy-Nagy, Pratt Institute
Mark L. Peisch, Columbia University
Adolf K. Placzek, Columbia University
Vincent J. Scully, Jr., Yale University

Guests of the Symposium
Alfred H. Barr, Jr., Museum of Modern Art, New York
Richard Chafee, Yale University
Patricia May Sekler, Harvard University
Howard Pederson, Columbia University
Herman G. Pundt, Manchester, Massachusetts
Robert Rosenblum, Princeton University
Eugene Santomasso, Columbia University
Péter Serényi, Amherst College
Suzanne Shulof, Columbia University
Arthur R. Sprague, Columbia University
Robert A. M. Stern, Yale University

Statement by the Organizers

George R. Collins and Adolf K. Placzek
March, 1963*

In May 1962, the Avery Architectural Library and the Department of Art History and Archaeology of Columbia University were hosts to the Modern Architecture Symposium (MAS), attended by a number of architectural historians from the United States and Canada. The working sessions of the symposium were chaired by Professor Henry-Russell Hitchcock of Smith College with the assistance of Professor Henry Millon of Massachusetts Institute of Technology. The subject under investigation by the symposium was the decade 1918–28, "From the Novembergruppe to the CIAM." Discussion was organized specifically around the origin and applicability of the terms "functionalism" and "expressionism" during that period.

The purpose of this symposium was to provide for scholars and graduate students concerned with the history of modern architecture a series of small closed meetings in which a selected group of experts could exchange views on specific problems in the field in a systematic manner. It is intended that the symposia be held at two-year intervals, preferably at Columbia where there are available the resources of the Avery Library and of the metropolitan area in general.

The idea for such a meeting grew out of the remarkable success of the discussion session "Frank Lloyd Wright and Architecture around 1900" chaired by Mr. Hitchcock at the XXth International Congress of the History of Art at Columbia in September 1961. An organizing committee was formed, somewhat spontaneously in the fall of 1961, consisting of Mr. Hitchcock, Philip C. Johnson, Adolf K. Placzek, and George R. Collins. Early in 1962 invitations were sent to participants along with the chairman's statement of purpose. The participants submitted their suggestions about topics for discussion, and these were organized by the chairman and his assistant, Mr. Millon, into the program. Each participant was permitted to invite two guests (students or colleagues) to attend as part of the small audience. The names of these guests who participated in the discussions or assisted with the arrangements are listed on the Roster of Participants. There were also others present.

The sessions were not taped. A record was taken by Mrs. Patricia May Sekler and Mr. Arthur R. Sprague; their notes were collated and then typed by Mrs. Sekler. After editing by the undersigned, these proceedings were distributed to all those who contributed for their corrections and emendations. Although all such corrections were received back almost immediately, while the event was still fresh in memory, there has been a delay of several months in preparation of the final manuscript.

In connection with the symposium, an exhibition of architectural books was arranged in the Avery Library. This was so pertinent to the theme of the meetings that it may be considered the "bibliography" of the sessions, and therefore a complete inventory of it has been appended to these proceedings. Also scheduled to coincide with the symposium was an exhibition in the School of Architecture on the structural theory of Antoni Gaudí (the gist of which appears in the spring 1963 issue of *Perspecta*). The Frank Lloyd Wright drawings were on view at the Museum of Modern Art at the time.

The Avery Library was host to the participants, their guests, and university faculty and officials at a party the evening before the symposium. Another such social gathering was held privately for the participants and guests the evening after the sessions. The entire project and its realization were made possible by the generous financial assistance of the Graduate Faculties of Columbia University and of Mr. Johnson.

*Written to accompany a mimeographed version of the proceedings made available at Columbia University

Saturday Morning Session: Functionalism
May 5, 1962
....

[Henry-Russell Hitchcock, chairman of the symposium, opened the meetings by welcoming the participants and their guests. After noting that for each session the morning and afternoon topics were closely related aspects of the same question, he called upon Peter Collins to begin the symposium by defining "functionalism," considered with a capital "F."]

Peter Collins: Arnold Whittick, in *European Architecture in the 20th Century* of 1950–3, cites J. E. Barton as the first to use the term "functionalism." This was in Barton's *Purpose and Admiration* (1932), a popular work probably written in 1931:

> In architectural discussion today a good deal is heard about "functionalism." The vogue of this term has been largely inspired by the work and propaganda of the French architect Le Corbusier, who is the author of the now-famous saying, "A house is a machine to live in." The gospel of functionalism which he preaches, and which many designers all over Europe have taken up with ardor, asserts that function and beauty are twins. *It recognizes no beauty except that which comes from the perfect adaptation of an object to the function which it exists to carry out.* There is nothing new, of course, in the broad idea that beauty and purpose are related.... What is novel in present-day functionalism is the merciless French logic of its application, stripping architecture to the bone, rejecting all the accretions and fancies that have gathered round it from age to age, shaping it anew in the strictest conformity with practical requirements, and re-clothing the skeleton only so far as mere health demands.[1]

Barton assumes that this notion stems from Le Corbusier (pseudo. of Charles-Édouard Jeanneret); but as anyone familiar with Le Corbusier's writings knows, it is at variance with them. Compare Barton's remarks in italics in the above quotation with Le Corbusier in *Towards a New Architecture*: "When a thing responds to a need, it is not beautiful; it satisfies all one part of our mind, the primary part, without which there is no possibility of richer satisfactions; let us recover the right order of events."[2]

Why did Barton make such a patently false attribution? I suggest that it was inspired, not by a misunderstanding of Le Corbusier's text, but by Frederick Etchells's translation of Le Corbusier's *Vers une architecture* from 1927. Barton's notion of functionalism specifically occurs in Etchells's translation at the end of the chapter entitled "Eyes Which Do Not See: I. Liners," yet it does not appear in the original text at all. Compare Etchells's translation with the original text:

Etchells translation:

> The creations of mechanical technique are organisms tending to a pure functioning, and obey the same evolutionary laws as those objects in nature which excite our admiration.... A seriously minded architect, looking at it as an architect (i.e. a creator of organisms) will find in a steamship his freedom from an age-long but contemptible enslavement to the past.[3]

Original French:

Les créations de la technique machiniste sont des organismes tendant à la pureté et subissant les mêmes règles évolutives que les objets de la nature qui suscitent notre admiration.... Un architecte sérieux qui regarde en architecte (créateur d'organismes) trouvera dans un paquebot la libération des servitudes séculaires maudites.[4]

As to why Etchells should be shy of the word "*pureté*" and prefer the words "pure functioning" is perhaps a problem more in the domain of a psychiatrist than an architectural historian. It should be noted, however, that in Etchells's introduction, the concept of functionalism is even more explicit, as the following quotations show:

Now, in modern mechanical engineering, forms seem to be developed mainly in accordance with function. The designer or inventor probably does not concern himself directly with what the final appearance may be, and probably does not consciously care. But men are endowed in varying degree with an instinct for ordered arrangement, and this can come into operation even when least thought of. The ordinary motor-car engine is a conspicuous example of this.... In structural engineering the same thing appears. The modern concrete bridge or dam may be a crude and ungainly affair, or it may possess its own grave and stark beauty; the structure being equally good and functional in either case.[5]

And:

The modern engineer, then, pursues function first and form second, but it is difficult for him to avoid results that are plastically good.[6]

It will be noticed that Etchells makes no distinction between structural function and organic function, whereas Le Corbusier was concerned with the organic sense of function, i.e., with the way people live, the circulation of the house, etc. Etchells says that a concrete bridge "may possess its own grave and stark beauty." But Le Corbusier would here have used "harmony," not "beauty," since for him the engineer's aesthetic equaled harmony only, whereas the architect's aesthetic equaled harmony plus beauty. Etchells makes similarly tendentious references in his introduction later on:

It is precisely Le Corbusier's originality in this book that he takes such works as the Parthenon or Michelangelo's apses at St. Peter's and makes us see them in much the same direct fashion as any man might look at a motorcar or a railway bridge. These buildings, studied in their functional and plastic aspects, emerge in a new guise.[7]

And later:

Already the average user of the motor-car is beginning to take a keen pleasure in good bodywork, in cleanness of line and general design.... It is not too much to hope that this interest may soon include within its scope our modern architecture, passing from, it may be, an appreciation of works of a functional or purely constructional character to embrace works of even greater significance.[8]

Thus Etchells, in his introduction, uses the word "functional" where Le Corbusier in his text speaks of an organism. For example, Le Corbusier's text, even in Etchells's translation, reads, "If we feel the need of a new architecture, a clear and settled organism, it is because, as things are, the sensation of mathematical order cannot touch us since things no longer respond to a need."[9] And then, "A plan proceeds from within to without, for a house or a palace is an organism comparable to a living being."[10]

From these texts we see that the use of the word "functional" and much of the confusion which surrounds it seems to stem from the Etchells translation. If we now turn to consider the popularity of the word, it seems that the term "functionalism," used in a mechanical-determinant sense, began to appear in the architectural periodicals about 1930. A book review by James Burford of three books on modern architecture appeared in the August 1930 issue of *Architectural Review* and contained the following remark:

> Let me say a word at this point to the mechanistic school which tells us that
> if a building meets its purpose, and its construction is the logical outcome of the
> means employed, it has done all that good architecture has any right to require.
> It is said to be "functional."[11]

Similarly, P. Morton Shand, writing on Alvar Aalto, with respect to the Turun Sanomat at Turku [*figure 77*] in the September 1931 issue of the *Architectural Review* defined functionalism by saying: "Aalto is a 'functionalist' in the sense that he moulds form in the semblance of basic construction and purpose, working outwards from plan instead of inwards from elevation."[12] Thus Shand interprets Le Corbusier correctly but uses the term "functionalist" inappropriately. Finally, "functionalism," used in a structural sense, became so popular that it even appeared in an article entitled "Mediaeval Functionalism," in the *Architectural Review* of July 1931: "The dread word *functionalism* must be applied to timbering because it is so frequently connected with all that is not functional in the more unhealthy branches of modern architecture."[13]

Henry-Russell Hitchcock: Concerning the use of the word in 1931, I had been asked by Reyner Banham, in correspondence prior to the publication of his *Theory and Design in the First Machine Age* (1960), just how the word was considered at that time. For Alfred Barr, Philip Johnson, and myself, the term was not new in the early 1930s, and we used it with a small "f."[14] But it did not come into use as we know it until the late 1930s. The two-sided use of the term stems from various writers, including J. M. Richards, Charalambos Sfaellos, and Edward Robert DeZurko.[15]

Today we are concerned not so much with how "functionalism" was first used but with its validity as a term. How useful is it? How should it be interpreted? The only way to make it apply is to interpret it broadly — it always expressed an aspiration more than a reality. The term "*Zweckbau*," that is, "building to a purpose," is also important in this connection.

[Hitchcock then called on Sibyl Moholy-Nagy.]

Sibyl Moholy-Nagy: So far we have concentrated on the English use of the term in the early twentieth century. We must also look into developments in Germany before and after the World War I, especially the work of Hermann

Muthesius, a charter member of the Werkbund, who formulated the Werkbund Resolution of 1911, "Die Einheit der Funktion."[16] This was a reaction against the Arts and Crafts movement and art nouveau. The Werkbund was the last great movement encouraging architects of stature to do low-cost building schemes of social importance—*Siedlungen*. Great figures of this movement toward the social responsibility of architecture were Ernst May, Bruno Taut, Walter Gropius, Hans Scharoun, and Otto Bartning. They rallied after World War I around three major catchwords denoting three aspects of functionalism, on the economical, aesthetic, and social planes: *Rationalisierung der Bauwirtschaft* (rationalization of the construction industry; also, *Normierung*, standardization), *Neue Sachlichkeit* (the new objectivity), and *Gesamtkultur* (literally, total culture).

The *Rationalisierung der Bauwirtschaft* was based on two demands: the unification of component parts according to spatial and structural measurement, tabulated in the *Deutsche Industrie-Normen* (German industrial standards), or DIN format, and an attempt to fix absolute standards of taste. Taut, who had been made the city-architect of Magdeburg, said in 1923, "One must organize the building of apartment houses after the example of automobile fabrication." And Gropius: "Houses must be reduced to their fabricable components and must be mass-produced." Thus he advocates the mass production of building parts and their assembly on the site "like toy boxes."

The second goal of "rationalization," that of norms for taste, was clearly formulated in points one and two of the "Ten Guiding Principles" put by Muthesius before the Werkbund meeting in Cologne of July 1914:

1. Architecture, and with it the whole area of Werkbund activity, urges on us a move toward standardization. Only through standardization can we recover the general significance which architecture had in times of a harmonious culture.

2. Only standardization, which must be understood as the end result of a wholesome concentration, can open the way for a generally valid unfailing taste.[17]

The term *Neue Sachlichkeit* was probably first used by Gustav Hartlaub, the director of the Mannheim Kunsthalle. In 1923, Hartlaub was exhibiing the paintings of Otto Dix, Max Beckmann, George Grosz, and others. *Neue Sachlichkeit* was formulated as the opposite of *Stil* (style). The new objectivity was opposed to any ornament on facades and any expressionistic deviation from reality in the arts. Among the documents is an article by H. Imhauser, "Gibt es eine neue Architektur?" in *Pyramide* of 1927 (a very rare publication):

Style has gradually descended to connote irrelevant external matters. It is too worn out to be appreciated at all…. The demand of *Sachlichkeit* should at this moment be viewed as a reaction against the preceding lack of meaning. It is a concept which, since it permits a comparative, permits yet an ultimate degree of *Unsachlichkeit*.[18]

"Style" is still being discussed; therefore it was an important challenge. Or Gropius: "The result of such a changed and deepened spirit and its new technological implementations is a changed building form (*Baugestalt*), which has not been created for its own sake but grew from the essence of the building, from its function, which it must fulfill."[19]

Gesamtkultur, the third of the three catchwords of German functionalism, was neatly classified into expedient and universal function by Taut: "Simple human huts need only protection against cold, rain, and hunger. Simplicity around our bodies must keep a long distance from the dwelling-place of ideas."[20] This, as against Taut's: "The ideal dwelling has nothing to do with aesthetics, but only with ethics. The practical and the ethical become a unit, and therefore the new dwelling becomes completely beautiful."[21] And Gropius: "The ethical power of industrial functionality."[22]

The striving toward *Gesamtkultur* climaxed in the founding in 1928 of the Congrès Internationaux d'Architecture Moderne (CIAM). Many heterogeneous convictions were represented in the CIAM group, which Sigfried Giedion and Le Corbusier tried to unify through a somewhat acrobatic and contradictory universalism in their draft for the CIAM Town Planning Charter, where they wrote, "It should assure on the spiritual and material planes individual liberty through the benefit of collective action."[23] Its first working session (held at the second congress, in Frankfurt, in 1929) was devoted to "The Subsistence Minimum Dwelling"; the second working session (held at the third congress, in Brussels, in 1930) was devoted to "Rational Methods of Siting." The key to CIAM functionalism is to be found in the CIAM Charter, which declared: "The course to be taken by all town-planning projects will be influenced basically by political, social, and economic factors existing at the time, and not, in the last resort, by the spirit of modern architecture."[24]

Adolf K. Placzek: We always seem to be coming back to that ugly word *Zweckbau*.

Moholy-Nagy: No, it is not an ugly word. It is a nice word, and merely implies a building devoted to a practical purpose.

Hitchcock: What is the relation of Le Corbusier, a pure Swiss, to the Central European events? This has never been fully detailed. We know of his contact with Peter Behrens, the Werkbund, and his first book, *Étude sur le mouvement d'art décoratif en Allemagne* (1911). What about other sources?

Péter Serényi: Le Corbusier's relation to Central European thought goes back to the late nineteenth century and to Jean-Jacques Rousseau, Henri de Saint-Simon, Charles Fourier, and other social thinkers. An ethical ideal seems to have helped formulate the architecture of Gropius, Taut, and Le Corbusier. Therefore we need to know the ethical concerns—when they were adopted, when abandoned. Both Le Corbusier and Frank Lloyd Wright go back to Rousseau, but Wright's more poetic heritage is through Ralph Waldo Emerson, Walt Whitman, Johann Wolfgang von Goethe, and Gotthold Ephraim Lessing, while Le Corbusier's is through Saint-Simon and Fourier. The latter were concerned with a total concept of the world, a *Gesamtkultur*, and were interested in unity as such.

World War I itself did much to influence modern architecture by inspiring the architects to formulate and write down their ideas; many of their ideas were fulfilled after the war. In reaction to the unsettled conditions brought about by the war, Gropius and Le Corbusier sought a unity, a concept of a total culture, which could overcome the chaos of the world in many realms—social, economic, cultural, etc. As Sibyl Moholy-Nagy says, the major purpose of architecture at this time was ethical.

Hitchcock: Mention of ethical concerns brings to mind immediately such people as Adolf Loos and Henry van de Velde, and the development treated in Nikolaus Pevsner's *Pioneers of the Modern Movement* (1936). We tend to feel that England and America were outside this story until the "importation" in the late 1920s of Continental ideas. But Muthesius, for example, was in England to study housing before World War I. Is England just remote background?

Walter Creese: As Mr. Serényi observes, Wright looked back to Emerson, Whitman, Henry David Thoreau, and the Naturalists, and so did a number of the members of the English domestic school. The point here is that the English had already adjusted the house to nature, essayed a functionalism of the environment, before they felt the impact of World War I. That manifested itself as a moderate acceptance of greater mechanization, but I believe the basic modern search among the British was for a renewed sense of locus or place which they had earlier lost. Therefore it was an "environmental" ethic. Muthesius makes a good tie, I would say.

Hitchcock: In the U.S. there seems to have been a lack of interest in international movements. European happenings were little known here; there was little dissemination of new ideas. A. D. F. Hamlin's article on the art nouveau was one of the first of the good ones.[25]

Professor Fitch and his students have made a survey of American periodicals from 1918 to 1930. How was this done and what were the results?

[Fitch called on Howard Pederson, who had conducted the research.]

Howard Pederson: The two publications checked were the *Architectural Record* and the *Architectural Forum*. The aim was to see where the modern movement was mentioned and how it was interpreted. In both publications there was a great lack of information. The City Planning Conference in Amsterdam in 1924, reported in the *Architectural Record*, was the first event to be given good coverage. Before this, reports were accidental; after this, more systematic attention is given. As to writers, book reviews around 1918 were of some importance, as were Professor Hitchcock's later reviews of foreign periodicals. The first Hitchcock article appeared in 1928 in the *Architectural Record*.[26]

Hitchcock: Turning to the new visual ideals of the period, many are related to functional aspirations—for example, references to steamboats and automobiles (in Le Corbusier and others). They admired the concept of *Zweckbau* and its results. Also, many of the architects of the 1920s had connections with painters or sculptors. J. J. P. Oud, for instance, who was the first to produce low-cost housing, well before Gropius.[27] What about De Stijl?

Theodore M. Brown: Oud has been writing an article in German to try to revise what has been said of his connections with De Stijl.

Hitchcock: Gerrit Rietveld is also related. What is the connection between functionalist ideals and De Stijl?

Brown: The concept of functionalism was not a part of De Stijl. De Stijl was concerned purely with aesthetics—the visual. As for the Bauhaus and De Stijl, the Bauhaus formulated the functional problem; De Stijl said, "here is how you can do it; this is how it should look."

Moholy-Nagy: There was the famous fight between Gropius and Theo van Doesburg. Gropius called Van Doesburg a useless aesthete, and Van Doesburg called Gropius a Prussian boor.

Brown: De Stijl had ethics plus aesthetics.

Moholy-Nagy: Van Doesburg called the Bauhaus a socialist labor movement.

Hitchcock: Getting back to the relation between painting and architecture, was there "painting toward architecture"? Which came first? How do you place the development in painting (e.g., purism) that was in opposition to surrealism and expressionism? Was it a major current?

Alfred H. Barr, Jr.: It was indeed a major current. In the Soviet Union, the aesthetic of constructivism, as formed by Vladimir Tatlin, Antoine Pevsner, and Naum Gabo, the first two of whom were painters who became sculptors, was worked out and then adapted by architects [figure 40].[28] In De Stijl, the aesthetics and the forms were developed in painting before architecture. Oud's Café de Unie of 1925 in Rotterdam was his most unfortunate work [figure 59]; it was too dependent on Piet Mondrian in design.[29]

Brown: Also the Schroeder House of 1924 [figure 60]. That seems the closest adaptation of the painting of Van Doesburg and Mondrian.

Barr: Another factor which should be looked into is the relationship between Van Doesburg and Le Corbusier. What about the works shown in Léonce Rosenberg's gallery in 1923—the models by Rietveld and Van Doesburg? Van Doesburg was also involved with the Bauhaus. There was a conscious clash. You can clearly see the influence of De Stijl in Gropius's work in the mid-1920s [figure 66]. Gropius told me emphatically that he felt he was uninfluenced in his Bauhaus buildings. Indeed, Gropius had an almost fanatic insistence on his independence from De Stijl, but the influence shows in the forms. Possibly it was unconscious.

   In De Stijl there was a mystical desire to make the artifacts of man all show the same spirit. Mondrian had a mystical hope in the power of his own paintings to save the world—a touching ambition. The work of Kasimir Malevich is metaphysical too.

Mark L. Peisch: One aspect we have not discussed is the role of the so-called Chicago School. Hendrik Petrus Berlage was here in 1911, and Frank Lloyd Wright was published in Germany in 1910. Willem Marinus Dudok was Wrightian. Is there a relationship; do they really share a common background? The Progressive movement in the Midwest led by Robert M. La Follette, Sr., and others, which had such an impact on artists and intellectuals of the time, has only a remote relation to European happenings. How far can we go in relating Wright with Germany and the Lowlands?

[At this point Hitchcock requested the visual material that had been brought by Moholy-Nagy.]

Moholy-Nagy: This material was selected to show housing as a mirror of the architectural development of the 1920s. Slides:

BEHRENS, ROW HOUSE SETTLEMENT, 1910
Adaptation of cottage architecture to row housing, stemming from the Arts and Crafts movement.

GROPIUS, DIAGRAM OF HOUSING FORMS, 1923
Idea of breaking down the house into seven different basic forms to be assembled in various combinations.

GROPIUS, MODEL OF THE ABOVE CONCEPT
Merely typical Werkbund houses of which the roofs have been shaved off. The exteriors were to express the internal functions.

ANONYMOUS, HOUSE IN DANBURY, CONNECTICUT, REAR VIEW
Its many external projections indicate that there is nothing new in the idea of the external expression of function; therefore the functionalist claims of the Bauhaus were its weakest point.

GEORG MUCHE, HAUS AM HORN, 1923, GENERAL VIEW *[figure 52]*
This was published by Adolf Meyer in 1925.[30]

MUCHE, PLAN OF ABOVE
Central plan with living area lighted by clerestory and the utilities occupying the choice east and west exposures.

GROPIUS, FIRST BAUHAUS SETTLEMENT AT DESSAU-TÖRTEN, 1926
[figure 65]
Part of the building set into the ground; called "iceberg architecture."

GROPIUS, HASSELHORST PROJECT, 1928–9
Apartments divided by central corridor. Some given east-west, some north-south orientation; therefore idea of functionality on shaky legs.

De Stijl had great influence on housing in the 1920s:

WEISSENHOF BUILDING EXPOSITION, STUTTGART, 1927
Two highly formalistic schemes by Le Corbusier and Oud show how far the idea of functionalism could be distorted.

ERNST MAY AND C. H. RUDLOFF, NIEDERRAD QUARTER,
FRANKFURT-AM-MAIN, 1926–7
A sober, honest functionality.

HUBERT BITTER, SIEDLUNG "RUNDLING," LEIPZIG-LÖSSNIG, 1929
This is a formalistic arrangement with no relation to function, no evidence externally of internal use.

ERNST MAY, SIEDLUNG RÖMERSTADT, FRANKFURT-AM-MAIN, 1927–8
[*figure 68*]
May, an engineer turned architect, had been hired as city architect in 1920. He was disdained because he rejected theory. Built according to site and materials.

MAY, RÖMERSTADT, DETAIL
Two-family houses with school included, as well as proverbial vegetable gardens. All others perverted concept of functionalism; May did not. Question arose of flat roof versus roof garden. Le Corbusier preferred the roof garden.

DIAGRAM OF ROOF TYPES, FROM A PAMPHLET ISSUED IN 1934 BY THE GARDEN CITY ASSOCIATION OF LONDON
Justifies use of flat roof through absurd reasoning, thus indicates the folly of functionalism.

DIAGRAM OF FLAT ROOF TYPES, WITH SUNLIGHT AND CAST SHADOWS PLOTTED

DIAGRAM OF FLAT ROOF

WEISSENHOFSIEDLUNG, STUTTGART, 1927 [*figure 72*]
Mies was the general director. Site planning was still in its infancy. Disregard for circulation.

GROPIUS'S BUILDING, WEISSENHOF
Obviously influenced by De Stijl.

MIES, BLOCK OF FLATS, WEISSENHOF, FRONT
Already the Miesian elegance and inhumanity.

MIES, BLOCK OF FLATS, WEISSENHOF, REAR

According to presented evidence, the two approaches to functionalism seemed to be the greatest refinement of exterior form relationships according to doctrine, on the one hand; and the acknowledgment of collective needs, on the other. Thus, the conflict between the concern for preconceived design motivations and the regard for human inhabitants. The two sides of functionalism were Mies versus May.

Hitchcock: "Machinolatry" versus new visual ideals. Futurism is related to this. Were functionalist aspirations present in Antonio Sant'Elia? How were his ideas so rapidly diffused?

Carroll L. V. Meeks: By 1914, Sant'Elia had gathered his ideas together. These included the total environment, the importance of the machine and—in his case—a mania for transportation, the worship of the engineer (as was also the case with Filippo Marinetti), the elimination of the past. All these ideas seem to be held in common. Beginning in 1913 his drawings were shown all over Europe, in exhibitions promoted by Marinetti. In Italy itself they had no direct influence until much later. Sant'Elia held many ideas in common with the others but never got to asymmetry.

Hitchcock: Turning now to economic ambiguity, the problem was how to put the new social ideas into effect. For example, mass housing was difficult to solve economically. In Germany the functionalist leaders were not the most productive. Less extreme men such as May did the bulk of the significant work in the low-cost housing tradition. How does a building like the Philadelphia Saving Fund Society Building (PSFS) by Howe and Lescaze (1932) [*figure 87*] relate both to the idea of dissemination and to the economic question? How did George Howe "sell" the building?

Robert A. M. Stern: Purely on rationalization of the design features: better suitability to needs, better sunlight, circulation, etc.

Hitchcock: Do you have comparative costs?

Stern: On the PSFS itself, the original bids were $10,000,000; the final construction cost was $6,000,000.[31] This is a special case because of its timing with the Depression. Much was specially tooled for the project, and many interiors were handcrafted. The project goes back to 1926 when Howe prepared the original scheme, Beaux-Arts in nature.

[*A question was posed regarding how those costs compared with the Empire State Building and Rockefeller Center.*]

Stern: These figures are not available at the moment. The present scheme is from 1929. The final decision to build was not made until after the Crash. It was thought to be good publicity for the bank.

Hitchcock: How did the rentals hold up?

Stern: Pretty well. The building was air-conditioned, hence good economics.

Hitchcock: What were the actual economics of building in the 1920s with respect to maintenance? Many of the structures appear to be in very bad condition today.

Moholy-Nagy: This is not entirely so. Jungfernheide and Siemenstadt in Berlin have held up very well. In the Weimar Republic the State did the building and then leased to cities or districts, which were responsible for upkeep. Therefore, no private capital was involved. Private architects were not able to compete easily, and many railed against the extravagance of public housing. Evidence of this was given at the 1960 Stuttgart housing conference with a comment to the effect that there was no longer a Weimar Republic to maintain housing.

Barr: The durability of the materials used has a lot to do with it. Didn't Michel de Klerk use brick?

Hitchcock: Many of the sites, especially in Holland, were bad, hence the cost of foundation work was high.

[Participant unknown] **Question:** Does anyone know what the minimum costs were?

John M. Jacobus: There's one famous project in Los Angeles (near Wright's Freeman House), much of it tar paper, that ran three dollars a square foot.

Philip C. Johnson: All economic talk is silly. There is no truth in any economic report. When it comes to finances, all the magazines and the architects, including Frank Lloyd Wright, are damned liars.

Hitchcock: Mr. Brown, what about Holland, especially the economics of the Van Nelle factory [*figure 63*]? It is in good shape today. Was that an extravagant building? And who did design it?

Brown: Much of the work in Holland was stuccoed brick.

Johnson: Oud said it was expensive at the time, but of course he was jealous.

Meeks: Wasn't it refurbished after the war?

Hitchcock: Also, to what extent did all this involve the belief in the 1920s that each generation was to rehouse itself completely? Did the architects of the 1920s mean for their buildings to survive? Many, such as Le Corbusier's Villa Savoye at Poissy [*figure 78 a and b*] and Gropius's Bauhaus building [*figure 57*], have had very difficult circumstances. But others have not and have held up. Isn't one part of the architect's job to consider maintenance?

Johnson: This depends on who maintains it.

Jacobus: Several slides of the Villa Savoye, taken in 1956, show its condition at that time. The building was structurally intact; the roofs and terraces were sound, but one large piece of glass was beginning to slip from a rusted frame. It is my understanding that the house has not been lived in since the early 1940s.

[Four slides were shown.]

Hitchcock: Has Poissy been repainted?

Jacobus: There did not seem to be any evidence of repainting. The original colors have faded. They are described by Hitchcock in 1932 as follows:

> The painted color at Poissy is at once restrained and full of interest. Most important is the strong contrast of dark and light, not of black and white but of dark green below and cream above with dark chocolate window trim. Then on the roof shelter, whose functional [*sic*] and structural requirements are so slight as to justify an absolutely free treatment, the pale rose and pale blue emphasize the adjustment of the curved and straight planes.[32]

In 1958 this color scheme could still be seen albeit in a somewhat ruinous condition.

Johnson: Now can't some of you art historians tell me why those roof elements are so similar to certain of Viking Eggeling's basic shapes?

Moholy-Nagy: No, there is no connection, except that both designers, Le Corbusier as well as Eggeling, were in love with the *angle droit*. But so was Phidias!

Barr: What is the present status of the building?

H. Allen Brooks: It is a playhouse for teenagers. The living room is crowded with ping-pong tables, and they have built a low masonry wall to protect the glass between the living room and the terrace. That "flow of space" has been interrupted.

Herman G. Pundt: Does anyone know the condition of the Bauhaus, and is it accessible?

Johnson: One of the members of my staff saw it last year. She was driving by and could just drive in. She said it looks fine. The glass wall has been replaced.

Moholy-Nagy: This must have been done since 1957: it was missing at that time.

[At this time a short break was called by the chairman.]

Hitchcock: Much more information is needed on the problem of West Coast developments. Rudolph Schindler, coming from Vienna and working with Wright, preceded Neutra in bringing something close to Europe in the 1920s to the United States.

Jacobus: Much of his work I have seen recently, and although I am not as qualified as people like Esther McCoy or Gregory Ain to talk about Schindler, I do have recent visual material. Schindler came to Los Angeles with Wright. Slides:

FRANK LLOYD WRIGHT, BARNSDALL, 1921 (HOLLYHOCK) HOUSE AND
STUDIO RESIDENCE, OLIVE HILL, LOS ANGELES *[figure 47]*
Schindler was in charge of their construction beginning in December 1920.

DETAIL OF TERRACE
The fountain (1923) is definitely Schindler, and this sector of Olive Hill was built over the site of Wright's "Little Dipper" kindergarten, begun in 1923 but demolished by Schindler in 1923 at Miss Barnsdall's instruction.[33]

WRIGHT, SAM FREEMAN HOUSE, LOS ANGELES, 1923–4
While the building was done by Wright after Schindler left Wright's employ, according to the original owner's statement of 1962, the furnishings were subsequently designed by Schindler.

SCHINDLER, PUEBLO RIBERA APARTMENTS, LA JOLLA, CALIFORNIA, 1923
[figure 53]
Poured concrete slab with movable forms, a technique he is said to have
learned from Lloyd Wright (who is supposed to have built a hotel in
Riverside, Illinois, according to Neutra's *Wie Baut Amerika* of 1927).

TWO DETAILS OF ABOVE

SCHINDLER, HOUSE FOR DR. LOVELL, NEWPORT BEACH, CALIFORNIA, 1926
[figure 69]
The same patron as Neutra's in Hollywood, 1927–9.

NUMEROUS DETAILS OF ABOVE
This was the third of three projects that Schindler did for the same
patron. Two-story studio and living quarters—an arrangement analogous
to Le Corbusier's Citrohan projects [figure 48]. Now it is sought out by
innumerable architecture students. The sleeping porches are functionally
reminiscent of Greene & Greene. Subsequently glassed in by Schindler,
they were originally open (at the top of the building). Reinforced concrete
frame, wood studs, double stair ramp, window detail consistent with the
structural forms. This dramatic open structure shows Schindler's degree of
separation from Wright. We do not know how he arrived at it, nor can any
exact European and Viennese contacts be specified as yet. Neutra's 1927 book
includes a photo of the house under construction. The facing is stucco.

P. Collins: In the *Architectural Review* of June 1931, in an article on American
architecture, a caption to a photo of Neutra's Lovell House [figure 75] contains
the following, which purports to be a quotation: "The essential functional
requirements of a modern house have created this form as the most efficient
and expressive solution to the problem posed."[34]

Meeks: Isn't the upper corner of the rear of the Schindler house like Rietveld?

Jacobus: Yes. De Stijl shows here, and the date of 1926 certainly indicates
that stylistic communication between Europe and America was swift.

Creese: But must we not look also within the region as well as outside, particularly in the buildings of architects like Bernard Maybeck and Irving Gill?
Neutra, after all, was influenced by Gill. Gill used pergolas in some
such fashion.

Vincent J. Scully, Jr.: The big armature is what is significant.

Creese: That does not seem unlike Wright, Otto Wagner, or Josef Hoffmann
to me. I believe these people came to Wright from Austria because they felt
the affinity of his work. Schindler studied with Wagner before he came to the
United States in 1913. Recall Wagner's own villa outside Vienna, his Steinhof
Chapel, or his Franz Joseph Fountain. All had space frames with other solids set
in among them. Go further with the interior of Hoffmann's Stoclet House, with
its frames supporting the hovering planes of the balconies [figure 14]. That delicate little space frame outside the Gropius House porch at Lincoln [figure 106]

tells a lot. In interpreting the Schindler elevation, one has to remember also that the plot was narrow.

Jacobus: Schindler is a Viennese bringing, among other things, Chicago ideas to the West Coast—an architect of considerable individuality, trying to break loose from the influence of Wright.

Scully: Why did Neutra break loose from concrete and go to steel?

Jacobus: In 1927 there was a split between Neutra and Schindler. And in 1931 there was an architectural exhibition in California, and both Wright and Schindler were invited. This gave Wright a chance to denounce Schindler again. Clearly these architects were all too individualistic to get along together.

Creese: Wasn't Lovell some sort of health enthusiast? He was called "Dr." Lovell, and believed in sleeping in the open air, swimming, breakfast foods, etc. His house by Neutra was published as the "health house." All this is connected with ideas of hygiene, public health, and purity. That suggests an important component of prewar functionalism. Neutra often mentions in his earlier houses the dust-free qualities of the rooms. I feel that the first functionalisms were functionalism of the heart (as in the British search for *locus*) and hygiene (coming out of the nineteenth-century association of health with better housing). I heard Neutra give a talk in which slums were featured in just this way, in contrast to his own "clean" buildings.

George R. Collins: Going back to De Stijl, it shows here in the suspended or hovering effect. This was not like the Wright that Schindler knew. Two documents may be of interest here. One is a letter from Van Doesburg to Adolf Behne, dated 7 November 1928, regarding the Aubette in Strasbourg [*figure 74*], which illustrates the De Stijl search for the art of total design that Mr. Barr mentioned earlier:

> The Aubette in Strasbourg has taught me that the time is not yet ripe for an "all-embracing creation." When the Aubette was just finished, before its inauguration, it was really good and significant as the first realization of a program which we have cherished for years: the total artistic design (*Gesamtkunstwerk*). Yet as soon as the proprietors heeded the opinion of their customers (who, of course, considered it cold and uncomfortable) all sorts of things which did not belong were carried into it. The public cannot leave its "brown" world, and it stubbornly rejects the new white world. The public wants to live in mire and shall perish in mire. Let the architect create for the public.... [T]he artist creates beyond the public and demands new conditions diametrically opposed to old conventions, and therefore the work of art contains a destructive power. Rietveld has formulated this very well in the jubilee issue of *Stijl* [1927]. Constant values are only created by a 100% art. This is now my firm conviction. Architecture is on the wrong track, as is applied art.[35]

The second is an article of 1922 by Oud in Taut's *Frühlicht*, the expressionist periodical. It deals with the aesthetics of "hovering" forms:

But furthermore it is possible that by deviating from the old support and load system in which one could construct only from the bottom upward and back (battered toward the rear), one can also build upward and projecting forward (cantilevered out). With the latter the possibility arises of a new architectural plasticity which...may lead to the creation of an architecture of visually immaterial, almost suspended character.[36]

P. Collins: Most of this discussion seems to have dealt with domestic architecture. Perhaps we should remember here John Summerson's essay, "The Case for a Theory of Modern Architecture," published in the *RIBA Journal* in 1957. Summerson contends with good justification that the source for unity in modern architecture is in the architects' program. It is thus clear why those who sought a "new" domestic architecture as an expression of functionalism had to change people's ways of living if they wanted to create it; they had to promote artificially new ways of life for the people in order to build something "modern" to correspond. I suggest that it would be better to look for the best and truest examples of functionalism in the larger buildings for new uses such as Le Corbusier's Swiss Pavilion and Centrosoyus [*figure 73*].

Hitchcock: There was an article important here in the Dutch periodical *i 10*. This is almost impossible to get hold of.

Moholy-Nagy: I have one.

Hitchcock: I shall remember that! On the question of hovering, Frank Lloyd Wright called buildings with *pilotis* "boxes on stilts," but his own hovering roofs converged with them in the late 1920s. Mr. Scully, did Frank Lloyd Wright owe anything to the European functionalists?

Scully: He did by the early 1930s, by the time of the House on the Mesa, the Usonian houses, and Fallingwater. Here he seemed to be redirecting his own ideas of how to put a building together in order to bring them into line with European planar developments. Compare Corbu's Citrohan [*figure 48*] with the Millard House [*figure 54*]. The *parti* is the same, and they have many elements in common. There is the problem of the date. When was the Citrohan first published?

Hitchcock: This is complicated because there are two versions of the Citrohan houses, one on the ground.

Serényi: The Citrohan with *pilotis* was not in *L'Esprit Nouveau*. It was the first version that was published there (in number 13).

Hitchcock: The second version was in *Vers une architecture*, but it is unlikely that Wright ever saw it. After his 1909 flight from Chicago, Wright turned to a more fortresslike architecture (e.g., the Barnsdall [*figure 47*] and Millard houses). They fit less into the site. Wright's pre-1909 work hovers in a way that creates a close relationship with the earth. The European hovering separates from the earth, produces restlessness.

Scully: Wright's buildings became heavy with the site, with an exaggerated attention to mass and weight — he turned to Mayan forms. They are related to hollows and gullies around the buildings.

Serényi: The Barnsdall and Millard houses are very similar in concept and relation to the site.

Scully: No, they are very dissimilar.

Serényi: They are both very stark.

James Marston Fitch: When the Barnsdall House was designed, the land was not yet irrigated. The starkness goes with this. The house was designed for the site, but the site has changed.

Edgar Kaufman, Jr.: Not so. The early sketches for the Barnsdall in the current show at the Museum of Modern Art show that Wright had always thought of the building as situated in a densely wooded area.

Scully: I think the relation of Wright in 1922–3 to Le Corbusier is accidental.

Hitchcock: I agree. But by the time of the Noble Apartments project in 1929 [*figure 83*], the situation changed. Wright was always conscious of the *genius loci*. The Millard House was vertical because of the conditions of the site. The Hardy House was an earlier vertical development. Le Corbusier's Citrohan House had no relation to the site at all. In fact, the concept was so isolated that it could also be piled up into blocks of apartments. In type, the Citrohan falls between his early minimal housing projects (e.g., the Dom-Ino [*figure 33*]) and more elaborate works like the Villa Stein. Citrohan, neither sumptuous nor minimal, was the middle-income dwelling. Why did Le Corbusier abandon his concept of low-cost housing and turn to building more expensive houses in the mid 1920s?

Serényi: Don't you think Le Corbusier knew that good architecture is always expensive?

[Hitchcock adjourned the meeting for lunch at 12:45.]

Saturday Afternoon Session: Expressionism
May 5, 1962

....

Henry-Russell Hitchcock: Various aspects of a definition of expressionism are needed, and we especially need to determine the theoretical basis. You cannot describe it merely as nonfunctionalist. When the word "expressionism" was first used is not of such consequence; it was taken over into architecture from painting. The problem is whether it should be limited to a narrow German movement in the few years after World War I or given broader international application. Mr. Meeks, would you care to comment?

Carroll L. V. Meeks: I am not prepared for a definition. I am primarily interested in Italy at this time. There is nothing on Italy in the Avery Library exhibition; nothing is in Madsen.[37] Italy seems to be a no-man's-land. We are faced with the basic problem of what went on there.

Hitchcock: Few of us seem ready to contribute on this question. Mr. Placzek is interested in the sources.

Adolf K. Placzek: When I set up the exhibition in Avery Library, I was surprised by the richness of material on German expressionism. I could have filled all the cases easily with it, at the expense of the rest. Incidentally, I was also surprised by the lack of any French sources on expressionism. It is as if architectural expressionism had bypassed France completely, at least until Le Corbusier's Ronchamp, in the way in which, as has been often said, baroque architecture bypassed Cartesian France. The question of course arises: what is expressionism? Is it simply the son or daughter of German Romanticism in music and art? If so, who was the father? The philosophy of G. W. F. Hegel, F. W. J. Schelling, et al.? Indeed, what are its literary sources? They patently go back a long way—not only to Romantics like Novalis, but also to the Sturm und Drang, to the expressionistic genius of a Georg Büchner; and it is no mere coincidence that Alban Berg chose Büchner's *Woyzeck* as a libretto, just at the time of the beginning of the new expressionism with which we are concerned today.

What then is expressionism? Can it be defined as the expression of inner experience, as different from outer, visual experience? Or the expression of form (i.e., the visual) as different from structure? And can inner experience be equated with emotion—which would bring us right back to Romanticism, where emotion prevails over the structure, or imposes its own structure not rooted in function. That, in turn, leads us to music, particularly to Wagner (and I mean Richard, not Otto!), and from there to Robert Schumann and possibly to the Beethoven of the late quartets. Admittedly, this is a far cry from Bruno Taut, but after all, architecture has its roots in culture as a whole—whether consciously or unconsciously.

Hitchcock: Certainly there is a relation to Romanticism, especially high and late Romanticism. Let me now read the questions which Mr. Kaufmann has sent in:

1. Did expressionism include the expression of the individual personality?

2. Did it place emphasis on the creative personality? Gropius versus the functionalists.

3. Emphasis on the expression of the nature of the materials? The attitude to structure and the expression of the materials was not based on efficiency, although some very efficient solutions of definite importance were arrived at (e.g., Gaudí). Link to Frank Lloyd Wright through his preoccupation with materials.

4. Emphasis on social ideals? Their expression?[38]

This last one is hard to deal with. The two Goetheana of Rudolf Steiner seem to have been an attempt to express social, religious, and humanist ideals—an otherworldly idealism [*figure 76*]. On the other hand, functionalism has socio-practical ideals. Occasionally these two have come together.

Turning to a different topic, when did expressionism begin in painting?

[Hitchcock called on Robert Rosenblum.]

Robert Rosenblum: Expressionism existed in painting and sculpture before World War I. In architecture it is post–World War I and during the 1920s. The painters and sculptors began to make their statements from about 1905 through 1914 and continued later. Therefore the cycle in sculpture and painting was about a decade earlier than that in architecture.[39]

Placzek: Much of the decisive writing also occurred before World War I. See for example Kurt Pinthus's *Mënschheitsdämmerung*, first published in 1919. This was the great anthology of the works by the German expressionist poets. But all the decisive poems were written before 1914.

Rosenblum: Also in music—Arnold Schoenberg.

Hitchcock: Could one subsume such things as fauvism under expressionism?

Rosenblum: No. This would just lead to confusion. It is better to narrow the definition. It is a very national problem, particularly German.

H. Allen Brooks: What about the Dutch again, especially the Amsterdam School in the 1910s?

Hitchcock: Munich? Relations to art nouveau? Were there Dutch expressionists?

Rosenblum: Of course, there is the question of how much is a continuation of the 1890s. Art nouveau had an expressionistic flavor in the Low Countries.

Hitchcock: A book has come out which brings together much of the material we are concerned with and includes new examples: *Phantastische Architektur*, by Ulrich Conrads and Hans G. Sperlich.[40] George Collins is working on a translation. But I have not read it yet—I am waiting for George to finish.

G. Collins: Actually, I am not doing it; my wife is. It brings up many things that are necessary in order to straighten this out.[41] There are many types of expressionism. One type is of broad definition: expressions of use, of structure, of materials. This includes statements concerning function. Another is liturgical expressionism, for example Antoni Gaudí and Dominikus Böhm [*figure 62*]. Liturgical changes in the church called for new architectural expression of them. A third is German expressionism after World War I, a type in and of itself: a self-contained, cohesive movement; pacifist and internationalist, not nationalist. The new book is important here.

Expressionism in Germany at this moment was not out of step with painting and sculpture. However, little seems to have derived from painting; few of its forms are from painting. Many ideas were exchanged with Amsterdam, and much theory may have come down from art nouveau and symbolism. From 1919 to 1922–3, the German movement was a unified phenomenon of its own. The weakness of the recent *Casabella* article is that the writer is unable to understand many things because he lacks much of the documentary information contained in this new book.[42] There was too much reliance on painting and too little on the architecture in his article. It was an incredible architecture!

The translation of the new book, by the way, will not be called simply *Fantastic Architecture* but *The Architecture of Fantasy: Utopian Building and Planning in Modern Times.* One interesting section we have inserted deals with Steiner's theory of architecture, including empathy (or eurythmy, as he described it). The interior architectural surfaces were shaped by hand in wood at Dornach, to be in resonance with the body moving in eurhythmic dance in the interior space.

Hitchcock: Dornach was a center for Anthroposophy.

Philip C. Johnson: Let's go back to Mr. Rosenblum's statements. I would include only the German developments, 1919 to 1922–3. This leaves out Gaudí. It includes Mies's Friedrichstrasse skyscraper [*figure 45*], Gropius's Weimar monument, and Fritz Höger's Chilehaus [*figure 55*]. Some of the forms are found in woodcuts up to the late 1910s.

George R. Collins: Paul Scheerbart is important for theoretical writings from before World War I.

Hitchcock: Böhm's early churches were intended to be the new ecclesiastical architecture of the twentieth century. And expressionism was intended to be a new architecture, as art nouveau had been, with a certain "form will." Some forms delight, others do not. Expressionistic architecture is overtly emotional, not *sachlich*. It is aimed at emotional response. It is not subjective, but it has some subjectivity in it.

Sibyl Moholy-Nagy: Here is a test case. There was a specific point of changeover from expressionism as an architectural program to functionalism. Johannes Itten had dominated the early Bauhaus — he was strongly expressionist. See the early *Bauhausbücher* for examples. When Gropius came in 1919, there began a literal life-and-death struggle with Itten. Gropius with Moholy then took over in 1923. You can see the changes in Moholy's Bauhaus books.[43]

Much of expressionistic feeling goes back to Novalis, as mentioned — the deepest of the German Romantic poets. The definition of Romanticism in 1801 went somewhat as follows: Romanticism gives sense to the vulgar, hope to the lost, and a sense of eternity to the ephemeral. Two important books from the 1920s were Taut's *Modern Architecture* (1929) and Walter Müller-Wulckow's *Wohnbauten und Siedlungen* (1928). A statement in the latter book is that what counts in building art is the immediate emotional involvement. When you look at the buildings illustrated, you get the feeling that expressionism is inherent in the German character, that there is a constant move toward expressionism, and that the functionalist theory actually never "took."

Placzek: It is interesting that Mrs. Moholy-Nagy should bring up Novalis. I have always considered him one of the great fountains of Romantic intuition, particularly in his little-known notebooks. I found another gem by him the other day: "All true communication is symbolic."[44] Doesn't that anticipate twentieth-century thinking? Even Steiner?

G. Collins: Both Gropius and Taut were involved in a show at J. B. Neumann's *Kabinett* in 1919 in Berlin. Gropius shows himself as a bit of a Romantic in the catalogue of the occasion, in which he says:

> Ideas perish as soon as they are compromised. Therefore distinguish clearly between dream and reality, between everyday work and a longing for the stars.... [G]o into the buildings...engrave your ideas onto their naked walls" and build in fantasy without regard for technical difficulties. To have the gift of imagination is more important than all technology, which always adapts itself to man's creative will. Today there really does not yet exist a true architect, all of us are only the forerunners of the one who will some time again deserve to be called "Architect," a name signifying Lord of Art, who will make gardens of the desert and will heap wonders to the sky.[45]

And from Taut:

> Art—that is the thing, if it be there! Today such art does not exist. The disrupted tendencies can achieve a unity only under the auspices of a new art of building, in such a way that each separate discipline will contribute to it. At that point, there will be no boundaries between the crafts, sculpture, and painting, all will be one: Architecture. A building is the direct carrier of spiritual values, shaper of the sensibilities of the general public, which slumbers today but will awake tomorrow. Only a total revolution in the realm of the spiritual can create this building; yet this revolution, this building, does not happen by itself. Both have to be sought—today's architects must prepare the way for this edifice.[46]

In the manifesto of the Novembergruppe of 1918–9, the author of which is unknown to me, we read the following:

> Spiritual warriors of the world: The blood, roaring, gushed from the heaps of the slain, millions of cadavers piled up and their skeletons chiseled their own sarcophagi. The sweat of hunger demolished lungs and fertilized the withered grass.... Salvation is near. Brothers in the world, bend your knees, our innocence is proven, our conscience pure.... The proletarian armies of the world have grasped at the stars, destroying and building at the same time in a heavenly

craving for justice and love—free men.... [B]rothers, lift up your hearts and eyes high to the firmament, and the ridiculous national boundary stone will be no obstacle to a single fatherland for us all—the World—the Earth![47]

This kind of thinking explains a great deal about Taut's *Alpine Architektur* in the Avery exhibition.

Hitchcock: Better insight into the period will probably also be gained from the book on Mendelsohn's letters, which has been prepared by Mrs. Mendelsohn.[48]

Walter Creese: But as Johnson suggests, we ought to be as specific as possible about the forms themselves so as to observe how ambiguous they are. Expressionism and symbolism can come close together and yet do not quite fuse. There are many questions we have left unanswered about the juxtaposition of these themes and functionalism, too. For instance, what do you do with Mendelsohn's Einstein Tower, which seems to be a key monument [*figure 44*]? Is it out of the Jugendstil, Henry van de Velde's flowing plasticity, or is it the "movement" of the building suggested by expressionism and the new astrophysics? When you change sciences, from the nineteenth-century botany to the twentieth-century physics, do you then automatically and unconsciously change styles, or the meaning of styles? Second, with functionalism, if we follow a branch of it back into the nineteenth century and to the advent of the Industrial Revolution, it becomes evident to me that it is the neutrality of its meaning that counted. The urgent idea was to discover the cheapest and most easily duplicated structure for factories and worker housing. The architect-artist was told "hands off," and the old craftsman squeezed out. Without exaggerating the case too much, it might be maintained that the initial impulse toward functionalism was the initial impulse toward "no-meaning" in the culture and the elimination of the architect. Although it has to be admitted that William Morris, Gropius, and even Wright attempted to fight against this, the question in the long run may be, were they fighting a losing battle? Maybe functionalism as standardization is anti-architectural, and expressionism is trying to tell us so.

James Marston Fitch: Is Mendelsohn on record as calling himself expressionist in his sketches of "ideal" buildings during the 1910s?

Hitchcock: Mendelsohn never felt himself a member of the functionalist camp.

G. Collins: Mendelsohn seemed to be straddling. In 1923 in speaking to the *Wendingen* group on "Dynamics and Function," he said:

In iron, the building material of our time, the revolutionary play of the forces of tension and compression elicits movements which are always astonishing for the professional and are still totally incomprehensible for the layman.
It is our task to find the architectural expression for these dynamic forces, to express through architectural configuration the adjustment of these stresses, to master the vitality of the forces which are pressing internally toward actual movement.... Just as when dealing with dynamics, so when defining "function" there are several points of departure. The reduction of all outward forms to their simplest geometric basis is, properly speaking, the primary requirement

for an original beginning. Knowledge of the elements has always been the prerequisite of creativity.[49]

And in his early wartime letters he commented:

> Spatial geometry, the theory of the control and interrelationship of spaces, of the disposition of bodies and of the layout of space includes all configurations: the simple equations from cube to sphere, the highly complicated ones for any celestial curvature.[50]

Creese: It is the same change within functionalism again, from the ideograms of botany to those of physics. Anthropology is important here also. From 1880 on, the revival of the "noble savage" cult was a factor, in painting with Paul Gauguin, Henri de Toulouse-Lautrec, Vincent van Gogh, Franz Marc, and others. The dilemma was that modern man could not make up his mind whether he was a primitive or a sophisticate. And it really contradicted Darwinian thought too. Don't we still see this in Corbusier, in Aalto, in the younger men like Aldo van Eyck, Jørn Utzon, and even Eero Saarinen? The cave instinct (Ronchamp and the TWA terminal) and field instinct (the Air Force Academy and the GM center) are never done.

Placzek: The noble savage figure *par excellence* is Friedrich Nietzsche's Zarathustra, even including the caves. This, of course, exerted an enormous influence.

Hitchcock: We have touched on the relations to painting and architecture. What about the stage, the theater?

Moholy-Nagy: The Bauhaus stage was very important in 1924–5. It attempted a synthesis of expressionism and constructivism. The Bauhaus stage was the key experimental ground to depersonalize the actor, to make him the carrier of pure universal expression. Oskar Schlemmer, particularly in his mechanical ballets, tried to find out where the limits were [*figure 61*]. What was there in man that could not be subjected to constructivism of movement, expressing the basic identification of man and machine?[51]

Rosenblum: The stage designs of Adolphe Appia and Gordon Craig are of interest, especially Appia's sets for works by Richard Wagner. The forms were important—many of Gothic character.

Hitchcock: Expressionistic architecture is similar to expressionistic painting in taking architectural members and distorting them. This extreme distortion is, in a manner, similar to stage design.

Rosenblum: Appia's Wagner sets look like Mies's skyscraper [*figure 45*] and Gropius's Weimar memorial [*figure 51*].

Hitchcock: We obviously need more information on particular people, such as Hugo Häring and things like his farm buildings at Gut Garkau [*figure 67*]. The *Casabella* article mentions some new literature, including an article on Häring. Mendelsohn, whose letters have just been published, was never wholeheartedly expressionist. Scharoun is still alive today and producing. Who are some of your personal heroes that need to be listed and reevaluated? Taut, for instance, is taken too much for granted.

G. Collins: Miss Suzanne Shulof has passed me a note recalling the work on various aspects of the cinema: the sets for *The Golem* were designed by Hans Poelzig and Fräulein Marlene Moeschke (later Madame Poelzig). There were the theaters and opera houses of Poelzig. Gaudí was pictured in a volume of *Wasmuths Monatshefte* (1920–1), which also includes an article by Heinrich de Fries on space in the cinema — *The Cabinet of Dr. Caligari* [*figure 41*], etc., Poelzig's Salzburg Festival Theater project [*figure 46*] was pictured there, near to illustrations of Gaudí buildings: many things came together at the time. The famous movie *Metropolis* (1927) by Fritz Lang is from our period.

Hitchcock: At this point, let's look at Professor Meeks's visual material on Italy.

Meeks: Slides:

RAIMONDO D'ARONCO, VILLA, TURIN, 1902
Not Floreale, but influenced by Darmstadt, Paris, Belgium.

ANONYMOUS, VILLA, FLORENCE, CA. 1905
View of the upper house with balcony.

HOUSE TOWER
Experiments with ironwork.

ANONYMOUS, FACADE, FLORENCE
Arts and Crafts overtones.

HOUSE AND GATE OF TYPICAL FLOREALE, FLORENCE, CA. 1905

GIULIO ARATA, PALAZZO BERRI-MERRIGALLI, MILAN, 1913

ERNESTO BASILE, VILLA ON VIA ABRUZZI, ROME, 1903, DETAIL

GINO COPPEDÉ, APARTMENTS ON VIA PO, ROME, 1921 [*figure 42*]
Picturesque asymmetry.

GINO COPPEDÉ, VILLA, ROME, 1921

This emphasis on diagonals was carried over from futurism. But Italian publications up to 1928 do not include what was talked of today. Expressionism and futurism were not published in Italy. But they did publish art nouveau, floreale, etc. Good art nouveau was usually derivative in Italy. The floreale was usually imposed on a traditional core without innovations in form or structure — a flamboyant frosting on an old tradition. Therefore, from 1914 to 1927 in Italy there was a general thrashing about — no new architecture. There was good futurist architecture, but it was unbuilt. An influence comes back in 1927–8 in De Stijl buildings, International Style, etc.

G. Collins: Professor Hitchcock has asked for heroes to be revaluated. Another unknown has been Hermann Finsterlin.[52] His drawings are fantastic—all curved surfaces [*figure 43*]. [*Collins shows slides of a sketch from* Wendingen *of 1924 and a study for a bedroom of 1920.*] His is a purely sensuous type of tactilism. He wrote in 1921–2:

> Just as the basic idea of the New Architecture can be expanded to great scale, so it also penetrates down to the minute elements of an architectural entity. The type of form represented by the last great ingenious invention of the Spirit of the Earth (*Erdgeist*)—the organic form—lies between the crystalline and the amorphous. In this in-between area my architecture also blossoms. In the interior of the New House one will not only have the experience of inhabiting a fairy-tale crystalline geode, but also that of being the inhabitant of the insides of an organism, wandering from organ to organ—the giving and receiving symbiont of a giant "fossil mother body." A small portion of the interchangeable set of boxes of World Forms consists of the sequence of city, house, furniture, and vessel: these hollow things must grow one-out-of-the-other like the gonads of an organism; they should no longer be disparate foreign bodies as they were heretofore. Such furnishings as we glue into our large boxes for living would, in the New Space, have the effect of annoying, destructive, irritating strangers. Tell me, have you never been irritated by the brutal system of your six walls and by the intrusion of caskets for your thousand material necessities?—has never the secret desire come over you to re-arrange yourself according to the rhythm of the breathing of your soul?—have you never, like an oxygenic creature, wished to bore and gnaw into the stubborn masses of an erratic Methuselah and to let your impulses play freely within the mellow substance of the stone? The furnishings of the New Room will have to be built-in—subforms, particles of the house organs, inseparable and immovable within them, organs within the organ, containers within the container. It is obvious that their basic materials must then be identical or at least akin. So, for instance, a wardrobe could swell from its root in the wall of a concrete structure, changing into majolica, and finally for its decorative surface other materials can be considered. Imagine beds made out of majolica with their legs growing out of their sub-strata and carrying the eiderdown in their chalice as the mushrooms do the spores of their next generation. Just as "outside in Nature" a body seeking rest will be welcomed by snug crater-like depressions; so the foot will tread on glassy transparent floors that allow the antipodal bas-relief to be fully appreciated—relegating to the illusionary the necessary but dreadful horizontal which, if solid and opaque, would cut through the New Room and Building like a pathological diaphragm. However, the transparent material of the floors allows the diffusion of a full dimensional sense of space, and it holds the dweller in unprecedented equilibrium. This reflecting floor, however, will be crossed by carpets of new forms and colors like streets of vegetation, on which will play the dawn light streaming through "organic" windows, through the thinnest sections of the wall, those sections which, owing to the furniture growth, were thinned down to the point of transparency and glassiness. Or the bare foot will caress the floor sculptures with every step, bringing new life to the neglected tactile sense and enriching the reactions which nowadays reach the level of our consciousness only as the grossest fragments, instead of as inconceivably delicate and pure melodies of the material world by which we are surrounded.[53]

Also Frederick Kiesler's Endless House and the bedroom for an Arabian sheik's daughter—a glass floor with goldfish swimming underneath and the walls covered with fur.[54]

Hitchcock: What do you do with pre-1914 Max Berg in Breslau? His *Jahrhundert Halle* is very dissimilar internally to Auguste Perret's classical world. Like Giovanni Battista Piranesi, it is a romanticism of classical elements.

Richard Chafee: I would like to hear more about expressionist dance and its possible relations to architecture. The great theoretician was Rudolph von Laban in Zurich in 1918—an architect. Others involved were Kurt Jooss, Mary Wigman, and Harold Kreutzberg. Is expressionist dance a symptom or an influence?

Hitchcock: We are also interested in the relation of expressionism to the International Style or functionalism. What was the status of expressionism in the late 1920s? Mendelsohn was in some sense a convert to functionalism. Was there expressionism in the late 1920s, and what was its outcome, particularly in view of events of the last fifteen years? The current estimate was that at the end of the decade it was as dead as a doornail.

Johnson: Then, people even refused to look at Häring. That was a mistake!

Hitchcock: Was Scharoun working then?

G. Collins: First there was the expressionist program of the German groups. See *Ja! Stimmen des Arbeitsrates für Kunst* (1919) for this first stage.[55] Then came the Berliner Secession exhibition of 1923. That was the breaking point. The new architecture was shown there—*Neue Sachlichkeit*. What has been happening since the late fifties finds many parallels in the expressionist forms of 1918–23.

Hitchcock: But I cannot accept that it is a revival.... Expressionism never died out entirely: It just went underground and then broke out again. Aalto did not look at De Klerk and then build the House of Culture. In the early 1930s there was the work of Le Corbusier, and shortly certain work in Latin America (e.g., the parabolic-vaulted churches of Enrique de la Mora, beginning circa 1939).

Fitch: Our search for expressionism in the *Architectural Record* and the *Architectural Forum* was not very successful.

Edgar Kaufman, Jr.: But it seems to come out in the American skyscraper—Radio City.

Mark L. Peisch: I would suggest that Hugh Ferriss, the most popular of the architectural draftsmen, was quite expressionistic. The search for extreme forms pops up in strange places. Even on top of the Chrysler Building.

Creese: There were several expressionist-symbolist painters of skyscrapers in the 1920s, such as John Mann and Georgia O'Keeffe. Some even came here from abroad just to paint skyscrapers, like the English futurist C. R. Nevinson.

Stefan Hirsch, Kenneth Hayes Miller, Louis Lozowick, and Abraham Walkowitz would be other men who painted skyscrapers for their dramatic effect.

Kaufmann: Then America seems to have been the "underground"?

Robert A. M. Stern: Much work in Sweden was important, and a great deal of it appeared in American magazines in the 1920s. The *American Architect* is filled with expressionistic architectural renderings.

Hitchcock: [P. V. Jensen-] Klint's Grundtvig Church in Copenhagen [*figure 50*], other churches in Sweden.

Stern: [Hugh] Ferriss's *Metropolis of Tomorrow* is from Sant'Elia [*figure 79*]. This came out at the end of the 1920s. Raymond Hood carries on from this.

Hitchcock: Yes, and there is Hood's relation to the elder Saarinen, Eliel — the American Radiator Building, the Daily News Building.

Kaufmann: Has anyone done research on the Daily News [*figure 80*]? Walter Kilham remembers working on it, especially the entasis.

Hitchcock: Also Francis Barry Byrne's church in Oklahoma.

Brooks: Barry Byrne did work in Oklahoma, Kansas City, and other parts of the Midwest. The Church of Christ the King in Tulsa, Oklahoma (1925), was expressionistic [*figure 64*], as was the Church of Christ the King in Cork, Ireland (1928). He thought he was reflecting liturgical changes, but they really come later.

Peisch: Böhm was also working with the new liturgical changes [*figure 62*]. The pontificate of Pius X (1903–14) marked a new effort to bring the people closer to the liturgy. A deeper understanding of the Mass And the encouragement of frequent reception of the Holy Eucharist were two aspects of the liturgical revival which had such an important effect on the design of churches during the 1920s.

Johnson: Russell, are you going to include the Dutch in all this?

Hitchcock: This has always troubled me. Berlage and perhaps Eduard Cuijpers were important, as well as work in the Louis Sullivan tradition.

Theodore M. Brown: A very telling comparison of the concurrent themes is between the expressionist cover of *Wendingen* no. 6 and the cover of *De Stijl* from the same period.[56]

John M. Jacobus: *Wendingen* is available today and *De Stijl* is not. This means that *Wendingen* had a larger circulation.

Placzek: It is hard to get *De Stijl*. In spite of many years' efforts, we have not been able to buy it for Avery.

Brown: Do not forget *Wendingen* was supported and sponsored by an architectural association, Het Genootschap Architectura et Amicitia, Amsterdam, whereas *De Stijl* was supported and sponsored largely by Van Doesburg. *De Stijl* began in Delft and moved to Leyden.

G. Collins: Notice that *Wendingen* is bound in raffia by hand. This indicates an Arts and Crafts continuation and hence a localism, regionalism.

Hitchcock: It is rather Indonesian, with a Chinese type of page binding.

G. Collins: But it means that some local vernaculars were important. Many different expressionisms may also fall into the category of Arts and Crafts. Frank Lloyd Wright is relevant here. In many cases there are no real expressionist qualities in what we are discussing other than a strong feeling for materials.

Kaufmann: No, I disagree.

Creese: Isn't Bruce Goff related to Finsterlin?

Hitchcock: What are other sources for expressionism? Were there any of those secret little magazines?

G. Collins: There were two runs of *Frühlicht*. Avery has the first one (as supplement to *Stadtbaukunst* during 1920): the Museum of Modern Art has the second, published by Taut in Magdeburg in 1921–2.

Placzek: The former is on paper that has become very fragile.

Johnson: Scharoun has kept all his drawings. They are much like Taut's and Finsterlin's.

Hitchcock: One help is that many young groups published photos of the work that interested them. This helps to show where they were going.

Brown: *Wendingen*, for example, has Wright, odds and ends of *De Stijl*, oriental material, and stage designs.

Johnson: I would like to know what was going on in other places as well, such as with constructivism in Russia.

Hitchcock: Russian ballet popularized Russian constructivist forms.[57]

Rosenblum: There was Sergei Prokofiev's "The Age of Steel" of 1927.

Hitchcock: What came out of Russia was never architecture as such, even Tatlin—just monuments [*figure 40*].[58]

Kaufmann: But Malevich's work was architecturally conceived.

G. Collins: Selinski's comments on "Style and Steel" of 1923 are significant as a reflection of ideas then current:

> Stone is dying out. Stone becomes a characteristic of retrogression. It holds back architectural development and thus becomes socially reactionary. Inflexible, restricted, and tortuous in its dynamic possibilities, stone is incapable of keeping up with the rapid pace of life. Life becomes more dynamic, and at an accelerating rate. Today people still travel in carriages and cabs in the streets of the city, but tomorrow the sidewalks will be set in motion, just as advertisements, neon signs, pneumatic doors, etc., are already mobile.... Why not construct upon a gigantic self-rotating steel foundation a great building of glass and aluminum walls that can be easily disassembled? Such a palace would be capable of transferring masses of people from one room to another, opening up into magnificent halls, bringing audiences on various levels close to the speaker. Instead of elevators, continuously rotating spiral escalators would take the people up to the roof. Why should one not install, for instance, some rooms, lecture halls, laboratories, operating rooms, which can alternately rotate southward toward the sun or at night throw light into the street in order to utilize the rooms fully for general artistic and educational purposes? [59]

Hitchcock: Mr. Johnson, as a practicing architect, does any sort of expressionism count for you?

Johnson: But what can we call expressionist? Is Scharoun's Philharmonic Hall expressionist? That is being built. Is Ronchamp expressionist?

Hitchcock: No, we are concerned with 1918 through the 1920s.

Johnson: Well, International Style is a dirty word now. There is a great renewal of interest in things from early Poelzig through work in Hamburg and in Amsterdam. Gaudí to De Klerk has more importance now for eclectics than the International Style of the 1920s.

Fitch: Mr. Johnson, do Saarinen's TWA and Dulles Airport fit in here?

Meeks: There are formal analogies.

Stern: It seems that today we can now build what they envisioned; we can do almost anything. Mendelsohn could not build his Einstein Tower as he wanted it [*figure 44*]. There seem to be two directions: structural emphasis in imaginative shells, and a symbolic use of materials. The last issue of *Progressive Architecture* was devoted to brick—a reemphasis on craftsmanship. [60]

Johnson: Ronchamp is *Schmier*-masonry. Mendelsohn also, and many forms of that period. If you are going to "schmier" your forms you might just as well "schmier" them organically as any other way.

Péter Serényi: Is expressionist painting anti-architectural and antisocial? Is expressionist architecture in its most extreme form so personal as to be anti-architectural? Here I am referring, among others, to Finsterlin's "houses" [*figure 43*] or Poelzig's project for the Salzburg Festival Theater [*figure 46*].

P. Collins: In the last chapter of his *Modern Architecture* of 1929, "The Architecture of the Future," Professor Hitchcock wrote about "symbolic functionalism."[61] Since most of Mendelsohn's expressionist designs were for automobile factories, cinema studios, etc., and were intended to express or symbolize, by "dynamic" contours, the function of these buildings, "symbolic functionalism" would seem to me quite a good alternative to "expressionism."

Hitchcock: I used the term "symbolic functionalism" in 1929. What, I wonder, did I mean by that?

Placzek: I have made notes this afternoon whenever a new term was used — either simply as a synonym for "expressionism" or as something closely related. Here are a few examples, and does this not shed a light on our confusion in terminology?

Romanticism
Machine romanticism
Fantastic architecture
Liturgical symbolism
Utopian architecture
Symbolism
Futurism
Emotionalism
Sensualism
Visionary architecture
Symbolic functionalism

Kaufmann: We could add *architecture parlante*.

Hitchcock: We should distinguish between what expressionism was intended to be *à la lettre* and how the term was actually used. We lack seriousness in this respect. The Russian attitudes at the recent London Congress are a case in point.[62] They spoke of "purist architecture"; this just seems out-of-date and naive. To hear them talk you would think Stalinist architecture never existed.

Louis Kahn has an extremely 1920s feeling to his vocation. Then there is the theater question again — it all implies a certain illusion. Perhaps expressionism is not a concerted movement but a collection of individual responses.[63]

What about Frank Lloyd Wright and the International Style?

Kaufmann: Frank Lloyd Wright has a relation to Romanticism. The Imperial Hotel interiors — the ballroom especially — are close to Behrens's lobbies. Both led to Paris in 1925.

Hitchcock: Yes, and what about his late fantasies?

Kaufmann: Remember Wright and what he knew about his clients. He had a very quick sense of when a commission was realistic and when it was just a friendly gesture. When he knew it was just a gesture, he was quick to sail off and let his imagination run free.

Hitchcock: Mile High Center is probably just his response to what he knew was going on elsewhere in the architectural world. His late projects are often megalomaniac, sort of his answer just to show off what he could do.

Kaufmann: The Interfaith Cathedral project of 1926 was an early example of this.[64]

Hitchcock: You can always find sources for things. Why are the 1920s so difficult? [65] American periodicals show little American architecture of interest. What happened in California in the late 1910s and 1920s was an exception. The San Diego Fair was not all Spanish colonial, was it?

Jacobus: And the Wright houses of 1920 to 1924 were not a *détente* in his work but were a particular response to a new environment.

Hitchcock: There was great difficulty in his private life in these years.

Kaufmann: Yes, but this went on all during his career. Wright went through a programmatic "destruction of the box." He destroyed the walls before his Florence period and began to destroy the roof when he came back.

Hitchcock: Perhaps we can conclude by saying there is no formal conclusion.

[The session adjourned at approximately 4:50, the participants and guests going on to what Webster terms "a drinking together...a social gathering at which there is free interchange of ideas...a symposium."]

Notes

1. J. E. Barton, *Purpose and Admiration* (London: Christophers, 1932), 217, quoted in Arnold Whittick, *European Architecture in the 20th Century* (London: C. Lockwood, 1950–3), 206.

The problem of when the term "functionalism" was first used in connection with modern architecture was not systematically discussed in the symposium. In the course of their checking the manuscript of the proceedings later, however, the participants offered several bits of information. On the use of 'functionalism' in regard to modern architecture, Henry Millon noted: "For what it is worth, I quote Fiske Kimball and George Harold Edgell, *History of Architecture* (New York: Harper & Brothers, 1918): '[P]art of the tendency toward natural science. It is at one with the biological concept of adaptation of form to function and environment…. Most recently there had been a tendency not to remain satisfied unless all the forms employed… owe as little as possible to the historic styles…are…peculiarly and emphatically modern.'[499ff.] Page 516 has a photo of Behrens's AEG Turbine Factory [*figure 5*] as an example of the 'new approach.' There seems to be enough evidence to show that functionalism in *almost* as narrow a definition as we used in the symposium was current in the minds of the really bright young architects (Kimball) *even* in the United States, in spite of what the magazines seem to indicate."

George R. Collins added, "It is strange that Whittick cited its use as beginning so late, because Mendelsohn discussed 'Function' and 'Dynamics' at considerable length in his 1923 lectures (quoted in the afternoon session), and Whittick reported this fact in his book on Mendelsohn."

Theodore M. Brown contributed another continental source: Theo van Doesburg, "Tot een beeldende architectuur," *De Stijl* 6, nos. 6/7 (1924): 78–83; rpt. *The Work of G. Rietveld, Architect*, tr. Theodore M. Brown (Utrecht: A. W. Bruna, 1958), 66–9:"The new architecture is *functional*, i.e. it evolves from the accurate determination of practical demands which it establishes in a clear groundplan…. Division of functional spaces is strictly determined by rectangular planes…. The new architecture is *open*; the whole exists as one space which is divided according to functional requirements."Italics in the original.

2. Le Corbusier, *Towards a New Architecture*, tr. Frederick Etchells (New York: Payson & Clarke, 1927), 110.

3. Ibid., 102–3.

4. Le Corbusier, *Vers une architecture* (Paris: Les Editions G. Cres et cie, 1923), 80.

5. Frederick Etchells, in his introduction to Le Corbusier, *Towards a New Architecture*, vi.

6. Ibid., viii.

7. Ibid., x.

8. Ibid., xiii.

9. Ibid., 111.

10. Ibid., 180.

11. James Burford, "Old Wine in New Bottles," *Architectural Review*, Aug. 1930, 131. The three books on modern architecture reviewed in the article were all part of the series *Neues Bauen in der Welt*, ed. Joseph Gantner (Vienna: Anton Schroll & Co., 1930); the books were El Lissitzky, *Russland*; Richard Neutra, *Amerika*; and Roger Ginsberger, *Frankreich*.

12. P. Morton Shand, "The Work of Alvar Aalto," *Architectural Review*, Sept. 1931, cap. to pl. V.

13. "Mediaeval Functionalism," *Architectural Review*, July 1931, 16–7. Peter Collins would expand his examination of the term "functionalism" in his *Changing Ideals in Modern Architecture, 1750–1950* (London: Faber and Faber, 1965); see esp. "Part Three: Functionalism," 147–81.

14. Hitchcock here refers to his collaboration with Johnson and Barr on the *Modern Architecture: International Exhibition* held at the Museum of Modern Art, New York, in 1932. See the resulting publication, *The International Style: Architecture Since 1922* (New York: W. W. Norton, 1932).

15. J. M. Richards, *An Introduction to Modern Architecture* (Harmondsworth: Penguin Books, l940); Charalambos Sfaellos, *Le Fonctionnalisme dans l'architecture contemporaine* (Paris: Fréal, l952); Edward Robert DeZurko, *Origins of Functionalist Theory* (New York: Columbia University Press, 1957).

16. Sibyl Moholy-Nagy is likely referring to Muthesius's address to the Werkbund conference of 1911; see Hermann Muthesius, "Wo stehen wir?" *Jahrbuch des Deutschen Werkbundes* 1 (Jena: E. Diederichs, 1912); tr. and rpt. as "Aims of the Werkbund," in Ulrich Conrads, *Programs and Manifestoes on 20th-Century Architecture* (Cambridge, Mass.: MIT Press, 1970), 26–7. See also Muthesius, *Die Einheit der Architektur* (Berlin: K. Curtius, 1908). —Ed.

17. From Henry van de Velde, *Geschichte meines Lebens* (Munich: R. Piper, 1962), ch. 16; tr. from a manuscript published in *Bauwelt* 27 (Berlin: 1962).

18. H. Imhauser, "Gibt es eine neue Architektur?" *Pyramide*, 1927.

19. Originally: "Folge dieses veränderten und vertieften Geistes und seiner neuen technischen Mittel ist eine veränderte Baugestalt, die nicht um ihrer selbst willen da ist, sondern aus dem Wesen des Baues entspringt, aus seiner Funktion, die er erfüllen soll." In Walter Gropius,

Bauhausbuch 1, Internationale Architektur (Munich: A. Langen, 1925), 6.

20. Bruno Taut, *Die Auflösung der Städte* (Hagen in West: Erschienen im Folkwang, 1920), 7.

21. Bruno Taut, *Die Neue Wohnung: Die Frau als Schöpferin* (Leipzig: Klinkhardt & Biermann, 1924).

22. For similar arguments in English, see Walter Gropius, *The New Architecture and the Bauhaus*, tr. P. Morton Shand (London: Faber and Faber, 1935), 33, 89–91. —Ed.

23. See Le Corbusier, *The Athens Charter*, tr. Anthony Eardley (New York: Grossman Publishers, 1973), 96. Originally published as CIAM, *La charte d'Athènes* (Paris: Plon, 1943).

24. Ibid.

25. A. D. F. Hamlin, "The Art Nouveau: Its Origin and Development," *The Craftsman* III (1902–3): 129–43.

26. Henry-Russell Hitchcock, "Modern Architecture," part I, *Architectural Record*, April 1928, 337–49; and "Modern Architecture," part II, *Architectural Record*, May 1928, 452–60.

27. Hitchcock published the monograph *J.-J. P. Oud* (Paris: Cahiers d'Art) about 1931.

28. Sibyl Moholy-Nagy added a note to the transcript explaining, "El Lissitzky felt he had found the bridge by calling his pictures 'Prouns'—'the transfer point from painting to architecture.'"

29. For more see Alfred H. Barr, *De Stijl, 1917–1928*, spec. ed., *Bulletin of the Museum of Modern Art* 20, no. 2 (New York: Museum of Modern Art, 1952). —Ed.

30. *Bauhausbuch*, no. 3, *Ein Versuchshaus des Bauhauses* (1925).

31. At the time of the symposium, Robert A. M. Stern's edited collection "The Philadelphia Savings Fund Society" appeared in the *Journal of the Society of Architectural Historians*; see vol. 21, no. 2 (May 1962): [entire issue].

32. *Modern Architecture: International Exhibition*, ex. cat. (New York: Museum of Modern Art, 1932), 77.

33. Frank Lloyd Wright, *Drawings for a Living Architecture* (New York: Bear Run Foundation and the Edgar J. Kaufmann Charitable Foundation by Horizon Press, 1959), 109.

34. Dorothy Todd, "Some Reflections on Recent Tendencies in American Architecture," *Architectural Review*, June 1931, 210.

35. George Collins later added the note, "The letter from Van Doesburg to Adolf Behne, 7 Nov. 1928, regarding the Aubette in Strasbourg, illustrates the De Stijl search for the art of total design that Mr. Barr mentioned earlier." Theo van Doesburg to Adolf Behne, Paris, 7 Nov. 1928, rpt. Ulrich Conrads and Hans G. Sperlich, *The Architecture of Fantasy*, ed. and tr. Christiane Crasemann Collins and

George R. Collins (New York: Frederick A. Praeger, 1962), 155.

36. J.-J. P. Oud, "Über die zukünftige Baukunst und ihre architektonischen Möglichkeiten: ein Programm," *Frühlicht* I, no. 4 (1922): 117; rpt. Conrads and Sperlich, *Architecture of Fantasy*, 112.

37. Meeks appears to be referring to Stephan Tschudi-Madsen, *Sources of Art Nouveau* (New York: G. Wittenborn, 1955), which covers the international origins of art nouveau (a critical forerunner to expressionism) but does not include information on Italy. — Ed.

38. See "Chairman's Memorandum" soliciting questions in advance of the 1962 conference, 89–90.

39. Robert Rosenblum, a professor of art history at Princeton University, published *Cubism and Twentieth-Century Art* (New York: Harry N. Abrams) in 1960. — Ed.

40. Ulrich Conrads and Hans G. Sperlich, *Phantastische Architektur* (Stuttgart: G. Hatje, 1960).

41. Conrads and Sperlich, *Architecture of Fantasy*. George Collins used this soon-to-be-published translation as source material throughout the morning and afternoon sessions. — Ed.

42. Vittorio Gregotti, "L'Architettura dell'espressionismo," *Casabella* 254 (1961).

43. Moholy-Nagy co-edited the Bauhausbücher series with Walter Gropius and wrote two volumes. See László Moholy-Nagy, *Bauhausbücher*, no. 8, *Malerei Fotografie Film* (Munich: A. Langen, 1925), and *Bauhausbücher*, no. 14, *Von Material zu Architektur* (Munich: A. Langen, 1929). — Ed.

44. This quote—*Alle ächte Mitteilung ist also sinnbildsam*, in the original— comes from Novalis, "Fragmente oder Denkaufgaben," *Vorarbeiten zu Verschiedenen Fragmentsammlungen* (1798), rpt. in Novalis, *Schriften*, vol. II, ed. Richard Samuel (Stuttgart: W. Kohlhammer Verlag, 1960), 564.

45. Walter Gropius, pamphlet for *Ausstellung für Unbekannte Architekten* [Exhibition for Unknown Architects] *veranstaltet vom Arbeitsrat für Kunst im Graphischen Kabinett* (Berlin, Apr. 1919); rpt. Conrads and Sperlich, *Architecture of Fantasy*, 137.

46. Bruno Taut, *Architekturprogramm* (Berlin: Arbeitsrat für Kunst, 1918); rpt. Conrads and Sperlich, *Architecture of Fantasy*, 135.

47. See Will Grohmann, *Zehn Jahre Novembergruppe* (Berlin: J. J. Ottens Verlag, 1928).

48. See Erich Mendelsohn, *Briefe eines Architekten,* ed. Oskar Beyer (Munich: Prestel-Verlag, 1961); tr. as Erich Mendelsohn, *Eric [sic] Mendelsohn: Letters of an Architect,* ed. Oskar Beyer,

tr. Geoffrey Strachan (London and New York: Abelard-Schuman, 1967).

49. Erich Mendelsohn, "International Conformity of the New Architecture or Dynamics and Function," *Gesamtschaffen des Architekten* (Berlin: Mosse, 1930), 22–34; rpt. Conrads and Sperlich, *Architecture of Fantasy*, 152.

50. Erich Mendelsohn, "Ideas about the New Architecture" (at the Front in 1914–7); rpt. Conrads and Sperlich, *Architecture of Fantasy*, 152. — Ed.

51. Oskar Schlemmer, László Moholy-Nagy, and Farkas Molnar, *The Theater of the Bauhaus* (Middletown, Conn.: Wesleyan University Press, 1961).

52. George Collins noted an exhibition of Finsterlin's work in Berlin; Nikolaus Pevsner, "Finsterlin and Some Others," *Architectural Review*, Nov. 1962, 353–7; and "Postscript on Finsterlin," *Architectural Review*, Jan. 1963, 5.

53. Herman Finsterlin, "Innenarchitektur," *Frühlicht I,* no. II (Winter 1921–2): 36; rpt. Conrads and Sperlich, *Architecture of Fantasy*, 149–50.

54. Edgar Kaufmann added, "Roger Wolfe Kahn used to conduct his band in a New York nightclub with a floor just like this." See "The Endless House," *Architectural Forum* 95 (Nov. 1950): 124–6.

55. *Ja! Stimmen des Arbeitsrates für Kunst* (Charlottenburg: Verlegt bei der Photographischen Gesellschaft, 1919).

56. *Wendingen* 6 (June 1919); *De Stijl* 1, no. 1 (Oct. 1917); *De Stijl* 5, no. 12 (Dec. 1922).

57. Sibyl Moholy-Nagy added, "One cannot ignore Lissitzky, the ballet *Victory over the Sun*, and Leger's *Ballet Mécanique*."

58. George Collins instructed, "But see forthcoming master's essay by Arthur Sprague of Columbia University for evidence that it was impressively architectural in character." Arthur R. Sprague, *N. A. Miliutin and Linear Planning in the U.S.S.R., 1928–1931* (Master's thesis, Columbia University, 1967).

59. K. Selinksi, "Style and Steel," *Neue Kultur-Korrespondenz* (Berlin) I, vols. 4/5 (1923), quoted by Adolf Behne, *Der moderne Zweckbau* (Munich, Vienna, and Berlin: Drei Masken Verlag, 1926), 65; rpt. Conrads and Sperlich, *Architecture of Fantasy*, 53–4.

60. "Contemporary Masonry," *Progressive Architecture*, April 1962, 126.

61. *Modern Architecture: Romanticism and Reintegration* (New York: Payson & Clarke, 1929), 215–8.

62. Hitchcock is referring to the Sixth Congress of the International Union of Architects, held in London in 1961. — Ed.

63. Sibyl Moholy-Nagy amended the transcript, declaring, "Now you're talking!"

64. Kaufmann is likely referring to Wright's unbuilt project for a Steel Cathedral for a Million People of 1926. — Ed.

65. Sibyl Moholy-Nagy quipped, "Three guesses: Because the Renaissance ended and a totally new period was born. All births are messy."

MAS 1964

THE DECADE
1929-1939

Chairman's Memorandum

Henry-Russell Hitchcock
January, 1964*

Two years ago the first Modern Architecture Symposium devoted to the history of modern architecture considered the architecture of the 1920s primarily under the two headings of functionalism and expressionism. As the subject of a second symposium held in May 1964, the committee proposed the succeeding decade of the 1930s, the eleven years preceding the outbreak of World War II.

The historical problems of the period—a period which many of the participants have known firsthand and in which several were in some sense actors—are perhaps not of as deep significance as those of the 1920s. In part, doubtless, because personal memories of those years have dimmed, the issues seem, paradoxically, less clear-cut than those of earlier periods that have already been subjected to impersonal historical examination. Yet certain controversies were sharp at the time and have even continued, if usually in much altered form, through the following thirty years.

Briefly stated, and phrased in relation to what had immediately gone before, one may perhaps say that among the major strands of theory and practice in the 1930s were, on the one hand, the continuation and spread of the new architecture that had come to early maturity in Europe toward the end of the previous decade—such continuation at the center being by no means, however, identical with the spread at the periphery—and, on the other, nationalistic reaction against earlier internationalism, all the way from the utter rejection of the new architecture under several totalitarian regimes to the regional nativisms that began to flourish from California's Bay Area to the Scandinavian North of Europe.

To one or the other of these topical groups many additional subtopics can, but need not, be closely related. There is, for example, the matter of technical innovations, from drastically new ways and new forms of using concrete to the increased importance of various improvements in building equipment: even houses were becoming containers for machinery. This is part of the broader theme of continuation but with the emphasis on development. Some of the development was certainly quite revolutionary in practice, even if largely foreseen in principle, and well beyond what the new architecture of the 1920s had actually known and used. So also the social intentions of the new architecture, though hardly new in themselves, were yet finding new support from governments in the 1930s.

One must further consider as unexpectedly important facets of the scene in the years before World War II the revival of Frank Lloyd Wright's activity and the appearance of Alvar Aalto on the international stage, not to speak of the modulations, chiefly in projects rather than executed work, of such established international masters as Le Corbusier and Mies van der Rohe. For Wright and for Aalto the support was primarily at home, in the United States and in Finland, respectively: for Le Corbusier and for Mies, as also for Gropius as an educator, it was increasingly from the New World. Strands of ideas still crossed and recrossed the oceans, even if doctrinaire internationalism had received a severe setback.

As they appear in retrospect from this slightly awkward point in time, only a generation later, the many individual topics of real significance seem too various to justify intellectually any merely dichotomous grouping for the 1920s. The extreme, or polar, topics do not seem to be the most important ones historically, but rather those national situations or cases of individual architects that reflect several not necessarily closely related aspects of the contemporary scene in the 1930s.

The committee this year has therefore taken upon themselves more responsibility than two years ago. Instead of inviting a range of scholars to propose topics and then attempting to organize those topics into intelligible groups under two or more main headings, they have this time selected out of innumerable possible topics and subtopics about a dozen to be discussed individually. Furthermore, there has been assigned to each of the speakers a particular topic, with which that speaker may be thought to be especially familiar, either from direct participation in the 1930s or from special study later. Naturally these assigned topics are intended to be broad enough to allow each speaker considerable freedom of treatment, beginning with a more precise or cogent title for his own contribution than the somewhat vague but suggestive words or phrases tentatively worked out by the committee. Since the main theme is different, the composition of the panel is also different from that of 1962.

* Circulated to prospective participants in advance of the symposium

Agenda of the Symposium

Saturday Session
May 9, 1964

Relevance of the Decade
Robert A. M. Stern

The International Style in the 1930s
William H. Jordy

Le Corbusier's Changing Attitude toward Form
Péter Serényi

The Diaspora
Sibyl Moholy-Nagy

World's Fairs in the 1930s
Paul F. Norton

Frank Lloyd Wright's Years of Modernism, 1925–35
Edgar Kaufmann, Jr.

A Brief Review of the Decade's Architectural Literature
Adolf K. Placzek

Doldrums in the Suburbs
Vincent J. Scully, Jr.

The Social Front of Modern Architecture in the 1930s: More than a "Style"?
Promising Principles Unfulfilled
Catherine Bauer Wurster

The Role of History of Architecture in Fascist Italy
Henry Millon

Spain: A Case Study in Action and Reaction
George R. Collins

The Committed Architect
Colin St. John Wilson

Yale and the Ivy League Tradition
Carroll L. V. Meeks

The Architectural Reaction in Austria
Eduard F. Sekler

City-Planning Theory in Nationalist-Socialist Germany
Christian F. Otto

The Rise of Technology
James Marston Fitch

Modern Architecture and Architectural Criticism in the United States
Mark L. Peisch

Sunday Session
May 10, 1964

General Discussion
Led by Henry-Russell Hitchcock

....

Roster of Participants

Henry-Russell Hitchcock, Smith College
Chairman
Robert A. M. Stern, Yale University
Assistant to the Chairman

Catherine Bauer Wurster, University of California at Berkeley
George R. Collins, Columbia University
James Marston Fitch, Columbia University
Philip C. Johnson, New York City
William H. Jordy, Brown University
Edgar Kaufmann, Jr., Columbia University
Henry Millon, Massachusetts Institute of Technology
Sibyl Moholy-Nagy, Pratt Institute
Paul F. Norton, University of Massachusetts
Adolf K. Placzek, Columbia University
Vincent J. Scully, Jr., Yale University
Eduard F. Sekler, Harvard University
Péter Serényi, University of Pennsylvania

Guests of the Symposium
Stanford Anderson, Massachusetts Institute of Technology
Alfred H. Barr, Jr., Museum of Modern Art, New York City
John Belle, Cornell University
Robert Branner, Columbia University
H. Allen Brooks, University of Toronto
Theodore M. Brown, University of Louisville
Percival Goodman, Columbia University
John M. Jacobus, Indiana University
Elizabeth Mock Kassler, Princeton, New Jersey
Carroll L. V. Meeks, Yale University
Christian F. Otto, Columbia University
Mark L. Peisch, Columbia University
Robert Rosenblum, Princeton University
Colin Rowe, Cornell University
Colin St. John Wilson, Cambridge University
Patricia May Sekler, Harvard University
Joseph M. Shelley, Columbia University
Kenneth A. Smith, Columbia University
George B. Tatum, University of Pennsylvania
D. Dean Telfer, Columbia University
Andrew Weininger, New York City
Rudolf Wittkower, Columbia University

Statement by the Organizers

....

George R. Collins and Adolf K. Placzek
March, 1965*

The second biennial Symposium on Modern Architecture was held at Columbia University on May 8, 9, and 10, 1964. It was devoted to a historical reappraisal of the architecture of the years 1929–39. The previous decade, 1918–28, had been the subject of the first such symposium at the university in May 1962. That symposium, in turn, had been inspired by the success of the discussion session on "Frank Lloyd Wright and Architecture around 1900" at the XXth International Congress of the History of Art held at Columbia in September 1961.

All of these sessions were chaired by Professor Henry-Russell Hitchcock of Smith College. He was assisted in this successively by Professor Henry Millon of MIT (1961, 1962) and by Mr. Robert A. M. Stern of Yale University (1964). Organization of both the 1962 and 1964 symposia was in the hands of a committee composed of Mr. Hitchcock, George R. Collins, Philip C. Johnson, and Adolf K. Placzek. The symposia have been sponsored jointly by the Avery Architectural Library and the Department of Art History and Archaeology of Columbia University.

The purpose of the symposium was to provide a series of closed meetings for the benefit of invited participants: architectural historians, all of whom were chosen for their particular interest in the theme under discussion. A number of distinguished colleagues were also invited by the committee to attend the sessions, and each of the panelists was encouraged to invite two or three students to sit in the audience.

This year the panelists were asked to prepare themselves to discuss special aspects of the decade in question and each to submit in advance a brief written statement of his views. These statements were read, with some amplification, during the Saturday sessions. At this time the chairman also called upon several of the guests in the audience to speak on particular subjects. On Sunday morning the entire group met again, less formally, in the Avery Library for a discussion of questions that had arisen the previous day. Printed here are the Saturday "papers"—in most cases somewhat modified and expanded by the speakers—and an extract of the Sunday discussion.

The success of the working sessions of both the biennial symposia owes itself in large part to the imaginative control of the discussion by Mr. Hitchcock. It had been planned, as a surprise to him, that the 1964 symposium would serve as one of the public celebrations of his sixtieth birthday, and there were several testimonials offered to him during the weekend.

During the meetings considerable doubt was expressed as to whether a decade, and in particular the years 1929–39, could have much significance in the writing of architectural history. It seems appropriate, therefore, to put on record the reasoning by which our committee selected the period that it did for study. In the first place, a ten-year span seemed to be of a satisfactory size—not too large, not too small a snip—for scrutiny. The years 1929–39 were then chosen simply to follow the period 1918–28, which had been treated in the previous symposium. As it happens, the decade 1929–39 has a built-in historical significance: it starts with a great depression and ends with the outbreak of a major war, and, being an eleven-year "decade," it neatly comprises those years known as the "1930s." As to whether a year that is important to history is also important to architecture is, of course, an open question. The 1962 symposium had carried an "architectural" date, in that it had examined events between the formation of the Novembergruppe with the 1918 Armistice and the establishment of the CIAM in 1928.

The symposium was made possible financially by contributions from the Graduate Faculties and the School of Architecture of Columbia University and, especially, from Mr. Johnson. The Department of Art History and Archaeology of Columbia University assumed virtually all the secretarial chores and paper work of organizing the meetings. Preparation of correspondence, notices, and tape transcription, as well as the typing and duplicating of the papers, was carried out almost entirely by Mrs. Nancy Edgerton of that department. Appreciation is due the several students from the Department of Art History and the School of Architecture who assisted with the mechanics of the sessions and to members of the Avery Library staff for their assistance to our wives in arranging the social functions of the symposium.

The undersigned want also to take this opportunity, in the name of the entire panel, to thank the editor of the *Journal of the Society of Architectural Historians*, Robert Branner, for making the pages of this publication available as a lasting and accessible record of our discussions, and for the time, care, and skill he has exerted in preparing the complex material for publication.

* Published as an introduction to the proceedings in the *Journal of the Society of Architectural Historians* in March, 1965

Relevance of the Decade
Robert A. M. Stern

The years 1929–39 constitute a chronological convenience and not a meaningful architectural era. The period we should be talking about extends from 1927 through World War II to about 1950 and, indeed, lingers on in certain recent works of Walter Gropius and some of his students. I should like to discuss the inadequacies of 1929 as a beginning date for this period. Later on today Mr. [Vincent] Scully will discuss the inadequacies of 1939 as a terminus—a point which he has already suggested elsewhere.[1]

Nineteen hundred and twenty-nine is less meaningful a beginning for this period than is 1927, niggling though such a distinction may seem to be. Yet it is difficult to recapture the special spirit of "modernity" which suddenly came to form in 1927. Although two significant monuments date from 1929 (the Villa Savoye [figure 78 a] and the Barcelona Pavilion [figure 81]), it was in 1927, especially at the Weissenhof housing exhibition in Stuttgart [figure 72], that, as Reyner Banham has written, the "mainstream of modern architecture found its International Style."[2] So it was that in 1927 the leading "form givers" of the period to come produced their first significant works. Ludwig Mies van der Rohe's apartment building at Stuttgart, a far cry from his apartments on the Afrikanische Strasse, was his first experiment with the steel cage. The double house at Stuttgart by Le Corbusier (pseudo. of Charles-Édouard Jeanneret) culminates his development from the Citrohan projects of 1920–2 [figure 48], and his Villa Stein at Garches, also completed in 1927, is unquestionably his first masterpiece, although it can in turn be traced back to his work at La Chaux-de-Fonds and to the Maison La Roche. Alvar Aalto, a comparative newcomer, was already pointing to the future with his preliminary designs for the Viipuri Library.

Nineteen hundred and twenty-seven was also the year when the League of Nations competition brought the question of the monumental possibilities of the new architecture face to face with the established forces of the old guard. Ironically, it was Baron Victor Horta, the pioneering architect of the art nouveau, who presided over the jury which was to veto the scheme on a technicality.[3] Similarly, Gropius's Total Theater project for Erwin Piscator and his Civic Center project for the town of Halle, both of 1927 as well, mark the first of a series of projects for mass-democratic programs which were to become a central preoccupation of the period to come. It was also in 1927, at Stuttgart, that Gropius began to experiment in earnest with prefabrication—another major interest in the following twenty years.

But it is to America that we must turn, for more than any other country, this period was hers. Consider the impact the following events must have had on such conscience-stricken conservatives as George Howe, A. Lawrence Kocher, and Raymond Hood as they contemplated, with wavering commitment (and some confusion), the new architectural styles ranging from Paris Jazz-Modern through the various International modes embodied in works by such men as Bernard Bijvoet and Johannes Duiker, Le Corbusier, Hans Scharoun, Hugo Häring, and Bruno Taut.

In America, 1927 was a year of tremendous technological progress: radio-telephone service was established between New York and London, San Francisco and Manila; the first national radio networks were established; television was given its first public demonstration; the movies began to "talk"; the Holland Tunnel — the first underwater vehicular tunnel in the world — was opened to carry automobiles under the Hudson River; Henry Ford, after producing his fifteen-millionth car, ceased production of the Model T and brought out the consumer-oriented, highly styled Model A.[4] It was the year in which the stage designer Norman Bel Geddes, having conceived the first "streamlined" train and the first "streamlined" automobile, established himself as an artistic consultant to industry.[5] Calling himself an "industrial designer," Geddes gave birth to the profession which was to challenge seriously the position of architects throughout the next twenty years and, in a number of key instances, to set the pace. From the point of view of technology, the most provocative challenge to architecture during this period was the work of Buckminster Fuller, who, in unveiling his Dymaxion House in 1927 [figure 71], hurled the first volley of his extended polemic against the International Style.[6]

Nineteen hundred and twenty-seven was also a time when America began for the first time to sense her cultural independence from Europe — and, indeed, to feel that Europe, broken by the war and the ensuing economic chaos, was no longer able to lead. America's new role was perceived first by a French writer, André Siegfried, who wrote in his book of 1927, America Comes of Age, that America had evolved an "entirely original social structure...[which] may even be a new age, an age in which Europe is no longer the driving force of the world."[7] Our own writers (especially our critics and historians) reinforced this sense of cultural independence. Vernon L. Parrington's book of 1927, Main Currents in American Thought, was posited on a belief that American literature was not merely a provincial branch of English thought but a full-blooded literature in its own right, while Charles and Mary Beard's book of the same year, The Rise of American Civilization, was predicated on the belief that there was not only civilization in America but that there was an American civilization.[8] At the same time that these events were bespeaking a kind of nationalism, Charles Lindbergh's solo flight across the Atlantic on the night of May 21, 1927, may be said to have announced a new international age.

Nineteen hundred and twenty-seven saw the establishment of the first museum devoted to modern art, Albert Gallatin's Gallery of Living Art at New York University. It was also an important year for our painters. After ten years' wrestling with European cubism, many of them, in their insistence on the direct representation of recognizable objects, finally acknowledged their inability to accept either the analytic or synthetic approach. A new and thoroughly American kind of "modernism" emerged which can be best described as precisionism, though many other terms have been employed.[9] Charles Demuth's enigmatic painting of 1927, My Egypt, reflects the American artistic temper at this decisive moment. Aware of the inherent beauty of industrial structures, though not completely enchanted by them, Demuth's typically American concern for the recognizable image — in this case two grain elevators — and for the material object prevents him from attempting a reorganization of the shapes into a new pictorial order similar to the attempts of the cubists and their more contemporaneous descendants, the purists. Instead, My Egypt is, as John McCoubrey has written, a depiction of "twin commercial colossi," an unmistakable expression of Demuth's "wry comment on the nonexistence of an American past."[10]

Stuart Davis's decisive *Egg Beater* series of 1927–8 and Charles Sheeler's photographs of the Ford plant at River Rouge, also of 1927 (Sheeler was the first American photographer to use the forms of industrial buildings and processes as landscape subjects), announced that American machine art had come to maturity. Indeed, Sheeler's development away from the cubistic abstraction and manipulation of his early work to the precise realism of such important canvases as *Upper Deck* of 1929 may be seen as the principal example of American unwillingness to romanticize the machine; American architects, lagging behind the painters, would not come to a similar point until about 1932.

A good many Americans in 1927 were reading Oswald Spengler's *Decline of the West*, the first volume of which had just been translated into English. Spengler's extraordinary comparison of the Temple of Poseidon at Paestum and the Münster at Ulm suggested to many Americans that, as George Howe put it, there was "an intimate relationship between mathematics and science on the one hand and architecture on the other, a relationship of form and spiritual content and not of dry technology."[11] Henry-Russell Hitchcock was himself in a Spenglerian mood when he wrote in 1927, in his first article in the new magazine *Hound and Horn*, that we stand "beyond the downslope of the 19th century and the apparent gap of the war, and, regarding our architecture, we are led to demand whether the time of its discard is at hand or whether, after the superficially historical wastes of the last century, it may be reintegrated as a sound organ in an aging body."[12]

The architectural scene in America in 1927 was electric with the spirit of "modernism," although it was in no way clear which way the profession would go. Americans were just beginning to realize that the best European architects had shed the neoclassical forms of Beaux-Arts academicism once and for all. A most perceptive American commentator on this was Samuel Chamberlain, who, after an extensive trip to Europe "in search of modernism," reported that "out of the wilderness of wails of discontented modernists, chafing at the artificiality of the academic and calling loudly for a new vision, a new impulse, there comes a strong and sonorous and uncompromising voice, setting forth the case of modernism with unexpected logic, the voice of the pensive and earnest Le Corbusier."[13] In addition to word-of-mouth reports, such as Chamberlain's, there was Le Corbusier's own emphatic polemic, *Vers une architecture*, which had just been translated by the English architect Frederick Etchells. Its awesome challenge—"Architecture or Revolution"—could not be ignored. The mood of the American Institute of Architects (AIA) convention was one of some uneasiness,[14] but it was generally felt that hope lay in the stripped forms of Bertram Goodhue and Paul Cret or in the Paris Jazz-Modern of Ralph Walker, Ely Jacques Kahn, and Raymond Hood. Walker's Barclay-Vesey Telephone Building in New York had been just completed and was at the forefront of everyone's imagination,[15] as Joseph Urban's Ziegfeld theater[16] and James Gamble Rogers's Medical Center for Columbia would be later in the year.[17] Frank Lloyd Wright was at the nadir of his influence and prestige. Relegated by historian Thomas Tallmadge to the limbo of lost causes along with Louis Sullivan, he was without work, besieged by bill collectors and lawyers, and thought by some internationalists to be dead.[18] Toward the end of the year, however, things began to look up. He was occupied with a project for Dr. Chandler at San Marcos-in-the-Desert, and Michael Mikkelsen, editor of the *Architectural Record*, offered to pay him $10,000 for a series of articles, "In the Cause of Architecture," which were to go a long way toward his architectural "comeback."[19] The *Record* was unquestionably the most innovative among the American professional journals and, under the direction of Mikkelsen and A. Lawrence Kocher (who became managing editor late in 1927), the format was completely modernized and the magazine transformed into a sounding board for new ideas.[20]

In 1927, there was, as Sheldon and Martha Cheney put it, "a spreading machine age consciousness."[21] It was the year of the *Machine Age* exposition in New York, which, more than any other single event, opened American eyes to the wealth of new forms at their disposal. The *Machine Age* exposition was the brainchild of Jane Heap, coeditor with Margaret Anderson of the most influential of the so-called "little magazines," *The Little Review*.[22] For the first time, the American public was asked to look at machine parts, machines, and machine products and to recognize in their purely utilitarian shapes significant artistic form. In addition, models and photographs of many important European buildings were shown as well as a sizeable number of examples of Russian constructivist art, set designs, and architecture. Because of the novel Russian art, the exposition received considerable attention in the daily press and was well attended.[23] It can surely be regarded as the first major event of the modern movement in America.

In addition to all this intellectual agitation, there were some serious attempts at building in the International Style in 1927.[24] In New York, William Lescaze succeeded in building the Capitol Bus Terminal, while in California — where Schindler had erected his constructivist Lovell Beach House the year before [*figure 69*] — Neutra built the more conventional Jardinette garden apartments with strip windows (as superficially conceived as those of Hood's McGraw-Hill Building of 1930–1), white walls, and other trademarks of the new style. Neutra's book *Wie baut Amerika?* was published in 1927 as well, presenting, in addition to a discussion of technology, Neutra's futurist urban vision, "Rush City Reformed."[25] The projected office tower in Rush City was to influence the design of the Philadelphia Saving Fund Society Building (PSFS) of 1930–2 [*figure 87*], the only significant skyscraper to be built during the period. Most important was the "Health House" for Doctor Lovell, which Neutra has long claimed was also conceived in 1927 [*figure 75*].[26] Clarence S. Stein and Henry Wright's "City of the Motor Age" at Radburn, New Jersey [*figure 82*][27] — the first section of which was completed in 1927 — was perhaps more humane in its separation of pedestrian and motor traffic than Neutra's Rush City but was surely less exciting in its architectural forms. Stalled by the Depression, Radburn never grew to its full size; yet its principles dominated new-town planning in America throughout the 1930s and early 1940s.

There are surely other events which can be added. The point is that all of these I have mentioned belong, it seems to me, far more to the future than they do to the past. If we confine our discussion to the years after 1929, we will cut ourselves off from the roots and will find ourselves afloat in a phase of development already well under way.

The International Style in the 1930s
William H. Jordy

Surely the first observation to make about the International Style in the 1930s
is that the 1930s saw the style baptized with the name—and by two who are
with us today. If one were to mention the documents of cardinal importance for
the International Style during its first phase, one would surely include
Le Corbusier's *Vers une architecture* and *The International Style*, and probably at
the top of the list. Conveniently, they are precisely a decade apart: one of 1922;
the other of 1932. The tenor of the books is very different. Le Corbusier stated in
1922, "There exists a new spirit." Alfred Barr, in his introduction to the text by
Henry-Russell Hitchcock and Philip C. Johnson, could say, "There exists today
a modern style as original, as consistent, as logical, and as widely distributed
as any in the past." In short, during the decade between 1922 and 1932 the "new
spirit" had become a widely distributed "modern style."

If the first observation to be made about the International Style in the 1930s
centers on a book rather than on buildings, so might the second: that is, on
Sigfried Giedion's *Space, Time and Architecture*. Its initial publication occurred
only in 1941; but the perspective of this phenomenally successful book is that of
the 1930s. That two books, both historical syntheses, might be cited as the outstanding contributions of the 1930s to the International Style suggests in itself
that the most important buildings in the style were completed around 1930.

More precisely, they were realized by 1932, since the first three years of the
decade saw the design and completion of a number of buildings significant
for any corpus of the style. Hence the Hitchcock and Johnson volume, with
its brisk summary of the formal characteristics of the style, could hardly
have appeared at a more opportune moment—though the import of the book
is rather that "this is the start of a style" than that "this is its legacy." To be
sure, the International Style, as formulated by Hitchcock and Johnson, did
characterize most of the progressive architecture of the decade. The modifications and changes of emphasis effected within the style during the 1930s were
hardly more than this. Even Frank Lloyd Wright, as Vincent Scully has pointed
out,[28] was tangentially influenced by some aspects of European modernism
during the 1930s. If, however, one interprets Hitchcock and Johnson very
narrowly—more narrowly than they would wish, but it is worth doing so in a
symposium of this sort—and if one seeks the outstanding buildings designed
after 1932 which continue in the image of the style described in their book, few
are to be found.

For example, it came as a surprise to me that the major contributors to the
International Style prior to 1932 contributed so little *after* 1932. J. J. P. Oud contributed nothing at all. Until the very end of the decade, Walter Gropius's most
substantial building was his school at Impington in England of the mid-1930s,
which he designed with Maxwell Fry. It is surely a minor work. He did not again
hit his stride until 1937, when he began to work in the United States on suburban houses with Marcel Breuer, who, in the light of work subsequent to that
of the period of their collaboration, seems to have provided the partnership
with its most creative ideas. During the decade Ludwig Mies van der Rohe was
primarily interested in his projects for houses in courts. Although these may
be related to the International Style in the same way in which Hitchcock and
Johnson included the Barcelona Pavilion in their exhibition, they do not fully
accord with the canons of the International Style. Their brick walls would have

been barely tolerated by Hitchcock and Johnson.[29] The sense of gravity felt in the relation of the walls of the houses to the plane of the earth differs from the container of space lightly enclosed by a seamless, membranous wall which was characteristic of the International Style as Hitchcock and Johnson formulated it. This kind of container was at variance, too, with Mies's definition of space by discrete "constructivist" elements.[30] During the 1930s, Mies also designed projects for the Reichsbank and for the Silk Administration Building in Krefeld. Both buildings more specifically meet the norms of the International Style than his court houses; but both, like Gropius's school at Impington, seem rather dry, more the tired residue of old enthusiasms than fresh assertion. Among the major figures of the 1920s, Le Corbusier was the most active, and most creative, in the 1930s. Yet as I shall indicate, his work of the decade is of special interest for its modification of the canonical International Style.

In the strictest sense of the Hitchcock and Johnson criteria, were any outstanding buildings produced in the International Style after 1932? There are none of the importance of the major buildings in the style that were erected between 1926 or 1927 (dates which Mr. Stern also considers significant) and 1932. Of those buildings in the style put up after 1932, none purely within it matches the importance of the Bauhaus; nor that of the Stein and Poissy [figure 78 a] villas, nor the League of Nations project [figure 70], the Hook housing, the Barcelona Pavilion [figure 81], the Wolf house, the Stuttgart complex [figure 72], the Chemnitz Schocken store, the Sanitorium at Paimio, the Van Nelle factory [figure 63], the Lovell House [figure 75], or the somewhat idiosyncratic Philadelphia Saving Fund Society (PSFS) skyscraper [figure 87]. All of these buildings, in which the International Style culminates, were designed before 1932. After 1932, there are Breuer's Harnischmacher House [figure 86] and, what is more important, the Dolderthal Apartments in Zurich [figure 93]. There is Giuseppe Terragni's Casa del Popolo in Como [figure 100]. (Here, however, some influence of fascist neoclassicism is evident, as I shall specify later.) There is the Museum of Modern Art by Philip Goodwin and Edward Durell Stone [figure 114]. There is the Peter Jones Department Store in London by William Crabtree and others [figure 107] — a gently picturesque version of the International Style. There are the Tecton apartment towers at High Point. There are some production plants by Albert Kahn, such as the Dodge Truck Plant for the Chrysler Corporation [figure 108], although by no means are all of his factories in the International Style. There are certain buildings by Richard Neutra, notably, it seems to me, his elementary and junior high schools in Los Angeles [figure 97]. Perhaps his house for John Nicholas Brown on Fishers Island [figure 99] should be included as well.

More interesting, however, than this continuation of building severely within the International Style are buildings within the style which nevertheless reveal modifications of the canons enunciated by Hitchcock and Johnson. The most evident tendency of the period is one that I fear I must term a "psychologizing tendency" within the International Style: that is, the adaptation of the style to normative human needs and desires rather than the forging of an avant-garde image symbolic of l'esprit nouveau. There was much loose talk during the decade of a "humanized" modernism[31] — and again I use the neologism deliberately. Should this manner of characterizing the decade seem pejorative, one may prefer the stuffy rubric coined by the *Architectural Review* in the 1940s: the "new empiricism."[32] Either way, for better *and* worse, the International Style became physically more comfortable in the 1930s than it had been in the 1920s; it tended to be achieved more easily from prefabricated products specifically in accord with its visual qualities; it revealed a greater concern with history; it assumed more diversity of aspect. In the process, the avant-garde International Style of the 1920s was popularized. All too often, the more "humanized" modern merely betokened a more popular modern.[33]

With respect to developments in physical comfort and prefabricated components, the modification of the International Style was technological. Such developments did not necessarily alter the style. In this instance, as in others, technological advance was merely catching up to the International Style. It provided controls so as to make living behind plate-glass walls tolerable. It furnished ready-made flush doors, simplified hardware, ribbon windows, wall panels, and many other items which had previously been custom designed. There was something of a concomitant fetish during the period for studies of construction from prefabricated parts, but the prefabricated building remained more a much-discussed experiment than an actuality. There were also many time-and-motion studies of the typical use of the kitchen, the bathroom, and, in fact, every other room in the house. As Mr. Stern pointed out in his remarks—and it seems to me that this was among the most significant aspects of the 1930s—the industrial designer came into his own during the decade. No longer was he an exception in industry. He began to become big business within big business. The industrial designer typically considers architecture not as building, but as a product, more specifically as an assemblage of products. In the 1930s he was still principally concerned with product design per se; but he established a position of power from which he could compete directly with the architect after World War II, and particularly once the metal-and-glass, panel-and-skeleton building of the 1950s had illuminated the way. (In this connection, do certain buildings at the Chicago and New York world's fairs of the 1930s mark the first instances in which industrial designers are responsible for major buildings?)

A second trend in the International Style during the 1930s was the influence on it of vernacular and regional traditions. At its best this tendency provided modern architecture with the denser appeal and denser meanings possible from form called forth by concern for historical values. At worst, this influence resulted from sentimental nostalgia: redwood siding, the "family room," outdoor living, barbecue cooking, ad nauseam—all too familiar to need elaboration.

With respect to these trends, the development of Neutra's architecture and his philosophy of architectural design during the 1930s exemplified that for the period as a whole. Accepting the forms and symbolism of the International Style at the beginning of the decade, he himself confessed to the technological and psychological bias of his philosophy. From 1937 on, he became less concerned with advanced technology (with the metal house, for example), and more concerned in both theory and practice with the psychic values of regionalism, of natural materials, of the intimate relation of the building to its site, and increasingly aware of the complexity of the diverse requirements for psychological comfort. Or, to mention another architect's career of the 1930s that reveals a parallel evolution of more consequence for design, although less for theory, Breuer's seems as normative as any. Indeed, it might be argued that of all the careers important to the development of modern architecture, the evolution of Breuer's career is prototypical. From his admission to the Bauhaus as a student in one of its first classes, his work faithfully records, and has helped to determine, the successive concerns of the movement as a whole, not only through the 1930s but (unlike Neutra's) throughout the postwar decades as well. If Breuer never quite achieved the pinnacle of leadership within the movement, his creativity made him consistently influential in the vanguard.

More than Neutra, Breuer could also exemplify the impetus within the International Style after 1932 toward individuality of expression. Whereas the Harnischmacher House and Dolderthal Apartments were thoroughly of the style at the beginning of the decade, his houses done with Gropius at the end of the decade were personal expressions within the style (although they eventually generated a sub-style of their own). This trend was to be expected once the group style had been formulated, and after the battle for modern architecture was substantially won through this concerted attack. Expectedly, too, with few exceptions, the quest for individuality of expression initially produced no more than tentative results, with pronouncements toward this end on the whole more sweeping than radical change in the International Style. By way of conclusion, I should like to suggest some specific changes which occurred.

I have already alluded to the regional vernacular development, which Le Corbusier's Villa de Mandrot [figure 84] especially heralded at the beginning of the decade. On the other hand, the appeal to the grand tradition of historical architecture (in contrast to vernacular historical architecture) became dominant, it seems to me, only after World War II, and largely as a result of Johnson's making explicit the recall to historical principles implicit in Mies's work. But it is nevertheless true that during the 1930s there were neoclassical developments which tended to give new emphases, however tentative these may have been, to the neoclassicistic predilections of the International Style. Again, I have alluded to these developments. They centered in Germany and Italy, and would seem to represent the infusion of fascist neoclassicistic monumentality into modern architecture. Neo-Schinkel tendencies characterize Mies's entire career. From the Barcelona Pavilion through his projects for court houses, however, there is, if anything, a greater insistence on the plane of the earth and on the grave equilibrium of discrete units rising from it. These are basically horizontal in character and of traditional materials. The change is more dramatic in Erich Mendelsohn's work done in Israel [figure 98], where (ironically) the influence of fascist monumentality seems more overt. His masonry walls, predominantly horizontal like Mies's, and heavier, are not discrete constructivist entities but rhythmically punctured by long rows of separate windows with deep reveals. In Italy, there are buildings in the International Style, such as Terragni's Casa del Popolo [figure 100], in which framing or stilting takes on a columnar force by virtue of its conspicuousness and the conspicuous manner in which it rhythmically organizes elevations of intense purity of outline and planarity. The elevations of this and certain other modern Italian buildings of the period also seem to have been conceived with a greater sense of frontality and formality than most in the International Style. And of course there is the podium of Le Corbusier's Villa de Mandrot, and the intensified physical presence of his stilting, beginning with that for the Swiss Pavilion.

While the full-modern drew historical traditions to itself, noticeably with respect to the vernacular, and gingerly with respect to the grand tradition, this decade more than any other saw the International Style eroding the Beaux-Arts aesthetic. The outstanding example from the 1930s of this admixture of modern with Beaux-Arts was Rockefeller Center [figure 105].

Regional interests intensified feeling for site. This concern for site depended partly on the influence of Wright, partly on the movement of the center of the International Style to England, Switzerland, the Scandinavian countries — where of course Aalto's influence loomed large — and the United States, countries in which modern architects seem to have been more concerned with the intimate relation of the house to site than they were in France, Holland, and Germany. Most interesting in view of later developments, however, are those buildings which in themselves take on something of a topographical character. One of the most important is Aalto's project at Sunila [figure 111]. Another is Le Corbusier's planning at Algiers, beginning in 1930. Here he envisioned the city comprising the large continuities of modern public works in violent juxtaposition to the small discontinuities of the jumble of existing streets and buildings, and he considered both in relation to the panoramic sweep of dominant landscape features.

Le Corbusier's Maison de week-end [figure 96] represents a modification of the International Style in a different way. Although the structural or spatial unit rhythmically making or conditioning both interior space and exterior elevation revived such early works of his as the Monol project and even the duplex apartment project exhibited in the Pavillon de l'Esprit Nouveau [figure 56] at the Paris Exposition of 1925, its reappearance has pervasively affected first Le Corbusier's architecture, then that of other modern architects, as the earlier schemes did not.

An innovation of the 1930s which worked toward a more palpable wall than was characteristic of the International Style, and eventually worked to make the interior compartmentalization of space more evident on the exterior, was Le Corbusier's invention of the brise-soleil. This was the most important architectural invention of the decade to enlarge the grammar of the International Style. Appearing first in various projects for skyscrapers for Algiers [figure 90], the device became familiar with the completion of the skyscraper for the Ministry of Education in Rio de Janeiro. In this connection, there are a number of Italian buildings of merit which have as yet received little notice.[34] They are interesting because they show within the window area a layering of elements in space which seem to be related to the brise-soleil while at the same time maintaining the membranous planarity of the International Style. A house by Luigi Figini in Milan illustrates the type. Another, extensively — even overly — publicized at the time, was Ignazio Gardella's Tuberculosis Clinic in Alexandria [figure 102]. The best is a house in Cernobbio by Cesare Cattaneo, this one complicated by certain constructivist skeletal influences.

Cattaneo's house suggests a final development during the decade. There was some influence of constructivism during the period, other than that evident in Mies's court houses. Le Corbusier devised ingenious tents for two exhibitions, and a projected stadium suspended from a mast. His most notable constructivist project is, of course, that for the Palace of the Soviets, which he designed at the very outset of the decade. Some of the buildings in Breuer's scheme for the Civic Center of the Future, done with F. R. S. Yorke in England and influenced by Le Corbusier, were constructivist in character. So are the projecting columns of Howe and Lescaze's PSFS.

In summary, the International Style surely dominated progressive architecture during the decade, but the most interesting work modified the principles set down by Hitchcock and Johnson. Of these principles, that of the seamless, membrane-like wall was most modified by the work of the decade, together with the mechanomorphic imagery of the style of the 1920s, about which Hitchcock and Johnson said little. There was some tendency to move away from the open plan of the 1920s simply enclosed in large, rectangular containers, and some tendency to complicate their austerity by constructivist devices. Most of these developments were less visible as "trends" during the decade itself than they were to become in retrospect.

Le Corbusier's Changing Attitude toward Form
Péter Serényi

No discussion of Le Corbusier's architecture of this decade can begin without considering, however briefly, his earlier development. Between 1919 and 1922 Le Corbusier embarked on a new path which he has never entirely abandoned since. In the realm of domestic architecture, the Maison Monol of 1919 and the Maison Citrohan of 1920–2 [*figure 48*] mark the beginning of a new style. In these two projects lie the roots of all his later houses, culminating in the Maison Jaoul of 1954 and the Villa Shodhan of 1956. Moreover, all his *unités* owe their origin to the Immeubles villas of 1922, while the Ville Contemporaine of 1922 is the ancestor of Chandigarh.

The historical events that preceded Le Corbusier's "period of invention" provide us with the best clues to a better understanding of the origins of his style, for the chaos and disorder resulting from World War I made him painfully aware of the need to create a new order based on a more stable world. It is not surprising, therefore, that both the *maisons* Monol and Citrohan as well as the Ville Contemporaine revert to a distant past. While the former find their sources in the architecture of the tribal societies of the eastern Mediterranean world, the latter recalls a Platonic order based on numbers. In his desire to create order in face of disorder, Le Corbusier conceived two kinds of utopias altogether too familiar to Western thought: the "ideal paradise," with its particular emphasis on the individual, and the "ideal city," with its primary concern for the many. His private houses, placed in a garden setting, embody the rural concept of the good life, which Plato called "*Kronos*"—the seat of a distant tribal world characterized by peace and tranquility. The Ville Contemporaine, on the other hand, corresponds to Plato's Republic and its later derivations, expressing an urban concept of an ideal world.

More than once Le Corbusier has referred to the immediate years after World War I as the starting point for modern architecture. "If we pose the question," he proclaimed in 1928, "'Has the architectural moment of our epoch arrived?' the answer is 'It has; because since the end of the war period we possess a modern conception of architecture.' This fact is certain and can be verified in every country."[35] Let me add that Walter Gropius, who has always been more articulate in verbal than in visual images, summed up the effect of World War I on modern architecture even more precisely. He declared:

[T]he full consciousness of my responsibility in advancing ideas based on my own reflections only came home to me as the result of the war, in which these theoretical premises first took definite shape. After the violent interruption... every thinking man felt the necessity for an intellectual change of front. Each in his own particular sphere of activity aspired to help in bridging the disastrous gulf between reality and idealism. It was then that the immensity of the mission of the architects of my own generation first dawned on me.[36]

As mentioned earlier, Le Corbusier invented two kinds of private houses shortly after the war: the Monol and Citrohan. The latter, angular and firm, stands erect on the ground, dominating the setting, while the former, undulating and soft, rests on the ground, absorbing the setting. To use Le Corbusier's own words: "In the one, strong objectivity of forms, under the intense light of a Mediterranean sun: *male* architecture. In the other, limitless subjectivity rising against a clouded sky: *female* architecture."[37] In his private houses, then, it is the individual human figure—isolated and lonely, to be sure—that is expressed symbolically. It is no coincidence, therefore, that most of his houses were built for single men or women, who were either artists or intellectuals.

Before turning to the period under discussion, let me preface my brief remarks by proposing a chronology for Le Corbusier's artistic development:

1. Formative years, 1905–19
2. Period of invention, 1919–22
3. First mature phase, 1922–8
4. Period of reassessment, 1928/9–45
5. Fulfillment, 1945–present

Although the terminating date for this symposium has no particular relevance to Le Corbusier's development, the years 1928 and 1929 do mark a turning point in his style. As is well known, it was during these years that he designed the finest and, indeed, the last house in the purist style: the Villa Savoye [*figure 78 a*]. Yet it was also during these very same years that he conceived the Villa at Carthage—an entirely fresh interpretation of the well-known Citrohan type. This renewal of artistic imagination was made largely possible through his encounter with Gerrit Rietveld's work, more specifically with the Schroeder House [*figure 60*] and with his project for a house of 1923–4. On the facade of the Villa at Carthage, for example, two earlier elements—the studio and the ribbon window—are fused with the help of De Stijl vocabulary. As in Rietveld's project of 1923–4, there is a strong interplay between lines and planes, between solids and voids, and between verticals and horizontals. But unlike Rietveld's design, the various parts of the Villa at Carthage enjoy a lesser degree of independence, owing this quality, among others, to the tightness of the composition and to the uninterrupted nature of the roofline. But in later versions of the Villa at Carthage the spaces and masses are gradually loosened up, culminating in the dynamic composition of the Villa Shodhan.

Another example of the Citrohan project, the Maison Errazuris of 1930, marks the second change in his style during the period under discussion. In this case it is primarily Le Corbusier's attitude toward nature that leads him to a reassessment of form. For example, the exterior silhouette now becomes an active form, jutting upward from the ground itself. During the 1920s such visual activity was restricted to ramps or stairs, carefully concealed behind the external envelope. In fact, a comparison between this house and the Villa Savoye shows how the outline of the ramp is transformed into the space-enclosing mass, thus anchoring the entire interior volume to the site. There are, of course, a number of variations on the theme of the Maison Errazuris which were designed during this period, but with one exception, none of them was ever executed.[38] The exception is the house in Mathes of 1935. Here the functional independence of the wall—so characteristic of his houses of the 1920s—is entirely given up in favor of creating a masonry structure that serves as both a space-defining and load-bearing element, hence foreshadowing his houses of the past ten years.

Unlike its opposite, the Maison Monol had no successor during the 1920s. Some of its basic features, such as the vaulted roof and the long, continuous spaces, first appeared in Le Corbusier's own studio-apartment of 1930–3. Yet the first Monol-type house was built only in 1935. This well-known structure, located in the suburbs of Paris, occupies an important place in Le Corbusier's oeuvre [figure 96]. Unlike the Maison Citrohan and its later derivations, this weekend house does not stand upright on the ground, dominating the setting; instead, it rests on it, spreading its parts on the terrain itself. In this house—as in all Monol-type structures—Le Corbusier expresses a more subservient attitude toward nature. This is most visible in the low, earth-hugging structure, built partially of natural materials, and covered with grass. Moreover, the area defined by the external walls of the house and the small pavilion is transformed into an outdoor room, whose space becomes one with nature. As is well known, the later descendants of this house range from the project of La Sainte Baume of 1948 to the Maison Jaoul of 1954.

Before leaving the discussion of Le Corbusier's houses, let me turn, however briefly, to their interiors. During the 1920s his houses were built around staircases and ramps, creating an air of tension which was only resolved in the roof garden. As Le Corbusier has pointed out, the roof garden is a place "where the sky is always open; and far from the street, one can experience a feeling of security and well being."[39] This secluded area, high above the street and removed from the tensions of everyday life, must be understood as an Arcadia—an earthly paradise, as it were, an area where the isolated and lonely man can become one with nature in peace and tranquility. In this decade, however, Le Corbusier abandoned the roof garden in favor of creating a more restful interior space. Moreover, the importance of the ramps and stairs was taken over by the fireplace. In the 1920s his fireplaces were isolated and often fragile sculptural forms, whose primary function was to define or to divide space. This can best be seen in the living room of the Villa Church at Ville d'Avray and in the library of the double house at Stuttgart. In the 1930s, however, Le Corbusier's fireplaces acquire a more plastic quality, serving as a means to anchor the house more emphatically to the ground. Such fireplaces can be found in the house of Madame de Mandrot [figure 84], in the Errazuris project, and in the house at Mathes, not to mention in his numerous unexecuted projects.

Turning to his public buildings, let me restrict my comments to some aspects of his apartment houses and office buildings, mentioning only two important changes that occurred during the decade under discussion. First, the flatness of the roofline, so characteristic of his projects for large buildings in the 1920s, is abandoned in favor of creating a more complicated superstructure on the rooftops. Moreover, while the roof garden is gradually given up in his private houses during this period, it acquires a significant role in his public buildings, foreshadowing the spacious roof gardens of the past twenty years. Also, the relationship between the public space on the roof and the natural surrounding is now firmly established. The project for the Rentenanstalt of Zurich, designed in 1933, serves as a good example to illustrate these points.

More important, however, is the realization of Le Corbusier's best-known trademark: the *brise-soleil*. One of the first projects in which this feature appears is the apartment house for Algiers of 1933 [*figure 90*]. To enumerate the various sources for this motif lies outside the scope of this brief essay. Let me mention only one source whose origin goes back to Le Corbusier's peculiar use of window frames in the 1920s. In one of the windows of the living room of the Villa Church, for example, the glass pane is surrounded by a freestanding frame so as to give it the effect of a painting. In Algiers, on the other hand, the freestanding window frame of the previous decade is turned outside and is treated monumentally.

There is another kind of *brise-soleil*, which has, as it were, a life of its own. This type first appeared in the project for a law court for Algiers of 1938. Its composition has many visual sources. The one which I would like to emphasize particularly is Theo van Doesburg's project for a house for an artist of 1923. As in the Van Doesburg project, large rectangular frames make up the facade of Le Corbusier's law court, creating a rich, plastic effect. Although the rigidity of Le Corbusier's *brise-soleil* has little to do with Van Doesburg's looser and more fragmented composition, the original qualities of the De Stijl spirit were later incorporated into the *brises-soleil* of Chandigarh.

The year 1929 also marks an important change in Le Corbusier's attitude toward the city. His various projects of the 1920s for the rebuilding of Paris were essentially utopian diagrams, based on a neoclassical tradition best summed up in Marc-Antoine Laugier's dictum: "uniformity in detail and variety in general effect." The Mundaneum of 1929, intended for an actual site near Geneva, marks the first real effort on Le Corbusier's part to create a civic space based on the Acropolis. In this city plan the rigid symmetry of the earlier 1920s is given up in favor of a more open composition so that the various buildings acquire a greater sense of independence. Moreover, the axis of the city links the mountains with the lake. But it was only in the project for the University of Brazil of 1936 that most of his ideas first adumbrated in the Mundaneum were more fully developed. Here the dynamic asymmetry of the Acropolis is reinterpreted in a vigorous modern language. The buildings of the university are indeed "animated by a single thought, drawing around them the landscape and gathering it into the composition," to use Le Corbusier's own earlier words.[40]

Needless to say, the development of what one might best call Le Corbusier's "Acropolic style" of city planning was not the only significant event of this period of reassessment. There were also his "anti-city" city plans and the plan for a farm, which played an equally significant role in preparing the way toward fulfillment. Let me begin with the former.

Ever since 1920, when Le Corbusier made the first sketches for the Ville Contemporaine, his cities contained an element of fear—a fear of the big city, to be more exact. The most amusing illustration of this fear can be found in the various cartoons reproduced in *The City of Tomorrow*, accompanying the chapter "Newspaper Cuttings and Catchwords." The best of these, of course, is at the head of the chapter, with the caption: "Heartrending farewells of the father of a family about to cross the street in front of the Gare de l'Est."[41] On the more serious side, there is his long diatribe on the evils of the street, first published in 1929.[42] Here he condemns all conventional streets and boulevards, urging the immediate adoption of his elevated arteries of circulation, which would, as we know so well, not only separate pedestrian from vehicular traffic but also trucks from cars and cars from bicycles. But this is not all. There are also his Ville Contemporaine and Plan Voisin for Paris in which, to paraphrase Sir John Summerson, the park is not in the town but the town in the park.[43] Nothing done before or after, however, surpasses the plan for Hellocourt of 1935 in terms of being an "anti-city" city. With the pretentious title "Urbanisation d'Hellocourt," Le Corbusier introduces a few scattered skyscrapers, separated by wide-open spaces and large areas of greenery. Aristotle once said that "men come together in cities in order to live; they remain together in order to live the 'good life'—a common life, for noble ends."[44] In Hellocourt, however, men stay apart; in fact, they escape from one another by isolating themselves in lonely towers—or "lookouts," to use Le Corbusier's term—to live a private life freed from communal responsibility.

It should be noted, however, that the degree of isolation that permeates the plan of Hellocourt is rather rare in Le Corbusier's city plans. It first appears in the Plan Maciá for Barcelona of 1932, where two isolated skyscrapers are placed in a vast and deserted landscape, far outside the city boundaries. It again reappears, although in a considerably modified version, in the project for Nemours of 1934. Here the plan calls for eighteen *unités*, each housing 2,500 people, with every building standing separately on a sloping terrain, facing the sea.

It seems that during the decade under discussion Le Corbusier devised two entirely different approaches to city planning. The first, embodied in the plans for the Mundaneum and the University of Brazil, can best be called classical, following the tradition of the Acropolis. The second, expressed in the plans for Hellocourt, Barcelona, and Nemours, to name just the most significant examples, can perhaps be called "existentialist." In the former, Le Corbusier envisages a collective order based on the interaction between man and man, and between man and nature. In the latter, he views man as an isolated being, fulfilling himself through the act of living a solitary life in nature.

While addressing himself to these two entirely different attitudes toward human order, during these very same years Le Corbusier also searched for a means to reconcile them. For if seen in the proper light, the Ferme Radieuse of 1934–8 must be understood as a desperate effort on Le Corbusier's part to reconcile the one and the many, the country with the city, individuality and collectivity, indeed existentialism with classicism. In it, he combined the sense of freedom and openness of such plans as Hellocourt with the more formal organization of his "Acropolic style" of city planning. Unity between these two is achieved with the help of De Stijl vocabulary. As a comparison with Van Doesburg's painting *Rhythm of a Russian Dance* of 1918 indicates, the fragmentation of form combined with the continuity of space—so characteristic of De Stijl compositions in general—reappears in Le Corbusier's plan for this civic space. The two buildings at each end serve as primary space definers, while the others mark the boundaries for the space that flows between the first two, creating a spatial and formal rhythm that is closely reminiscent of Van Doesburg's painting. Though each building is treated as a separate unit, the whole composition is brought into unison by a flowing space. Unlike in the plan for Nemours, for example, where only a series of diagrammatic roads links the buildings together, here the whole town revolves around and emanates from a space that is both living and active. Moreover, in order to achieve a greater sense of unity between man and nature, each building is covered with a Monol–type vaulted roof, which firmly anchors the interior spaces to the ground.

Although it is an ideal town, planted not on an actual site but simply on a blank sheet, the Ferme Radieuse is far removed from its ancestor, the Ville Contemporaine. The gradual reassessment of form and content which is first visible in the plan for the Mundaneum of 1929 comes to an end here. It is a process of transformation without which such mature plans as St. Dié and Chandigarh would remain incomprehensible.

To conclude, the numerous important changes that took place in Le Corbusier's style during the decade under discussion were realized, first, through his reassessment of nature; second, through his renewed encounter with De Stijl; and third, through his fresh attitude toward his own work of the 1920s. All these changes paved the way for his most mature style of the post-1945 period. One can therefore justly call these years a period of reflection and reassessment.

The Diaspora
Sibyl Moholy-Nagy

"Diaspora" means a scattering of the faithful and was first applied by St. James to Christian Jews having to live among heathens. There are two sides to every diaspora. One is so dark and tragic that no novelist has ever succeeded in formulating the agonies of the creative mind made homeless. The other side of any diaspora is so excruciatingly funny that, again, no writer has ever conveyed the comedy of errors played out by the alien mind anxiously disguised in native costume.

I am a beachcomber of history. This is why I responded so enthusiastically to an assignment that sent me back to the desolate shores of our emigration decade. But in spite of an intense search for clues that would explain the astonishing impact of a handful of refugee designers on the environmental concepts of this country, I found no fascinating pieces of driftwood, shaped by the complex currents that fill the vast void between Europe and America. Only the images of small, repetitive boxes had washed ashore, their disingenuous simplicity pointing to a common dogma as their only possible justification.

And with the interpretation of this dogma starts the drama and the farce of diaspora architecture. The design revolution on which America staked the beginning of a new era in her architectural history was in reality neither a beginning nor a revolution. It was the conclusion of the anti-academic protest that had started more than a hundred years ago. Nikolaus Pevsner was more right than he perhaps intended when he subtitled his popular book on the pioneers of modern design "From Morris to Gropius." As with all reformations, the architectural one that had started with Sir John Soane and Karl Friedrich Schinkel never discarded first principles: boxed-in spaces, form equilibrium, and an anxious guardianship over the anthropometric scale. It merely subtracted what it considered superfluous, without a flaming desire for new potentialities. In a precise historical analogy to the decay of the Gothic Reformation toward the close of the fourteenth century, Palladian purification classicism around 1580, and the strangling of baroque by a host of theorizing friars in the eighteenth century, the twentieth-century conclusion of the academic liberation was mere paper. The Bauhaus program and the charters of the Congrès Internationaux d'Architecture Moderne (CIAM) took up where architectural creation left off. CIAM was conceived from its beginnings in 1928 as an endless succession of congresses with an endless publication chain of subcommittee findings. The Bauhaus program in its final crystallization in 1923 defined functionalism as the interaction of art and technology, with the artist as the guilty escapist who had "to be liberated from his otherworldliness and reintegrated into the everyday working process."

It is puzzling to consider that functionalism should have acquired such an aura of ideological revelation in Cambridge, Chicago, and the lectures of Sigfried Giedion, when American builders had practiced it uncompromisingly since constructing the first hogan in Plymouth Colony. This historical irony rests on a total misunderstanding of the term. For the American designer, functionalism meant, and still means, building as economically and as technologically as possible, with minimum consideration of personal or aesthetic principles. To the diaspora architects, functionalism meant pure ideology, visualizing self-evident truths of ethical, aesthetic, and social *Weltanschauung*. What Germany admired most during the 1920s was pure Kantian non-empirical idealism. Perhaps the misunderstanding between the two functionalisms would have been cleared up earlier if fortuitous timing and ample publicity had not maintained the myth of a "new" architecture. The Great Depression had made it clear that a stable economic future had to be grounded on more than successful stock market manipulation. As after all crises, the public outcry was for better education. In the design field, John Dewey's *Art as Experience*, published in 1934, propounded educational tenets that were straight Bauhaus theory: "Science as the organ of social progress," "continuous sensory experience to replace learning by recapitulation and retrospection," "search instead of research," and "art as the tool of education and therapy." [45] Neither the Deweyites nor Dean Joseph Hudnut, who played such a decisive part in bringing Walter Gropius and ultimately Ludwig Mies van der Rohe to American universities, caught on to the fact that "science" and "technology" were purely poetic terms for the European functionalists—as "sin" and "salvation" are for modern theologians. "The tumultuous transformations by the triumphs of science" [46] which Hudnut promised to Harvard would not be made by the diaspora reformers. Not a single structural system used by them up to 1946 was invented later than 1900.

The other passport that secured the entry of the "makers of modern architecture" into this country was *The International Style* by Henry-Russell Hitchcock and Philip C. Johnson, published in 1932. In its unconcerned mixture of truth and opinion, quality and cliché, this is an astonishing document, declaring Le Corbusier, Mies van der Rohe, Gropius, and, of all people, the Dutch architect J. J. P. Oud the unquestionable leaders of modern architecture. Taking a firm, disdainful stance *against*—not for—functionalism, Hitchcock and Johnson slew the anti-aesthetic, expedient, economic, and socially conscious tendencies of the day with arguments that would have expelled them instantly from Le Corbusier's CIAM, Gropius's Bauhaus, Mies's Werkbund, and Oud's De Stijl. It is hilarious to read in 1932 about the necessary separation of architecture and building (on whose absolute unity the whole Bauhaus idea was founded); about a hierarchy of aesthetic significance (against the fierce renunciation of "taste and form" in all the patristic utterances); about regularity of design based on bilateral symmetry (as if "*Fassadenarchitektur*" had not become the dirtiest work in the trade); about stone-granite-marble exteriors as the only worthy architectural materials (when it was *sozialer Wohnungsbau* that gave to all four heroes of the book their reason for being); and about "plan fetishism" (flung into the pictorial evidence of "expressed interior function" as the law of laws). But no one caught on to this schizophrenic sleight of hand, least of all the diaspora architects who only wanted to be accepted.

Architectural school programs were reformed in the Bauhaus image. This was such an improvement over what the watered-down Beaux-Arts education had offered that the lack of distinguished building design was gladly over-looked by the imported architect-educators. With a tactful shrug, America looked the other way when Gropius and Marcel Breuer built those astonishingly ugly little houses, leading up to that permanent diner, the Harvard Graduate Center. Bexhill Pavilion, by Erich Mendelsohn with Serge Chermayeff, had still a faint echo of the bold curves of the Schocken store and the soaring staircase of the Metal Workers' Building. But his buildings in Israel proved that a decent standard of subtractive simplicity, shared by the functional ideologists of the 1920s, had been destroyed by the diaspora. Mies van der Rohe seemed to be wholly a part of that slow death when he finally arrived in this country in 1937. His first scheme for the campus of the Illinois Institute of Technology [*figure 116*] is painfully reminiscent of his deadly fascist designs for the German Reichsbank, and the Krefeld factory of 1937 proved the old German proverb that he who lies down with dogs gets up with fleas. Yet he was the only one of the diaspora architects capable of starting a new life as a creative designer fol-lowing World War II, because to him technology was not a romantic catchword, as it had been for the Bauhaus program, but a workable tool and an inescapable truth. There can be little doubt that the spark that ignited his talent was the Chicago School, just as the Tugendhat House and the Barcelona Pavilion [*figure 81*] of his European phase owe an acknowledged debt to Frank Lloyd Wright. His finest achievement, the Seagram Building in New York, carries John Root's Reliance Building of 1893 to its ultimate perfection.

The halo of greatness and originality surrounding the Bauhaus teachers gradually became questionable, and the misunderstanding of the two func-tionalisms has resolved itself in a new architectural beginning. The historian, however, must never forget that more enduring than the ironies of history is the testimony of an essential evolution. A new beginning is predicated on a total conclusion which had been achieved by the reformers of the diaspora. In 1949 at the CIAM in Bergamo, Helena Syrkus, a Polish state architect, buried ideological functionalism. Although her motivations were certainly not purely architectural, she had the insight and the courage to tell the old lions that their days were over: "We must revise our attitude," she said, "The Bauhaus is as far behind us as Scamozzi." [47]

[The following comment was made by Hitchcock, at the suggestion of Philip Johnson that he speak about the International Style *book.]*

Henry-Russell Hitchcock: I seem to remember that toward the beginning something was said about the presumptive possibility of taking a series of striking monuments of a given, rather limited period and attempting to derive from those monuments some cohesive, though unconscious, program, for example, at very great length (much greater length than Mr. Johnson and I) but also with many more monuments to lean on, as Paul Frankl did with the Gothic. We didn't have a great many monuments to work from. In fact, when one looks back now on the architectural production of the 1920s that was rele-vant to the International Style, it is *fantastically* small. In spite of the fact that we think of the 1920s as a period of boom production and the 1930s as, on the whole, a period of limited production, the number of relevant buildings was enormously greater, of course, in the 1930s than in the 1920s, whether or not, as it seems to us at the present point, there occurred a certain "dilution"—that is to say, that the intensity there was in *one* Le Corbusier house of the 1920s was vastly diluted in however many in the whole world—thousands, at least—of vaguely Corbusian imitations that went up in the 1930s.

But looking back at the buildings, where they still exist and are in good condition, it is obviously true that they do not, in retrospect, seem to make as intense an impression as they made when they were new. The situation was somewhat like what occurred later on Park Avenue: when the Lever House was built and was alone, it was very exciting; but now that there are ranges of Lever houses all up and down the avenue, you can't always pick out Lever House itself. And it seems to me that one thing that happened in the 1930s was that what had been rare and special became *common*. I suppose in that sense what we *wrote* was a kind of prognosis; but worse than that, it has been suggested by some unkind people that the very fact that we wrote the book helped, at least in this country, to produce the later situation, that if we had kept quiet there wouldn't have been such a spread of mediocre imitations of the great monuments in the 1930s. I am afraid that I myself can't believe that writers about the arts influence history to that extent.

The really influential writers were not people like Mr. Johnson and myself. They were still people like Le Corbusier and Frank Lloyd Wright. Today Mr. Johnson's pronouncements on architecture are backed up by his work; they were not then. Whereas when you have any point of time in mind—and this was especially true, it seems to me, in the 1920s and 1930s—the configuration of vigorous theoretical writing about architecture with actual, though limited, production is significant. When you have both precept and practice to lean on, the influence of the new is very great; and, at least in the case of the two twentieth-century architects who seem so far to be surviving best—Le Corbusier and Wright—that combination of being skillful, if not technically perfect, writers—exhorters perhaps more than expositors—with their executed work, even though in many cases what they said seemed to be in the opposite direction, had a great deal to do with the total direction of the period.

When we come to a new figure of the 1930s like Alvar Aalto, it seems definitely true that the fact that Aalto has never been his own interpreter in books and that, indeed, he has had very few serious interpreters who are as close to his thought as, say, Mr. Johnson was close to Mies van der Rohe's thought, may explain the fact that Wright's architecture or Le Corbusier's architecture is a much more comprehensible thing than Aalto's architecture. I thought Aalto's architecture was more comprehensible before I saw it, that is to say, before I went to Finland last year. I knew it only from a few specimens in other countries. Now that I have seen the whole—well, hardly the whole, but a great range of Aalto—I feel that his interpreters have been neither close to his thought nor sufficiently informed of the totality of his work. But that means that we have not had, in the case of Aalto, who has moved about the world and built a good deal, the same kind of situation that existed with the German diaspora. There may actually be an important difference of temperament also. Undoubtedly it is the ghost of G. W. F. Hegel in the background of certain Germans that motivates them to form a total system. That is certainly not so true of other architects.

World's Fairs in the 1930s

Paul F. Norton

The real importance of world's fairs in the 1930s can be measured by considering them only as a few in a long series of such events dating from 1851, the year of the Crystal Palace Exposition in London. Before the Crystal Palace, all expositions had been national. The 1851 exhibition was international and included innumerable examples of craft and industry as well as art. The United States sent, as part of its collection of 1760 exhibits, false teeth, chewing tobacco, artificial legs, and air-exhausted coffins. Prince Albert, sponsoring the affair, looked at it with lofty idealism as symbolizing the unity of mankind. He spoke of it as "a living picture of the point of development at which mankind has arrived, and a new starting point from which all nations will be able to direct their future exertions." [48] At any rate, it was clearly international. As you all know, the most influential part of the exhibition was not, paradoxically, any of the seventeen thousand individual exhibits but the exhibition building itself. For the next seventy-five years, builders of railroad terminals, palm palaces, and further exposition halls were to rely heavily on Joseph Paxton's provocative crystalline effects and his utilization of mass-production methods in making prefabricated components.

By the 1930s what was revolutionary in 1851 — namely, the great glass container lighting exhibits with daylight — was passé, and instead, the opposite condition became desirable. Exterior light was generally excluded, and windowless interior spaces were electrically lighted with what one critic of the Chicago World's Fair in 1933 called "gas-filled tubes." The neon light, so brilliant and gay at night, and the use of intense color values turned what used to be, through the British Empire exhibition of 1924, a comparatively dignified policy of exhibition into an atmosphere of the carnival. "A Century of Progress," the slogan for Chicago's fair referring to the time elapsed since the founding of the city, brought before the public many a new scientific discovery or improvement. But (and here is the weakness) the exhibitions were frankly commercial advertising, privately financed, whereas the Chicago fair of 1893, and most others, were financed with public subsidy. Perhaps because of the "spirit" of progress, the Chicago Fair Commission in 1933 chose as architects men with a forward-looking point of view. [49] To repeat the architectural debacle of 1893 would only have played into the hands of reactionaries and revealed to the immense Depression-era crowds a real lack of progress. Thirty-eight million people went there in two years to saunter up and down the three and-one-half miles of lakefront.

Paul Cret designed the all-important Hall of Science. Blatantly, though somewhat confusedly, modern, its carillon tower was flooded with red and blue neon light, its height only bettered by the ugly sky-ride towers. Nearly of equal importance was Raymond Hood's Electrical Building, sparkling with lighted fountains and ever more neon. Hood joined several pieces of gay, brilliant design into a length of disunity. Nevertheless it was a grand architectural achievement coming forth full-blown as it did from a country not yet aware of contemporary European standards nor of its own Frank Lloyd Wright. [50]

One other structure deserves mention: the House of Tomorrow. It was greeted by a critic as that part of the fair showing "a new and probably transitory architectural ideal." [51] Never was the word "transitory" less appropriately used. The House of Tomorrow was designed by George F. Keck, who was then age thirty-eight. It had twelve glass walls and a most peculiarly inconvenient arrangement of rooms, but at least here was an idea.

Barcelona and Stockholm, the sites of Europe's fairs of the early decade, were vastly different in influence. Yet they both brought forth the best from their architects, and in both cases the works were clearly contemporary and even revolutionary within tbeir own spheres. Mies's German pavilion [*figure 81*] could hardly be matched for sheer brilliance, precision, slickness of material, and clarity of plan. This was his real break with the past. But it was not so much a building as it was an abstract design—the same kind of nonhuman abstraction he has used ever since.

The case of the exhibition of arts and crafts of 1930 in Stockholm was quite different. In the first place, it was not really an international exhibition, and perhaps for this reason it should not be compared with those that were. Furthermore, all the architectural work was assigned without competition to one man: Gunnar Asplund. It was said that previous expositions in Sweden had emphasized architecture to the detriment of the exhibits. Now the objects themselves were to be emphasized. The buildings were to be "machines with which to demonstrate the objects exhibited." [52] As it has now turned out, all is forgotten *but* the architecture. The airy white buildings ingeniously grouped amid displays of colorful flags and flowers with an evening array of brilliant lights became Asplund's way of awakening himself and provincial Sweden to the new style—the International Style. Le Corbusier, Walter Gropius, and Mies, all of whom had progressed beyond experimentation by 1930, must have inspired Asplund to design his splendid, tasteful buildings. Before the Stockholm exhibition, Asplund was local and rather traditional; afterward he was inventively international.[53]

Two other world exhibitions particularly noteworthy because of their size and volume of attendance must be mentioned, but it may be worth recalling that there were many others of less importance in the 1930s, for instance, at Antwerp, Leipzig, Liège, Brussels, Glasgow, Jerusalem, Oslo, and San Francisco, some of which may have added strength to the modern movement.

At Paris in 1937, the French managed to organize successfully a veritable exhibition city within a city. They chose not a vacant lot in the suburbs but a place not only intimately connected with previous Paris exhibitions but planted loosely along the banks of the Seine and reaching into the density of the city, along avenues prepared nearly one hundred years earlier by Baron Georges-Eugène Haussmann. Thus for a year the fair and the city intermeshed to the advantage of each. The slogan in Paris was "Arts and Science as Applied to Life Today," though an official commentator found the fair valuable for promoting world peace as well and said, "I am sure [the people] will enjoy the poetry of its decorations—which has come off victorious in a duel with the integral nudism of recent architecture." [54] The last phrase indicates that our commentator found the International Style architecturally indecent. However, on close inspection of the published sources, with the exception of structures included from previous fairs, it is clear that the outstanding examples of architecture are nevertheless International Style. Perhaps what the commentator meant—and this is quite true—was that most of the buildings had appliqué decoration, breaking up the smooth, flat, and rounded surfaces with patterns of lettering, murals, and sculptural contrivances.

Serge Chermayeff, partly in jest, has said that the best thing at the exposition was the Eiffel Tower. There were, though, a few other interesting, if not world-shaking, structures. Sweden, educated by Asplund and provided with designs by S. I. Lind, built an impressively clean, well-proportioned pavilion of welded steel. The Japanese, as might be expected, toyed with new materials and produced varying effects of design. The Swiss gave a sense of up-to-date-ness but were misguided in using a factory-style window of too large size. Poor in design, and even in promotion of nationalism, were the Italian and the Russian contributions. An Italian gallery, a pastiche of irresponsible pleasant-ries with Corinthian columns standing free of the walls but also of the ceiling, shows a widely separated point of view from a similar gallery of the Dutch pavilion. The Russians, evidently unhappy with their site, became obstreper-ous and built nature literally into their structure. The best of the architec-ture at the Paris exposition was in the foreign pavilions. Nothing sponsored by the French government is worthy of mention—all was retrogressive.

Finland naturally put the problem of designing its pavilion for Paris into the hands of Alvar Aalto. To say that this was significant for Aalto would be wrong. He had already developed his own vertical-stick style, so that, although it was probably the handsomest of all pavilions in the exposition, it did nothing for Aalto's personal style, but probably increased his international prestige.[55]

One may now inquire as to what use was made of architecture at fairs up to this point in the 1930s, namely 1937. Along with peace, said to be sponsored at Paris, there certainly was an increase in international rivalry in architec-ture, which tended to produce many different ideas, if not always good ones. In opposition to the rigidity of academies, freely moving, openly eye-catching architecture had the chance to impress the holiday public without their having to take it all too seriously. After all, the structures were mainly temporary. What actually happened at Paris, I believe, is that the unsuspecting public became aware of many new architectural possibilities and liked what they saw, even though the whole exposition must have exuded the usual smell and appearance of an immense carnival.

Finally, in New York in 1939, the World of Tomorrow, the most gigantic car-nival ever thrown together, demonstrates again the point reached at Paris. Frankly and openly modern, with many a seducing and playful piece to suggest the weirdness of the future, and with even more emphasis than before on mass production of industry through the innumerable buildings constructed with seemingly unlimited private funds, this heterogeneity of weekend escapism produced little of significance. The past was ruled out, to be sure, but the past might have been preferable to the pre–Pop art of Walter Dorwin Teague's National Cash Register Building, with a cash register forty feet high counting the customers as they entered the gates of the fair. In fact, commercialism not only was allowed by the promoters but encouraged. What can be salvaged architecturally? Whose names are attached to the interesting bits and pieces of Flushing's madness? Many exhibits, particularly the scientific ones, turned out to be of more interest than the buildings housing them. I can remember how exciting the experimental TV was in the AT&T building and have no mental picture now of its structural container.

Albert Kahn and Norman Bel Geddes made a mock-up of the center of a model city for General Motors with smooth, slick surfaces: the Street of Tomorrow, a sheet of uncompromising iciness [figure 115]. Harrison and Fouilhoux, for some quite incomprehensible reason, was commissioned to design a house and barn in Tomorrow Town. The architects were unable to imagine a barn (or a house for that matter) of tomorrow, so they justified their work by stating that "traditional forms of barn and silo inspire a clean-cut honesty of design."[56] In a more positive way, Voorhees, Walker, Foley, and Smith designed for the E. G. Budd Manufacturing Company a corrugated, stainless-steel umbrella system reminiscent in form of Wright's Johnson Wax Administration Building in Racine. The Budd Company, of course, makes stainless steel, which adequately accounts for their choice of materials but not for the sophisticated display. For this the architects deserve great credit.

William Lescaze, with J. Gordon Carr as associate, designed the Aviation Building. It was as successful as any at the fair because they did not try to make it like an airplane or dirigible but rather made it into a great wind tunnel, embracing the spirit of air flight without mimicking the obvious shapes.

For Sweden, now used to superior exhibition design, Sven Markelius designed a pavilion impermanent in feeling yet beautifully finished with wood and welded metal, and created a sense of informality without detracting from a sense of elegance. It was reported at the time that "Even the advertisers have been persuaded into cultural restraint, the names of businesses being neatly carved on some of the limestone paving slabs." With a few other possible exceptions, Flushing's first fair was, architecturally speaking, an abysmal failure. Economically, it must have pleased the city; otherwise we would not have with us again another monstrous carnival.

In New York today there is another fair of enormous proportions. I visited it on the fourth day after the opening and found many pavilions still under construction, yet the pattern was clear. This fair is without a slogan. It serves no worthy purpose. Yet a vast section, including all exhibits of industry and many foreign pavilions, is devoted exclusively to enormously expensive advertising. It is 250 million dollars' worth of conspicuous holiday atmosphere with only the slightest pretense of providing education, useful information, beauty, or the precious ideas of man. Most impressive is the exterior dark wall of the Japanese pavilion, cut to the design of a sculptor who knew how to introduce subtle pattern without detracting from the qualities of stone. The interior of the same pavilion is filled with gross industrial displays.

In conclusion, it is clear to me that whereas exhibitions of the early 1930s had architectural offerings to make, particularly through the energies of certain individuals, by the end of the decade contemporary design had already been accepted by the best of professional architects and by large masses of the public for industrial problems, public buildings, schools, and even churches, although the private house — the center of man's traditional way of life — remained an area where, in large measure, advanced architectural ideas were not wanted. Thus, the fairs of the *late* 1930s were not apt to produce a sense of wonderment and excitement anymore. The stuff of the fairs had already been accepted as normal, and what few advanced architectural concepts may have occurred went unseen in the midst of carnival confusion.

Frank Lloyd Wright's Years of Modernism, 1925-35

Edgar Kaufmann, Jr.

Through almost five years, from 1925 to 1929, the very air Frank Lloyd Wright breathed was thick with catastrophe. His home, Taliesin, was once again fully destroyed by fire. Debts drove him to the verge of bankruptcy. Hysterical persecutions pursued him and the new, beloved family who were to remain close to him for the long rest of his life. These blackest years were survived only through personal love and a secure sense of creative accomplishment. This accomplishment was posited, in 1925, on the sumptuous pages of *Wendingen*. Soon, at the urging of his wife, Wright started to evoke his childhood, beginning *An Autobiography*.

Unsurprisingly, the architectural yield of these years is strange and ideal, especially in contrast to the immediate past when Wright had built the Barsnsdall (Hollyhock) House [*figure 47*], his most lavishly embellished design, and the block houses for Mrs. Millard [*figure 54*], the Storers, the Ennises, and the Freemans, all in California, and had planned elaborate Death Valley and Chicago projects for A. M. Johnson, an adventuresome insurance magnate. These works and those that followed in the later 1930s bracket a unique decade of architectural ideation in Wright's career. Building almost nothing, he surveyed a number of important avenues that were to lead him to major achievements. And (perhaps stimulated by the extravagant coterie centered on the mistress of Hollyhock House) Wright became an advocate of the idealistic modernism we recognize as the essence of the 1920s. World horizons, technological miracles, the thrill of speed, the challenge of untried potentials were as stimulating then to his imagination as to the rest of the Western world's. In so regarding the spirit of Wright's work in these years I am returning to insights published by Henry-Russell Hitchcock more than twenty years ago and little examined since.[57]

In 1925 and 1926, two dreams arose in Wright's mind, both worthy of close attention: the Gordon Strong Planetarium and Automobile Objective, and the Steel Interfaith Cathedral. Both projects celebrated modern technology with, for Wright, unprecedented vigor.

At the crest of Sugar Loaf, a 1,200-foot mountain some thirty miles northwest of Washington, D. C., Wright planned a planetarium, then the newest symbol of the popular appeal of science; the Carl Zeiss Corporation had just opened their panetarium at Jena, Germany to international applause.[58] Around the required dome Wright spiraled a broad roadway to a viewing platform that commanded the Potomac Valley and the Catoctin Ridge. Motoring was coming of age; over smooth highways created by the expanding economy of World War I sped new, small family cars and the sleek, roaring imports of sporting enthusiasts. Wright projected an ideal excursion for them.

Less specific, the vast glass pyramid of the Interfaith Cathedral was to rise, braced by steel, as high as Sugar Loaf and its superstructure together, a 1,500-foot, man-made summit: the highest ever. Like Bruno Taut a decade earlier, it would seem Wright was conjecturing some kind of "alpine architecture."

The formal elements Wright used in these two projects were portents of many of his latest and freest works of the 1940s and 1950s. Circles, triangles, and polyhedra rose openly from their long abeyance in Wright's ornamental details and romanticist roofs to become the substance of his architectural thought. Wright's originally eloquent roofs had dwindled to invisibility in his

California block structures, but a reversal typical of him — roof victorious over wall — began with the tepee-play of the Tahoe and Nakoma projects of 1922 and 1924, respectively. By 1926 such surface-Indianizing was absorbed into the superhuman scale and sheer crystallinity of the cathedral. In the Sugar Loaf scheme, likewise, archaeology was dissipated in a ziggurat for Isotta Fraschinis.

In 1927 Wright began his Arizona desert experiments for the San Marcos resort hotel and the nearby Young and Cudney villas. The liberated triangle acquired new meaning in this arid air; it appeared now less as roof or silhouette, more as the generative module of plan — reiterated, rhythmic, sharply responsive to sun and shade, the source of shimmer which every desert-lover knows is characteristic. The freedom of the 30-degree angle on plan, intuited for the Nakoma project, here was seized and understood. It was to yield a grammar for some of Wright's most livable and intriguing works.

The 1927 experiments evolved in a temporary camp called Ocatilla (after the ocotillo plant), where rough lumber and canvas flaps were used, as they later were for Taliesin West [figure 110]. Transcontinental journeys to and from Wisconsin by car meant more to Wright than his earlier, regular steamship crossings of the Pacific. The automobile had caught his attention. In 1927 and 1928 Wright developed several ideas for motor courts and service stations: crisp, modest architecture for rootless "grass-roots" America.

The fateful year 1929 opened well for Wright. The *Architectural Record* welcomed him to its pages month after month. The Arizona projects were amply developed. The little church of St. Mark's-in-the-Bouwerie was ready to introduce his most advanced ideas of apartment planning and furnishing to New York City, where he had never built. Wright had on the boards for Elizabeth Noble in Los Angeles different and ingenious solutions to the same problem. St. Mark's towers, especially, were notable for the structural advance they marked over the scheme for the insurance company's building. In the New York towers, cell and skeleton interacted more vividly than in the inert (and today still standard) cagework for Chicago.

Also in 1929 Wright was able to demonstrate, in a rare actual building, full victory over the wall without any assist from the roof — a maneuver he had been working toward throughout the decade. In the house at Tulsa for Richard Lloyd Jones, his cousin-client accepted regularly alternating, vertical piers and glass strips, equally wide, that resolutely elude the concepts of window or wall. The Jones House has usually been criticized for its exterior, but the experience inside is gratifying as well as extraordinary (so that one may expect happy results within some narrow-glazed, exoskeletal skyscrapers).

Then, the Crash. All Wright's commissions vanished. Nineteen hundred thirty brought only the Kahn Lectures at Princeton University, published the following year as *Modern Architecture*. The word "modern" was in the air; in 1929 the Museum of *Modern* Art (MoMA) had been founded in New York.

Nineteen hundred and thirty-one again brought purely ideal notions of Frank Lloyd Wright's to paper projection. Two out of three seem clearly inferior to his great conceptions of the late 1920s. Especially the Century of Progress skyscraper regulation schemes offer little but gigantism, picturesquely massed glassiness, and ornament hardly better than the imitation-Wright ornament in which Peter Behrens weltered in 1924 and 1925. The House on the Mesa, a project exhibited in 1932 at MoMA, had a daring cantilever over the open swimming pool, reminiscent of the extended free horizontals of Ludwig Mies van der Rohe's 1924 project for a reinforced-concrete country house. But in many sketches, only the living-room roof of the House on the Mesa is cantilevered, less daringly, and the counterbalancing slab over the pool is omitted. The result is cold, almost Auguste Perret–like, perhaps because of the rigid module which governs both plan and elevations. Only the stepped-in windows were salvaged in Wright's later work, the Walker House at Carmel.

The third 1931 project was a Cinderella. A modest proposal for a newspaper plant in Salem, Oregon, contained the seed idea of the Johnson Wax Administration block built in Racine — hollow, tapered, wide-capped columns with skylights between. Here Wright envisioned a dissolution of the roof as drastic as that of the wall at the Jones House two years earlier.

In 1932 Wright's grip on modernism was steady. Various, largely unconventional ideas for theater designs that he had assembled over the years were reworked and integrated into a project called "The New Theatre," substantially built late in Wright's life in Dallas. Prefabricated farm buildings, stamped in quantity like automobile bodies, and related roadside markets (incipient shopping centers) were designed for Walter Davidson. The theme of the cantilever was very modestly resumed in a project for Dean Malcolm Willey of Minneapolis, a wonderfully relaxed revision of a self-conscious project of 1925 for Mrs. Samuel W. Gladney.

My grudging attitude toward Wright's architectural projects of the first and deepest Depression years cannot extend to the magnificent, moving autobiography published in 1932. Together with the contemporary founding of the Taliesin Fellowship it demonstrates Wright's creative resourcefulness even in the least promising situations. Long after most of Wright's buildings will have been razed, *An Autobiography* will carry his spirit to new generations. The other book published in 1932, *The Disappearing City*, was sufficiently unsatisfactory for Wright to rework it twice subsequently; yet it launched him on his Broadacre City scheme [*figure 88*] that is perhaps now about to receive the renewed attention it deserves from serious students of planning.

Nineteen hundred and thirty-three saw the struggle to build facilities for the Taliesin Fellowship; a large drafting room and dormitories were added to a remodeling of the old Hillside Home School buildings that Wright had designed near Taliesin for his aunts in 1902. With very little money a good deal was accomplished, and the wide-trussed drafting room in particular added new vigor to the rich Wisconsin landscape.

The winter of 1933–4 was spent almost entirely on the Broadacre City model and on models of its details at larger scale. All these were shown in Radio City, first of several public exhibitions. To a general public, bewildered and frustrated by the Depression, here was a vision of the good life they had always hoped for. But it had no place in the reconstruction that pulled America out of the trough. A more modest house than that projected was built in 1934 for the Willeys — the first commission for someone other than himself or his family to be designed, supervised, and executed by Wright since the Freeman House in Los Angeles ten long, eventful years before.

In 1935 a wittily daring project was designed for Mary and Stanley Marcus of Dallas: a crisp, roomy house sheltered under a single, generous envelope of insect screening. Mrs. Marcus liked her screens at the windows.

Thereafter, modernism contributed to Frank Lloyd Wright's familiar masterworks of the later 1930s, but it no longer was the dominating characteristic as it had been in the years between the Freeman and Willey commissions. The change was due in part, no doubt, to a shift from paper to actual construction. Even more, it was due to the natural maturation of Wright's genius. The automobile, prefabrication, One-Worldism, and New-Worldism were accepted as ingredients of his thinking rather than as leitmotifs in works after 1935: Fallingwater, the Johnson Wax Administrative Center, the Hanna House, Taliesin West, Florida Southern College, and Auldbrass Plantation. After 1935 Wright, like most of the world, could widen his horizons and deepen his responses with a richness that included and superseded his modernism of the previous decade.[59]

A Brief Review of the Decade's Architectural Literature
Adolf K. Placzek

Long before Vitruvius first put pen to papyrus, architecture commanded an extensive literature. It is apparent that architectural literature is now more voluminous than the one accompanying painting, sculpture, or even the decorative arts. One obvious reason for this is that architects like to write—not only about themselves but also about other architects—and seem to be able to do so more articulately than painters and sculptors. A deeper reason lies in the fact that socially, economically, materially, politically, and ideologically, architecture is most directly and tangibly connected with the reality of time, place, and circumstance. It is, of course, fairly obvious that the relation between the actual architecture of a period and its attendant literature is a rather unpredictable one. Great breakthroughs in design and technology are not automatically reflected in equally great books; nor are great books always the harbingers of great buildings. However, an immediate relationship between building and writing about building does exist; and it is an ironic fact that the most casual and half-hearted illustration often survives and thereby guarantees a sort of survival of the sturdiest and most durable of structures, to say nothing about evanescent masterpieces like the Barcelona Pavilion [figure 81].

If we survey the vast literature of the period 1929–39 with these reservations in mind, we will find all the contradictions of the decade actually exaggerated in it. On the whole we will find technology advancing but utopia faltering. We will find ideas receding and propaganda mounting. These were years, particularly in Western Europe, of much publishing, frequently of a certain slick and glossy sort, the forerunner of much of today's type of illustrative material, but it was not a decade of great writing.

To begin with France, it is evident that this was no longer the period of Le Corbusier's Vers une architecture. It was, however, typically the period of the first volume of the architect's Oeuvre complète, the first codification of his achievements and as prototypal for all later architectural-biographical collected works as it was reflective of the great publishing tradition of Jacques Androuet du Cerceau, Jean Marot, and François Blondel. Le Corbusier published several other important books; his literary drive was not slowed down by the change in the intellectual climate. Then there was André Lurçat. But there also was the over-publicized and rather facile Robert Mallet-Stevens, and Michel Roux-Spitz. Among periodicals, L'Architecture d'aujourd'hui was continuing rather unexcitingly. L'Architecture vivante, one of the great periodicals, expired in 1933.

In Germany, historical events were sharply reflected in architectural publishing. In fact, design became politics because of the adamant hatred by the

Nazis of what we can call "modern architecture." Between 1929 and 1933, we find the Bauhaus as a publishing venture barely surviving; numbers 12, 13, and 14 — the last of the great series of *Bauhausbücher* — came out in 1929 and 1930. Erich Mendelsohn did publish, as we know. Bruno Taut rather faded out between 1929 and 1933. Then came 1933, the Hitler dictatorship. It would, of course, be oversimplifying to say that all quality ceased immediately. This was not the case; there were fine books around Hans Poelzig, Paul Bonatz, Fritz Höger, and others. There was brick regionalism and neoromanticism. But then came a deluge of publications which smothered any real thought. Behind people like Albert Speer, Paul Troost, and Werner March there was the whole propaganda apparatus of the State.

In Austria, a period of uncertain grace lasted until 1938. Adolf Loos's book came out in 1931 with "Ornament and Crime" in it, which, of course, was written much earlier. There were people like Oskar Strnad, who in spite of fine writing about them are now almost forgotten. There was the decorative genius of Josef Hoffmann and the regionalist Clemens Holzmeister. These two were successful architects and much publicized, but they were not themselves articulate in words. Loos, on the other hand, whose architectural career was blighted by enmity and lack of success, was one of the most articulate and brilliant architectural writers of his time.

In Italy the situation differed from Germany. There was considerable enthusiasm for modern design under the Fascist regime. Futurism was interwoven with Fascist ideology. The International Style and neoclassicism coexisted, and many architects and architectural writers walked a political tightrope between them. The richness of architectural literature is actually rather surprising when compared with the poverty of poetry, drama, and cinema of the decade in Italy. There was the intellectually highly influential Alberto Sartoris, whose book on functional architecture had a great impact also in France and in the whole Latin world. There were among the modernists Agnoldomenico Pica, Pietro Maria Bardi, and Luigi Moretti. Giuseppe Terragni was adequately recognized. On the other side there were the cabinet minister and bigwig Marcello Piacentini, who had prestige and a facile pen; Francesco Fichera; Giuseppe Vaccaro; and many others. The official organ was the heavy-handed *L'Architettura*. Giuseppe Pagano edited the much more worthwhile *Casabella*. And as late as 1935, there was a short-lived magazine called *Stile futurista*.

Turning to Scandinavia, we find that actually not very much appeared in print there. Alvar Aalto was not articulate, nor had much yet been written about him. Holland was, of course, different. There the literature was vigorous, rich, and interesting. There were J. J. P. Oud and Willem Marinus Dudok themselves, and books about them — particularly Mr. Hitchcock's classic study on Oud — and there were the last publications by Hendrik Berlage, who died in 1934. *Wendingen* lasted until 1931, although the last issues were mainly devoted to sculpture and painting. *Moderne Bouwkunst* was a great series which came out between 1932 and 1935.

Spain seems to have been stronger in architecture than in architectural literature, possibly because of the particularly volatile political situation during the decade. The monarchy was overthrown in 1931 and the civil war already started in 1936.

In England, as so often in her history, traditionalism and modernism were neatly balanced. There were on one side the MARS (Modern Architecture Research Group) publications, the Tecton Group, Herbert Read, and F. R. S.

Yorke, and the important "survey of constructivist art," the *Circle*. On the other side were Edwin Lutyens, Banister Fletcher (a book about him as an architect), the Liverpool Cathedral crowd, and Charles Reilly. The latter was a professor at London University, who wrote a book about representative (i.e., presentable) architects of his day. However, when Mendelsohn came to England, it was Reilly who welcomed him there in print—a very English story.

In Russia, the contrasts were striking. It was almost reminiscent of Germany that one phase (the reactionary) succeeded the other and extinguished it. El Lissitzky still published actively in the 1930s. Iakov Chernikhov's *Fantasy and Construction* came out at the same time. Then emerged the *Akhademiia NAUK* literature and, for a while, the printed matter about the Palace of the Soviets.

Finally, the United States. This is, of course, a famous tale and often told. It began with Hitchcock's *Modern Architecture: Romanticism and Reintegration* of 1929, followed by the *International Style* of 1932, the latter written jointly with Philip Johnson. These two were among the most important and consequential books of the decade. Much of the publishing activity from then on centered on the Museum of Modern Art (MoMA), which had published the *International Style*. The catalogue to the *Machine Art* exhibition of 1934, with a foreword by Johnson, was important. Then there was Sheldon Cheney's now almost forgotten book, *The New World Architecture* of 1930; and then the influx of the refugee writers. Their first great voice was Walter Curt Behrendt with his *Modern Building* of 1937; and then came the MoMA book on the Bauhaus, edited by the Gropiuses and Herbert Bayer. Buckminster Fuller must be mentioned, and the utopian books—in such contrast to the European mood—of Hugh Ferriss and Norman Bel Geddes. This was also the decade of many of Frank Lloyd Wright's writings, including his *Autobiography* (1932), the Kahn Lectures (1930–1), and *The Disappearing City* (1932).

The story in the United States would be incomplete without mentioning the social movement of the decade which had such an impact on architectural thinking, as reflected and generated in the prolific writings of Catherine Bauer, Edith Elmer Wood, Henry Wright, Clarence Stein, and Carol Aronovici, to mention only a few.

All this is confined to literature actually concerned with contemporaneous architectural development. Historiography is another matter, not really relevant to our discussions. However, the fact that the decade was also a fertile time for the writing of modern architectural history may have some significance. It was the decade when Sigfried Giedion prepared his *Space, Time and Architecture*, Nikolaus Pevsner wrote *Pioneers of the Modern Movement*, and Emil Kaufmann rediscovered Claude-Nicholas Ledoux—in other words, a time of looking at the origins of it all, since the direction into the future had become cloudy.

Doldrums in the Suburbs
Vincent J. Scully Jr.

I must apologize for the fact that my talk is not written out, as those of many of my colleagues seem to be; it will therefore not be as smooth as I should like. Fortunately, the theme of my topic is a childishly simple one. It is as follows: that during the 1930s in America architectural theory suburbanized itself up to the point where it became almost nonexistent; and where, indeed, architecture itself, or architecture as a topic of general urbanistic meaning, almost ceased to exist.

I personally came in contact with this phenomenon at a symposium at the Museum of Modern Art (MoMA) in 1948. At that symposium two points of view, or what we were told were two points of view, were presented. One was supposed to be that of the International Style and was upheld largely by Alfred Barr, Jr. In his description of work like that of Walter Gropius's house in Lincoln, Massachusetts, of 1938 [figure 106], Barr fundamentally confined himself to the arguments of Henry-Russell Hitchcock and Philip Johnson in 1932 and enunciated once more the ringing words of that earlier decade: "We have an architecture still." On the other side was Lewis Mumford, who told us that there was, in fact, another kind of architecture, that this architecture was not inorganic like that of Gropius but was, in fact, organic and was best seen in the work of the Bay Region architects. It is exemplified by a house of 1949, not from the Bay Region but more or less of that type—a house in Los Angeles, the Johnson House by Harwell Hamilton Harris. And these two *modes* of buildings were held up to us in 1948 as what architecture was; and between these two, apparently, the polemic was to take place. That polemic had already been developed a little bit by Walter Curt Behrendt in his *Modern Building* of 1937 and was to be carried further by Bruno Zevi in his book *Towards an Organic Architecture* of 1950. Zevi, picking up many of Behrendt's concepts, said that between these two kinds of architecture there was indeed a very great difference. You had, on the one hand, an organic architecture and, on the other hand, an inorganic architecture. We were told that organic architecture was a native art, like the Harris House. We were told that the inorganic was a fine art, presumably like the Gropius House. We were told that organic architecture had to do with intuitive sensation and that inorganic architecture was a product of thought, and so on and so on, making it perfectly clear that what we were being shown once more was the old false polemic between classic and romantic, which had served so long as an excuse to escape from thought in the criticism of much of the art of the past 150 years. We were more or less being told that Gropius's art was classic, or classicizing, and that the art of the Bay Region school was romantic.

Now I would suggest that the polemic was false, and that the reason we got nowhere with it was that there was basically no difference between these architectures at all: no important difference between Gropius's house at Lincoln and Harris's house at Los Angeles. Both are small, single-family suburban houses. Both of them are built of wood; both of them are light in weight; neither of them has anything whatever to do with the problem of urbanism. In fact, both of them, in the suburbs, embody an attempted escape from the larger questions of monumental architecture and city building as a whole. Now it may be argued that the Harris House, dating from 1949, is outside the period stated for the symposium. But in fact, like Robert A. M. Stern earlier, I find the stated period not too useful. I would suggest that the suburbanization which took place in the 1930s continued, largely because of the war, until 1949. It was only in 1949, for a number of reasons, that a significant shift began to be apparent—away from it to something new. Thus the Harris House of 1949 was continuing a development that in the 1930s had been carried on in California, especially by the work of William Wilson Wurster. In Wurster's Campbell House of 1938, a traditional construction of vertical board-and-batten siding is employed, showing a conscious attempt to reconstruct local traditions of wooden small-scale building. Hence the Harris House of 1949 grows out of developments of the 1930s and can therefore be considered there.

To get back to the main point, these are both suburban architecture: they are small in scale and anti-monumental, and they have nothing to do with the larger architectural problem of urbanism with which, in its own way, the International Style as a whole also had a rather curious record. That is to say, as in an "ideal" scheme for New York which is typical of the city-planning fantasies of this decade, they are fantasies which hate the city and all preexisting urban architecture. In them the city—indeed the whole past—is conceived as something which simply needs to be destroyed. The town is to be spread out across the landscape in a garden city sense or to be built up thoughtlessly in the towers of the Ville Radieuse in a Corbusian sense. For example, in a project from Yale of 1940 by Richard Bennett (a very important critic there at the time) entitled "New York in the Future," the city is destroyed. There is a project for Philadelphia by Louis Kahn of almost the same period and of exactly the same kind. I think it might be noted that the great Stonehenge down at the end of Manhattan in Bennett's scheme was supposed to be the regional planning center. The planners give themselves the cult place. The city is gone.

I would suggest, therefore, that modern architecture as it had developed and was being taught in America by the late 1930s was small in scale, anti-monumental, and urbanistically destructive. Despite the sociological pronouncements of its pedagogues, it was in fact neither functional nor structural in its methods and in its forms. Instead, it was pictorial. That can be seen I think in these two projects, one from Yale and one from Penn. A project of 1933 for a memorial for Johann Sebastian Bach looks to us today a little bit like a building by Philip Johnson. But in 1940 when this project for a microfilm library, or something of the sort, was designed, the architecture of the Bach memorial was seen as the enemy. It was the Beaux-Arts enemy. It was the enemy for two reasons: first, because it was heavy, which meant probably that it was fascist; and second, because it was symmetrical, which probably meant the same thing—or even worse, that it had some relationship possibly to Renaissance rather than to Gothic design. So the one architecture was seen by Mr. Bennett and the other architects and critics of the time as something too heavy and too symmetrical to be modern architecture. Bennett's building is maximally light. All its solids are made as evanescent as possible, and in the drafting technique those solids are made even lighter than they would in fact have been structurally able to be. Therefore I submit as follows: that both of these architectures are pictorial. The first is developed with a kind of baroque sense of modeling of forms by chiaroscuro in light and shade. The method of the second I think you will recognize as essentially a Bauhaus one of graphic devices: thin lines, planes behind, transparency, passage of planes, movement and flux of light, and so on. It is no less pictorial than the other; it simply deals with different pictorial devices. Therefore I would suggest that in the America of 1940 architecture was still as fundamentally pictorial as it had been earlier in the American Beaux-Arts.

Now I think you can see all that very quickly in a drawing from Yale of 1946 which shows the whole thing. It is by a critic named Eugene Nalle, who became extremely important at Yale in the middle 1950s; here he is in his late Bauhaus phase. His architecture is as light as possible. Indeed, it is exaggeratedly so: his perspective—as he himself used often to point out later—is distorted to give a sense of the passage and float of planes. The space is constructed purely by graphic tricks: a line, a little bit of shadow up above, and the *snap* of the black plane down below. Passage, transparency, flux, flow, no weight, no symmetry, and in front, demonstrating, I think, a good deal of the distrust with which Western civilization as a whole was held by the practitioners of this period, what is apparently the head of a Fiji Islander heaves into sight—so introducing in the project the necessary purity of primitive art. Now it seems to me that the fundamental prototypes for all these visions of form are the constructions painted by László Moholy-Nagy in the early 1920s at the Bauhaus, such as the one now in the collection of the Société Anonyme at Yale. The passage of planes, the graphic creation of space in terms of transparency, flux, flow, light and dark, forward and back, is already developed, and Nalle's rendering of the mid-1940s represents no visual advance beyond its image.

The same is true in the architecture of the Bay Region style, as shown in a house of this period from Lafayette, California, by Clarence Mayhew. This photograph appeared in 1946 in a book by Elizabeth Mock of MoMA—a book poignantly entitled *If You Want to Build a House*. This was the end of everyone's desire in 1946. The preoccupation is on the house, but again you will see that the passage of planes, the maximum thinness, the lightness, the asymmetry, and so on, is that of Moholy-Nagy. Ergo: Bauhaus and Bay Region all in one. The same is true of the Graduate Center at Harvard by Gropius and The Architects' Collaborative of 1949–50. The changes of plane, the small lally columns as against the larger columns, the shadow, the light—even the way the photographer has been instinctively trained to take the picture—are all part of the pictorial method whose prototypes can be seen in Moholy-Nagy's constructions.

I think it should be pointed out that the relationship of the International Style to a pictorial sensibility goes back to 1929 at least. It certainly goes back before that in practice, but in historical perception it can clearly be traced to that point. We owe that perception to Henry-Russell Hitchcock, who in his great book of 1929, *Modern Architecture: Romanticism and Reintegration*, decided that the difference between those architects whom he called "of the New Tradition" and those whom he called "the New Pioneers" was precisely that "the New Pioneers" were aware of the aesthetic inventions and experiments of the painters of the early twentieth century and of the teens. The difference for him between the "heavy" architecture of early Frank Lloyd Wright or Peter Behrens, or of the Scandinavians, and that of Le Corbusier, J. J. P. Oud, Gropius, and so on, was that the latter architects had been aware of the experiments of De Stijl and so on and their buildings participated in its pictorial perception. Now, in 1932, when *The International Style* by Hitchcock and Johnson appeared, the pictorial side, while still mentioned, was played down a little bit. And I feel—if I may comment within this talk on some of the comments made earlier here by Mr. Hitchcock—I feel that their comments were perhaps not quite candid. That is to say, it seems to me that Hitchcock's book of 1929 was a work of pure history and one of the most beautiful works of history we have seen in this century, one in which he tried to bring together all the disparate happenings of the past two hundred years and to state gropingly what *was* in fact the development which had occurred. But the book of 1932 was, I think, under the influence of Mr. Johnson, primarily a polemic. It was a statement of what architecture ought to be, and I think this is important because I do believe, as was suggested earlier, that a good deal of the character of the architecture of the 1930s in America does, in fact, derive from the statements of what architecture ought to be which Mr. Hitchcock and Mr. Johnson made in 1932.

I think the point is this: that certainly the great Bauhaus by Gropius of 1925–6 is stronger than its prototypes, is stronger than its pictorial prototypes. It lays its elements out strongly and stiffly and proudly in space, and you feel that it is as tough as a set of gears. But Gropius's house in Lincoln of 1938–9 is weaker than the prototypes, it seems to me; it is more compromised than the prototypes, and the set of pictorial elements with which it is involved are those which are more concerned with the subtle transparencies, the diminution of scale, the play of very thin planes—in a word, with flow, change, and ambiguity, which the stronger, much more monumental Bauhaus does not have. Now again I think that we find all these elements—the slide, the movement, the transparency, the flow, the ambiguities of form—in Bauhaus pedagogical experiments like those of László Moholy-Nagy.

It seems to me that Marcel Breuer, who has been cited as a sort of archetypal modern architect by Professor William Jordy, is the perfect expression of this period: the outgrowth—the archetypal outgrowth—of Bauhaus education, its prime expression and its victim. That is to say, in Breuer's own house in Lincoln of 1939, it should be perfectly clear that the space is made by light and decorative planes. The stone becomes a mosaic much thinner than the mosaics of Le Corbusier upon which it is based; indeed, it becomes almost wallpaper—a weightless plane back there in space—behind a set of transparencies derived from Moholy's experiments. Now Breuer keeps right on after this decade, right into the 1940s, with basically the same pictorial, small-scale, designer's sensitivity. And it seems to me that he does it splendidly for a time. He does it with all the attention to work at very small scale and with all the strangeness and ambiguity that Klee himself had been able to develop at the Bauhaus; so it seems to me that the pointing arrow, odd in scale and utterly without weight, in the house in Williamstown, Massachusetts of the 1940s by Breuer is very close to Paul Klee's *Precious Container for Stars* in the Société Anonyme collection. Breuer's great quality here is that of an insectile tension, a positive development of the characteristics of small scale, anti-monumentality, asymmetry, tension of line, and so on, which had been characteristic of his pictorial education. And his house in New Canaan of 1948 is a perfect expression of that, suspended like a little insect, like a little creature, off the ground with all the old stabilities of architecture overset; now everything is utterly light, held together by wires, and so on. But when Breuer came into the 1950s and received large projects, the continuation of his small-scale graphic sensibility made it impossible for him to build a monumental building—a properly scaled urban building—and has so far continued to make it impossible for him to do so.

This point is not an attack upon Breuer but only an expression of what the character of the 1930s *was* and afterward of the 1940s (Breuer continuing it into the 1950s) toward small scale and anti-monumentality with an avoidance of monumental mass, a lack of structural weight, and a preoccupation with small-scale graphic effects. It is all these things that turn Breuer's Bell Tower at St. John's Abbey in Collegeville, Minnesota of 1953–61 into a little plywood object. I think the point is clear. If we compare it with the development that is characteristic of the 1950s, as in the late work of Le Corbusier, we see the difference between a graphic sensibility and a sensibility which is concerned with monumental architecture. One would say, looking at the work by Le Corbusier, that the force that Chandigarh has derives from the fact that it elevates to heroic

scale the standing figures of men, whereas in the Breuer there is *no* possibility
to associate oneself empathetically with the form lifted. The relationships
are insectile, small-scale, and related to furniture design. The same thing is
true of the *brise-soleil* in both buildings. In each the *brise-soleil* is essential.
It is essential so that the eye will believe the sculptural lift of the other parts.
If there were only the thin plane of glass we could not physically believe that
one building could be both a thin container and an active sculptural force.
Therefore the box must be masked. But the difference is that Le Corbusier,
when he masks his glass wall, makes his *brise-soleil* plastically active itself,
precisely because he relates it architecturally to human scale, whereas Breuer
is thinking only in terms of graphic textures, scaleless repetitions. I think you
can see the difference—Le Corbusier's magically makes you read it both as an
abstract structural force and as something which also indicates the sizes of
men and the building's use by them, because the basic unit is the door height,
and moreover he lets you see where each floor is. But then he breaks it across so
as to confuse all that for the eye and to make the thing move in and of itself. He
does not cheat one bit; it is all there, whereas in Breuer's screen, with the simple
repetition of the element which is that of graphic design, what is created is a
radio cabinet much like the radio cabinets of the late 1930s or the early 1940s.
Again I cite Bauhaus methods. It is industrial design, not monumental architecture; it is abstractly graphic, not humanistically active in space.

I only want to point out that this change begins at the end of the 1940s.
Indeed, it begins in 1948 when Le Corbusier begins to construct his Unité
d'Habitation at Marseilles. And the difference between it and the *pilotis* of
Breuer's recent IBM building is again the same. In Le Corbusier's swelling
shapes we can read muscular force. At IBM, in La Guade of 1960, we have not
only an over-scaling in relation to the height of the building but also a set of
graphic devices which do not convince us that they relate to the noble sense
of lifting a great weight which we can feel in our own bodies as men. And this
seems to me the basic shift.

Now if that is the case with the "inorganic" International Style by the
late 1930s, what is the case with what was supposed to be its "organic" alternative—with the Bay Region wing? Was that capable of developing into a
monumental urban architecture? Again I would suggest "no"—here largely
because of that mode's preoccupation with the single-family house, but also
because of its special preoccupation with wood and also with a conscious desire
to make architecture as shack-like as possible. I would suggest, by the way,
that these limitations were not confined to architects at this period. My own
first work, carried on under the direction of Professor Hitchcock in 1948–9, was
with American domestic architecture, with what I came to call the Stick Style
and the Shingle Style, of which an early Stick Style house at Newport (1845) is
an example. Between the two, with what I was able to conceive as being architecture and what seemed an appropriate subject for historical investigation
in the late 1940s, on the one hand, and what Harwell Harris was doing then,
on the other, there is an exact concordance—just as, in fact, Mrs. Harris was
at this time studying the work of Greene & Greene, which is part of the whole
tradition. The limitations are the same: what architects do and what historians
study are, of course, intimately bound up with each other.

Now so far as the California group or the West Coast group is concerned,
how far could they go with this articulated Stick Style of architecture? Well,
about as far as a small church. And I think you can see that in the work of

Pietro Belluschi in his Central Lutheran Church in Portland, completed about 1950. This was apparently as far as it could be pushed, because when, in 1949, Belluschi built the Equitable Building in Portland he totally left this mode; he completely abandoned whatever might have been a development out of the articulated skeleton structure of the Stick Style and instead sheathed the whole thing over in a kind of screen wall, a cellophane envelope which had nothing whatever to do with his smaller-scale works. Therefore, the Bay Region school, too, was not capable of creating a monumental architecture. It could not deal with large city buildings.

So I come back to the same thing: a California house of 1949 that goes perfectly with, for example, Gropius and Breuer's Hagerty House in Cohasset of the late 1930s. The composition is almost the same, the light, pictorial elements are similar, and the anti-monumental suburbanization of architecture seems complete. When does all this change? It begins to change in 1939. It begins to change with the late work of Mies van der Rohe at the Illinois Institute of Technology (IIT). However, as already pointed out, it was still going on in a fairly late example in the Harvard Graduate Center of 1949. Here all the shapes are, as it were, purposely tentative in their organization of space, purposely asymmetrical, weakly curved, loosely connected with each other, interpenetrating, sliding, indeed laden with all those qualities that we found characteristic of the pictorial devices we have looked at already. Whereas Mies's first project of 1939 for IIT is symmetrical, with a strong cross-axis formed by big separate shapes, hollowed out inside as clear building blocks that define a large, confident volume of space, here is a return to a simple projection of architectural symmetry, mass, and space, which had been regarded as anathema during the 1930s.[60] I remember a very good student at Yale, Duncan Buell; about 1952 he was working on a space frame and suddenly he said, "I can't make it asymmetrical—it won't *become* asymmetrical, so what am I to do?" And then he said, "Why, a great many great buildings have been symmetrical!" and his project was published by Mr. Meeks in his book on railroad stations. Buell is now working for Louis Kahn.

Mies therefore was the beginning and, it seems to me, the return. I would suggest also that late Mies was not begun to be understood until about 1949. And I would suggest also, as I have done elsewhere, that the publication of Professor Rudolf Wittkower's 1949 *Architectural Principles in the Age of Humanism* was of considerable relevance here. This book, whose influence has been amply acknowledged by English architects such as Peter and Alison Smithson, who have also related its principles to those of Mies at IIT, indicated a return to all those things that were considered useless or even harmful by the American Bauhaus—for which the Renaissance was evil because it was symmetrical; it was bad because it was not made by happy craftsmen but was instead laid out in a strong, symmetrical, urban sense. And it was Mies's strong shapes—shapes indeed related to those of Louis Sullivan himself—that began to make us feel once more the possibilities for city building. He began to get us out of the suburbs, back into the city to make monumental architecture once more. True enough, it has turned out that Mies's method cannot solve everything, and that a truly urban architecture demands more than he had to give. The point here is that by 1939 his work began to point out a reasonable direction for us.

And of course by 1950, following Dr. Wittkower's lead, we had the *Architectural Forum* putting a picture of Vignola's urban facades together with one of Mies's constructions at IIT and indicating concordance between them.

Now it seems to me again that 1949 is the critical date here. It is the date when Philip Johnson began to give his splendid talks which those of us who first heard them regarded almost as the pronouncements of the devil. He stood up on the platform at Yale University, and he said to a shocked hush across the room, "I would rather sleep in the nave of Chartres Cathedral with the nearest john two blocks down the street than I would in a Harvard house with back-to-back bathrooms!" This terrible and even rather frightening pronouncement was the one after which, for the first time, I remember students saying to me, "He's talking about architecture as an art!" And suddenly I realized that that is what it was all the time.

In this way began in 1949 that particular classicizing mode of monumentality in the 1950s which Mr. Johnson knows that I feel to possess very strong limitations. I do think there are many limitations in it, growing more apparent all the time. That is something we might discuss later. But it seems to me that in 1949 the complement and the antidote of that classicism had already been stated, indeed constructed in America, especially as seen in the dormitory at the Massachusetts Institute of Technology by Alvar Aalto. Here we had an architecture which was massive and solid, which, most of all, physically released functions to make forms and went far beyond simple symmetry to a noble generosity in the fullness of its shapes. Strong, big, masculine, and powerful, it outstepped the small, hermetic, pictorial world of the late 1930s in America and reached toward the possible grandeurs of architectural form. And if I may not seem overly chauvinistic, it seems to me that in these two things together—Johnson's order and Aalto's generosity—you have the beginning. You have by the early 1950s such a combination of the two as that which resides in the Yale Art Gallery by Louis Kahn. Therefore, it seems to me that if, in 1948, the statement "We have an architecture still" was the correct one, by 1951 we should have said, "We have an architecture again." [61]

The Social Front of Modern Architecture in the 1930s: More than a "Style"? Promising Principles Unfulfilled
Catherine Bauer Wurster

Vincent Scully took a rather similar line to Jane Jacobs in defense of cities against suburbia. I agree with almost everything he said, although I am going to talk about the opposite side of the urban architectural scene: not the monumental aspects but the vernacular. Mr. Scully is young enough that he is probably not aware of some social and civic contributions that were originally promised by the Internationalists in the late 1920s and the early 1930s.

Instead of the princely patronage which had traditionally sponsored architectural innovations, it was the housing and community planning movement in northern Europe which first opened up major building opportunities to the pioneering theorists of the 1920s. This was an eminently suitable testing ground for their early principles because both movements had much the same goal: a rationale for improving human environment in a modern industrial society. [62]

At that time the new architecture was wedded to a pair of principles which gave the word "functional" a double meaning: 1. the full use of modern technology and its honest expression in design; and 2. a scientific approach to human needs and uses in programming, planning, and design. (This was the basis for the claim that it was more than a "style," a claim which Sigfried Giedion still defends and which still makes him angry at Philip Johnson and Henry-Russell Hitchcock for perpetrating the term "International Style.")

At the same time, the everyday condition of the "common man" was a rising issue in northern Europe, due to the strong influence of popular political forces, particularly in England, Holland, Scandinavia, and pre-Nazi Germany. The chronic housing shortage was a major concern, as was the demand for better schools and other community facilities. When the Depression came there was further demand for public works to stimulate employment and for social measures to avert communism. The political leadership of the housing and planning movement was largely democratic-socialist in philosophy and utopian enough, except in England, to welcome innovations in design as a symbolic break with the past. The rationalist and anti-snobbish principles of the new architecture were therefore appealing.

For a brief period, much of the resulting architecture fulfilled the principles of both movements to a very considerable extent. What I saw in Europe in 1930 was so exciting that it transformed me from an aesthete into a housing reformer. The earliest, of course, was J. J. P. Oud's public housing work as city architect of Rotterdam, although the standards were minimal. The Weissenhof Siedlung was epoch-making, quite as much in plans, social criteria, and construction methods as in aesthetic expression. By 1930 the Bauhaus principles were being applied, more or less, to thousands of dwellings all over Germany. Martin Wagner, as *Stadtbaurat* of Berlin and political representative of the trade unions, made it possible for Walter Gropius and many of the other pioneering architects of the time to design a number of large housing developments, notably Siemensstadt. The most voluminous and interesting city-wide program, in Frankfurt under Ernst May, included a new system of construction, all kinds of innovations in planning and community facilities, and even specially designed kitchen equipment which was mass-produced and sold in packages. Housing schemes were quite carefully designed for varied social uses: old people, single women, families at different income levels, and so on. Everywhere, technical, economic, and social research was going on, including Alexander Klein's ingenious studies of minimal-dwelling plans, based on analysis of family functions and household circulation. The Congrès Internationaux d'Architecture Moderne (CIAM) published *Die Wohnung für das Existenzminimum* (1930) and *Rationelle Bebauungsweisen* (1931), respectively presenting the latest dwelling and site plans for numerous cities and countries at the same scale and with comparable descriptive data.

Both the criteria and the means were still crude in all this innovation, but it seemed to have established a whole new approach, in both purpose and method, which could insure steady improvement in the urban vernacular by the application of increasing knowledge. Even then, however, I did have a few doubts. Dogma was evident here and there, a kind of too early jelling of the experiments, and distortion for technocratic symbolism. At the CIAM conference in Frankfurt (I think it was in 1930), there was exciting evidence of fresh social and technical thinking all over the city in a rich array of honestly experimental building. Just at that time, however, Ernst May and his fellow architects decided they had achieved the perfect site plan, the ultimate, universal solution. It was a rigidly geometrical *Zeilenbau* scheme, solely geared to a narrow system of standardized solar orientation. With this dogmatic approach, the May team soon set off for Russia, where it doubtless contributed to their failure, along with their inability to cope with a backward building industry. And their failure contributed to the whole Russian reaction against modern architecture in favor of Rome and Napoleon.

Both the verbal and three-dimensional production of that era had enormous influence, in many different ways often quite at variance with the original dual principles. Perhaps the Bauhaus had its most direct and salutary effect on the cultural status and design of simple mass-produced objects (including advertising and packaging). I think almost everyone would agree that the general level of industrial design has greatly improved, despite the "styling" requirements of our economy.

In architecture and urban design, however, the results have been highly "ambiguous," to borrow an epithet from Douglas Haskell. The tags were copied all over the world, often irrationally in the local context. Maximum glass, for instance, may have been desirable in northern Germany but hardly in South America or Chicago. The simple rationalist standards promulgated in 1930 had a useful cathartic influence later in the decade, when government housing policies began to take shape in the United States and elsewhere, but they also contributed to the institutional character that is now deplored. The skyscraper utopias of Le Corbusier, Ludwig Mies van der Rohe, and Walter Gropius have had a compelling attraction for many architects, but when the big chance came in America with postwar redevelopment and public housing, the results have hardly been a great step forward in social architecture, to put it mildly. The fact is — and it is a strange fact, remembering the promise of 1930 — that any real progress in rational design to meet social and civic needs over the past thirty years has been little influenced by exponents of Bauhaus principles or by the famous CIAM leaders.

The greatest overall success in coping with the modern urban environment has probably been in Scandinavia, with a number of quite independent regional leaders in architecture and planning including Sven Markelius, Alvar Aalto, and Steen Eiler Rasmussen. Holland is roughly comparable (but it must be acknowledged that Cornelis van Eesteren, Amsterdam's official planner for many years, was a dedicated co-founder of CIAM). In England, it was the old garden city idea — anathema to most of the Internationalists — that produced the New Towns movement which has been gathering steam everywhere since the end of the war, recently even in the United States. The same can be said of the greenbelt concept, and of course the superblock, no-through-traffic principle of neighborhood planning was invented by Raymond Unwin and refined by Clarence S. Stein in the Radburn plan [*figure 82*], well before it was taken over by the Bauhaus. Frank Lloyd Wright inaugurated the free-flowing house plan and also anticipated the "disappearing city." But it was primarily in northern California, quite removed from both Wright and CIAM, that the forms suited to an informal, outdoor-loving, family-oriented, automotive society — in houses, schools, shopping centers, and factories — first evolved in the 1930s. As for "science," however, the application of systematic research methods and modern technology to social and civic problems has been little advanced by architects anywhere, whatever their social or aesthetic principles and however much they may talk about the need for it. Only the transportation engineers and now the planners, most of whom never heard of the Bauhaus, have been making a serious start.

Meanwhile, the three original leaders who went on to become the most famous and influential world leaders in architecture — Le Corbusier, Mies, and

Gropius—contributed, I think, nothing further to the rational solution of social or functional problems, or even to technological progress. The same can be said of most of their direct disciples. I need not explain here the various directions they took, but the differences have been wholly in terms of aesthetic expression. They have been equally unconcerned with the advancement of practical solutions for the urban and regional environment.

Most would agree with Haskell that "form alone remains of the great upheaval." Few (except Giedion) would even argue now that it had been more than a style, or rather a great many styles. Many have forgotten—or never knew—that modern architecture was once primarily concerned with social and civic improvement.

But there is still room, I think you would agree, for considerable improvement in the functional quality of the human environment—even in an affluent society. Indeed, many of our most urgent problems are the *result* of affluence. So why did the pioneers, and those they particularly influenced, give up after such a promising start? One can have any number of theories about it, but I shall offer a few personal hunches.

There were two basic reasons, I think. In the first place, the Nazi era and the war made a big break. Postwar conditions were entirely different, and the original ideology did not always fit. Revolutionary design principles jelled into stylistic tags. Also, perhaps of basic importance, the rational approach was largely abandoned. The three leaders who had embraced "science" reverted to the old prima donna architect's role, little concerned with the application of advanced technology and social science to the human environment.

On the matter of changed conditions, we have to remember that the decade of the 1930s was a very constricted era. The international economic crisis created a kind of depression in thinking. There was no expectation *ever* of great economic growth; the only hope was for a more rational organization of the limited resources available. Therefore a whole series of principles, adopted by the pioneers to interpret a Machine Age culture in architectural and urban terms—the "morality of the machine"—turned out to be essentially fallacious.

One of these principles was the German concept of *Existenzminimum*, of course. Actually in the 1930s some very real and important contributions were made in terms of minimum standards, but they were all at an extremely simple level. This spartan oversimplification was well exemplified in our own Housing Act of 1937 (which I helped to write), whose goals were "decent, safe, and sanitary" homes. These goals were likewise the ultimate ideal (perhaps with the addition of "sunny") expressed in most pre-Nazi German housing design, which greatly influenced the later American product.

But the social aspects of postwar housing design turned out to be far more complex. This is even true for the poor, who have yet to achieve the simplest minimal standards in most sections of Europe and the United States, while for the burgeoning middle class it is obvious that housing choices and housing ideals are far removed from the old "decent, safe, and sanitary" criteria. For what modern technology has done is to increase productivity, raise incomes and the birth rate, enhance mobility, create new demands, and greatly complicate all the issues involved in housing design and city planning. But instead of seriously investigating these fascinating new problems in order to develop rational new criteria, the former pioneers clung to the old principle and turned it into a doctrinaire stylism. In fact this started rather early.

In 1932, just before Erich Mendelsohn had to leave Germany, I went out to see him at his famous, handsome, and expensive house on the Wannsee, where he was trying to prove that he was as pure a technocrat as anybody. It was the first time I ever saw a whole glass wall that went down into the ground at the touch of a button, and I was dazzled. He took me into his study, set up so that he could have a little independence when he wanted to. He pointed proudly to a Murphy bed imported from the United States, and said "Existenzminimum." A later example is in the house that Vincent Scully showed, at Cohasset (I think it was really more by Gropius than by Marcel Breuer). It has one of the meanest entrances of any house I have ever been in. (I must say that no house by my husband [William Wilson Wurster] or any Bay Region architect was ever that inhospitable.) The front door opens onto a narrow landing, and you are confronted by open stairways going both up and down, so you have no idea which to take. And of course Mies, in the whole theory of "less is more," to a considerable extent reflects this Depression-born ideology.

The second fallacy is closely related: standardization in design as a necessary and desirable expression of the Machine Age. The early housing projects were standardized far beyond the requirements of construction technology, and the purists still apply this principle. But present trends push in the opposite direction. As the economy produces more wealth, more leisure, and more education, what it mainly does is open up more choices and wider tastes for everybody. Many products are standardized, of course, but there is much greater effective demand for individuality and variety than would have been imaginable in either the United States or Germany in the 1930s. Now we are even rich enough to buy craftwork too, and we like it just because it is not standardized. When I came back from India, I decided that sooner or later all the handicraft will be in the United States, and all of the ugly, mass-produced things will be in India. Of course, Frank Lloyd Wright always sensed this, and Le Corbusier recognized it very early. But even they never saw that as we become more sophisticated, we also grow more interested in history as well as in distinction and richness. Now the big design problem in cities is how to preserve the past, and how to relate new buildings to old buildings because we do not want to destroy everything in order to be *ganz moderne*.

The third fallacy was collectivism. At that time, quite apart from one's political belief, it seemed inevitable to almost every sophisticated person that collective ways of living would result from modern technology. Nobody quite imagined that we would choose to use technology, beginning in the United States, primarily to enhance individual and family independence. It was assumed somehow that utopia would mean good mass-produced meals, in great apartment complexes where all the services were done for us. Mama would not have to cook or clean any more. But of course, rightly or wrongly, we used technology for exactly the opposite purposes. We used it for gadgets to make ourselves freer and more self-sufficient in the house, rather than less. We used it to mass-produce tracts of one-family houses and, above all, automobiles—i.e., auto-mobility. We chose individualism rather than collectivism. Mies and Gropius, when they came to the United States, had little feeling for these developments (although Gropius tried to understand). They were always primarily interested in high-rise construction as truly "modern." And Le Corbusier, who had always envisioned skyscraper cities, provided the ultimate model for minimal collective living in his Marseilles apartments.

Instead of rationalism, the influence of these great architects has promoted technocratic symbolism in various modes and manners. The machine is God, the symbol of human power, hope, and progress, therefore to be glorified in all architecture. But of course what the machine has done has been to create vast new problems which will destroy us unless we can develop social knowledge in time to cope with them, from atomic warfare to race relations to traffic. But our social imagination and our social science and our politics have not been keeping up with the possibilities and dangers of technology. Aesthetic excitement derived from the "morality of the machine" seems as outdated as the excitement in the Renaissance about the aesthetic values of ancient Greece and Rome. But why were not the early modern principles of dual functionalism adapted and refined?

The rational approach was abandoned because it would have required open minds and a real kind of collaboration and teamwork: architects working with engineers and social scientists, continuously trying to find better solutions, making experiments and testing them, working with business and government to encourage more research, experiment, and improvement. This is exactly what did not happen in the main line of "International Style" modernism. What did happen was that the famous innovators reverted to the old prima donna role: papa has all the answers, and personal aesthetic expression is paramount, even if it fails to function properly or to improve the cityscape. I have heard it said quite often recently that the trouble with the Bauhaus was not only that it destroyed any sense of the past but also that it did not develop a real discipline, even to the extent that the Beaux-Arts did. Certainly there has been much less concern with urban design.

The success of the three International Stylists and their disciples has, of course, been enormous. They have had particular success, ironically, in building monuments to an affluent society — monuments which are competitively novel, sometimes beautiful in themselves, often sculpturally interesting, very expensive, and seldom contributing to better functional solutions. Even the old technocratic tags are disappearing in the push for richness and visual novelty. At best, these men have added to our capacity for monumental architecture, and here Le Corbusier has of course been extremely important. But I think they have made little or no contribution to urban design or to the ordinary vernacular, whether in aesthetic, social, or technical terms. Things are happening in these realms, but it is partly in reaction against the prima donna dogmas, and partly by architects and planners who were never greatly influenced by them.

The Role of History of Architecture in Fascist Italy
Henry Millon

In the middle 1920s, Mussolini stated that the past — interpreted, invigorated, brought up to date — serves as a source of training and encouragement for the advancement of the aims of the nation. Italian publications on the history of art and architecture in the 1930s repeat this quotation again and again. It contains the kernel of what I would like to speak to you about this afternoon, that historians of art and architecture in Italy in the late 1930s directly aided the Fascist regime by advocating an expansionist policy based on the scholarly evidence they were able to gather concerning the extent of Italic or Latin (both words were used interchangeably) control, power, and influence from antiquity to the rise of the Fascist regime. Such evidence of previous Italic domination was used by the regime to argue the inevitability of Fascist expansion, to achieve what destiny had indicated belonged to Italic people.[63]

It would be easy, I think, to argue that what is said in the art-historical journals did not really indicate a concern on the art historians' part to propagate these ideas. In order to dismiss such an argument, I would like to quote a work by Gustavo Giovannoni. Giovannoni was, politically, probably the most important art historian and, intellectually, one of the most important scholars of the history of architecture in Italy in the 1930s. The book appeared in 1945 and internal evidence indicates this chapter was probably written by him just before publication. Giovannoni says,

> For this resurgence of the cult of antiquity, some wish to put the blame on the archaeologists. But there is no accusation more foolish. Archaeologists study the monuments of antiquity, they find remains, they defend their integrity; there is not a thoughtful or cultured person who is not grateful for the activity of the archaeologists and not thankful for the Providence that assures the preservation and improvement of the objects of their study, which represent the noble titles of the lineage, the sacred testimonials of memory and of art. But these archaeologists, in their serene researches, do not have anything to do with an imperialistic infatuation that looks for an impossible return. To put upon them the responsibility is the same as, for example, making the paper manufacturer guilty of what is written on the pages of books.[64]

What does this statement indicate? First of all, that Giovannoni knew what he advocated in the 1930s; second, that he knew he had been attacked for his writings; and third, that in this particular article he presents his defense, his explanation—he is trying to expiate his guilt. To compare with the paragraph above, written in 1945, I would like to quote a paragraph of his written in 1940. The statement appeared in *Palladio*, the official journal of the Italian equivalent of the Society of Architectural Historians. *Palladio* was in its fourth year of publication. Giovannoni said,

> In this our journal, which is the only one remaining in the world to occupy itself expressly with the history of architecture, we intend to illustrate Italian monuments, to create around these an awareness and affection, to demonstrate what grand and almost uninterrupted means of a dominant civilization these are still able to document. We have wished that an issue be dedicated almost entirely to our architectural works found in regions that should be returned to Italy by undeniable rights of history and of lineage.[65]

These two quotations, five years apart, are undeniably contradictory. In 1940 Giovannoni used history to advocate and justify the military expansion of Italy. In 1945 he ridiculed the possibility of such an attitude.

One of the reasons this examination should be made, even though it may be trivial, is that Nikolaus Pevsner, in an appended chapter to the recent Jubilee edition of the *Outline of European Architecture*, has suggested that the Fascist architecture of the 1930s will have to be reevaluated, and he implies that such reevaluation will show the architecture to have been of greater quality than we thought before.[66] The depressing sight that greets us today in Lincoln Center suggests there has already been extensive reevaluation. Where does an aside such as that get us? Nothing much is gained by noting the superficial semblances of exterior forms of loggias, arcades, arches, obvious plan arrangement, and so forth, between Lincoln Center and Mussolini's EUR, when there are major differences in circulation, internal disposition, structural organization, and mechanical services—but above all, major differences in purpose. And it is to this aspect, to this point of purpose, I would like to address my remarks today; partly to the architectural objectives desired by Fascist architects, but primarily to the intellectual, social, and political environment as it was formed, at least partially, by art historians.

Architecture in Italy, after Piacentini convinced Mussolini that his approach to building was the only sure way to achieve an architecture that would both demonstrate continuity with the past and provide adequate, permanent evidence of the imperial glories of the present, cannot adequately be discussed solely in terms of its forms, lighting, and spaces, nor its technological and industrial achievements. Fascist architecture must also be seen, I believe, in its context, as a social and political document.[67] Only then will the forms and spaces become understandable. And only then can relevant technical aspects be examined. The social, intellectual, and political background of Fascism has perhaps been recently overworked. I would like only to call your attention to one small aspect, which, when it is seen in the context of Fascist ideology, aspiration, and propaganda, may help us see what effect imperialist ideas might have had on Italian architects.

The Fascist reaction of the decade of the 1920s to "rationalist architecture," as they called it,[68] occurred both in Germany and in Italy. But the reaction was not only a Fascist phenomenon, and we have already seen how in the 1930s rationalistic architecture was being attacked on political, social, scientific, and economic grounds. It is becoming increasingly clear, also, that in spite of their denials, the historians of the modern movement were not only chronicling the emergence of a new way of analyzing, relating, and achieving architecture but were themselves involved as apostles of the new order.[69] Their mission was persuasion and conversion to the new faith, a new set of principles, that appeared to have more extensive and pertinent application to contemporary problems. The end justified the means, within limits, and whatever arguments—ideological, social, or political—could be sustained to demonstrate the superior qualities of this new approach were, of course, emphasized. About architecture other than rational, as a consequence, there was a virtual information blackout, or at the very least, it was simply ignored by the official publication of the propaganda arm of the modern movement. Today we still find very little written about the "other" architecture of the 1930s, and it is to the credit of Henry-Russell Hitchcock, our chairman here today, that both two years ago and at this symposium we were asked to turn our ideas toward material only summarily treated elsewhere. We must certainly look more closely at the works of Paul Troost, Wilhelm Kreis, and Albert Speer in Germany and to Marcello Piacentini, Arnoldo Foschini, Franco Petrucci, and Mario Tufaroli Luciano in Italy to see in the architecture of the 1930s its other manifestations as well as what we, in true deterministic fashion, look back to as the original protagonists of the contemporary scene.[70]

I am not, however, going to attempt to chronicle the major events leading to the official Fascist reaction to rationalist architecture in Italy that occurred when the Gruppo Sette and the Movimento Italiano per l'Architettura Razionale were wiped out by Piacentini and his followers through a calculated policy of (to use Zevi's words) "threats, corruption, and compromise." [71] Nor will I try to trace those movements that exhibit the triumph of "stripped classicism" over the notable rationalistic works of Giuseppe Terragni, Edoardo Persico, Luciano Baldessari, Luigi Figini, Gino Pollini, and Gianni Mazzocchi.

In order to demonstrate the changing official policy, however, I have chosen to turn to two of the official publications of the art-historical world, the journals *Le Arti* and *Palladio*. It would, of course, be somewhat easier to search through issues that came out in the 1930s of such magazines as *Roma*, *Capitoliurn*, or *L'Urbe* to find semi-historical articles arguing the primacy of Rome, the superiority of the Roman Empire and the Italian peoples, and their rights and their destiny, but while such articles abound they do not have the scholarly distinction and dignity conferred by appearance in either *Le Arti* or *Palladio*.

An explanatory word about these two journals is appropriate here because they are fundamental to the discussion. *Le Arti* replaced the *Bolletino d'Arte*, which was, up until 1938, the official art-historical organ of the Direzione Generale delle Antichità e Belle Arti. *Le Arti* began publishing in 1938 and was published bimonthly thereafter until the end of the war. The *direttore delle Antichità e Belle Arti* was Marino Lazzari, a man of no particular intellectual distinction, and he was the overall director of the journal. The editorial board included Giulio Carlo Argan, Guglielmo De Angelis D'Ossat, Giuseppe Petrocchi, and Ermenegildo Scaccia Scarafoni. Argan was the *segretario di redazione* and, one imagines, the real editor of the journal. The advisory board had an interesting composition, including, among others, Carlo Carrà, Silvio D'Amico, Roberto Longhi, Giovanni Michelucci, Ugo Ojetti, Giuseppe Pagano, Marcello Piacentini, Ardengo Soffici, and Pietro Toesca. These are names that were then, as now, well known as painters, architects, and art historians. *Le Arti* was not a Fascist propaganda organ with an editorial board composed of a few people who liked to wear black shirts but a journal advised by the major art historians of the country.

The other journal, *Palladio*, devoted to the history of architecture, was founded as the result of the resolution made at the first Congresso Nazionale di Storia dell'Architettura, which was held from October 28 to 31, 1936. The first issue appeared in 1937. The journal was published under the auspices of the Sindicato Nazionale Fascista Architetti. In other words, they received financial support from the AIA of Italy. The Union of Fascist Architects was also publishing at the same time the architectural journal *Architettura*, headed by Marcello Piacentini, who was, in addition, on the board of *Le Arti*. Gustavo Giovannoni, the man who trained an entire generation of architects who later turned architectural historians, was the president of the Consiglio Direttivo. Also on the advisory board were Alberto Calza-Bini, an undistinguished but ubiquitous architect; Carlo Cecchelli; Gino Chierici; Enrico del Debbio; Vincenzo Fazolo; Giulio Giglioli; and Mario Salmi. Among these names are several major architectural historians (Chierici, Fazolo, Salmi). Luigi Crema was the editorial secretary whose duties corresponded to those of Argan on the board of *Le Arti*. Others on the editorial staff were Bruno Maria Apollonj, De Angelis D'Ossat (who served on both journals), Fausto Franco, Piero Gazzola, Arnaldo Rava, and Ferdinando Reggiori. By 1939 Crema had Roberto Vighi as coeditor, and Constantino Baroni, Piero Tomei (one of the most brilliant architectural historians Italy produced), and Mario Zocca had been added to the staff. Such names establish these journals as, indeed, the official publications supported by the major historians in Italy.

The changing editorial policy of *Le Arti* and *Palladio* from 1936 to 1944 delineates the role played by art historians in the spread of Fascism. The acts of the first Congresso Nazionale di Storia dell'Architettura, held in October 1936, contain Professor Ambrogio Annoni's remarks that non-Italians who write about Italian art do not know Italian art and as a result "wish to minimize the originality of our architectural conceptions." Annoni added that even some Italians were guilty of such practices.[72]

The Congresso set the stage for a reevaluation of Italian art. Giovannoni, who was elected president of the Convegno by acclamation as well as director of the newly formed journal, said the following (this quotation indicates that as late as 1936 the position was stated rather mildly, but the arguments became more aggressive later on): "In preparing ourselves with pure Italian feeling and with the intent to make known and increase the value of that which we may call our true *materia prima*, our thoughts turn dutifully to him who is the invigorator of all our energies, to *Il Duce*. Now, while the empire returns to the fated hills of Rome" (this is another oft-repeated quotation of Mussolini), "and new glories are joining with the old" (Ethiopia was invaded in October 1935), "from our heart comes the solemn promise that architecture of the Fascist times will once again, in returning to our great tradition, take the path of power which was that of the past, the object of all our studies."[73] The language is unmistakable but as yet there is no more than a hint of the use to which history will be put.[74]

In 1937, the first issue of *Palladio* came out, and a large portion of one of the first issues is devoted to, interestingly, Ethiopia! In this issue, Guglielmo De Angelis D'Ossat, who is today unquestionably a splendid historian, said, "It is certain that even today, all over Ethiopia—and the tradition cannot be anything except extremely old—the name of Rome has a prestigious significance, and a value of exceptional moral importance."[75] In 1937 in Rome there was the great exhibition of the Augustan age, and again in *Palladio* the somewhat immodest statement was made that the modern world was born of Imperial Rome, which constitutes the single source for everything that has developed into the present.[76] Giovannoni said, "The *Mostra Augustea* is the most eloquent affirmation of the constructive civilization of Rome, especially important now that the 'Empire returns to the fated hills of Rome.'"[77]

The first issue of *Le Arti*, October–November 1938, appeared with a two-page propaganda statement (in capitals) by Minister of Public Education Giuseppe Bottai. Bottai would make an interesting study because he came into office in 1936, when a definite policy change took place; by 1938 he published as many lines as any art historian in each of these journals, but eventually, in 1943, he was among those who voted to depose Mussolini. Bottai said,

> The journal *Le Arti* will be a direct expression of the politics of art of the regime;
> it should demonstrate concretely the validity of principles of the Fascist state in
> its unitary doctrine, which considers art an indispensable element for the educa-
> tion of the masses.... I wish that the journal *Le Arti* demonstrate to the world that
> Italian art and criticism are in every way conscious of their function, which is of
> extreme importance politically.[78]

Further on in the issue is a report of an address by M. Lazzari, who spoke about the mission of Italian architects. In this speech of 1938, at the same time that the Nazi state began to increase its emphasis on racist propaganda, we find Lazzari and art historians beginning to talk about race. While addressing a *convegno di soprintendenti*, Lazzari said that the inherent virtues of our race and the values affirmed by our people through the centuries of history are those which will guide the production of the history of the future.[79] After this great inaugural address, the assembled *soprintendenti* went out to the tomb of the unknown soldier, the altar of the fallen Fascist at the Campidoglio, and the martyrs' shrine at the Palazzo Littorio, and were received by Mussolini.

Bottai, in an article entitled "Modernity and Tradition in Italian Art Today," spoke more concretely about race and attempted to dispel the arguments advanced against connections between "race" and "art." Bottai maintained that the racial concept taken in its largest view, as common human destiny, implied the entire achievement of the Italian people, the self-awareness of the Italian people and of their secular mission.[80] In Bottai's view, distinctions between Italians, Romans, and the Latin peoples became unnecessary categorizations.[81] He maintained, for instance when speaking of art education in Italy in the same issue of *Le Arti*, that history made Italians aware of "those virtues of Latin peoples that reveal themselves again in the forefront of the great battle for world civilization being fought by Il Duce."[82] Once again, for Bottai, Latin (or Roman or Italian) peoples would save civilization from the barbarians.

Late in 1939, Roberto Vighi gave a paper at the third congress, in which he claimed that Ticinese art, although produced in the southern part of Switzerland, was really Italian, and it was a mistake to see it as Swiss. *Palladio* contains a report on the congress and notes that a solemn vow was taken by the entire *congresso* to rewrite history in order to make the art of Ticino part of Italian art instead of Swiss art.[83]

It was in 1940, after Italy entered the war, that both journals began stating openly that Italy had a right to all those lands formerly held by any of the Latin, Roman, or Italic peoples. In an article on the work of Caravaggio and Mattia Preti at Malta, Valeriano Mariani argued that these works constituted a secure confirmation of the Italian nature of the island and justified the action already undertaken (i.e., World War II) to restore Malta to Italy.[84] Giovannoni, in the editorial quoted at the beginning of this paper, said that works of architecture found in North Africa, Crete, and Nice indicate that these regions should be returned to Italy in accord with the "undeniable rights of History."[85] Further on in the same editorial, Giovannoni, after quoting both John Ruskin and Gabriele D'Annunzio on the relationship between war and architecture, outlines the influence on the Mediterranean world that has flowed from the architecture of the "narrow peninsula," including that of prehistory (Malta), the Roman empire (in the Near East as well as Africa), Christian Rome, medieval maritime cities (all over the Mediterranean including particularly Corsica and Sardinia), the Renaissance (all over Europe), and the vernacular (Tyrrhenian, Aegean, Ionian). He concludes from his survey that "as if in sacred language" the presence of these monuments confirms "the character of *Mare Nostrum* to the entire Mediterranean."[86]

In reporting the activities of the art-historical group of which *Palladio* was the official organ, there is notice of the last meeting of the spring of 1940 that included a "noble contribution" to knowledge about "those regions that by secular right should at the victorious completion of the war return to Italy." The papers delivered included Pietro Romanelli, "I monumenti romani della Tunisia" (The Roman Monuments of Tunisia); Enrico Clausetti, "Le fortificazione venete di Candia" (The Venetian Fortifications of Crete); and Giulio Giglioli, "Il trofeo di Augusto alla Turbia" (The Trophy of Augustus in Nice).[87]

If it were not already clear that Italians had a "right" to the Mediterranean, in an article entitled "On the Threshold of a New Mediterranean Empire" that appeared in *Le Arti* in 1940, Gioacchino Volpe, professor of modern political history at the University of Rome, outlined in greater detail than Giovannoni the geographic unity of the Mediterranean and the role Italic peoples played in it. He added a new point, the large emigrations of Italians in the late nineteenth and early twentieth centuries. Volpe argues that Italians made barren land of North Africa habitable through irrigation and worked as artisans, laborers, and white-collar workers in Egypt, Malta, Tunisia, Algeria, and Morocco. He states that this is further evidence of the civilizing influence of Italy. Volpe terminates the article with the stirring words,

> [T]he works of the fathers [confer on the followers] a kind of right and even impose duties. The new Empire of the Mediterranean will be truly formed only when men appear that are capable of feeling its fullness, of governing it, evaluating it even in its archaeological and historical richness and thereby in its continuity from the Roman fathers to today.[88]

From June 1940 on, *Le Arti* published two pages at the beginning of each issue (slick paper and very nice black ink) devoted to the official communiqués of the war itself. All the declarations of war and announcements of victory became an integral part of this art-historical publication.

These "official" journals and "official" art-historical statements clearly served the State. Historians of art and architecture wrote and rewrote the history of Italian art to serve as inspiration for the Italian people and to make them conscious of the part played by Italic peoples in Mediterranean history. There is little doubt they hoped to justify Fascist expansionist policies.

Spain: A Case Study in Action and Reaction
George R. Collins

Spanish architecture has in the recent past begotten three episodes of modernity. First came the turn-of-the-century activity in Catalonia with which we are now well acquainted.[89] Second was an exciting outbreak of the International Style and other advanced design that coincided almost exactly with the decade of the 1930s, which is the subject of this symposium. And finally, there has been the work of the last ten years or so in which we have seen young Spanish architects—inspired by the example of both these previous periods—step to the forefront of today's progressive movement.[90]

Apart from the intrinsic artistic interest of the buildings they produced, these three episodes hold special fascination for the architectural historian and are of peculiar relevance to the decade under consideration here because their "modernity" in each case came on almost overnight and without apparent local antecedent, seeming to result instead from rather abrupt changes in socio-cultural conditions of which at least three significant characteristics can be noted. There was an interval of an international—or at least pan-European—outlook, in contrast to the usual peninsular isolation; there was a self-generated and radical renovation in architectural education, arising largely outside the official educational establishment; and there was a relatively liberal, even democratic, political atmosphere or, at least, an assumption of the role of political revolutionary by the architects concerned.

I am not aware of a case of more sensitive correlation between modernity in architectural activity and modernity in educational, cultural, and political developments.

The way in which avant-garde building and planning came about in Spain during the second of these phases (the 1930s) is a particularly neat instance of this reciprocity. The architectural movement actually began to stir a bit before the year 1929, with which we start our decade; it lost its physical momentum with the fascist-military uprising of 1936; and it was halted as though by the drop of a guillotine blade with the triumph of Franco in 1939.

Like so many other events in Spain, the cultural activity with which we are here concerned grew up and concentrated itself in two centers that are polar opposites: Mediterranean Barcelona and Castilian Madrid. However, in this instance, as with the grassroots political movement that was to produce the Republic in 1931, there were other influential regions, such as Aragon and the Basque provinces; in fact, the architectural renovation was *officially* launched in the city of Zaragoza in Upper Aragon. In 1930 a young architect of Madrid, Fernando García Mercadal, who had been trained in central Europe and had participated in the founding of the Comité International pour la Résolution des Problèmes de l'Architecture Contemporaine (CIRPAC) and the Congrès Internationaux d'Architecture Moderne (CIAM) at La Sarraz, met in Zaragoza with representatives of the Basque provinces and Catalonia to form the organization Grupo de arquitectos y técnicos españoles para el progreso de la arquitectura contemporánea (GATEPAC).

Control of GATEPAC was exerted largely by the majority party—the Catalans—and, under the leadership of one of them, José Luis Sert, the group studied carefully the recent architectural activity of northern Europe from the Atlantic to the Urals and chose Le Corbusier as its apostle. CIRPAC, the parent organization, itself met in Barcelona in 1932, the year that Le Corbusier drew up his well-known plan for that city, which was named Plan Maciá after the left-wing leader of the autonomous Catalan republic. GATEPAC published from 1931 to 1937—the years of permissible republican activity in Barcelona—a periodical entitled A.C. (*Documentos de actividad contemporánea*). This magazine conducted several vigorous campaigns, one being directed against the sterile teachings of Spanish architectural schools and another against outdated municipal ordinances. In an illustration accompanying an article of 1935 in the magazine, the forms employed by Antoni Gaudí are caricatured, although at the same time his "surprising modernity" is admired.

Equally polemical is an article contributed by GATEPAC to another Catalan modern art magazine that argues that the modern architecture of northern Europe had been evolved there not from native formal tendencies but by artists who were working in the memories of their Mediterranean travels and vacations (on the island of Ibiza, for instance), during which they had imbibed the cubist, elementarist principles of the age-old Mediterranean tradition of building.[91] The argument ran roughly as follows: Architecture of the Mediterranean littoral naturally tends toward the employment of pure forms, clearly demarcated volumes, and extensive sheer surfaces that are frequently devoid of ornament. Northern styles—by nature more pitch-roofed, complexly ornamented, and somber in tone—tend to simplify themselves in the direction of this Mediterranean form when they move to the south: witness Catalan Gothic architecture. Official and sumptuous work in the Mediterranean area tends to be shot through with imported tendencies that contradict these principles, but the true repository of this Mediterranean spirit is its popular architecture (as seen in the Greek isles, the Balearics, and so on), where instead of monumental pretensions one finds a human scale, and the masses are simple, flat-sided, stuccoed, painted in elementary colors, and so forth. How, then, could anyone think that modern architecture, marked by these characteristics, was Germanic in origin? Visual demonstration of this theory could be seen in a page from the article. This current of opinion, called "Mediterraneanismo," played an important role in the Spanish arts in our century; outside of Spain we know it from Benedetto Croce, Paul Cézanne, Aristide Maillol, and others. As a further example of the interest that the International Style architects of Spain took in indigenous forms of building I refer you to some illustrations from a book about the regional house traditions of Spain that was published by García Mercadal the very year that he collaborated in the founding of GATEPAC, 1930.[92]

To appreciate the caliber of this group of young Spanish artists of the Republican period, one has only to recall the circumstances surrounding the Spanish government pavilion at the Paris World's Fair of 1937 [figure 103]. As is well known, Pablo Picasso painted his Guernica for it, in that type of political-artistic act mentioned above. The pavilion also housed some large sculptures by Picasso, a propagandist painting by Joan Miró, and Alexander Calder's mercury fountain (an advertisement for a basic item of Spanish export). The building was designed by Sert and Luis Lacasa of the GATEPAC group. Installed late and in great haste (two months), it received relatively little professional comment at the time but was quite outstanding in what was otherwise a rather dismal fair, architecturally speaking. Rather less derivative and "international" in style than much of GATEPAC's work, it emphasized rational design, simple inexpensive materials, and humanized spatial scale in a way that was, prophetically, similar to much Spanish architectural design of today; in fact, in its modest way it calls to mind the luxurious Spanish Pavilion at the 1964 New York World's Fair. This architectural and political statement by GATEPAC in Spain's most desperate moment was a masterpiece that has gone unstudied for too long.

The GATEPAC, which became largely a Catalan and Basque organization, was paralleled in Madrid by what the Spaniards call their "Generation of 1925," a less organized group of individuals whose executed modern works date from as early as 1927–8. Rafael Bergamín, one of their number, was concerned with the design of several low-cost housing developments in the 1930s which, because of their excellence, have since been largely preempted by the upper middle class. The most unified enterprise of the Madrid group was the laying out, from 1930 on, of the University City, which was unfortunately almost entirely gutted when it served as no-man's-land during the long siege of Madrid. An important ingredient in Madrid was the remarkable cultural life that flourished around its Residence of Students and that supplied the necessary intellectual ferment for the modern movement. Finally, the presence of the engineer Eduardo Torroja as collaborator in Madrid permitted the Spaniards to achieve in those years an architecture of 'pure structure'—an ideal about which much was said but little actually done by the moderns elsewhere in Europe.

All of this then disappeared overnight: its members scattered, betrayed, killed, or suppressed, their works left standing about like the rusty machines of Erewhon. We are told that when, at an international meeting of architects in 1949, a young man invoked the forbidden name "GATEPAC," he was publicly reprimanded by a professor of the School of Architecture. The course in "Modern Architecture" given at that school during the 1940s ended with the Paris Opera of 1861–74. One of the leaders of today's progressive architects has pointed out that during the eight years of his professional training in the 1940s he never once heard the name Frank Lloyd Wright mentioned in public.[93] When the rebuilding of devastated Spain began after the civil war ended, it typically took the form of folkloric regionalism or Hapsburg imperialism. Our decade had closed, slammed shut.

The Committed Architect
Colin St. John Wilson

It seems true that architecture for certain groups in Europe is believed to be a revolutionary activity, the first "modern" architect being Claude-Nicholas Ledoux, who, without being asked to do so, stood up and told the world what it should do in order to be cured of its many ills. And, growing up and around the ideas formulated at the Congrès Internationaux d'Architecture Moderne (CIAM), there is very strongly this notion of architecture as carrying a body of ideas and turning them passionately into the body of a building in some way. These two things had to go together; merely to tell the story of the develop-ment of a plastic system or merely to talk of "existenzminima" was not good enough. And this clearly is why Le Corbusier is important for us, because he has always achieved this embodiment. But it is also, I think, very important to realize how the De Stijl people intended their forms to be understood. I don't think the analogy with painting-to-building is so important as the fact that the forms of De Stijl were abstract forms which carried considerable theosophical meaning—so much so that their abuse by Theo van Doesburg could lead to the breakup of his great friendship with Piet Mondrian.[94]

All of this has absolutely nothing to do with good taste. It was not on sty-listic grounds that the Nazis closed the Bauhaus, and not for nothing did Le Corbusier himself refer to futurism as "*bien dangereux*." [95] I think that there is a certain realm of ideas to be defined which is not that of morality but for which the nearest word I can get is "probity." It constitutes a border zone that lies between aesthetics and morality and politics—a zone which is hard to define, but one which Le Corbusier himself has always established as an axis of in-tention and which has always been advanced under a revolutionary banner.

Now I am truly surprised to hear so much talk purely at the level of forms, and all I can say now is that to have called the International Style the "International Style" in 1932 was indeed to point out that it had died. To men-tion the battle which started within CIAM and which is still perhaps being waged now by the young angries and the brutalists or whatever you would like to call them—the younger generation which feels this architecture of ideas has been betrayed in some way—is to raise a note which has been absent here today.

I must apologize for being a little incoherent. I speak with little warning but as a sort of foreigner in your midst, and with this view of what modern architecture is supposed to be, I make this one point. I think Le Corbusier perhaps stands for us as the man who carried this message right through into building, as in the Unité d'Habitation, which, after all, took thirty years to build and was being designed throughout the 1930s. It has a stature quite beyond any of our postwar buildings precisely because it carries a load of ideas.

Yale and the Ivy League Tradition
Carroll L. V. Meeks

This is in the nature of a reminiscence. I was in the architecture school at Yale University when the official decade 1929 began. One of the texts which we were assigned was a book called *The Significance of the Fine Arts*. A good deal of its architectural content was by Ralph Adams Cram and that on sculpture was by Lorado Taft, and so on. Lecturers in the school included Arts and Crafts people like C. R. Ashbee. We knew about Hitchcock's book,[96] and we knew about Le Corbusier, but this did not appear in the work in the drafting room. Our chief critic was Otto Faelton, who had been the chief designer for James Gamble Rogers.

Then a slight breath of fresh air came in when the Rockefeller Center people began to be important to Yale. As students in 1928 and 1929, we admired the work of Bertram Goodhue; we admired the work of Paul Philippe Cret and the elder Saarinen, Eliel. We knew about Buckminster Fuller. We admired Raymond Hood. We thought that Ralph Walker was pretty adventurous. George Howe and William Lescaze came along in due course. But Faelton disappeared from the scene and we had Fred Hirons; some of you may remember him, celebrated in his day as the winner of great competitions and maker of magnificent drawings. Our projects were completed, sometimes, in broken glass and whiskey.

Then we heard that something new was happening in Cambridge and so (as you know, Yale always follows Harvard if it can) after the appearance of Walter Gropius at Harvard, Yale, spurred on by Fred Godley, tried to do something at the end of this decade, in 1938 and 1939, and we again called upon the Rockefeller Center group: Wallace K. Harrison, who came with Max Abramovitz. And they did start things up, I must say, in quite a novel way. In fact, it was so novel it was unpopular with the administration. They did, however, follow an ancient American tradition in architecture schools, because they constantly brought Europeans into the drafting room. Most of the American architecture schools had chief critics from Europe, and so did we in 1938 and 1939, just as did Harvard. Among the people to whom we were exposed then were Paul Nelson, Amédée Ozenfant, Fernand Léger, Oscar Nitschke, and Sandy Calder.

This happy boom for us lasted until the war, when Harrison and Abramovitz had to leave and everything went into a slump. But that one decade showed the tremendous transformation between the Beaux-Arts system, which lasted very long at Yale, and the breath of new life which came in 1938 and 1939.

The Architectural Reaction in Austria

Eduard F. Sekler

When this topic was assigned to me, I thought everybody else was also going to talk about some aspect of the architectural reaction in the 1930s, and then to my horror I discovered that there are only two others who have this particularly unpleasant aspect to deal with. But having accepted the topic, I began to pursue it and soon discovered that I was not particularly familiar with the events, because I was really too young when they happened. At the same time, I had tended to pass the period over in my mind as being a rather distasteful interval. Nor did this decade seem particularly significant in Austria to be studied from the point of view of architectural history.

I was also reminded forcefully that there is a tremendous difference between "personal time" and "historic time," and that it was impossible for me to achieve the kind of dispassionate judgment in the handling of material for this period which we all at least *aim* for when handling historical evidence. I was at the same time too close and too personally involved, although I had of course not been close enough to be able to speak about the events in terms of personal reminiscences.[97] "Personal time" is something very non-homogeneous; some events assume enormous importance and others seem to have faded out; personal judgment prevails and significance may be apportioned in a very different fashion from the way in which it is distributed by later historians. I think this distinction, which I had to rediscover for myself here, though I knew about it in theory from my methodological training, is something which is rather important to keep in mind in our entire discussion.

As to the question of significance, I think it would be like beating a dead horse to insist on how insignificant architecturally a great deal of the production of these years was. But at the same time one realizes how tremendously significant these buildings were as embodiments of momentous social, historical, and political events. Because of the visual insignificance of most of the material and because I know that most of these buildings are familiar, I omit all illustrations. Our concern is not chiefly with architecture but with the forces behind architecture.[98]

When I looked for an approach to the topic, it seemed best to take just one piece of historical evidence and then try to build up a context around it. I chose a written statement in facsimile which was addressed in June 1933 to all members and friends of the Österreichische Werkbund, the Austrian parallel organization to the Deutscher Werkbund. This statement is very little known; even people who were involved with the events — former members of the Österreichische Werkbund — did not seem to remember it. It was written by Josef Hoffmann. He accompanied it with a brief covering letter in typescript dated March 26, 1933, which in translation reads as follows:

> In conclusion of our Werkbund activity I want to permit myself to send the enclosed confession of guilt so that at least my intentions, as I feel them, appear clearly established. All the rest, time will surely bring forth. At any rate, I thank you and the few friends for the trust which you have extended to me and for the strong support.

This is followed by a handwritten statement of twelve pages of which only the beginning and the end need to be given here in translation:

What we are really concerned with is to feel what can be done in the interest of enriching the image of the world within our more narrow borders.

Every soil carries its special fruit and without doubt shelters certain forces which can develop and unfold only there.

Everyone who possesses an outspoken feeling for his homeland (*Heimatgefühl*) will be able, if talent exists, to create something worthy of note, something particular.

The Germano-Austrian (*Deutschösterreicher*) not only possesses a charming, firmly harmonious character, but he also has an understanding for creative volition.

He has to bring forth works in which one can sense his homeland and the experience of the period.

For us it is important, therefore, to recognize all these impulses, whether they lie dormant or are awake, and to bring them to unfolding.[99]

The following excerpts are from the end of the statement:

We are not interested in disturbing any circles but we are fed up with being negatively criticized in a schoolmasterly manner....

[S]pirits who feel themselves high above anything tied to the soil will have to hover in the air and will not find [their way] back.

Think of the decline of all ancient cultures of the Orient, China, and Europe, and beware of being forced by foreign influences to approach a premature end.

Everyone who means well must understand everything and as a sage he must strive to grasp and admire only what is positive.

Malicious criticism, even if its form is most witty, is always the achievement of a passing, weakly period. Let us leave this to journalism.

What was the meaning of this letter in 1933? What could it refer to? And what kind of insight does it give us into the situation of architecture at the moment? It was a momentous year — 1933. On January 28, Adolf Hitler was appointed *Reichskanzler*. In February, the Reichstag went up in flames. In March, the president and vice-presidents of the Austrian parliament, in a very stormy session, handed in their resignations, which immobilized parliament and ushered in the period of Austro-fascism under Engelbert Dollfuss. In the same year, to remind you of some significant architectural events in Vienna, Adolf Loos died; a new periodical, *Das Profil*, began under the editorship of Hans A. Vetter; and Professor Clemens Holzmeister presided at the Allgemeine Deutsche Katholikentag (General German Catholics' Day), which was held in Vienna that year. The Werkbund Siedlung in Lainz, a suburb of Vienna, was still very new;[100] this parallel undertaking to the Weissenhof Siedlung had just been opened in 1932, and one of its most energetic sponsors was Dr. Hermann

Neubacher, for a time president of the Werkbund. The Werkbund Siedlung once more — and for the last time before World War II — brought together leading architects from all over Europe; among them were designers whose names are well known today and who stood for the most progressive thinking at that time: Josef Frank, Gabriel Guevrekian, Hugo Häring, Ernst Lichtblau, Adolf Loos, Richard Neutra, Gerrit Rietveld, and Oskar Strnad. This reminds us that the Österreichische Werkbund was meant to be an extremely important and essentially progressive association. But in this very year of 1933 — less than one year after the Wiener Werkstätte had been finally closed by Hoffmann — the Werkbund split into two groups.[101] One was centered around people like Frank and Strnad, and the other around Hoffmann and Holzmeister. Apparently it was in connection with this formation of two camps that our statement was written, and the last part, cited above, probably refers to criticisms that had been forthcoming from more internationally minded circles within the Werkbund. But criticism of the aims and productions of the Wiener Werkstätte in its last years was not the only reason for the split, nor was it only a quibble about a commission which both Frank and Hoffmann had hoped for.[102] The underlying cleavage went deeper and touches the domain of divergent political attitudes. There were, it seems, currents of hidden prejudice and suspicion; there were ties to both the Socialist and Austro-fascist parties of the day; and finally, there were both open and secret connections with Germany and its Werkbund.

This leads us to inquire as to what had happened to the Deutscher Werkbund under the impact of Nazism in Germany. What role was played by the members of an organization that in its earlier days had certainly counted among the forces for progress in the field of design?

Among the founding members of the Deutscher Werkbund were Peter Behrens, Wilhelm Kreis, and Paul Schultze-Naumburg. All of these had prominent positions after 1933, and Schultze-Naumburg was, in fact, *the* architectural authority as far as racist theories and *Blut und Boden* architecture were concerned.

How was it possible for something that obviously started as a positive movement to lead directly into a reaction? What happened on the Austrian scene, in that poor, strife-torn country, only mirrored what happened on the larger scene in Germany. Who were the "pioneers of reaction"? How could what in retrospect seems a monstrous perversion actually come about? These seem to me the key questions.

Perhaps a lead is provided by a little-known periodical that came out in Vienna a long time before the 1930s. It appeared for the first time in 1904 and was called the *Hohe Warte*, no doubt in reference to the Viennese garden suburb of identical name where Josef Hoffmann built his first important houses. Among its editors and contributors we find side by side the Austrians Josef August Lux,[103] Kolo Moser, Josef Hoffmann, and Otto Wagner, and the Germans Alfred Lichtwark, Hermann Muthesius, and Paul Schultze-Naumburg. The first issue featured a long translation of Ebenezer Howard, and the second issue had quotations from John Ruskin and William Morris. In later years the periodical became the official mouthpiece of the German garden city movement.

The four years during which the *Hohe Warte* appeared coincide with a formative and most successful period in Josef Hoffmann's career. He designed some of his most important buildings and furnished them through his newly founded Wiener Werkstätte, whose program explicitly referred to Ruskin and Morris. He attempted to create a miniature garden suburb in his group of houses at the Hohe Warte, just as in his later suburban development at the Kaasgraben, Vienna. It must have been in those years that he became deeply committed to a set of values that still found expression in his statement of 1933, when he defended a "feeling for the homeland" and what is "tied to the soil."

The four years from 1904 to 1908 also witnessed a significant change of mood that definitely altered the balance between progressive and reactionary tendencies in Austrian and German architecture. It was faithfully mirrored in the pages of the *Hohe Warte*. What began as an understandable enthusiasm for the English country house, garden suburb, and garden city and for the teachings of Ruskin and Morris gradually seems to have degenerated into an increasingly reactionary nationalism. In an article in 1908 Lux sounded a first cautious warning: "Recently in architecture a strong national sentiment makes itself felt.... [F]requently it takes as a model that which is old, past, and used up, and in its form tries to suit itself to that which is small and no longer sufficient. It is questionable whether this will mean progress." [104] Four months later Lux gave up his editorship of the *Hohe Warte*, and his farewell article was a much more strongly worded, strangely prophetic appeal against exaggerated *Bodenständigkeit* (being tied to the soil) and *Heimatkunst* (art tied to the homeland). "There is no art for the people," Lux concluded, in contradiction to Morris's famous doctrines. [105]

The process which Lux had watched starting in those early years went on, however. When in 1939 Gottfried Feder, in his book *Die Neue Stadt*, proposed the layout for an ideal Nazi settlement, his plan could hardly deny its derivation from English prototypes such as Hampstead Garden Suburb. We are reminded of the fact that it was easy to make the transition from reform movements based on a romantic medievalism to certain tenets of National Socialism; you have to convert and misinterpret the teachings of Ruskin and Morris just a little in order to have an excellent ideological foundation for going back to anonymous architecture, folkloristic trends, and the national (often "Nordic") elements in a country's past.

There remains one question: where does architectural classicism come into the picture? It did not exist in Austria in the 1930s in a manner comparable to the architecture of the Third Reich, but no discussion of reactionary trends would be complete without including classicism. It was a tacit assumption of reactionary doctrine that there are only two approaches to architecture—either in the folkloristic manner or in a pseudoclassicist vocabulary. This fundamental assumption was never questioned, and a discussion was only permitted concerning the handling of detail. Again, our search for beginnings leads us to the period around 1907–8 when in reaction to the Jugendstil there was a strong swing to classicism. Olbrich's Haus Feinhals and similar buildings come to mind. Architects like Peter Behrens and Bruno Paul at that time found the expression of the national past in classicism, usually in its Biedermeier or Empire variety. Friedrich Ostendorf illustrated numerous prototypes in his *Sechs Bücher vom Bauen* (1914), and even the unassuming, rather charming simplicity of Heinrich Tessenow had its roots in the same soil where folklore and classicism grew side by side.

We found that what came to fruition in the reactionary tendencies of the 1930s really had its seeds further back, but we are far from having a clear picture of the Austrian situation. It was not just a question of black and white; it was, as so often, a question of many shades of gray. This came out clearly in what evidence I could get from architects who lived through the period and who knew about the split in the Österreichische Werkbund and all it stood for. There were shifts in allegiance; there were compromises and paradoxes. Under the Nazi regime, Holzmeister, whose architecture occasionally had affinities to folkloristic traditions, was absolutely out of favor and had to stay out of the country. But architects whose previous record included work well in advance of the average production of the 1930s became enthusiastic and aggressive adherents of the new party line, and their work showed a corresponding retrogression. Dr. Neubacher, the administrator behind the very progressive Werkbund Siedlung, even became the first mayor of Vienna after the Anschluss.

The warning which obviously results from all this is that you cannot simply equate attitudes and achievements. The connection between architecture as form-giving and its social and political background is not as direct, it seems, as one would have liked to believe. The need emerges for extreme caution when linking words and deeds, statements and meanings; there can be an enormous gap between them.

This reminds me of the statement by Mme. Syrkus which was quoted today by Mrs. Moholy-Nagy in such a manner that we could understand it as an admirable, profound plea for a deepening and enriching of the architectural vocabulary. But when it was made, it came forth in defense of the then party line of Socialist Realism in architecture and of schemes which were reactionary in many ways and embarrassing to look at because it was known from past record that those who presented them really could do better. Thus we have another example, as with the reaction in the 1930s, of how tenuous the connection can be between what is said and what is designed, and how extremely cautious historians have to be when handling topics and material of this kind, especially when both "personal time" and "historic time" are involved.

City-Planning Theory in National-Socialist Germany
Christian F. Otto

One might assume there is a general "totalitarian" style of town planning. The briefest comparison, however, of planning in National-Socialist Germany, Communist Russia, Fascist Italy, Franco Spain, and other twentieth-century totalitarian countries demonstrates that a constant planning form does not exist. Instead, each country displays its own individual manner, oriented toward the specific ideals it seeks to achieve and conditioned by the particular problems it attempts to solve.

National-Socialist architecture is generally considered to be Karl Friedrich Schinkel–derived. In public buildings the square columns, flatly modeled Greek architraves, and restrained cornices were all lifted out of nineteenth-century classicism and given a perverse twist by the Nazi megalomaniacal quest for size. The result was Brobdingnagian structure that commanded Gargantuan space: massive, mercilessly axial piles of unwieldy blocks that sought a singular effect by the endless repetition of hard, dead forms. One would naturally assume that Nazi city planning would be in accord with this quality of the colossal in building. One thinks of vast spaces ominously controlled by cruelly white structures, such as the boulevard projected to cut across Unter den Linden in Berlin: a wide thoroughfare to be lined with Party buildings, passing at both ends into infinity.[106] But a minimum of this kind of architecture and planning was realized or even projected. Far more prevalent was the ideal concept of *das Volk.*

The intention of New Towns as defined by National-Socialist planners like Werner Knapp was "Raum schaffen für die Entfaltung einer deutschen Lebensgemeinschaft" (to create space for the development of a German community-for-living).[107] The ideal New Town was to have 20,000 inhabitants,[108] a size calculated to avoid the disadvantages of both metropolis and village, and at the same time to include the advantages of both village and city [*figure 104*]. Two traffic axes—the primary one east-west, the secondary one north-south—constituted the framework of the New Town.[109] The crossing was to be the political center, where governmental buildings were to stand. Industry, public utilities, and both passenger and freight railroad stations were laid out to the east;[110] sport facilities, parade plazas, hospital, and cemetery to the west. Housing sectors were to be located between the arms of the cross. A sustenance zone was to be drawn up around each city to support it agriculturally and to serve as a market for the goods it produced.

Three-dimensionally, the New Town would appear as a very squat cone, with a wide, circular base. Buildings took their site, size, and shape in the hierarchy from periphery to center according to their significance in community life. This was a law of political order, *Bausozialismus,*[111] a stepped relationship of buildings that would express the relationship between the leader and the led within the community. Albert Speer wrote proudly, "[N]ew buildings of the State and the movement are being combined, for the purpose of achieving a closed effect, into large representative areas of streets and squares. They are to crown our new city and become the centers of today's cities."[112] The elements of each section of the city were to be oriented toward its center.[113] This center in turn would lead to the next highest one, and so on, until the apex of the cone—the center of the whole town—was reached. Only from here would the city be ordered into the higher echelons of county (*Kreis*) and state.[114] Achieving unity (*Einigung*) was considered to be basically a question of the correct placement and articulation of these political centers.[115] The creation of centers was looked upon as necessarily containing the solution to all other town planning questions.[116] The circle was considered the *Urbild* (archetype) of the communal form: it united people in a readiness to help, in mutual participation; it was the *Soziale Grundfigur* (fundamental outline of society). The circle created communities, whereas rows of houses resulted in social indifference.[117] A precise, geometrical form would seldom be possible, nor even desired; the circle was to be stretched and molded to the contours of the landscape. Important was only the circle-constituting principle (*kreisbildendes Prinzip*),[118] which creates communities.

Success in achieving the goal of settling people permanently was also considered to be strongly dependent on the accord achieved between the city and nature.[119] A diagram shows the components that would lead to permanent residency, the various triangles representing the basic necessities for settled life. [*The speaker shows a diagram from Knapp's article "Die Siedlung," page 5.*] Life grows out of race and the landscape with its geological and climatic and economic conditions (*Blut und Boden*)[120] and is based on man and space. The human part consists of a harmony between labor, home, and cult. Architectural grouping was to be experienced as a continuation of the world of forms created by nature; the houses were to be set in the landscape, so that the inhabitants could make the feeling of a homogeneity—of a cohesion with the soil of the mother country—their own. The streets must also conform; they could not be a grid but must "grow from the soil...be one with its natural form, the specific geomorphological surface relief." [121] The task of bringing the forms of nature, the character of the land, and the architectonic articulation of space all into a harmony, so that a unity would arise between nature and art, was left to the eye of the town planner.

In architecture, the gable-roofed house was considered the most perfect expression of the German nature and a proper antidote to the "international" flat-roofed cubes of the 1920s. The cue came in part from Oswald Spengler (in his *Decline of the West* of 1930 he asserted, "Of all expressions of race, the purest is the house" [122]) and in part from the German countryside and cityscape. The former offered myriad variations of a gabled farmhouse type, and the latter was thick with buildings, even some complete towns, from the German Middle Ages. The result could be seen in all parts of Germany; projects studded with small white cubes topped with red gables.

The medieval epoch, for that matter, was of basic significance in the creation of the Nazi New Towns. National Socialism drank deeply from the vial of German Romanticism, [123] and it was for this reason that its planners drew heavily on the German medieval town for content and affirmation. Romanticism held that Germany's national tradition in its purest form, unstained by foreign and cosmopolitan influences, was to be found in the medieval era. "The task of politics," wrote Friedrich Schlegel, "is to reestablish the constitution of the Middle Ages and to bring it to full realization." [124] Novalis certainly captured the spirit which was to appeal to Nazism when he claimed that "For all times will this society [the Middle Ages] be a model for all societies that feel an organic yearning for unending expansion and eternal existence." [125] Johann Gottlieb Fichte, whose exuberance of high nationalism in his *Addresses to the German Nation* (1807–8) made him one of those most frequently listed in the Nazi roster of its heroes, had asserted that "The history of Germany, of German might, German enterprise and inventions, of German monuments and the German spirit—the history of all these things during that period [again the Middle Ages] is nothing but the history of those cities." [126] Hitler confirmed all these extollings in *Mein Kampf* [127] and in a speech given at the Kulturtagung des Reichsparteitages at the Parteitag der Freiheit 1935 [128] in Nuremberg, on both occasions praising the character of the German medieval city. It is therefore not surprising that we find in the German Middle Ages several counterparts of the Nazi conception of the New Town, morphologically, architecturally, and in the manner in which the town is set into the landscape. [129]

The main roots of National-Socialist planning ideas—their New Towns—are, then, to be found in three factors: first, in German Romanticism, especially in the love for the German medieval city; second, in twisted applications of the reflections of great German thinkers such as Spengler; and third, in a perversion of the traditions of German architectural and planning theory that had developed from the late nineteenth century on, including expressionism. [130]

The concept of the "organic," for example (which had been used by Heinrich Tessenow and A. E. Brinckmann, to name but two sources), was taken over as a slogan [131] by the Nazi town planners and used to evoke stirring and powerful emotional reactions (as were so many words in the language of Party orators and writers who drew on the vocabulary of religious revivalism for their political exhortations). Or again, the concept of the *Stadtkrone* (city crown), which Bruno Taut had set into a universal religious context,[132] was applied by Nazi planners to justify the political hierarchy of the Party within the city; that is, to subject all buildings to the main Party structures in a line of descending importance from the center of the cone down, so that the absolute control of the leader over the led might be given clear visual denomination.[133]

The Rise of Technology
James Marston Fitch

Having been robbed of almost every point I had planned to make, I have still the great advantage of being able to comment upon a lot of things which have been said and yet feel fairly safe from counterattack. It has seldom, if ever, been my experience to hear as much, as dense, and as fascinating material as we have been given today. It seems to me fabulous, and I hope that funds can be found to print not merely the papers but also the critically important illustrations which accompanied them.

There is no question of the significance of the new material we have seen and heard today on the epoch 1929–39. But I do not so fully share many of the judgments which have been passed on that decade. It has been handled with a kind of levity—a graceful levity, admittedly—which seems to imply that we are viewing this epoch from some pinnacle of mature accomplishment. The implication here is that the issues that were so vivid to those of us who lived and worked through that decade have vanished, that they are either resolved or obsolete. This, at least, is one possible interpretation to be drawn from many of today's papers.

Such assumptions, if they exist, seem to me quite mistaken. I think Mrs. Wurster is entirely correct in pointing out that we have no cause for complacency—for example, that the architect today plays a very minor role in establishing the vernacular quality of the countryside, or in the development of the social architecture of this nation. I feel that—whatever the fallacies, mistakes, errors, or enthusiasms which were current in that decade—we have no reason whatever to pretend that even worse ones are not endemic in architecture and design today.

I took as my assignment for today's discussion a rather narrow topic: namely, to scan the architectural press of the country from 1929 to 1939, to see how it reflected, reacted to, the rise of modern technology. I studied not only the editorial material but also the advertising, which is often the more illuminating of the two. It was a sad and sometimes embarrassing experience for me; sad, because it involved my reading many issues of magazines in which I played an editorial role; and embarrassing because of the uncritical enthusiasms we had for the promised benefits of technology—promises which have scarcely been fully confirmed by subsequent developments.[134]

And yet I do not feel that we were essentially mistaken. The general program for the regeneration of architecture which dominated the magazines of the 1920s and 1930s was not mistaken in its essentials, in the fundamental arguments it advanced. If there is disagreement about this today, it may very well be due to the vantage point from which we view this decade rather than to the theoretical positions which the decade itself took.

The decade was, of course, full of all sorts of conflicting arguments and polemics. The literature of the period is astonishing in the variety of the panaceas that are advanced and the different points of view from which they come. It is easy enough to ridicule many of these panaceas today, but when one looks at the decade as a whole, one must recognize that there has seldom been another time when the problems of architecture and urbanism have been approached from so many differing points of view. It is astonishing how complete, how synoptic, this investigation was. Certainly, a candid review of the American architectural press of the decade 1950–60 will not offer anything of comparable stature. In fact, it is my own impression that speculative literature — the very technique and habit of speculative thought — has disappeared from the scene. I consider this a loss. One of the great virtues of this decade we have discussed was its absorbing interest in theory, especially utopian theory.

As far as technology proper is concerned, we can see the role it played, the reception it got, in the way the press handled Buckminster Fuller: his Dymaxion House, which was first published in 1927 [*figure 71*]; his Dymaxion auto, which was published in 1933; or his prefabricated bathroom, which was published (and exhibited) in 1937. The appearance of these prototypes, the enthusiastic reception they got, and their subsequent failure to materialize, to lead to fruition in any immediate sense: this seems to me to typify the epoch. If we contrast the architectural press before the Great Depression with its behavior toward Fuller's revolutionary proposals, the surprising thing is the great shift in editorial positions which had occurred. This enabled the magazines to handle the Fuller projects sympathetically when, a few years earlier, they would have either denounced them as nonsense or (more probably) completely ignored them as not being a fit subject for discussion.

It is clear from this handling that the whole field was coming to recognize the role of modern industrial technology as making possible the new architectural idiom. The same issues of these magazines were full of new buildings which illustrated what visible forms this new idiom would assume. And we editors had, of course, to prove that this new movement was thoroughly "American." I remember very clearly that on the magazine on which I worked there were always sharp limits as to how much foreign material we dared include. Each month it was a struggle; each month we tried to present a picture of evenly balanced progress right across the country. Actually, there were about three states in the whole nation — New York, Illinois, and California — which gave any evidence of this progress. So we were continually trying to juggle eight houses from California, one from the East Coast, and then, if possible, a bowling alley or a drive-in or *something* from the Middle West to afford at least the pretense that we were reporting a national movement. Yet none of us doubted for a moment that there was a national movement, that its future was assured, and that technology was the means whereby it would be accomplished. History surely has vindicated this confidence.

But the depressed level of economic activity during that decade, and the consequent lag in technological development, effectively precluded the appearance on the market of products like Fuller's inventions. One of the rare cases in which American industry decided to gamble on the viability of the new image of progress occurred when the Chrysler Corporation put out its famous, ill-fated "streamlined" car. This design was a parody — well, perhaps not a parody...a *copy*, an echo — of Fuller's Dymaxion car. It failed disastrously to win public acceptance and Chrysler quickly took it off the market. This is the picture with which the journals of the period constantly confront us: that technology actually stood at a level where it could have put all these prototypes into mass production but that, economically, industry was too weak and timid to try it. For example, it was one of the great copper companies which subsidized Fuller's prefabricated bathroom; and there was not a single missing element, technically, to prevent its mass production. Yet it did *not* go into production—in fact, such a bathroom is not even available today!

The journals present us with the paradox of a new technology which has been fully conceived and yet cannot be born. Almost every component of today's modern building—prefabricated panels, air-conditioning, radiant heating, automatic controls, indirect lighting, fluorescent tubes, welded steel construction, special glasses—were all known in 1939 to be perfectly practical: they were regarded as inevitable, "just around the corner." You will remember how movie theaters just before World War II proudly advised you to "go to the movies and cool off!" Summer cooling was still an exciting luxury, and the magazines reflect that fact. Nevertheless, they were all convinced that the actual mass distribution, mass consumption of these products was near. It only awaited some kind of qualitative change in the economy.

The whole concept of scientific research as applied to architectural problems makes its appearance during this decade. The John B. Pierce Foundation was carrying on its elaborate time-and-motion studies on how people actually used various parts of the house. The Yale School of Public Health had already done a great deal of work in environmental medicine, including studies of heating and ventilation in public housing. Perhaps the most sophisticated research was that carried on by Frederick Kiesler in the "Design-Correlation" research laboratory that he ran for a few short years here at Columbia. Here he carried on some remarkable work in what he called "correalism" (insisting on spelling it with two "r"s in typical Kiesler fashion). This was—and still is—a truly scientific approach to the problem of industrial design. Kiesler had a very great sense of historical development, and he tried to imbue his students with this concept. The one prototype he managed to get fabricated into full-scale form was the revolving bookshelf. This bookshelf was the end-product of a program in which his students began by studying the history of the book—what it was before it became a book, what it was like when it was a manuscript, what it would be like when it became a microfilm. On the basis of this kind of background, Kiesler then posed the problem of book storage. What were the environmental requirements of the book? What were the environmental requirements of the user? How should they be, how could they be, resolved in the final design? This is an approach to design which seems to me to require no apology whatever a quarter of a century later. In fact, I should say that there has been a qualitative drop in industrial design today. I see no evidence anywhere of products being subjected to this kind of critical analysis. If the research work of this decade strikes us as old-fashioned, perhaps we ought to reexamine *our* position again. Perhaps it is *we* and not Kiesler who have dropped behind.

There were, of course, many detailed developments during this period, and speculation about their possible significance fell into two broad schools. One dealt fairly narrowly with technology itself, with its potentials for human well-being. Kiesler's work would represent the most sophisticated level of activity here, as would, for example, the studies of Knud Lundberg-Holm and Theodore Larson on the production cycle. There were many other men working on much crasser levels. There were men like Corwin Wilson, an early advocate of everyone's living in trailers, an apostle of social mobility. There were the Technocrats and the Decentralists with their theories of mechanized subsistence-farming combined with power-tooled home crafts. (Frank Lloyd Wright's Broadacre City [*figure 88*] is a poetic projection of this particular petit-bourgeois utopia.) And Buckminster Fuller was always there, in the wings if not on the stage, agitating for prefabrication, modular construction, packaged utilities. So we find a whole range of committed men exploring a whole spectrum of possibilities.

Speculation was simultaneously rampant at other higher, more abstract levels. There was much discussion of the social role and responsibility of the architect in housing and in town and regional planning—Catherine Bauer Wurster is one of our most distinguished representatives of this kind of thought. After the inauguration of Roosevelt and the beginning of the New Deal, the magazines carried a great deal of material on these subjects from both foreign and local sources. Schemes for urban housing, for rural housing like those of Vernon DeMars for the Resettlement Administration in *The Grapes of Wrath* country—all of this activity received wide attention and was handled with increasing respect by the architectural press. The Tennessee Valley Authority and its implications were recognized as important. This interest was not, of course, accidental, since many hundreds of architects, landscape architects, and civil engineers were finding their only employment precisely in these areas of social architecture and planning. At the literary level, all this activity found eloquent spokesmen in men like Charles Harris Whitaker, the elder Henry Wright, Lewis Mumford, and the late Henry Churchill: a whole hierarchy of talented men were advancing rationales for various approaches to planning.

At all these levels, the period seems to me a pregnant one, a very rich and stimulating one, despite the fact that, if you look closely at its actual accomplishments, they may seem pathetic in their scarcity, their small scale, their inability to go beyond the schematic and the hypothetical. (But many great periods of history reveal the same flawed texture when examined closely: reading the daily accounts of the Civil War, you would never guess that the Union would win and the nation be preserved.) These conditions did not change—apparently *could not* change—until the outbreak of World War II. That event put an abrupt end to all idle speculation, though paradoxically it laid the material basis for its fruition in subsequent decades. The war put American industry back to work, an industry that had never been much more than fifty percent employed since 1929. The exigencies of war not only forced an enormous acceleration in productivity but at the same time laid the basis for a qualitative change in American technology. The whole pace of innovation, invention, and product development was fantastically accelerated, and this made possible the postwar realization of every prewar dream. (It made possible many other things, including the whole field of nuclear technology, which had not even been dreamed of before.)

Another interesting by-product of this period was that it provided an interregnum in which laymen, the potential users of buildings, could only daydream about them. Magazine advertising all during the war was actually subversive as regards postwar architectural conservatism. Manufacturers spent a great deal of advertising money to tell the American consumer what building was going to be like after victory. Five years of stasis created a great reservoir of consumer demand. Thus at war's end, the American architect confronted a wealthier, hungrier, and better-informed audience than ever before. At the very least, this audience had a common denominator of understanding what it had a right to demand and what to expect—a better one than it would ever have had without that interregnum.

It is on the basis of the momentum accumulated during World War II, added to all the lively speculation that went on in the decade prior to the war, that the progress of the last two decades is based. The most we can claim today is that we have taken the constituent elements of the earlier decades, 1918–28 and 1929–39, and put them into common circulation. We have smoothed off some of the rough edges of earlier stylistic invention; we have managed to synthesize the idioms of powerful innovators like Walter Gropius, Mies van der Rohe, and Le Corbusier into some kind of common language of form. But I feel very strongly that we have done little else. Of course, many of us here, who lived and worked through that decade, are in a very ambivalent position. This must be especially true of Russell Hitchcock: he is involved in architectural history at so many levels right now that he must often wonder whether he is the object of historical investigation, or the subject of it, or the agent of it. This dilemma is bound to color the judgments of anybody who was active during that decade. Nevertheless, I should prefer not to see it handled with levity. But then I am perhaps a humorless person.

Modern Architecture and Architectural Criticism in the United States
Mark L. Peisch

As a means of approaching the decade 1929–39 in the United States, let me raise the following question: How was the American public prepared for the new qualities inherent in the concepts of modern architecture? During its development and the period under discussion, architects emphasized spatial relationships and geometric forms. The juxtaposition of spatial areas in a practical and useful manner became, in itself, a thing of beauty. Then there was, of course, the elimination of ornament. This was a vast change, and the public was unready for it. A historical parallel might be drawn between the development of the skyscraper in Chicago during the late nineteenth century and the period which we have termed "modern architecture." In Chicago Louis Sullivan and Frank Lloyd Wright developed in print as well as building materials the critical fabric pertaining to their work.[135] Both ran into vocal opposition. The writings of Russell Sturgis and Montgomery Schuyler come immediately to mind as clear, discriminating voices which helped prepare the public for these new architectural developments, particularly the skyscrapers.

Turning to the period 1929–39 in this country, I find that no comparable critics spoke with authority and to a large audience through the architectural journals and press of this decade. I think it is significant that in 1931 Talbot Hamlin wrote an article deploring this fact, stating that architectural criticism was needed to emphasize and explain the momentous architectural events taking place.

As we know, this period was not without its astute and highly discriminating observers and historians—Messrs. Hitchcock and Johnson above all—and perhaps because of their own involvement in the developments of the day they preferred to eschew the critical approach. Events moved so rapidly, so dramatically, that a critical voice, a voice with detachment and distance, was almost impossible. Would Lewis Mumford qualify in these years? Hardly, where the International Style is concerned. Nor would Thomas Tallmadge and George Edgell qualify, nor even Hamlin.

The absence of a body of architectural criticism during this period makes it a particularly difficult one to study. It would seem therefore that we must look to criticism in the field of painting particularly as the source of some of our information about the architectural events which were taking place simultaneously. In the larger international framework of this period we have a movement of "painting toward architecture," the title of a later book by our distinguished chairman.[136] I would submit that the isolation in which some of the more important architectural figures worked resulted from this lack of criticism as well as from the more obvious social and political events which shaped the period in the United States.

Sunday Session
May 10, 1964

....

General Discussion
Led by Henry-Russell Hitchcock

[Hitchcock introduced the session and asked Catherine Bauer Wurster to speak.]

Catherine Bauer Wurster: Well, I was surprised to hear no disagreement with my thesis that after the 1930s the Bauhaus-CIAM (Congrès Internationaux d'Architecture Moderne) line made no real contributions to the rationale for housing and city planning. In fact, some people—including Mrs. Moholy-Nagy— seem even to doubt that the internationalists *did* make a major contribution in the late 1920s and early 1930s. I also claimed that there has been more progress in rational design and in developing a suitable modern vernacular in the areas where architects were less strongly influenced by the great technocratic prima donnas, notably the Scandinavian countries and northern California.

Already in the Stockholm Exposition of 1930, recognized by another speaker as one of the landmarks of modern design, there was a fresh and undogmatic realism—or humanism—which presaged Scandinavia's whole attack on housing and urban problems over the past three decades. In this approach to architecture and civic design, men as different as Alvar Aalto, Sven Markelius, and Steen Eiler Rasmussen have had more in common with each other than with the CIAM leaders. And there was an affinity from the start between the Scandinavian and Bay Area architects, far beyond their feeling for wood. In their houses, schools, and shopping centers, the Californians created a vernacular which was only "regional" in the sense that it suited the climate and the way of life.

Of course, the Scandinavians build tight cities, even in the suburbs. And Mr. Scully was right that the modern architecture of the 1930s in America was largely suburban, whether in California or New England. Only since World War II have there been major opportunities to design high-density or monumental types of developments, but that will have to be the subject of another conference.

But don't forget that the future of the traditional city is an open question. The nostalgia for tight, old-fashioned "urbanity," which Mr. Scully evinced so eloquently, is prevalent among architects and planners, even in southern California. But the way-out urban thinkers are now predicting that communications technology will make an even wider dispersal the inevitable and suitable pattern of the future. To them Los Angeles is the most important and prophetic community, however crude its logic thus far. I think there are fallacies in their arguments and believe there are other alternatives than these polar extremes, but "sprawl" cannot be scorned away. In the history of projective urban ideas, Broadacre City [*figure 88*] is far more significant than La Ville Radieuse. Moreover, Le Corbusier himself later produced a scheme much closer to Wright's, however misplaced in its geographic location. The Chandigarh plan is very dispersed, and this is crazy in India where almost everyone has to walk or bike those long, hot distances. In California, however, it would not be crazy at all. Those scattered sculptural monuments, so vast in scale, might fit very well into the Los Angeles region, where they would be mainly viewed from freeways at 70 miles per hour.

[*Sibyl Moholy-Nagy asked why America never took to the medium-rise block developed in Holland and Scandinavia but clung instead to the small, individual Siedlungshaus.*]

Bauer Wurster: Well, we always go to extremes, I guess. On the one hand, we have promoted individual homes on larger and larger lots; on the other, high-rise and higher-rise apartments, although in both cases it would often have been both cheaper and more suitable to have built row houses or walk-up flats. There is some fresh interest in "town houses" now, I am happy to say, but tall buildings have been overpromoted as much by architects as by commercial interests. Largely owing to Bauhaus-Le Corbusier influence, every group of architectural students still goes through a period of mystical addiction to skyscrapers. This technocratic hangover is one reason that most redevelopment projects are much too dense.

Colin St. John Wilson: I think it is quite clear that the high-rise building has a considerable symbolic significance. We know now that it has not got very much to do with density, and I still do find students who feel that they are only taking housing seriously if they do a high-rise building. I am not saying that there are not other reasons for which one would do one, but there is this kind of carry-on of an idea. Well, I found that if you are working on housing you almost have to work against the grain with this idea because it has its momentum.

Henry-Russell Hitchcock: There is one rather general comment that I would like to make about the 1920s and the 1930s. It seems to me that the architects in whom, on the whole, we are most interested in the 1920s thought for the future, they lived in the future, they had very little interest in the present. Partly this was because they had very little place in the present. One of the changes — one of the major changes — that occurred in the 1930s, it seems to me, was that architecture literally did come to some kind of terms with the then-present. Some of the things that we find unexciting or dull or *détente*-like are in fact due to this shift from designing "cities for 3,000,000" that, at the time, it seemed extremely unlikely would ever be built, and coming — in the case of Asplund in Sweden, for example — to actually design and execute a complete exposition. If you think back to 1925, the Pavillon de l'Esprit Nouveau [*figure 56*], which seems to us such a major historical thing, was hidden away behind the Grand Palais; and I, at least, among the visitors, never found it. That seems to me one of the differences that was really basic. But for that very reason perhaps — because the buildings of the 1930s generally seemed less seminal, less *urformend* than those of the 1920s — we tend perhaps to underrate them.

[*John M. Jacobus noted that there had been a lack of comment on specific build-ings and asked the symposium to agree on a list of five or six buildings that could unqualifiedly be called "masterpieces" of the 1930s and that had contributed posi-tively to the decade itself. Elizabeth Mock Kassler suggested Frank Lloyd Wright's Taliesin West (figure 110). Péter Serényi suggested, from Le Corbusier's work, the last version of the apartment house in Algiers of 1938–9. Hitchcock added the Ministry of Education in Rio, begun in 1937 by Lucio Costa, Oscar Niemeyer,*]

and others, and the work of Wright. He also noted that the decade opened with
Howe and Lescaze's Philadelphia Savings Fund Society Building (PSFS, figure 87)
in Philadelphia. William H. Jordy suggested Raymond Hood's Rockefeller Center
(figure 105) and Alvar Aalto's Sunila (figure 111).

*   Hitchcock then called on Alfred H. Barr, Jr., who was associated with the*
Museum of Modern Art in the 1930s, to speak.]

Alfred H. Barr, Jr.: Russell, I really came to listen. I would like to suggest
that the time that I might take, or waste, should be given to this question, as I
think it is extraordinarily interesting: some discussion or argument about the
half-dozen buildings of the 1930s which now seem to us in the 1960s to be of
prime importance.

[Hitchcock referred to Jordy's paper on the International Style, which included
Giuseppe Terragni's Casa del Fascio (later, del Popolo) in Como (figure 100),
two of Marcel Breuer buildings, Aalto's Sunila, his Villa Mairea (figure 112), Erich
Mendelsohn's work in Jerusalem, the Peter Jones Department Store in London (figure
107), the Suresnes open-air school (figure 95), and the Cité de la Muette (figure 89),
which Hitchcock thought was one of the major arguments against high-rise housing.
He added the Bergpolder Apartments by Brinkman & Van der Vlugt in Rotterdam
(figure 92), Richard Neutra's John Nicolas Brown House on Fishers Island (figure
99), his Bell School (figure 97), Philip Goodwin's Museum of Modern Art in New York
(figure 114), and some factories by Albert Kahn (figure 108). He then called upon
Moholy-Nagy.]

Sibyl Moholy-Nagy: I took the idea that we were going to speak about the
1930s very seriously, and concentrated on it. I am more interested in the general
mood of that time and the psychological basis of it. I know this is an un-
American activity, but I wanted to make a statement in defense of negativism
and levity.[137] There is something in seeing a historical conclusion. Conclusions
are as important as new beginnings, and I think it is a rather labored affair to
try now to make a virtue out of the 1930s, while in reality, as I tried to point out
yesterday, it was the conclusion of a long development. It really put to an end a
magnificent impetus that had started, as I see it, with the cast-iron revolution
of the 1850s and 1860s. Plato says at one point, "A new beginning is like a God
saving all things." For me the new beginning came after World War II. I see
there a potentially positive beginning—in contrast to many people who think
that all we are doing today is bad. This new beginning was only possible because the 1930s had finished off so much. It is—and I always want to make clear
again that Wright and Le Corbusier, being giants or geniuses, are not within
this discussion—it is important for the students and the younger men who
are here to see the overall level of the period. I have brought slides with me—I
hadn't wanted to show them yesterday because I felt it was perhaps too negative
to show these few comparisons I have, but by now I feel that we really should
look the facts in the face and see what actually happened in the 1930s. We
shouldn't gloss over Mies's desperate attempts to play up to National Socialism;
we shouldn't gloss over the fact that people like Breuer and Mendelsohn and
others absolutely collapsed in their architectural imagination once they were
no longer on native ground. And I think this is now something which is negative or, as Mr. Fitch said, open to levity, but I think we should see tragedies
when they occur, and drama occurs in architecture as well as in human life.

For me the 1930s — perhaps because I was very much involved in this — were a great tragedy from every standpoint, but quite particularly from an architectural standpoint.

If I may, I will show you a few paired slides and make a few comments on them, and perhaps this will bring out the following point: that a conclusion is something in the nature of organic life, just as death is necessary for birth. What we have in one case is Leendert van der Vlugt's Gewerbeschule (Trade School) in Holland [*figure 49*] and in the other, the Bauhaus building, which is four years later. Now the point I tried to make — this idea of the concrete band and glass curtains, in a modulation of bays that is very strongly influenced by the Werkbund — is that the Bauhaus building was *not* a new beginning but a rather interesting conclusion to a development that had started long before.

We are apt to forget this extraordinary talent of the 1920s, also outside of Germany. I remember that after the last meeting we had here two years ago I felt very badly that, instead of speaking on Germany, I had not concentrated on the short flowering of Holland. Between 1915 and 1925, Holland was incredibly fruitful in ideas, which were obscured by the strong publicity given the Germans by Sigfried Giedion. But when you look at Mies van der Rohe's apartments in the early 1920s and then Michel de Klerk's *Apartmenthäuser* in Amsterdam, you see quite clearly that a medium was developed which needed refinement, or was refined but which, in its origins, was very strongly influenced by the previous decades.

In another case, you have remarks by Mies about the tremendous influence of Wright on the German group, which is visible in their works but which is again obscured by historians. It is interesting to observe the role which Giedion has played with his book; its influence is still unbelievably strong today. Anything that Giedion chronicled has been accepted by the next generation of students, and Giedion's complete neglect of the cross-influence between Wright and Germany, and between Holland and Germany, has put the Germans into a position of original creators, but it just "ain't so." The Coonley Playhouse is one of the most amazing examples of space penetration [*figure 18*]. We are today very apt to think of the Coonley House as only the main building, but for me this building has a space-form continuity which anticipates something that only now is actually coming into its full force. And the immediate influence of Wright on Mies is completely clear in the Barcelona Pavilion [*figure 81*]. There is almost an emulation of Wright's space penetration, of the horizontal, of the movement of light and shadow, which by no means, I think, takes anything away from the talent of Mies at that time. One simply must not forget that America was not a no-man's-land to which the new Eden was borne. This has been completely and utterly faked in architectural history. If you compare the plans of the Robie House by Wright [*figure 8*] and the Gericke House by Mies, you have once again the very strong idea of the barely defined continuity of space which comes alive only in the movement of the inhabitant. It is no longer an aesthetic succession of unified rooms but the dynamic movement of the occupant that actually creates the space experience. And when you think of the fact that Mr. Wright was able in 1908 to persuade a bicycle manufacturer in Chicago to finance a plan of such absolutely scandalous novelty, this is for me infinitely greater than almost anything that was later done in Europe.

Take Le Corbusier's Villa Savoye [*figure 78 a*] and Mies's Tugendhat plans. What I wanted to say, what I had pointed out yesterday, was the fact that gradually the paring down of academic traditions created a sort of universal aspect.

If you compare the plans, which are from almost the same time, you will see in the emphasized space-experience, the turning, the changed view, what Corbusier was later to formulate as "space is the foot that walks, the eye that sees, and the head that turns." This is the vocabulary that had been developed at that time.

Here is a juxtaposition of the Tugendhat House and the House on the Rupenhorn by Mendelsohn. You know, Mendelsohn had the unspeakably bad luck of not being mentioned by Mr. Giedion. He is completely left out of *Space, Time and Architecture*, which at that time, and well into the 1950s, was absolutely synonymous with a historical death sentence. I still have today a very difficult time convincing my students that it might be worthwhile to look up Mendelsohn's work in the 1920s, although it is *not* mentioned in Giedion; and if Giedion ever comes out in paperback, that will finish up poor Mendelsohn. But you see here that within the period — the Tugendhat House of 1930 and the House on the Rupenhorn of 1929 — this subtractive vocabulary, this vocabulary that had been started by Charles Voysey and continued by Adolf Loos, has now reached its ultimate character. If you see the Tugendhat House without the sunshades down, these are almost interchangeable elevations.

Next we come to the extraordinary influence of Le Corbusier. It is quite clear that the Dolderthal houses by the Roths and Breuer [*figure 93*] would not have been possible without the two houses by Le Corbusier at the Weissenhof. I do not think that either the Roths or Breuer would have ever thought of their two buildings without the prototypes of the Weissenhof. But again one must look at this from the standpoint that it is a final subtraction, that after the Weissenhof houses you can vary to a certain extent the height, or the proportion of the row windows, but this is the final vocabulary that can no longer be pared down any further.

Now for me the great tragedy of Mendelsohn is the fact that he was a dreamer of architectural forms that were only to be realized thirty or forty years later by others. There is a stunning and almost eerie similarity in the role played by Louis I. Kahn and Mendelsohn. Both of them are dreamers of architecture who, in one way or another, are incapable of translating their visions full force into reality. This analogy between Mendelsohn's architectural sketch and Eero Saarinen's Dulles Airport is for me not a detrimental statement about the latter. (I would be far from accusing Saarinen, even if he had been conscious of the adaptation.) It is amazing that a man like Mendelsohn, who had these fantastic visions, had such a terrible struggle in his younger years to translate them into reality. This is the case of his two most publicized buildings, the Schocken Store and the Hat Factory in Luckenwalde. These are characteristic aspects of a man who struggled from a lofty vision into the reality of the third dimension. But at least in this case, part of his vision was realized. And then you take this man after his emigration, and you see him on alien ground, and what you get is an unbelievable downward curve into banality. The whole tragedy of the diaspora for me is completely realized in these two buildings: one is the pavilion on the English seaside which he did together with Serge Chermayeff, and the other the Weizmann House near Tel Aviv. They are just outright bad buildings from every standpoint and seem not to be related in any form to anything he had tried to achieve earlier.

And this goes for most of the other buildings of the 1930s. I said yesterday that the diaspora has a darkly tragic and a cynically comic side. This idea seems illustrated in two buildings: a project by Breuer and F. R. S. Yorke for a hotel on the English seaside, and the Papworth scheme by Walter Gropius and Maxwell Fry. Both of them look like the work of people who have lost all the certainty of designing for their native ground.

Now Mies van der Rohe is a case which I really think is not quite understood here, and I think by now these thirty years which have passed make it possible to speak without too much bitterness about this. When he accepted in July 1933, after the coming to power of Hitler, the commission for the Reichsbank, he was a traitor to all of us and a traitor to everything we had fought for. He signed at that time a patriotic appeal which Paul Schultze-Naumburg, as commissar, had made to the artists, writers, and architects of Germany to put their forces behind National Socialism. I would say that, of the leading group of the Bauhaus people, Mies was the only one who signed. And he accepted this commission. This was a terrible stab in the back for us, and we mustn't forget that in 1933 there was still a great hope that Hitler might not stay, that a concerted effort might liquidate the Hitler movement—after all, it was the eleventh government we had had since 1918. And so it was hard to realize at that time that this *was* going to stay. Look at his Krefeld Silk Factory; unfortunately I didn't bring the slides with me, but there are several government buildings in Washington of the same kind. The more Mies tried to identify himself with the Nazi government by doing the Krefeld Silk Factory, which was a state-subsidized enterprise, the more he identified himself with a type of architecture that was to be acceptable to what Giedion, in another desperate attempt at contemporaneity, called "the new monumentality." And it was for me yesterday a most extraordinary experience to see Mies's first scheme for Illinois Institute of Technology in 1938 [*figure 116*] shown as something positive. I think it is ghastly. It is one of the most brutal, symmetrical, and lumpish plans I can imagine, and I find it amazingly like the plan of the Krefeld factory. If you look at the two plans, if you will think of them in three dimensions, you will see an extraordinary resemblance between the two. And this in itself, I think, makes Mies's conversion during the war years the more amazing and the more extraordinary.

Now the America to which these people came was certainly one of the most bewildered and befuddled architectural scenes you can imagine. There is a remark in the *Architectural Record* of 1937 which says, "We are baffled by the so-called new Soviet architecture which beginning in 1932 bears the stamp of genuine Fascism. Could it be that Bolshevism and Fascism have much in common in their doctrines?" And then, of course, you see the Ministry of Foreign Affairs in Moscow and, lo and behold, the New York Municipal Building, by McKim, Mead & White. There is a peculiar ideological confusion here which I think is very characteristic of the tremendous opportunity missed by the diaspora architects to make a clear statement. Because the new architecture needed quite clearly to make a physical imprint, to show that it was capable of expressing a particular progressive doctrine. With some hesitation, I want to recall to you Norman Mailer's statement in the *Architectural Forum* of last month about the identity of totalitarianism in capitalist countries and socialist countries, which I think comes out very well in these particular examples of a Russian hotel and an American city hall.[138]

[*Collins, returning at Hitchcock's suggestion to the matter of individual "masterpieces" of the period, called attention to the Zarzuela Stadium near Madrid, by Eduardo Torroja (figure 94). He pointed out that, although seemingly outside the mainstream of European "modern" in its day, the building has always intrigued engineers, and it holds particular interest in our time for the architect who is in search of new forms" in both cases because of its dramatic employment of surface-resistant structures. Hitchcock expressed his surprise that Torroja and Pier Luigi Nervi were both passed over in the Saturday papers. He pointed out that Nervi was already a mature constructor in the 1920s and singled out his work at Orbetello as an example (figure 118). Jacobus felt that the Zarzuela Hippodrome was a test of alternatives, since it could be seen either as a benign connector between the earlier twentieth century and the present, without particular meaning for the 1930s, or as a work fundamental to the 1930s.]*

George R. Collins: It is part of the scattered and less "central" tradition of modern architecture that is illustrated in our book *Architecture of Fantasy*. It did not appear in the book, but it is of that character, and it may mean more now than it did to its contemporaries, as you suggest. But I was trying to indicate, both today and Saturday, that it was in its own historical tradition, in Spain at least, where a tradition of intuitive design in thin-shell forms had grown up in the nineteenth century, owing in part to a scarcity of the structural metals that were being employed by more technologically developed nations.

[Moholy-Nagy, Hitchcock, and Scully made some remarks about Louis I. Kahn and his ability to translate his visions into material form, to which Moholy-Nagy had referred. Scully defended Kahn, saying that major works of his, such as the First Unitarian Church in Rochester and the Salk Institute, were now underway and would soon bear witness to the realities.

Hitchcock regretted the lack of emphasis on Holland in the symposium and noted the absence of a major totalitarian reaction there in the 1930s. Moholy-Nagy said that after 1933 Holland was already a National-Socialist country to all intents and purposes. Hitchcock asked Theodore M. Brown to speak on Holland.]

Theodore M. Brown: I don't know the political situation in Holland intimately at all. I have some idea of what happened in architecture, and it looks rather sad, as has been indicated. Here are a few of the facts that should be kept in mind: to begin with, De Stijl vaporized in 1931. Theo van Doesburg died, and De Stijl was Van Doesburg, and Van Doesburg was De Stijl. He had some sort of asthmatic condition, and suddenly he collapsed at that point. The next thing that ended — also in 1931 — was the Amsterdam School, built around *Wendingen* and around Hendrik Wijdeveld. Wijdeveld left Holland and came to the United States, where, he claimed, he gave Wright everything that he had in the 1930s. Then this was also the time of the beginning of something else: a group of architects that called itself "Reconstruction," that built itself around a periodical called *De 8 en Opbouw*. They picked up on the materialistic aspects of the 1920s and the rather simple-minded notion of functionalism. They kept playing it in the 1930s as much as they could. A new, younger generation came in at that point — J. H. van den Broek, who is now Van den Broek and Bakema, and Willem van Tijen; Leendert van der Vlugt from the early period, Benjamin Merkelbach, and others were grouped with them; some of them worked on into the 1940s. Gerrit Rietveld, I think, looks rather sad in the 1930s. He never reached the level that he did in the 1920s. He did some apartments, a few small houses, and things of that sort.

On the positive side, of course, there was the high-rise housing in the late 1930s with Van Tijen, Van der Vlugt, and that crew; it seemed to be a materialization of the Bauhaus-y notion of the 1920s, as far as I can see. A couple of small, very high quality things could be cited from the 1930s: municipal works such as bridges that one still sees driving through the countryside, and clean reinforced-concrete and steel bridges—most of them done during the 1930s under a municipal program. They also produced the street telephone—those small glass boxes now found everywhere.

Oud never was a member of De Stijl, even though technically he was in at the beginning; he left in 1921, and during the 1930s he returned to an early nineteenth-century, Amsterdam School, decorative, "let's get back to the good old days" proposition. He was a very sad man at the end of his life. He sat in his little office, misunderstood; the world didn't understand his greatness, and he waited for someone to come along and describe his greatness. He died last year.

Then also during the 1930s there was a kind of formal reaction against the International Style, the School of Delft, led by Grandpré Molière. This was a formal, "let's get back to the farmhouse" type of thing, and I suspect that it could be linked to the political movement of the decade. I think in general, even though I don't see [an explicit manifestation of] the political situation, there was a quality of fear. The Dutch knew what was happening in Germany, I suspect; the things that were happening in Germany were filtering into Holland. There was definitely a lack of confidence. This is clear from talking to scholars, artists, and other survivors. I think definitely there was a lack of quality after the end of the 1920s.

Adolf K. Placzek: I think that a footnote should be made to Mr. Brown's and Mrs. Moholy-Nagy's statements. There is not only the agony of the diaspora open to the creative artist but also the shame of collaboration. There were a great many who left, but there were also many who stayed and made their skills available to despotic governments. If we list the great buildings of the decade, Terragni's Casa del Fascio *is* one of the great buildings. It was built for what we would consider a rather reprehensible purpose, a Fascist Party home. Almost sadder than the genius broken from his native context is the genius coming to terms with political reaction. Mies did not succeed at it. Others did, particularly in Italy, where Fascism was far less unlivable than Nazism in Germany. Nervi certainly did a great deal of work for the Fascist regime. In Germany there was Paul Bonatz, certainly an architect of stature, and less actively Peter Behrens.

This, of course, cuts across all fields. One of the greatest German writers of the time was Gerhart Hauptmann, and he collaborated; so did the greatest musician Richard Strauss. This too, is an aspect of the tragic decade.

Colin Rowe: Russell, I think one could also say as a further footnote to the discussion that at the end of the 1930s there did exist a remarkable school of architecture in Warsaw. The products of the school of architecture I have met, not in hundreds, but probably I have met almost a hundred of them. I knew many of them in Liverpool. They were, judging from the way they performed in the 1940s, probably the best-trained people at the end of the 1930s, and I think this Warsaw achievement is something obliterated and forgotten. This goes along with Mr. Placzek's remarks about Terragni, with whom, of course, one would associate Cesare Cattaneo and the apartment houses at Cernobbio [*figure 113*], which surely were one of the most remarkable achievements of the 1930s.

[*Hitchcock directed the discussion to America and asked Elizabeth Mock Kassler if she would care to name some outstanding individual buildings.*]

Elizabeth Mock Kassler: I cannot think offhand of anything that could be compared in quality, in lasting interest, to the work of Wright and Le Corbusier. Looking more at *Built in U.S.A., 1932–44* when I get home, I may find something better than I remember, but I don't think so.

Barr: She did say "Wright," but so low that no one could hear it.

Kassler: Yes, I always say "Wright."

Rowe: I would identify myself with Mrs. Moholy-Nagy and with Mr. Wilson's remarks of yesterday. I did feel yesterday that I was rather being an observer of a number of people perhaps taking the inventory of a deceased's estate. And I also felt there were a great many people, let's say, not seeing the wood for the trees. I thought that all the exotic trees in a forest were being itemized; but I felt, to some extent, the animating principle of the forest was not being discriminated, not being observed. This depressed me a little. I identified very strongly when Mr. Wilson made his remarks about architecture being a projection of ideas into building and a projection of a body of ideas into building. I identified when Mrs. Moholy-Nagy was speaking about the emotional tone of an era and its psychological aura. I think that my problem was that I was thinking of the period as a kind of amateur iconographer, and that most people were looking at it from the point of view of connoisseurs. I remain interested in what might have been the vital principle of the 1930s, what might have been the ideas which made things tick, and one could either be infinitely excited about this, or one could be very laconic. In the most laconic way I think one could insist that there was somewhere some rapport between modern architecture and millennial politics, or if you like between modern architecture and Marxism. I think one can make no sense of the 1930s without bringing into the picture something of this relationship. Now it is inevitable because of the climate of the present time that this sort of thing is going to be evaded. It is extremely difficult and unpleasant to deal with this sort of matter. But as one meets the relics of the 1930s, as one sees them around, as one smells the atmosphere which they breathe, one does sense the corpus of ideas to which they react. And one recognizes that throughout the 1930s there is a millennium-oriented personality which in its most extreme cases does become Marxist. Now one of the meanings of modern architecture in the 1930s — and in the 1920s too, for that matter — is surely that it is somehow an affirmation of a millennial condition which is assumedly going to occur. This explains why architects could get so extravagantly steamed up and obsessed, and why they could simultaneously embrace quite contradictory ideas. I am really interested, like Mr. Wilson (who I hope will help me out at this stage), in the matter of the architecture of this period as a projection of ideas. What I am really trying to do, Mr. Hitchcock, is inject into your territory a method which Mr. Wittkower used for the Renaissance. He produced the idea of the Renaissance as the projection of the

Platonic cosmos, and one is convinced that the 1920s and the 1930s, to be really alive, have to be treated in some way or other like this.

[Hitchcock pointed out that Rudolf Wittkower did not confine his image to one decade and asked him to comment.]

Rudolf Wittkower: Maybe I can bring the discussion back to a more easily negotiable problem. I found in yesterday's talks a certain, what I may call, easy use of terminology. For instance, I found that the term "neoclassicism" was used for the dictatorial type of architecture of the 1930s as well as for anything that looked vaguely symmetrical. We would therefore have in the 1930s the extraordinary phenomenon of the dichotomy between two types of classicism: that derived from the Bauhaus in a broad sense and that of the "dictatorial" reaction. I don't think that it is permissible to call both Le Corbusier or Mies and Hitler-architecture "neoclassical." Anything that did not appear symmetrical was called—again very loosely—"folk architecture" (and not, for instance, "baroque," because everyone knows that baroque is also symmetrical). Symmetry itself is, to my mind, not necessarily a sign of classical or neoclassical architecture. The main characteristic of any form of classical art and architecture is, it seems to me, anthropometry—human measure, that is—projected into the architecture; and perhaps the only modern architect who in that sense can be called a "classical" architect is Le Corbusier, because he has a very intense feeling for the anthropometric element in architecture. I think we might possibly get a little further with our statements about the 1930s by clarifying the use of our critical terms. This is one of the points that occurred to me while listening to you.

I want to add a remark to the discussion of the diaspora architects. We have heard very interesting comments, and surely Mrs. Moholy-Nagy's demonstration was extremely revealing. But I think it worthwhile investigating a little further as to what changes architects were exposed to who, as Mrs. Moholy-Nagy said, experienced the tragedy of people divorced from their native soil. Why did their architecture deteriorate? How would a man like Mendelsohn have developed if he had stayed in Germany? Would his development have gone in a different direction? This is a difficult question to answer. But we can say that the diaspora may lead to a psychological disturbance on very many levels (and this is true of some of us who have been going through the experience without being creative artists). As you know, the diaspora is not a phenomenon of our own days; it is a phenomenon that has existed throughout history, and one should attempt to explore the problem on as broad a basis as possible. In our particular context, it seems to me that the architects who emigrated from Germany and went first to England—as many of them did—and then to the United States had to cope with a specific set of problems, apart from the psychological difficulties of adjustment to an entirely new way of life. In terms of the architecture of the 1930s, many of the architects working in Germany were closely associated with the Weimar Republic. They were handling projects of a social nature, and I think the most impressive work done in Germany (and also in Holland) in the 1920s and 1930s concerned the planning of middle-class and lower-class living quarters. When these people came over here they were faced with completely new tasks: monumental buildings, skyscrapers, and the like—problems which had meant little to them before and which they had to tackle without the human background of the German social ambiance. The attitude of the diaspora architects is surely a question of immense importance in the exploration of the architecture of the 1930s. This is all I wanted to say at the moment.

Hitchcock: Sometime in the first year or two after Gropius was in Cambridge, the Institute of Contemporary Art (ICA) in Boston got Dean Hudnut to organize a series of lectures on high buildings. At that point, of course, no skyscraper had been built for five or six years, and many people thought the Empire State Building was the end, that high buildings were over. But we were all aware that among the theoretical proponents of high buildings, though not necessarily at that point terribly high buildings, was Gropius. So among the people who were asked to contribute lectures to this series at the ICA was Gropius. His reply was that he would be pleased to speak at a business luncheon to bankers and real estate men but he couldn't be bothered to speak in a museum. Which showed, of course, a curious misunderstanding of the American world, where I think Mr. Barr and I would say that what went on at the Museum of Modern Art probably had a lot more to do with influencing bankers and real estate men than anything they ever heard at business luncheons.

Vincent J. Scully, Jr.: I just want to say one word to that question of terminology because I think it is an important one and because I did use the terms "neoclassic" and "classicism" yesterday. You recall that I started by questioning the utility of considering "classic" and "romantic" as dichotomies in considering modern architecture, as was done over and over again, especially by people like Walter Curt Behrendt and Bruno Zevi. But I did use the term "neoclassicism" later by projection to Mies's late work and to Johnson's work and to the whole movement of the 1950s in which they play a very important part.

Wittkower: I noticed that in various talks the terminology was rather loose, and of course terminology may not appear terribly important; but if we really want to come to grips with certain problems just of the 1930s we can't use the same *differentiae* for Hitler-architecture and for Mies. It just doesn't work.

Barr: Just to create some further confusion, it seems to me that there is a connection between the admiration that both Mies and Hitler had for Karl Friedrich Schinkel in this area of neoclassicism. It is hard to find a general word of a historical nature other than "neoclassic" to apply to certain works of Mies and of Le Corbusier in the early 1930s.

Hitchcock: Well, consider the confusion in Nazi architectural doctrine: there were many purposes for which something *heimatkundlich*, something "folkish," was wanted. The relation to that of the extremely "unfolkish" and, one would have said arbitrarily, "un-Nordic" architecture of Schinkel is certainly very confused. My own conclusion is that it is rather pointless to look for automatic connections between political movements and architecture. There is the amusing cartoon by Osbert Lancaster of two identical facades, identical, that is, except that one has Nazi eagles and the other has the hammer and sickle. He says one is Soviet architecture and the other is Nazi architecture. But he could perfectly well have put in a third sketch of what was then the new State Department in Washington, with the American eagle on it, and said that that was the architecture of "free enterprise," or capitalism, or whatever you like.

In other words, my simple suggestion would be merely to say that it is all the monumental architecture of bureaucracy; it doesn't make much difference what the politics of the builders are, the results are much the same.

Placzek: Do you think perhaps the three have one thing in common, which is their attempt to overpower by mass?

Barr: Well, overpower by order, too, of the most obvious sort. Returning to Mies, there is a conflict between classicism and another strong influence on his work: Van Doesburg. Mies struggled between Schinkel and Van Doesburg, putting one on the inside and one on the outside.

[Hitchcock remarked, with respect to the connotational images of architecture, that the most advanced European architecture before the war was considered very un-American, but that after the war all modern architecture began to be considered American.]

Eduard F. Sekler: This obviously seems to me very closely related to what I tried to say yesterday about the difficulty we had in keeping historical time and topical or egocentric time separate. You notice how you repeatedly have to call back our discussion to the 1930s. Everybody gets carried away and presently we are speaking about what is happening now. And I don't think—and this is the source of the trouble of which Mr. Wittkower spoke—that you can expect to have, with what touches us so directly in our own work and in what we can criticize now, the kind of careful methodological clarity of diction which you have for your historical materials where it has been worked out over a long period. So there is one area where confusion can easily occur, and where the feelings pretty soon run high, because unwittingly you keep slipping from one into the other. At one moment you are the historian trying to be as absolutely impartial as you can, and then, of course, you are carried over into what touches you very directly. Now, a good example for this came to my mind trying to think of the tricky problem of what is an end and what is a beginning. Recent years have seen the reevaluation of art nouveau and the Jugendstil, which I can still remember as a thing that was scorned; we wouldn't deign to look at it. And I remember the statement of Adolf Loos writing about it when it was quite new, in 1898, when he said, "We have a new decorative art.... The old styles are dead, *viva* the new style! And yet one cannot be glad of it. It is not our style.... It almost appears at present as if Asia has given us the last remainder of its very own strength. For we already had to reach back into the most distant Orient, to Japan and Polynesia." [139] Fifty or sixty years later, we tend not to agree with Loos any more, nor with people who at that time welcomed art nouveau as the true beginning of a new era. We see it in a completely different historical perspective.

Finally, I want to come back to a man who was fortunately mentioned several times and who for me reigns very high in the 1930s—who for me has produced one of the few timeless buildings of that period—and that is Gunnar Asplund. I believe the Woodland Crematorium in Stockholm is built around 1939 [*figure 117*]; it was just finished at the beginning of the war. And it is for me a very moving building; it sums up a great deal, and it can also be understood only as an expression of principles that Asplund himself formulated for the Stockholm exhibition of 1930, in a manifesto that seems to me really to bring into focus all that was positive in the 1930s. It was his *Acceptera* (We Must Accept), which he wrote with several others. In it they explain where they saw the genuine challenge of their time and the principles for a new architecture. They sum it up in these words:

> WE MUST ACCEPT the existing reality—only in this way have we any hope of controlling it, of prevailing over it to modify it and create a culture which is a flexible instrument in our lives. We have no need for the outgrown forms of an ancient culture to uphold our self-respect. We cannot slip out of our own time into the past. Neither can we spring over something which is difficult and unclear into a utopian future. We can do nothing else but look at reality directly and accept it in order to control it.[140]

I think this was the only real *positive* attitude wherever it was followed, and it is one which to me has a timeless quality; this is what Le Corbusier speaks about when he says, "There is no beginning and no end, and only one answer—architecture and planning."

[Moholy-Nagy insisted that the political movements of the time must be interpreted in context or one gets a non-historical attitude toward architecture.]

Placzek: Particularly in regard to Mr. Sekler's remarks and to Mr. Stern's talk yesterday, it is rather significant how much trouble we had to agree on a take-off date. Mr. Stern argued that architecturally 1927 was far more decisive than 1929. This brings up a point of methodology. How should art historians properly date—in decades, or even centuries? Should we follow historical events of sometimes cataclysmic importance? These are rarely immediately followed by equally dramatic breaks in style. Undoubtedly the collapse of the German and the American economies in 1929 was such an event. Naturally, nothing equally drastic happened in architecture, nothing seemed to collapse, but I still think it is a valid date for a new era—if there is any reality, any principle behind architecture at all. This, of course, is again a problem which extends to all history writing or history arranging. Chopping off the head of a mediocre French king did not immediately change French architecture. Yet that was the end of an era in architecture too, and a new one began. Mr. Wittkower began his Pelican volume on art and architecture in Italy not with stylistic analysis but with the statement that with the Sack of Rome in 1527 an intensely optimistic epoch came to end. The same words, almost, could be used for 1929.

Moholy-Nagy: But you can only see that in retrospect. The Fall of Rome in 476 meant nothing to the Romans or to anybody there, but it is to us still a fantastic beginning. So I think that our whole enterprise here, speaking in decades, is merely a convenience, basically meaningless except that it forces us to a certain form.

Placzek: It is, of course, equally difficult to write *finis* under an era. Mr. Hitchcock's difficulty in finding a terminal date for his Pelican volume is an example. Was it 1949? Or 1950? The second edition has pushed it a little further, but the methodological question mark remains.

Hitchcock: But I tried to avoid that by stopping it roughly in 1955 and writing an epilogue.

[Hitchcock then asked H. Allen Brooks, as president of the Society of Architectural Historians, for his comments.]

H. Allen Brooks: Well, one thing that I have noted is that the patron or client, except where he may be the State, has not figured in our discussions. It seems to me that he should. Of the art nouveau we often say that its rapid end came about because the client lost interest in these forms. The same was certainly true in Chicago. Sullivan lost his patronage, as Wright and his contemporaries later lost their clients. This question should also be asked of the 1930s. If indeed the International Style was international, and not destroyed by its uprootings, or by the change of government and program in Germany, how critical or how important was the patronage, or lack of patronage, to the production of these architects' work in the 1930s and thereafter?

Robert A. M. Stern: Well, in America, if we can develop Mr. Scully's thesis, the single house, of course, becomes the typical case; the individual client becomes most important. It is not a social phenomenon at all. It is an individual client—often the rich and, if not, the upper middle class—that one thinks of in connection with Wright's houses in the 1930s and 1940s, as well as those of Gropius, Breuer, William Wurster, and the other leading architects of the period.

[The discussion revolved around Wright's attitude toward his clients: whether his "inexpensive" houses were really so and whether the "intellectual" client was treated in the same manner as the wealthy one. Moholy-Nagy pointed out that Wright at first built for anyone but later in his career largely for the rich. She also noted that he had a "fantastic disregard" for his clients' ability to pay.

Rowe suggested that the background of Wright's clients be investigated, and Wittkower said there was a recent Columbia University doctoral dissertation on the subject.[141]

The discussion turned for a moment to Philadelphia, where it was noted that, despite the generally conservative views of its clients in the 1930s, the decade saw there the first completely modern public housing project (Oscar Stonorov and Alfred Kastner's Carl Mackley Houses [figure 91]), the work of George Howe, and the writings of Catherine Bauer Wurster.

Hitchcock then asked Stanford Anderson to comment on Peter Behrens.]

Stanford Anderson: I could say something about Behrens, but I don't think that he is very important for the period under discussion. I would have to document a lot of dreary facts from the 1920s and 1930s about Behrens's proud turn toward Nazism and about many disparate buildings. He was a man who always worked in intricate ways and was hard to understand. So I don't think that a brief discussion of Behrens's late work would contribute very much to an understanding of what was most interesting in the 1930s. And finally, what I wanted to say today, if I had a chance, has been very well stated by Mr. Rowe, so the notes I made over breakfast I think can now be passed by.

[Hitchcock then asked Kassler to speak.]

Kassler: I am convinced that the International Style, as the dominant movement of the 1930s, produced no buildings of intrinsic value in this country. And I also now begin to question whether it really was very important in the development of our architecture. The work that is being done today that is really significant seems to stem from a certain aspect of Le Corbusier that had nothing to do with the International Style, or from Frank Lloyd Wright. The International Style has contributed very little.

[Hitchcock asked Dean Kenneth Smith to comment.]

Kenneth A. Smith: I am not a historian, but I would like to add two footnotes, the first to Carroll Meeks's remarks about education. I was brought here when Dean Hudnut left, and we in those first years had very much the benefit of what he planned before he left Columbia. The big change in our school was that we began to teach structures and construction and integrate them with design. The second footnote is to Mr. Fitch's remark about what was going on in the technical literature. I went to England in 1937 because I wanted to see what was happening. I didn't feel there was much in America, whereas things could be seen very quickly there. What I came back with was the sense of a tremendous movement in use of structure and techniques, in comparison with what we were doing: buildings like the Finsbury Health Centre by the Tecton Group [*figure 109*], with forty-foot spandrel girders in clear spans, are very much a forerunner of things that have been done since. Radiant heating was being used throughout England, but there were only a couple of examples in this country: the British Embassy in Washington, D.C., the Raymond Loewy House, and, I believe a DuPont house. These were all before the war and certainly were more than just ads promising things after the war. Another couple of interesting buildings were not great architecture, but there was Earls Court (1937) [*figure 101*], with tremendous spans bigger than Madison Square Garden, all done in concrete; they didn't have the steel, so they used concrete trusses. There were Sir Owen Williams's factories and a swimming pool with cantilevered trusses, which were to be a forerunner of some of the bicycle-wheel type of auditoriums that have been done by Lev Zetlin and several others.

Hitchcock: It is unfortunate that Peter Collins from McGill is not here because he was going to speak precisely on that matter — the development of concrete in structures in England in the 1930s. I would like to go back to something that actually came up yesterday, but which you probably can straighten us out on, and that is the precise date when Hudnut was here. When did he come and when did he move out to Harvard?

Smith: On the sixteenth of June, I believe, in 1935, and went to Harvard that September. I don't know what his staff was there; my recollection was that he went abroad to get Gropius over in 1936. Hudnut had been here at Columbia as a professor. He was the acting dean for about a year and a half and dean for a year before he resigned and went to Harvard. But he had been a professor of history here for a number of years.

Hitchcock: Alfred, since you were involved, I believe you could tell us just when Hudnut's negotiations which led to the appointment of Gropius took place. Was that in 1936?

Barr: Yes, it was. In the summer of 1936, at the request of Dean Hudnut of Harvard, I called on Gropius in England to ask him whether he would consider an important position at a great American university. Gropius said yes, he would.[142]

[Collins made some closing remarks on behalf of the organizing committee and presented to Hitchcock a letter wishing him a happy birthday, signed by all the participants. The symposium adjourned.]

Notes

1. See esp. Vincent J. Scully, *Modern Architecture: The Architecture of Democracy* (New York: Braziller, 1961), 32–3.

2. Reyner Banham, *Theory and Design in the First Machine Age* (New York: Praeger, 1960), 305. Gropius was also aware of the importance of 1927 in the evolution and establishment of the International Style. In the preface (written at Dessau in July 1927) to the second edition of his book *Internationale Architektur* he said, "Since the appearance of the first edition [in 1925] the modern architecture of the various lands of western culture has followed the line of development indicated by this book with a surprisingly rapid tempo. Then but an idea, it is today a solid fact." Walter Gropius, excerpt from *Internationale Architektur*, tr. Henry-Russell Hitchcock, *Architectural Record* 66, no. 2 (Aug. 1929): 191.

3. See John Ritter, "World Parliament: The League of Nations Competition, 1926," *Architectural Review* 136 (July 1964): 17–28. The problem of the potential for monumental expression within the International Style continued to be obsessive until the early 1950s. Nineteen hundred and forty-eight, a year in which this problem was discussed at two major symposia, was especially important. The first symposium, "What Is Happening to Modern Architecture?," was sponsored by the Museum of Modern Art in New York; for discussion of this symposium, see Vincent J. Scully, Jr., "Doldrums in the Suburbs," MAS 1964, 165–72. The second symposium, "In Search of a New Monumentality," was conducted by the English periodical *Architectural Review*; see "In Search of a New Monumentality," *Architectural Review* 104 (Sept. 1948): 117–28.

4. For a discussion of the significance of Ford's decision, see William Leuchtenburg's excellent survey of the 1920s in America, *The Perils of Prosperity* (Chicago: University of Chicago Press, 1958), 200–1. There is good reason to claim that Ford's Model A was the first car put into production to embody the principles and techniques of industrial design. This rules out much of Banham's elaborate treatment of automobile design at the end of his book *Theory and Design in the First Machine Age*. Surely the Model A and not Harley Earl's La Salle of 1934 was the first car to respond to consumer preferences in the matter of design, and certainly, if we take into account the availability of the Model A—it was a cheap car introduced in a period of prosperity, while the La Salle was a high-priced car introduced in a period of economic depression—as well as the tremendous publicity which accompanied its appearance on the market, the magnitude of its influence gives it a far greater historical role. See Allan Nevins and Frank Ernest Hill, *Ford: Expansion and Challenge, 1915–1933* (New York: Scribner, 1957), ch. 16, "The End of Model T," esp. 418–21, 431–6; and ch. 18, "Model A: A New Era." See also Charles Merz, *And Then Came Ford* (Garden City, N.Y.: Doubleday, 1929), ch. 13, "America on Wheels," esp. 271–86, and ch. 24, "The Mysterious Stranger." Sheldon and Martha Cheney also wrote about the importance of Ford's transition from the Model T to the Model A; see their *Art and the Machine* (New York: McGraw-Hill, 1936), 26–30.

5. See Norman Bel Geddes, *Miracle in the Evening*, ed. William Kelley (Garden City, N.Y.: Doubleday, 1960). According to Kelley's chronology, Bel Geddes "established the profession of industrial designer" in 1927; "that is, Norman Bel Geddes was the first designer of national reputation to surround himself with a staff of specialists and offer industrial design services." [344] The underlying commercial spirit of the industrial design movement in the late 1920s is suggested in Ernest Elmo Calkins's essay "Beauty, the New Business Tool," *Atlantic Monthly* 140 (Aug. 1927): 145–56. Calkins writes that "there is behind all these changes simply the desire to sell. Beauty is introduced into material objects to enhance them in the eyes of the purchaser. The appeal of efficiency alone is nearly ended…. This remarkable turn of the industrial world toward beauty in design and color is not really a new thing. It is merely the size of the movement that is startling." Sheldon and Martha Cheney see the emergence of industrial design as a result of consumer demands for "higher standards of appearance [that] resulted, in 1927, in the artists' being summoned to the factory for service in unfamiliar design fields." *Art and the Machine*, 7, 55. They also corroborate the primacy of Geddes's position. Buckminster Fuller has a good deal to say about the "myth of industrial design" in his recent "spontaneous autobiographical disclosure," *Ideas and Integrities* (Englewood Cliffs, N.J.: Prentice-Hall, 1963), 76–8.

6. Nineteen hundred and twenty-seven is a key date, often repeated, in Fuller's *Ideas and Integrities*, in which he devotes a considerable amount of energy to criticism of the Bauhaus and the International Style; for example, "Many people have asked if the Bauhaus ideas and techniques have had any formative influence on my work. I must answer vigorously that they have not." [9] Robert W. Marks, *The Dymaxion World of Buckminster Fuller* (Carbondale: Southern Illinois University Press, 1960), emphasizes the importance 1927 had in Fuller's career; see pp. 18, 21, 24–5, 27–8. Perhaps the most eloquent and influential exponent of Fuller's position in this matter is Reyner Banham, who concludes his book *Theory and Design in the First Machine Age* with a chapter entitled "Functionalism and Technology" in which he makes frequent reference to Fuller's achievement and includes "something like a flat rebuttal" of the International Style taken from his writings.

7. André Siegfried, *America Comes of Age*, tr. H. H. and Doris Hemming (New York: Harcourt Brace, 1927), 347.

8. Vernon L. Parrington, *Main Currents in American Thought* (New York: Harcourt, Brace, & Co., 1927); Charles and Mary Beard, *The Rise of American Civilization* (New York: Macmillan Co., 1927).

9. For a comprehensive view of precisionism from the period, see *Art in America* 3 (Nov.–Dec. 1960): 30–61. Especially relevant to developments in the late 1920s and to their prevalence in present attitudes toward form in that volume are the articles by Martin Friedman, "The Precisionist View," 31–7, and Vincent Scully, "The Precisionist Strain in American Architecture," 46–53.

10. John W. McCoubrey, *American Tradition in Painting* (New York: Braziller, 1963), 47.

11. George Howe, unpublished talk delivered before the students of the Graduate School of Design, Harvard University, ca. 1954.

12. Henry-Russell Hitchcock, Jr., "The Decline of Architecture," *Hound and Horn* 1, no. 1 (Sept. 1927): 28–35. See also the letter from Charles Crombie and Hitchcock's letter of reply, ibid., 140–4 and 244–5, respectively.

13. Samuel Chamberlain, "In Search of Modernism: Concerning the Dearth of Material in France for the Enquiring Reporter," *American Architect* 131 (Jan. 1927): 71–4.

14. Milton B. Medary, president of the AIA, reflected the apprehension with which the "old guard" greeted the spirit of modernism when, in commenting on "the myriad confusions and complications of twentieth century life [which tend to bewilder men with] the surface manifestations of constantly changing forms," he grudgingly acknowledged that "in literature, in religion, in sculpture and painting and music and drama, as well as in architecture, the world is in revolt." AIA, *Proceedings of the Sixtieth Annual Convention* (Washington, D.C.: Board of Directors of the AIA, 1927), 5–8. George C. Nimmons, a leading architect of industrial buildings, offered the following explanation for the new modernist spirit to a reporter at the convention:

"[T]he demand on the part of the press for a new style of architecture, as they call it...has been very strong and the effect of that has not been so much on the architect, because he knows the causes which produce loose styles of architecture, as upon the client. The client now demands a departure from the old line of work. He wants something new." *American Architect* 131, no. 2522 (June 5, 1927): 701.

15. The impact of this building on the profession (it was awarded the Gold Medal by the Architectural League of New York in 1927) and on the public was enormous. It established its designer, Ralph Walker, at the forefront of the profession; see George H. Allen, "Dynamic Energy and Modernism," *Architectural Forum* 54, no. 5 (May 1931): 609–10. The building's critical notices were enthusiastic.

16. See "The Ziegfeld Theatre, New York," *Architectural Forum* 46, no. 5 (May 1927): 414–6, and pls.

17. See Lawrence Moore, "The Medical Center," *The Arts* 14, no. 5 (Nov. 1928): 284–6.

18. Thomas Tallmadge, *Story of Architecture in America* (New York: W. W. Norton, 1927), ch. 9, "Louis Sullivan and the Lost Cause." By 1936, when Tallmadge brought out a second edition of his book, the complete resurgence of Wright's career and Sullivan's reputation is reflected in Tallmadge's new chapter title, "Louis Sullivan, Parent and Prophet."

19. For a discussion of Wright's difficulties in the late 1920s and early 1930s, see his *An Autobiography* (New York: Longman's, Green & Co., 1932), esp. 271–95. See also Finis Farr, *Frank Lloyd Wright* (New York: Scribner, 1961), esp. ch. 6. In January 1927, Wright's collection of Japanese prints was sold at auction in New York. Taliesin was in the hands of a bank and, in order to protect himself from complete financial ruin, he announced the formation of Frank Lloyd Wright, Inc., which eventually led to the establishment of the Taliesin Fellowship. Wright's only executed commission for the year—and his first since 1924—was "Greyston," the Darwin D. Martin House at Derby, New York.

20. Kocher became managing editor of the *Record* in August 1927, but the new format did not appear until January 1928. See Michael A. Mikkelsen, "A Word about the New Format," *Architectural Record* 63, no. 1 (Jan. 1928): 1–2. *The Architectural Forum* and the *American Architect* also modernized their formats in January 1928, but neither carried their reforms over into their editorial policies with the fervor and intelligence that marked the *Record's* efforts in the period 1927–32.

21. S. and M. Cheney, *Art and the Machine*, 8.

22. The exposition was held at 119 West 57 St., New York, 16–18 May, 1927. See Jane Heap, "Machine Age Exposition," in *The Little Review Anthology*, ed. Margaret Anderson (New York: Hermitage House, 1953), 341–3. See also Margaret Anderson, *My Thirty Years' War* (New York: Covici, Friede, 1930), in which Anderson states that Jane Heap made the *Little Review* the "American mouthpiece for all the new systems of art that the modern world has produced from the German expressionists and the Russian constructionists [sic] to the French surréalistes. She opened a Little Review Gallery at 66 Fifth Avenue, where the painting, sculpture constructions, and machinery of these groups were exhibited. In 1926 she organized an International Theatre Exposition in which Russian constructionist stage-sets were shown for the first time in America. In 1927, she gave a Machine-Age show—modern art in juxtaposition with engineering and the industrial arts, the first exposition of its kind to be shown anywhere." [265] Heap wrote in the last issue of the *Little Review* that the *Machine-Age* exhibition was the "first exposition of its kind anywhere...[and the] first showing of modern architecture in America." "Lost: A Renaissance," *Little Review*, May 1929, 5–6. The Cheneys confirmed Heap's claims (*Art and the Machine*, 7–8), as did Herbert Lippman, an architect who reviewed the show for the magazine *The Arts*. Mr. Lippman wrote that the *Machine-Age* exposition was "the first large aesthetically intended opportunity offered the New York public of seeing this new inspiration in process of development." *The Arts* 11, no. 6 (June 1927): 325.

23. The press coverage was, however, non-architectural. On Sunday, 22 May 1927, the very day the *New York Times's* banner headline screamed "Lindbergh Does It!," a small article devoted to the exposition was published in the real estate section of that newspaper; under a photograph of a small house by André Lurçat, it announced that the new style of architecture was "marked by an emphasis on the undecorated facade, flat roof and horizontal window." *New York Times*, 22 May 1927, sect. 7, p. 23. Coverage in the *Times* for the following Sunday was far more prominently placed on the first page of the editorial and general news section, and it carried the following headline: "New Architecture Develops in Russia / Exhibits at Machine Age Show Here Indicate Trend in Building and Art / Evidence of Vast Change / Industrial Civilization the Basis of New Forms / Skyscrapers Built on Horizontal Plan." The bulk of this article was devoted to the

remarks of the Russian-American painter Louis Lozowick, who delivered a talk on Russian architecture at a symposium called "Russian Night." *New York Times*, 29 May 1927, sect. 11, p. 1.

24. Nineteen hundred and twenty-seven was a significant date in the emergence of continental modernism in England as well. See for example *The Architectural Association Guide to Modern Architecture in London* (London: Architectural Association, 1957), whose earliest listing is Easton and Robertson's Royal Horticultural Hall completed in that year; see also Gerald K. Geerlings, "The Royal Horticultural Hall," *Architectural Forum* 54, no. 5 (May 1931): 567–8.

25. Richard Neutra, *Wie baut Amerika?* (Stuttgart: J. Hoffman, 1927).

26. Esther McCoy, *Richard Neutra* (New York: Braziller, 1960), gives 1929 as the date of the Health House, though she is referring no doubt to its date of completion. Neutra, on the other hand, insists on 1927 as the significant date; see his recent autobiography, *Life and Shape* (New York: Appleton-Century Crofts, 1962), esp. 220–6, "Health House, Vintage 1927."

27. See "A New City," *The Architect* 9 (Mar. 1928): 681–2; see also "Radburn, New Jersey, a Town of Modern Plan," *Architecture* 57, no. 3 (Mar. 1928): 135–6. Schemes for sorting traffic based on French and Italian precedents, fundamentally Beaux-Arts although subjected to futurist influences, were very current in America in these years. In addition to those of Stein and Wright and of Hood, Harvey Wiley Corbett's double-decked street plan should also be mentioned; see Harvey Wiley Corbett, "The Problem of Traffic Congestion and a Solution," *Architectural Forum* 46, no. 3 (Mar. 1927): 201–8.

28. Vincent Scully, "Frank Lloyd Wright vs. the International Style," *Art News* 53 (Mar. 1954): 32ff.

29. See *The International Style*, ch. 5.

30. I use "constructivist" here in the sense of its use in my "PSFS: Its Development and Its Significance in Modem Architecture," *Journal of the Society of Architectural Historians* 21, no. 2 (May 1962): 74ff.

31. See for example my "Humanism in Contemporary Architecture: Tough- and Tender-Minded," *Journal of Architectural Education* 15 (Summer 1960): 3–10.

32. "The New Empiricism in Denmark," *Architectural Review* 103, no. 618 (June 1948): 236ff.

33. See William H. Jordy, "The Symbolic Essence of Modern European Architecture of the Twenties and its Continuing Influence," *Journal of the Society of Architectural Historians* 22, no. 3 (Oct. 1963): 177–87.

34. Photographs of the buildings mentioned appear in Alberto Sartoris, *Encyclopédie de l'architecture nouvelle* (Milan: U. Hoepli, 1948).

35. Le Corbusier, "The Town and the House," *Architectural Review* 64 (Dec. 1928): 224. Serényi published on Corbusier throughout his career. His dissertation "Le Corbusier's Art and Thought: 1918–1935" was completed at Washington University in 1968. On matters relating to his MAS presentation, see his "Classicism and Anti-classicism in Le Corbusier's Architecture," *Journal of the Society of Architectural Historians* 29, no. 3 (Oct. 1970): 273–4; and his "Le Corbusier: The Formative Years, 1887–1917," *Journal of the Society of Architectural Historians* 31, no. 3 (Oct. 1972): 222. —Ed.

36. Walter Gropius, *The New Architecture and the Bauhaus* (London: Faber and Faber, 1935), 48.

37. Le Corbusier, *Modulor 2, 1955: Let the User Speak Next,* tr. Peter de Francia and Anna Bostock (Cambridge, Mass.: Harvard University Press, 1958), 224.

38. For other examples of the Maison Citrohan with the butterfly roof, see the Arundell Clarke House of 1939, Lannemezon House of 1940, and MAS Prefabricated House of 1939–40.

39. Quoted in Jean Badovici, ed., *Le Corbusier et Pierre Jeanneret,* vol. 1 (Paris: Éditions Albert Morancé, 1927), 13.

40. Le Corbusier, *Towards A New Architecture,* tr. Frederick Etchells (London: John Rodker Publisher, 1927), 188.

41. Le Corbusier, *The City of Tomorrow and Its Planning,* tr. Frederick Etchells (London: Architectural Press, 1947), 141.

42. Rpt. in Le Corbusier, *Oeuvre complète, 1910–1929* (Zurich: Girsberger, 1937), 118–9.

43. "Architecture, Painting and Le Corbusier," in Sir John Summerson, *Heavenly Mansions* (New York: W. W. Norton, 1963), 191.

44. Aristotle, *On Civics,* quoted by Frederick Hiorns in *Town Building in History* (London: George G. Harrap, 1956), 10.

45. John Dewey, *Art as Experience* (New York: Minton, Balch & Co., 1934).

46. For a discussion of Dewey's influence on Hudnut, see Jill Pearlman, *Inventing American Modernism: Joseph Hudnut, Walter Gropius, and the Bauhaus Legacy at Harvard* (Charlottesville: University of Virginia Press, 2007), 41–5. For a less balanced discussion by Moholy-Nagy on the ideology of functionalism "unloaded on America" by Breuer, Gropius, and Mies van der Rohe, see her article "Hitler's Revenge," published in *Art in America,* Sept. 1968. —Ed.

47. Quoted in Sigfried Giedion, *Architecture, You and Me* (Cambridge, Mass.: Harvard University Press, 1958), 87.

48. Prince Albert, quoted by Christopher Hobhouse, *1851 and the Crystal Palace* (London: J. Murray, 1950), 14.

49. All of the members of the commission were graduates of the École des Beaux-Arts, yet none of the architecture reflected this in style, except for the feeling of monumental organization in many of the large buildings and in the architectural plan of the fair in general. The architectural commission members were Harvey Wiley Corbett, chairman, New York; Edward H. Bennet, Chicago; Arthur Brown, Jr., San Francisco; Daniel H. Burnham, ex officio, Chicago; Hubert Burnham, Chicago; Alfred Geiffert, Jr., New York; Ferruccio Vitale, New York; Paul Cret, Philadelphia; John A. Holabird, Chicago; Raymond Hood, New York; and Ralph Walker, New York.

50. Edgar Kaufmann has told me in conversation that Wright was asked to contribute his talents to the fair, but he refused when he was not allowed to make the entire design. When asked by *Architectural Forum* in 1933 to write about the Chicago fair, Wright castigated the entire project saying, "To me, of course, the whole performance is petty, strident and base. The 'public,' whatever that is, may be partially weaned from pseudo-classic only to find another 'pseudo' thrust into its arms. How stale it all is." *Architectural Forum* 49 (July 1933): 25.

51. F. C. Brown, "Chicago and Tomorrow's House?" *Pencil Points* 14 (May 1933): 235ff.

52. Hakon Ahlberg, "Gunnar Asplund, Architect," in *Gunnar Asplund, Architect: 1885–1940,* ed. Gustav Holmdahl, Sven Ivar Lind, and Kjell Ödeen (Stockholm: Tidskriften Byggmästaren, 1950), 56.

53. Ibid.

54. M. Edmond Labbé, "The Meaning of the 1937 Exposition," *Paris 1937* 12 (1937). This was the official magazine published by the exposition's General Committee.

55. For pictorial coverage, see *Architectural Review* 82 (Aug. 1937): 85–110.

56. *Architectural Review* 86 (Aug. 1939): 62.

57. Henry-Russell Hitchcock, *In the Nature of Materials, 1887–1941: The Buildings of Frank Lloyd Wright* (New York: Duell, Sloan and Pearce, 1942).

58. The Zeiss Planetarium, whose projection system was designed by the engineer Walther Bauersfeld, opened in 1926. —Ed.

59. A collection of essays authored by Edgar Kaufmann, Jr., on the subject of Wright appeared in 1989, the year of Kaufmann's death; see *Nine Commentaries on Frank Lloyd Wright* (New York: Architectural History Foundation, and Cambridge, Mass.: MIT Press). —Ed.

60. Scully later added, "To call such symmetry 'Nazi,' as was oddly done by a participant during the Sunday discussion, because the Nazis preferred symmetrical architecture is like calling 'peace' communist because the communists continually use the word." Scully appears to be referring to Sibyl Moholy-Nagy's discussion of Mies van der Rohe's Krefeld Silk Factory; see 206. —Ed.

61. In addition to appearing in the March 1965 volume of the *Journal of Architectural Historians* as part of the MAS proceedings, a version of this essay was also published in *Perspecta* 9/10 (1965): [entire issue]. —Ed.

62. By 1964 Catherine Bauer Wurster had contributed much to the U.S. discussion on housing and social welfare. In print, see her *Modern Housing* (New York: Houghton Mifflin Co., 1934); and *Social Questions in Housing & Town Planning* (London: University of London Press, 1952). —Ed.

63. Millon published "Some New Towns in Italy in the 1930s" in 1978 in a collection of essays titled *Art and Architecture in the Service of Politics* (Cambridge, Mass.: MIT Press, 1978), which he co-edited with Linda Nochlin. —Ed.

64. Gustavo Giovannoni, *Architetture di pensiero e pensieri sull'architettura* (Rome: Apollon, 1945), 141. The volume is a collection of essays: one dates back to 1924; another is dated 30 May 1944; several appeared in journals in the late 1930s. The essay from which the quotation above is taken, "Edilizia Romana vecchia e nuova," contains two references to publications that appeared in 1945. The section in full reads as follows: "Di questo risorgere del culto dell'antichità classica si è voluto far colpa agli archeologi, ma non v'è accusa più stolida. Gli archeologi studiano i monumenti antichi, ne scoprono le vestigia, ne difendono l'integrità; e non v'è persona di pensiero e di coltura, che non abbia, 'cerchiato ii senno di fredda tenebra,' che non sia grato della loro attività e non lauda alle provvidenze che assicurano la conservazione e la valorizzazzione degli oggetti testimonianze di ricorde e di arte. Ma essi, nelle loro ricerche serene, nulla hanno a che vedere con una infatuazione imperialistica che auspica impossibili ritorni. Darne loro la responsabilità equivale ad incolpare, ad esempio, i fabbricanti di carta di quanto sta scritto sulle pagine dei libri."

65. Gustavo Giovannoni, editorial, *Palladio* 4, no. 4 (1940): 145–6.

66. Nikolaus Pevsner, *Outline of European Architecture,* seventh ed. (Baltimore: Penguin Books, 1963), 411. "The Fascists in Italy certainly were more successful in handling this style, whose terms of reference were to be imposing and easily understood. Their classical tradition was stronger and the revival came more naturally to them. They had also had less of the new style and could turn to the

Fascist idiom more easily and naturally. Moreover, for a noble, unvulgar display, no one can compete with the Italians. Hence such buildings as those in the new Bergamo and Brescia, in the new towns of Littoria and Sabaudia, as the Paris Exhibition pavilion of 1937 (by Marcello Piacentini and Giuseppe Pagano), as the Foro Mussolini in Rome of 1937, etc., and much that went up of commercial buildings and blocks of flats in the city centres will one day once again come into their own. They all combine a convincing rectangularity with fine shows of shining marbles inside and out."

67. One example should be cited here since it throws light on the character of the architecture that was being built. Gustavo Giovannoni, when speaking of restorations and of the impossibility of "matching" earlier works, argues that until a "national" style develops, it is better to fall back on classic architecture rather than the International Style; see his "Restauro dei monumenti e urbanistica," *Palladio* 7 (1943): [39]. To bolster this view he cites, revealingly, Hitler's *Mein Kampf*.

68. See for example the reversal of attitude expressed by Marcello Piacentini from 1930 to 1939. In his book *Architettura d'oggi* (Rome: P. Cremonese, 1930), he talks favorably of Mies van der Rohe's Barcelona Pavilion [39] and in many places speaks highly of the new "international architecture." In his essay "Evoluzione architettonica," (*Le Arti* 1, no. 3 [Feb.-Mar. 1939]), he says that Italian architecture must be liberated from the mortal poison of internationalism. [239–40] The original reads, "È belle dunque chiarire che non si tratta oggi di tornare indietro, di tornare all'antico, di ricopiare i classici; si tratta invece di ridestare lo spirito Italiano, si tratta di liberarci di questo tossico mortale che è l'*internazionalismo*." "International" is equated with "rational" throughout the book.

See also Giovanni Michelucci, "Limiti del 'razionalismo' e della decorazione nella nuova architettura," *Le Arti* 1, no. 3 (Feb.-Mar. 1939): 281–3; and Bruno Zevi, *Storia dell'architettura moderna* (Turin: Einaudi, 1950), ch. 5, "La vicenda italiana," 209–81, esp. 231–41.

69. See for example Ludwig Hilberseimer, *Internationale neue Baukunst* (Stuttgart: J. Hoffmann, 1926), and his *Grosstadt Architektur* (Stuttgart: J. Hoffmann, 1927); Peter Meyer, *Moderne Architektur und Tradition* (Zurich: H. Girsberger, 1928); Henry-Russell Hitchcock, *Modern Architecture: Romanticism and Reintegration* (New York: Payson & Clarke, 1929); Henry-Russell Hitchcock and Philip Johnson, *The*

International Style: Architecture since 1922 (New York: W. W. Norton, 1932); Alfred H. Barr, Philip Johnson, Henry-Russell Hitchcock, and Lewis Mumford, *Modern Architecture: International Exhibition* (New York: Museum of Modern Art, 1932); Catherine Bauer, *Modern Housing* (Boston and New York: Houghton Mifflin, 1934); Nikolaus Pevsner, *Pioneers of the Modern Movement, from William Morris to Walter Gropius* (London: Faber and Faber, 1936); Walter Curt Behrendt, *Modern Building: Its Nature, Problems, and Forms* (New York: Harcourt, Brace and Co., 1937); F. R. S. Yorke and Colin Penn, *A Key to Modern Architecture* (London: Blackie and Son, 1939); J. M. Richards, *An Introduction to Modern Architecture* (Harmondsworth, Middlesex: Penguin Books, 1940); and Sigfried Giedion, *Space, Time and Architecture* (Cambridge, Mass.: Harvard University Press, 1941).

70. For Germany see the recent Hildegard Brenner, *Die Kunstpolitik des Nationalsozialismus* (Reinbek bei Hamburg: Rowohlt, 1963).

71. Zevi, *Storia dell'architettura moderna*, 239.

72. *Atti del 1º congresso nazionale di storia dell'architettura* (Florence: G. C. Sansoni, 1938), x. "L'architetto Prof. Ambrogio Annoni quindi offerse una precisa documentazione circa quell'abitudine di critici stranieri, di voler diminuire l'originalità di concezione architettoniche nostre, a cui avveva accennato il presidente nel suo discorso, e notò come anche fra noi si presti fede a simili conclusioni."

73. Ibid., viii. The address ends with the following: "*Hic opus, hic labor*. Il nostro pensiero, nell'accingervisi con puro sentimento di italianità e con l'intento di far conoscere e di valorizzare quella che può dirsi la nostra vera materia prima, si rivolge doverosamente a colui che è animatore di tutte le nostre energie, al Duce. Mentre che l'Impero ritorno sui colli fatali di Roma e le glorie nuove si ricongiungono con le antiche, parte dai nostri anirni il voto che l'Architettura del tempo fascista riprenda, nel ritorno alla grande nostra tradizione, il cammino di domino che ebbero quelle del passato che sono oggetto dei nostri studi."

74. Ibid., xx, contains a resolution passed to ask the Ministry of Foreign Affairs to add studies of early Christian art and architecture to their programs of excavations in the east Mediterranean. "A cui si riferiscono importantissimi problemi d'Arte Italiana...nostra continua attività costruttiva."

75. Guglielmo De Angelis D'Ossat, "Su un particulare sistema costruttiva axumita," *Palladio* 1 (1937): 170.

76. G. G. Giglioli, "La mostra augustea della Romanità," *Palladio* 1 (1937): 203. "Si

troverà infatti che il mondo moderno, dalla casa alla basilica, dalla strada al porto, dall'acquedotto alla tomba monumentale, nasce tutto nella Roma Imperiale, dalla quale soltanto hanno origine le forme sviluppatesi fino alle attuali."

77. Ibid., 210.

78. G. Bottai, preface to the first issue, *Le Arti* 1, no. 1 (Oct.-Nov. 1938), reads in total: "La rivista 'Le Arti' sarà expressione diretta della politica artistica del regime: Dovrà dimostrarne in concreto, la validità di principi. Lo stato fascista, nella sua dottrina unitaria, considera l'arte elemento indispensabile dell'educazione delle masse. L'universalità dell'arte italiana, che ha conservato, nei secoli dell'avversa fortuna politica, il predominio morale di Roma, dev'essere, sempre, presente alla coscienza del popolo italiano. ¶L'organo di stato direttamente responsabile, in pratica, della politica artistica del fascismo, deduce norma d'azione dalla coscienza della storia dell'arte—e, forse, non soltanto dell'arte—Europea. Quell'azione politica, nei limiti naturale del settore artistico, è esattamente parallela all'azione politica che fu di Roma ed è, oggi del regime fascista. Questa verità molto semplice, ma degna d'essere meditata, esclude dall'azione artistica dello stato ogni pedanteria conservatrice ed ogni grettezza fiscale: far la storia significa determinare dei valori utili, nella realtà attuale, per la realtà future. ¶Non importa se quei valori appartengono, cronologicamente, a un passato estremamente remoto o immediatamente prossimo. Non chiediamo all raggio, che ci illumina, in quanti milioni d'anni o in quanti frazioni di secondo sia giunto a noi. Non poniamo cesure tra un passato ed un presente del pari vivi ed operanti sul piano storico dell'Italia imperiale. Gli Italiani sono tanto più giovani e pronte all'avvenire quanto più sono esperti della loro secolare grandezza. Questa certezza conferma la fiducia del regime nell'opera degli artisti d'oggi e nella riflessione degli storici che sostengono l'agire odierno con l'esperienza della tradizione. ¶Desidero die la rivista 'Le Arti' documente di fronte al mondo che l'arte e la critica italiane sono del tutto consapevoli della loro funzione, anche politicamente importantissima." [3–5]

79. "Report of an Address by Marino Lazzari to the Assembled Soprintendenti ai Monumenti," *Le Arti* 1, no. 1 (Oct.-Nov. 1938): 41. "Rilevando poi come l'azione politica del Fascismo, potenziando nel quadro di una concreta realtà attule le virtù conaturate alla nostra razza e i valori affermati dalla nostra gente in secoli di storia, il prof. Lazzari definisce il significato e la funzione dell'azione dell'Amministrazione artistica in rapporto alla politica del Regime."

80. Giuseppe Bottai, "Modernità e tradizione nell'arte italiana d'oggi," *Le Arti* 1, no. 3 (Feb.-Mar. 1939): 230–4. "Il postulato più recente delta dottrina fascista è, come è noto, quello di 'razza.' Questo nuovo dato deve, necessariamente, aggiungersi, attraverso una riflessione non precipitata e aggrappata a motive occasionali, al rapporto, già impostato, di politica e arte. Ne si insinui, com'è uso degli oppositori ostinati, che 'razza' è un fatto biologico; e che, pertanto, l'arte non possa tenerne conto, se non degradandosi nel materialismo veristico, cui si concede tutt'al più l'indulto d'un vago classicisimo. Il concetto di 'razza,' per sua natura riassuntivo, implica nella più estesa legittimità d'un commune destino umano tutte le definizione che, con progressiva chiarezza, dal Comune all'Impero, la civiltà italiana ha dato della politica della società. Nel concetto di 'razza' è riflesso e riassunto, in sintesi, il percorso della coscienza civile italiana, a tutt'oggi. ¶Se, dunque, il concetto di 'razza' è la definizione più attuale, più politica, nel senso classico ed etimologico della parola, più decisamente e intransigentemente moderna, del contenuto ideale della civiltà italiana, nessun vorrà negare, che il problema della razza sia in rapporto con quello dell'arte. Ma tal rapporto non agisce tanto tra l'arte e la razza, nel più corrente e accetato significato biologico, quanto tra ii *concetto* d'arte e il *concetto* di razza, che in sintesi enuncia la nuova coscienza, che l'Italia ha di se, della propria tradizione, delta propria missione civile."

81. Parallel to the interest in Roman, Italic, and Italian works of art and architecture abroad is the interest in vernacular (rural, indigenous, or popular) architecture. Many articles begin to appear in the 1930s devoted to, for example, "Architettura populare in Sicilia." It would be fruitful to examine the ideas behind these articles. There are, I think, two possible reasons—regionalism and a form of racism. Regionalism was probably a national reaction to the International Style, and there was hope of finding a refuge in that which was national, local, and indigenous. The other aspect, racism, is of even greater interest in regard to Fascism. I think it might be possible to delineate the desire to find a Mediterranean type that resulted from the influence of, say, Rome. An argument would then result, as Giovannoni suggests (see note 86 below), that the Latin people unified, ordered, and populated the Mediterranean world. At the common vernacular level this

is apparent. All the artificialities of national boundaries are unimportant when one sees the common people have a common heritage in Rome. This common heritage resulted, it would be argued, from the *Pax Romana* which was possible because Rome controlled the Mediterranean. And the *Mare Nostrum* (certainly one of Mussolini's aims) of the past that aided the civilization of the lands surrounding it would once again enable the unity of all peoples with a common heritage. The argument is implied in many places but needs to be tracked down.

82. Giuseppe Bottai, "Direttive per la tutela dell'arte antica e moderna," *Le Arti* 1, no. 1 (Oct.-Nov. 1938): 42–52. "La funzione culturale della tutela artistica si delineò parallelamente al sorgere di una cultura nazionale, al di sopra delle limitazioni pedanti dell'erudizione locale. Dalla valutazione complessiva di riferimenti e raccordi storici scaturì la visione unitaria dell'arte italiana; e si scoprì, che l'unità ideale d'Italia era un fatto compiuto, nell'arte, molti secoli prima che, con le armi, se avverasse l'unità politica. Ebbe a ricordarlo Mussolini in due discorsi del 1924 e del 1926, con queste perentorie affermazioni: 'Fu nell'arte, che gl'Italiani si sentirono e si ritrovarono fratelli,' 'Quando l'Italia era ancora divisa la sua unità era espressa dalla rinascenza dell'arte.' [42] ¶"Nell'adempiere scrupolosamente al nostro compito, noi tutti siamo consapevole dell'esigenza attuale, che la grandezza passata ci addita. È la piena coscienza dell'importanza storica dell'ora presente, che ci spinge all'indagine delle origini prime della nostra tradizione, alla ricerca delle fonte di quelle virtù civili della stirpe latina, che oggi si allineano sulla prima fronte della grande battaglia che il Duce combatte per la civiltà del Mondo. Come gli antichi guerrieri, anche noi portiamo fuori dal tempio, nel fervore della battaglia, le immagine sacre del passato, il palladio della nostra civiltà millenaria, che incuta reverenza ai nemici e nel cuore dei combattenti rinsalde la certezza e la volontà della vittoria. ¶Alla fine dei nostri lavori, noi diremo al Duce, che i militi operosi dell'Amministerazione delle Antichità e Belle Arti, ai suoi ordini, sono fieri di dare ogni energia alla grande battaglia." [52]

83. Reported in *Palladio* 3 (1939): 277. "Il Dott. Roberto Vighi, trattando il tema 'Gli architetti ticinesi e l'errata impostazione degli studi sulla loro arte,' pone in evidenza la grande importanza dello studio sui monumenti e sugli architetti ticinesi non solo dal punto di vista scientifico, ma anche da quella nazionale. Propone quindi, e ha proposta

viene unanimamente accettata, che il Congresso esprima un voto in proposito, per un maggiore interessamento da parti nostri studiosi su questo grande fenomeno artistice, e per una più retta valutazione di esso nel quadro dell'arte italiana contro le pubblicazione arbitrarie e tendenziose che si vanno diffondendo nel Ticino e all'Estero con scopi di schietta anti-italianità culturate."

84. Valeriano Mariani, "Malta (Caravaggio–Mattia Preti)," *Le Arti* 2, no. 5/6 (June–Sept. 1940): 305–7. "Questi documenti inoppugnabili di una civiltà italiana, così vicina nel tempo e così attuale nei suoi valori, sono sicura conferma della legittimità dell'azione che, vittoriosamente impegnata, suggellerà l'integrità del nostro mare restituendo all'Italia l'isola mediterranea. Così queste opere dovute al genio italiano, brani vivi di una storia che continua, saranno ricongiunte, e non soltanto nel sentimento degli italina e nella logica dei fatti, al nostro patrimonio artistico."

85. See note 64 above.

86. Giovannoni, editorial, *Palladio* 4, 146. "Così quando noi, ad esempio, in Malta ravvisiamo nei templi e nei sepolcri antichissimi (rilevati ed illustrati da due giovani studiosi italiani, l'Ugolini e il Ceschi) i primi segni della civiltà mediterranea; o quando nell'Asia Minore, nella Siria, nella stessa Grecia vediamo le grandi opere della Romanità sovrapposi all'ellenismo; o quando tutta l'Africa settentrionale, dall'Egitto al Marocco, reca i segni grandiosi della civiltà imperiale romana e poi della civiltà cristiana che, anche essa, muove da Roma; quando tutte le coste del mediterraneo si inghirlandano delle fortificazione medievali erette dalli grandi nostri repubbliche marinare; e le chiese della Corsica sono, come quelle della Sardegna, tutte di origini pisani; e le opere della maestranze lombarde, degli intagliatori in marmi toscani, dei nostri ingegneri militari della grande scuola cinquecentesca e seicentesca si affacciano per ogni dove, parlandoci tra tanti idiomi, con la unica, dolce favella italiana; quando infine l'architettura minore, schietta espressione del sentimento popolare, accomuna i tipi e le forme delle coste tirrene con quelle dell'Egeo e dello Jonio, e risale a prototipi, nobili od umili, di terme romani, come quelle di Leptis, di tombe romane, come quelle di Ostia, ne appare sicuramente affermato, come da termini sacri, il carattere di MARE NOSTRUM a tutto il Mediterraneo. ¶Su questo mare l'Italia ritornerà, per l'opera del suo grandissimo artefice, 'donna di province,' sicure delle sue vie, dei suoi confini, del progresso della sua civiltà nuova che riprende il cammino della civiltà antica."

87. *Palladio* 4, no. 4 (1940): 293. The articles are published in the same issue.

88. Gioacchino Volpe, "Su la soglia del nuovo impero Mediterraneo," *Le Arti* 2, no. 5–6 (June-Sept. 1940): 297–8. "Da quando gli Italiani che emigrarono per ragioni politiche e poi gli artigiani e contadini tornarono a riversarsi a Malta e Alessandria, a Tunisi e Algeri, e si misero ad esercitarvi professioni liberali e commercio, a far la guerra nella Legione Straniera francese e ad assumere uffici dello Stato egiziano, a travagliarsi per trovare le sorgenti del Nilo e per dissodare la terra, piantare aziende agricole, lavorare alle miniere di fosfati e ad ogni mestiere; da quando Crispi si arrolló per Tunisi e Biserta e tenne d'occhio il Marocco, e Caneva e Cagni e Ameglio sbarcarono nel 1911 a Tripoli e a Rodi; da quando il Fascismo ha riaddidato con nuova e più energica coscienza il Mediterraneo e l'Africa agli Italiani e riconquistato la Libia che era andata perduta e creatovi porti e strade, bonificato e rinnovato le città, riportato alla luce Sabrahata e Leptis e Cirene; da quando Balbo ha tracciato laggiù la grande strada litoranea, didotto migliaia di famiglie coloniche, creato diecine di villaggi, italiani e indigeni, trivellato la terra e impiantato poderi irrigui dove era steppa e quasi sabbia, creato la bella architetture delle piantagioni e quasi rinnovato il paesaggio, messi o rimessi su di esso i segni dell'uomo italiano; da quando fanti e Camicie Nere han debellato il Negus d'Etiopia e conquistato l'Impero, potenziando Impero mediterraneo, e i Legionari han combattuto in Spagna e aiutato la riscossa della nazione spagnuola; da quando Mussolini ha tenuto testa agli inglesi e la Home fleet è tornata ai suoi porti donde si era mossa con la solita orgogliosa presunzione di sè e la non meno solita disistima degli Italiani; da quando infine, spuntato il gran giorno della riscossa, animi e armi sono tesi verso Corsica e Tunisi e Nizza e Malta ed Egitto. ¶Grande lavoro, anche questo dell'ultimo secolo. Lavoro nuovo che si somma con l'antico, due volte compiuto. E il lavoro antico riappare sempre più nella sua giusta luce non di episodio dovuto a favorevoli e momentanee contingenze esterne, non di acqua passata che non macina più, ma di fatto organico e quasi necessario della vita mediterranea ed europea; e il lavoro nuovo di illumina della gran luce di quello antico, che è luce di Roma e delle città italiane della rinascenza, luce di politici e guerrieri, di dissodatori di terre e di creatori di opere d'arte; e il lavoro antico e nuovo additano il lavoro di domani. Ci sarà molto da fare per gli Italiani di domani. Le opere dei padri, se

conferiscono ad essi una specie di diritto, impongono anche dei doveri. E il nuovo impero del Mediterraneo sarà veramente formato solo quando saranno formati gli uomini capaci di sentirlo nella sua pienezza, di governarlo, di avvalorarlo anche nella sua ricchezza archeologica e storica e quindi nella sua continuità, dai padri romani ad oggi, di dargli in ogni sua parte l'impronta nostra, come impronta romana, veneziana o genovese diedero Romani, Veneziani e Genovesi a tante terre del Mediterraneo che erano parte del loro Impero fossero esse Africa o Malta, Corsica o isole del Levante o Dalmazia."

Volpe (1876–[1971]) was director of the *Rivista storica italiana* and *L'archivio storico di Corsica*, member of Accademia d'Italia and Accademia dei Lincei, and member of the Consiglio Superiore della P.I. After his early career as a social and economic historian of medieval Italy, Volpe devoted his research effort to modern political history. From the mid 1920s onward he published many works on Fascism, among which are *Guerra, dopoguerra, fascismo* (Venice: Nuova Italia, 1928); *Pacifismo e storia* (Rome: Istituto nazionale fascista di cultura, 1934); and *Storia della Corsica italiana* (Rome: Istituto per gli studi di politica internazionale, 1939).

89. See A. Cirici Pellicer, *El arte modernista catalán* (Barcelona: Aymá, 1951); and George R. Collins, *Antonio Gaudí* (New York: Braziller, 1960).

90. For this see Carlos Flores, *Arquitectura española contemporánea* (Madrid: Aguilar, 1961); and A. Fernández Arenas, *Iglesias nuevas en España* (Barcelona: Ediciones La Poligrafa, 1963). Also consult the periodicals *Cuadernos de arquitectura* of Barcelona and *Hogar y arquitectura* of Madrid. Flores's book is the best and the most thorough study of the whole development of Spanish architecture from the 1880s to the present.

91. "Les arrels mediterranies de l'arquitectura moderna," *Art* (Barcelona), Dec. 1933, 76–9.

92. Fernando García Mercadal, *La casa popular en España* (Madrid and Barcelona: Espasa-Calpe, 1930). See note 81 above, for a discussion of how, during the same years in Italy, the study of Mediterranean and vernacular traditions turned into a chauvinistic nationalism. — Ed.

93. See Antonio de Moragas Galissá, *Hogar y arquitectura*, Mar.-Apr. 1962, 16–27.

94. In connection with Mr. Wilson's remarks here, see his letter of 25 May 1964 about the symposium, which appeared in the journal of the Columbia School of Architecture *Program* 3 (Spring 1964): 72–4; and also Wilson's "Open Letter to an American Student," *Architectural Design*, March 1965, 5. — Ed.

95. Specifically, Le Corbusier used the phrase "futurisme bien dangereux" in a critique of Auguste Perret's take on the principles of the "Tower-City": "Car il a jeté ainsi sur cette idée saine un voile de futurisme bien dangereux et quelque peu incoherent" (For thus did he throw over this sound idea a veil of futurism [that was] quite dangerous and a bit incoherent). See Le Corbusier, *Toward an Architecture*, tr. John Goodman (Los Angeles: Getty Research Institute, 2007), 126, 314. See also Reyner Banham, *Theory and Design in the First Machine Age* (New York: Praeger, 1960), 254. — Ed.

96. Henry-Russell Hitchcock, *Modern Architecture: Romanticism and Reintegration* (New York: Payson & Clarke, 1929).

97. I was fortunate, however, to receive pertinent information from a number of architects who do have personal reminiscences from the 1930s in Austria. In this connection I wish to acknowledge the kind assistance of Mr. Felix Augenfeld, Professor Josef Frank, Professor Leopold Kleiner, and Mr. Walter Sobotka.

98. References to the illustrations may be found in Hellmut Lehmann-Haupt, *Art under a Dictatorship* (New York: Oxford University Press, 1954); and Franz Roh, *"Entartete" Kunst* (Hannover: Fackelträger-Verlag, 1962).

99. The German text reads as follows: "Das, um was es sich uns thatsächlich handelt, ist, zu fühlen, was im Interesse einer Bereicherung des Weltbildes innerhalb unserer engeren Grenzen geschehen kann. ¶Jeder Boden trägt seine besonderen Früchte und birgt zweifellos bestimmte Kräfte, die sich nur da entwickeln und entfalten. ¶Jeder der ein ausgesprochenes Heimatgefühl besitzt, wird bei vorhandener Begabung Merkwürdiges und Eigenartiges schaffen. ¶Der Deutschösterreicher besitzt nicht nur ein liebenswürdiges, fest harmonisches Wesen, sondern er besitzt auch Sinn für schöpferischen Willen. ¶Er muss Werke hervorbringen, denen man ihre Heimat und die erlebte Zeit nachfuehlen kann. ¶Für uns ist es daher wichtig, mögen sie schlummern oder wachen, zu erkennen und zur Entfaltung zu bringen.... ¶Wir denken nicht daran, irgendwelche Kreise zu stören, haben es aber satt, immer wieder...schulmeisterlich herunterkritisiert zu werden.... Geister, die sich hoch über allem Bodenständigen fühlen, werden in der Luft schweben müssen, und nicht zurückfinden. ¶Denkt an den Untergang aller alten Kulturen des Orients, Chinas und Europas und hütet euch durch fremde Einfluesse gezwungen, einem vorzeitigen Ende entgegen zu gehen. ¶Jeder der es gut meint, muss Alles verstehen und als Weiser darf er nur das Positive erfassen und zu bewundern trachten. ¶Böswillige Kritik in noch so geistreicher Form ist immer die Erungenschaft einer vergehenden, schwaechlichen Zeit. ¶Ueberlassen wir das der Journalistik."

100. See Josef Frank, *Die internationale Werkbundsiedlung Wien 1932* (Vienna: A. Schroll & Co., 1932).

101. It is significant that in 1934 *Das Profil* no longer appeared under the editorship of Hans Vetter and is described on its title page as the official publication of the Neuer Werkbund Österreichs (New Austrian Werkbund). In its May issue, Josef Frank is blamed for having criticized the Austrian Arts and Crafts in an English architectural periodical.

102. Sekler is referring to the commission for the design of the Austrian exhibit for the 1933 Milan Triennial. Hoffmann believed that Frank was attempting to steer the commission to Oskar Strnad. For a contemporary account of the split within the Wiener Werkstätte, see Christopher Long, *Josef Frank: Life and Work* (Chicago: University of Chicago Press, 2002), 187–90. — Ed.

103. Josef August Lux has not received the attention he deserves in the historiography of architecture. He not only wrote the first major appreciation of Otto Wagner and was chiefly responsible for the *Hohe Warte*, but he was also involved in the events preceding the founding of the Deutscher Werkbund and in the educational experiments at Hellerau, near Dresden.

104. *Hohe Warte* 4 (1908): 254.

105. See Lehmann-Haupt, *Art under a Dictatorship*, 10ff., for a full discussion of Morris's art for the people and by the people.

106. Hans Stephan, *Die Baukunst im Dritten Reich* (Berlin: Junker und Dünnhaupt Verlag, 1939), 14–8.

107. Werner Knapp, "Die Siedlung," *Architektur Wettbewerbe: Schriftenreihe für richtungweisendes Bauen* 1 (Feb. 1939): 8.

108. Gottfried Feder, *Die neue Stadt* (Berlin: J. Springer, 1939), 22, advocated this as the ideal size. Fritz Rechenberg, *Die günstigste Stadtgrösse* (Berlin: Deyhle, 1936), 58, claims that the proper size of a city is between 10,000 and 60,000 inhabitants. Adolf Hitler, *Mein Kampf* (Munich: F. Eher Nachfolger, 1932), 288–9, praising the medieval city as an *exemplum* for his present-day Germany, maintained that the city of the Middle Ages contained 50,000 inhabitants on the average. Alfred Kauss, *Die Pflege der Betriebsgemeinschaft durch Kleinsiedlung* (Berlin: W. Limpert, 1936), attempts to document the economic efficiency of the "Kleinsiedlung" (small New Town) but commits himself to no specific size.

109. Feder, *Die neue Stadt*, sect. 2, p. 3, and pl. IV ("Kristallogram"), alone of all Nazi planners, undertook an exhaustive analysis of how the New Town should be structured. He repeatedly emphasized, however, that his proposed disposition of elements was purely schematic and must not be considered a rigid system that could be imposed on any site. Such considerations as climatic and geographical peculiarities of locale influence the structuring of the New Town.

110. These elements were to be on the east side since the prevailing west winds in Germany would carry smoke, soot, and noise away from the city.

111. Knapp, "Die Siedlung," 8.

112. Albert Speer, *Neue deutsche Baukunst* (Prague: Volk und Reich Verlag, 1943), 10.

113. Feder, *Die neue Stadt*, 19; Werner Knapp, "Neubildung politischer Mittelpunkte I," *Architektur Wettbewerbe: Schriftenreihe für richtungweisendes Bauen* 7 (Oct. 1941): 5.

114. Feder, *Die neue Stadt*, 49; Knapp, "Die Siedlung," 9; Werner Rittich, *Architektur und Bauplastik der Gegenwart* (Berlin: Rembrandt-verlag, 1938), 86.

115. Knapp, "Neubildung," 5.

116. Speer, *Neue deutsche Baukunst*, 7.

117. Württemberg Landesgewerbeamt, *Zeitgemässe Forderungen an das Siedlungswesen* (Stuttgart: Hart, 1937), 12.

118. Ibid., 13.

119. Knapp, "Siedlung," 5; Württemberg, *Zeitgemässe Forderungen an das Siedlungswesen*, 34, 37–9.

120. Karl Sepp, ed., *Pflege und Gestaltung der Heima: Beiträge zur Kulturpolitik der Gemeinde* (Munich: Kommunalschriften-Verlag, 1938), 57.

121. Knapp, "Die Siedlung," 7.

122. Oswald Spengler, *Der Untergang des Abendlandes: Umrisse einer Morphologie der Weltgeschichte*, vol. 2 (Munich: C. H. Beck'sche Verlagsbuchhandlung, 1930), 141. "Das Haus ist der reinste Rassenausdruck, den es überhaupt gibt."

123. Koppel S. Pinson, *Modern Germany, Its History and Civilization* (New York: Macmillan, 1954), 1–11.

124. Friedrich Schlegel, *Vorlesungen über Universalgeschichte* (1805–6), vol. 14 (Munich-Paderborn-Vienna: Schöningh, 1960), 256.

125. "Die Christenheit oder Europa" (1799) in Novalis, *Gesammelte Werke*, vol. 5, ed. Carl Seelig (Herrliberg-Zurich: Bühl-verlag, 1945), 20.

126. Johann Gottlieb Fichte, *Reden an die deutsche Nation* (Hamburg: F. Meiner, 1955), 103.

127. Hitler, *Mein Kampf*, 288–9.

128. Adolf Hitler, *Die Reden Hitlers am Parteitag der Freiheit 1935* (Munich: F. Eher Nachf., 1935), 32. The speeches in which Hitler mentioned art for a paragraph or more include: Munich: "Laying of the foundation stone for the Haus der deutschen Kunst," 1933; "Die Deutsche Kunst als die stolzeste Verteidigung des deutschen Volkes," 1934; "Opening of the Haus der deutschen Kunst," 1937; "Beginning of the Munich subway," 1938; "Opening of an architectural exhibition," 22 Jan. 1938; "Opening of the second architectural exhibition," 1939. Nuremberg: Reichsparteitag, 1933, 1934, 1935, 1936, 1937, 1938. Berlin: "Laying of the foundation stone for the Wehrtechnische Fakultät," 27 Nov. 1937; "Beginning of the 'Neugestaltung' of the city," 14 June 1938.

129. A description of medieval Nuremberg, taken from the introductory pages of Feder's book, dramatically documents this attitude of Nazi planners. He includes a whole gamut of Nazi city-planning principles in his short descriptive analysis, touching on the conical shape of the city, the visual demonstration of leader over led in the building hierarchy (in this case the church and the German burghers), the "organic" character of the city, and the manner in which the city blends into the landscape. "Nuremberg, what a colorful, lively, serious, and yet festive and gay picture this city presented, how its interior rose in a clear rhythm and change across river and hills all the way up to the castle, how even the streets, like an ingenious rib structure of a leaf, satisfied the traffic requirements of the medieval city, how the market places and church squares were clearly and purposefully separated, and yet remained in close relationship. In short, how the whole city plan shows even today clearly and distinctly the spirit of a living organism, how it corresponds to the spirit of the sovereignty of the church as well as to the proud spirit of the German citizenry of the High Middle Ages. But it also clearly shows the development of industry and handicraft in the guilds. We see that the individual trades are being settled in the streets assigned to them." Feder, *Die neue Stadt*, 5–6.

130. For other possible, though less immediate, factors that lie behind Nazi architecture and city-planning theory, see Eduard F. Sekler's "The Architectural Reaction in Austria," 188–92.

131. A few examples will illustrate: Knapp, "Die Siedlung," wrote, "The New Town is an organism with its own ability to live." [5] To Feder, in *Die neue Stadt*, the objective of the New Town was to structure the elements in order to achieve an "artistic organism." [3] Rittich, *Architektur und Bauplastik der Gegenwart*, maintained that large cities must be ordered to enable "a continued organic growth." [83]

132. Bruno Taut, *Die Stadtkrone* (Jena: E. Diederichs, 1919).

133. Mrs. Bauer Wurster commented after Otto's presentation ended that she thought political symbolism was important. She recalled two almost identical housing projects, probably in Nuremberg, where everything—plans, facades, windows—was the same, except that one, for the Socialist trade union, had flat roofs while the other, for the Catholic trade union, had peaked roofs.

Otto would receive his master's from Columbia University in 1966 after successfully defending his thesis, "German Architecture and the November Revolution: Architecture in Berlin from the Surrender of Germany to the Stabilization of the Mark, 1918–1924. The 'Arbeitsrat fuer Kunst,' the 'Novembergruppe,' and the 'Glasserne Kette.'"—Ed.

134. Fitch had addressed the issue of technology previously; see his essays "The Impact of Technology," *American Institute of Architects Journal* 34 (Aug. 1960): 34–8; and "Architecture and the Avant Garde," *Four Great Makers of Modern Architecture* (New York: Columbia University, School of Architecture, 1961), 17–23.—Ed.

135. See Mark L. Peisch, *The Chicago School of Architecture: Early Followers of Sullivan and Wright* (New York: Random House, 1964).—Ed.

136. Peisch here refers to Henry-Russell Hitchcock, *Painting toward Architecture* (New York: Duell, Sloan and Pearce, 1948). —Ed.

137. Moholy-Nagy's remark refers to James Marston Fitch's comment of the preceding day in which he made reference to Moholy-Nagy's earlier discussion of the diaspora, a side of which she described as "excruciatingly funny...a comedy of errors played out by the alien mind anxiously disguised in native costume." See Fitch, 195, and Moholy-Nagy, 152.—Ed.

138. Moholy-Nagy here refers to a widely debated article by Mailer first published in *Esquire* magazine and subsequently reprinted in *Architectural Forum*, in which the author rails against modern architecture as inherently totalitarian in nature; for the article and a rebuttal by Vincent Scully see "Mailer vs. Scully," *Architectural Forum* 120 (Apr. 1964): 96–7.—Ed.

139. "Kunstgewerbliche Rundschau" (1 Oct. 1898), in Adolf Loos, *Ins Leere gesprochen 1897–1900* (Innsbruck: Brenner-Verlag, 1932), 175, 178.

140. "Acceptera den föreliggande verkligheten—endast därigenom har vi utsikt att behärska den, att rå på den för att förändra den och skapa kultur som är ett smidigt redskap för livet. Vi har inte behov av em gammal kulturs urvuxna former för att uppehålla vår självaktning. Vi kan inte smyga oss ut ur vår egen tid bakåt. Vi kan inte heller hoppa förbi något som är besvärligt och oklart in i utopisk framtid. Vi kan inte annat än se verkligheten i ögonen och acceptera den för att behärska den." Gunnar Asplund, Wolter Gahn, Sven Markelius, Gregor Paulsson, Eskil Sundahl, and Uno Åhrén, *Acceptera* (Stockholm: Bokförlagsaktiebolaget Tiden, 1931), 198.

141. Norris K. Smith, *A Study of the Architectural Imagery of Frank Lloyd Wright*, Ph.D. thesis, Columbia University, Department of Fine Arts, 1961.

142. Mr. Barr contributed the following note after the conference: "I have recently looked through my files and found a letter of December 14, 1936, from Dean Hudnut with the following paragraph, which provides the exact date announcing his appointment: Mr. Walter Gropius has accepted the appointment as Professor of Architecture in this School and we expect him here early in February. For this happy circumstance we are in no small measure indebted to you, and we are most grateful for all the help you gave us. The appointment will be announced on January 15 and until then this information is, of course, confidential."

MAS 1966

THE DECADE
1907-1917

Chairman's Memorandum

Henry-Russell Hitchcock
January, 1966*

The years 1907–17 do not constitute a recognized "decade" in the way that the 1890s do, or as does the 1920s, to which the first Modern Architecture Symposium was devoted in 1962. They were, however, rather more eventful in architecture than the decade of the 1930s, with which the last symposium was concerned two years ago. In America, the classic Prairie House period of Frank Lloyd Wright's production was drawing to a close, but the years that followed his departure from Chicago in 1909 were the busiest that the Midwestern architects whom we associate with him and with Sullivan were ever to have. Moreover, the publication of the Wasmuth portfolio in Europe in 1910–1, at once cause and result of his brief stay abroad, made his early architecture known to Europeans, while before the United States entered World War I and building halted he had been called to Japan to design and build the Imperial Hotel. Thus, the innovations of the Chicago School, or schools, were no longer associated with a merely regional American movement — paralleled though they were over these same years by the work of several notable West Coast architects — but could exert an influence upon the whole international development of modern architecture.

Both ends of this brief period are dates of considerable importance in Europe. The year 1907 saw the founding of the Deutscher Werkbund, whose activities in the field of both architecture and industrial design reached a prewar climax at the Cologne Exhibition of 1914. In 1917, in neutral Holland, the De Stijl group came into existence, just at the time the earlier Amsterdam School there was beginning to produce its finest works. Both of these were of seminal significance to the practice and the theory of the following decade. So also, though unbuilt, the projects of the Italian Antonio Sant'Elia and of the German Erich Mendelsohn in the early years of the war were, in related but contrasting ways, evidence of major innovations to come after 1918. Although the war closed down building construction in the combatant countries in 1914, the immediately preceding years had seen the construction in Germany of Peter Behrens's finest industrial buildings for the Allgemeine Elektricitäts-Gesellschaft (AEG) and the prophetic Fagus Shoe-Last Factory by Walter Gropius and Adolf Meyer [*figure 21*].

It would be pointless to set down in this preliminary statement, even briefly, a country-by-country accounting of these years. But I may note the contrast between the striking new developments referred to in the preceding paragraph and the *détentes* — not to say the outright reaction against surging new currents of the years around 1900 — that characterized British, Belgian, and Scandinavian production.

For the most part, the leading younger architects of the Western world (different in their training, in the particular traditional contexts with which they had to come to some sort of terms, and in their extra-architectural interests and connections both aesthetic and social) operated as individuals with less sense of coherence in their programs than there had been even a few years earlier, in the days of the art nouveau, and little sense as yet of the convergence apparent after World War I.

Merely to name a few of the men not hitherto mentioned, such as Lars Sonck and Eliel Saarinen, Auguste Perret and Albert Kahn, Adolf Loos and Irving Gill, and also to recall that postwar leaders like Mies van der Rohe and Le Corbusier, as well as Gropius, had built their earliest works (mostly houses) before 1917, suggests the remarkable variety of the international architectural scene in these years. It must indicate also with what an *embarras de richesses* the committee has been faced in determining the particular topics with which to deal. Many aspects of the period, many architects whose work was intrinsically distinguished, as we are now able to see again, must be omitted. There is a good chance, however, that by using the formally set topics as springboards, the participants in the discussion session will be able to broaden the consideration of these productive prewar years. It is less likely, even, than in the case of the symposia devoted to the 1920s and 1930s that any synthetic consensus will be reached; but the purpose of these gatherings has never been to arrive at conclusions, even tentative, but rather to revive historical and critical interest in topics that have long been taken too much for granted — to revive interest and to throw light on half-forgotten divergences in theory and in form that have often proved to be almost as lively matters for discussion today as they were in the periods reviewed. Just what confrontations, both in theory and in practice, between somewhat parallel but biographically unrelated figures like Loos and Gill, Kahn and Perret, Antoni Gaudí and Erich Mendelsohn, and — not forgetting that in these years the past continued to influence the present — Behrens and Schinkel, or the Greene brothers and the Orient, will receive new light it is impossible to foresee. If there are to be no conclusions, nonetheless new lines of study should at least be opened and relationships be glimpsed that the fragmented character of national activities in these years preceding World War I has largely masked. For in this short period, part late 1900s, part early 1910s, architecture was in a vigorous and productive condition. The variety of that production, in contrast to periods of more firmly organized aesthetic and social programs for architecture, is evidence of a real vitality. Even the outbreak of the war in 1914 could not bring significant activity to a stop, since actual building continued in neutral countries, even though it was only after the war was over, as the first of these symposia made evident, that a new and more concerted stage in the development of modern architecture finally got underway.

* Circulated to prospective participants in advance of the symposium

Agenda of the Symposium

Friday Evening Session
May 13, 1966

Comments on the Significant Buildings and Projects of the Decade
Philip C. Johnson and Robert A. M. Stern

Saturday Session
May 14, 1966

Introductory Remarks
George R. Collins and Henry-Russell Hitchcock

Frank Lloyd Wright's Years of Crisis
Edgar Kaufmann, Jr.

The Middle West
H. Allen Brooks

The West Coast Architecture Scene
David Gebhard

The Skyscraper
Winston Weisman

Scandinavian Architecture
Leonard K. Eaton

Rudolf Steiner and the Emergence of Expressionism
Eugene Santomasso

The Literature of the Decade, 1907–17
Adolf K. Placzek

Vienna
Eduard F. Sekler

Holland
Theodore M. Brown

The German Werkbund: Antecedents and Interpretations
Sibyl Moholy-Nagy

Behrens and Berlin
Stanford Anderson

Walter Gropius, 1907–17
James Marston Fitch

Some Observations on the Villa Schwob
Colin Rowe

Sunday Session
May 15, 1966

The City-Planning Scene
George R. Collins

Action History in Spain
David Mackay

The Problem of Mackintosh
Thomas Howarth

Futurism
Sibyl Moholy-Nagy

Le Corbusier and the Maison du Diable at Le Locle
Patricia May Sekler

The Purpose of Symposia in the History of Architecture
Rudolf Wittkower

General Discussion
Led by Henry-Russell Hitchcock

Modern Architecture Symposium 1966 Proceedings
May 13–15, 1966

Roster of Participants

Henry-Russell Hitchcock, Smith College
Chairman
Christian F. Otto, Columbia University
Assistant to the Chairman

Catherine Bauer Wurster, University of California at Berkeley
George R. Collins, Columbia University
James Marston Fitch, Columbia University
Philip C. Johnson, New York City
William H. Jordy, Brown University
Edgar Kaufmann, Jr., Columbia University
Henry Millon, Massachusetts Institute of Technology
Sibyl Moholy-Nagy, Pratt Institute
Paul F. Norton, University of Massachusetts
Adolf K. Placzek, Columbia University
Vincent J. Scully, Jr., Yale University
Eduard F. Sekler, Harvard University
Péter Serényi, University of Pennsylvania

Guests of the Symposium
Stanford Anderson, Massachusetts Institute of Technology
Alfred H. Barr, Jr., Museum of Modern Art, New York City
John Belle, Cornell University
Robert Branner, Columbia University
H. Allen Brooks, University of Toronto
Theodore M. Brown, University of Louisville
Percival Goodman, Columbia University
James Grady, Georgia Institute of Technology
John M. Jacobus, Indiana University
Elizabeth Mock Kassler, Princeton, New Jersey
Carroll L. V. Meeks, Yale University
Christian F. Otto, Columbia University
Mark L. Peisch, Columbia University
Robert Rosenblum, Princeton University
Colin Rowe, Cornell University
Patricia May Sekler, Harvard University
Joseph M. Shelley, Columbia University
Kenneth A. Smith, Columbia University
Eckhard Siepmann, *[affiliation unknown]*
George B. Tatum, University of Pennsylvania
D. Dean Telfer, Columbia University
Andrew Weininger, New York City
Colin St. John Wilson, Cambridge University
Rudolf Wittkower, Columbia University

....

Comments on the Significant Buildings and Projects of the Decade
Philip C. Johnson and Robert A. M. Stern

Philip C. Johnson: The historians among us architects should get ready to respond to our choices. Sibyl [Moholy-Nagy] has already sharpened her claws on the Behrens building. Mr. Stern and I overlap only on the Robie House. These are not the significant buildings of the decade, as we will find out tomorrow; I chose the buildings that amused me, completely off the top of my head. I at once thought of twenty more I could have chosen. During the course of my thinking I grew fond of the decade, much more than of the last symposium's 1930s. The sequence here reflects only the order of how I came upon them. There is no other meaning to the order. My first association with the International Style came through [Henry-] Russell [Hitchcock].

WALTER GROPIUS AND ADOLF MEYER, FAGUS SHOE-LAST FACTORY, ALFELD-AN-DER-LEINE, 1911–2 *[figure 21]*
It's quite an ugly building.

PETER BEHRENS, AEG TURBINE FACTORY, BERLIN, 1908–9 *[figure 5]*
I chose this for the use of steel and glass and the slope. It has the interest of an older man foreseeing what would happen later.

LUDWIG MIES VAN DER ROHE, KRÖLLER-MÜLLER HOUSE (PROJECT), WASSENAAR, 1912–3 *[figure 23]*
After the 1930s [symposium], I looked around a bit more at Mies and chose the Kröller-Müller House of 1912. It shows the Miesian influence on myself, modern fenestration, a twist of Schinkel.

PETER BEHRENS, GERMAN EMBASSY, ST. PETERSBURG, 1911–2 *[figure 19]*
This uses the regular massing to bind together the boring three-story facade. The regular spacing appealed to my classicism. I have personally used the regular spacing since.

JOSEF HOFFMANN, STOCLET PALACE, BRUSSELS, 1905–11 *[figure 14]*
I never liked the perfume tower but did like the marble and bronze. I never got over the use of decoration here.

ADOLF LOOS, KÄRNTNER (AMERICAN) BAR, VIENNA, 1907 *[figure 2]*
Loos has stayed with me because of the elegant use of materials. The coffered marble ceiling has stayed with me, and I have later done it myself without remembering the source. I have never seen it.

FRANK LLOYD WRIGHT, ROBIE HOUSE, CHICAGO, 1909 *[figure 8]*
Those of us under the influence of Corbu couldn't see the "old man," but then his breaking of the box had a most important influence. In 1936 I began to like Wright and have liked him ever since.

Le Corbusier, Maison Dom-Ino (prototype), 1915 [*figure 33*]

Antoni Gaudí, Crypt of the Colonia Güell Chapel, Barcelona, 1898–1914 [*figure 26*]
Later I came to like the personal interpretation of Gaudí. Everyone should visit this building, with its chipped columns and romantic, idiotic lines of force. This is a *good* building, according to my taste in 1966.

Antonio Sant'Elia, Città Nuova (project), 1914 [*figure 30*]
I started liking him in 1965 when I began to work with city plans. At best he broke with the functional element. Futurism had a lot to say about the automobile. Sant'Elia turns out to be the best man today.

Robert A. M. Stern: The Steiner House — and in fact all the buildings I have chosen — are multi-viewed and complex.

Adolf Loos, Steiner House, Vienna, 1910 [*figure 12*]
I show the front elevation because it is rarely reproduced. The garden side elevation is different.

Walter Gropius and Adolf Meyer, Werkbund Model Factory, Cologne, 1914 [*figure 27*]
The bubblegum towers so frequently commented upon.

Frank Lloyd Wright, Coonley Playhouse, Riverside, Illinois, 1911 [*figure 18*]
Two-story height with double space. Complex cross-axis and jump in scale.

Hans Poelzig, Werdermühle Factory, Breslau, 1906–7 [*figure 3*]
Interchanges of internal spaces. Bearing-wall construction frankly used.

Peter Behrens, AEG High Tension Factory, Berlin, 1910 [*figure 9*]
Each function expressed, including the stairs. Internal space pushing through the outside. Richness of space. Mixing structural connotations and systems.

Frank Lloyd Wright, Robie House, Chicago, 1909 [*figure 8*]
Unquestionably the greatest and most significant building of the decade. The extended horizontals destroyed the American street but brought richness.

Michel de Klerk, Eigen Haard Housing Block and Post Office, Amsterdam, 1913–20 [*figure 39*]
A regular system in housing with a freedom absent from J. J. P. Oud's projects. Space, freedom, whimsy, frankness.

Edwin Lutyens, Palace of the Viceroy and Capitol Complex, New Delhi, 1911–31 [*figure 85*]
Magnificent Beaux-Arts. Overall sense of order. Complex gardens. Here is a cross-section you never see.

REED & STEM AND WARREN & WETMORE, GRAND CENTRAL STATION,
NEW YORK, 1903–13 [*figure 24*]
The greatest built futurist project. Differentiation of space. Natural light
enters into the center of the building.

CHARLES RENNIE MACKINTOSH, SCHOOL OF ART, GLASGOW, 1897–1909
[*figure 7*]
For the entrance, the use of verticals, the adjustment to the irregular site
of a hill.

Saturday Session
May 14, 1966

....

Introductory Remarks
George R. Collins and Henry-Russell Hitchcock

George R. Collins: As one of the Columbia University members of our organizing committee, I would like to welcome you all to the working sessions of the third Modern Architecture Symposium. I want to thank you for coming and thank your institutions which made it possible for you to do so. At the risk of being somewhat repetitive, I would like to sketch in, for those of you who haven't been with us before, how these symposia arose. In 1961 we had at Columbia the XXth International Congress of the History of Art, at which Henry-Russell Hitchcock chaired a discussion panel on the early work of Frank Lloyd Wright. This inspired a number of us, so that during the following year Professor Hitchcock and Mr. Johnson, Mr. Placzek, and myself thought it should become a continuing affair.

In 1962, in the spring, we held our first symposium of this type, which was dedicated to the decade 1918–28 and had the subtitle "From the Novembergruppe to the CIAM." I don't think the Novembergruppe or the Congrès Internationaux d'Architecture Moderne were mentioned in the course of the day, but it seemed suitable. We no longer use subtitles. The proceedings of the occasion were taken down by Mrs. [Patricia May] Sekler and Mr. Arthur Sprague, and we published them privately in a pamphlet with which I think you are acquainted.

Then in 1964 we had our second symposium, moving to the decade 1929–39. (Notice that all of these "decades" consist of eleven years.) On this occasion the proceedings were taped, and they were published almost *in toto* in the March 1965 issue of the *Journal of the Society of Architectural Historians.* This was made possible through the Herculean efforts of its editor, Professor Robert Branner, and I think we produced the largest issue of the journal that has ever been put on the scales.

As you know, this time our subject is the decade 1907–17. We feel that the value of taking an inert subject like a decade, which has no meaning in itself, allows us to range quite freely in subject matter.... Our chairman on this occasion, as on all previous ones, will be Professor Hitchcock, who will now take over and describe the procedures.

[Hitchcock announced the sequence in which the presentations would take place and then introduced the first speaker.]

Henry-Russell Hitchcock: It is almost impossible to find something new to say in bringing up the name of Wright, but I think it is an interesting fact that the only building on which Messrs. Stern and Johnson agreed in their lists of the great monuments of this decade was the Robie House [*figure 8*]. It is true that they both also had buildings by Behrens, but not the same buildings. Once Mr. Johnson infuriated Wright by telling him that he was the greatest architect of the nineteenth century; I would slightly modify that to say that Wright was the greatest twentieth-century architect whose career began in the nineteenth century. That would perhaps justify asking Mr. Kaufmann to lead off with remarks on the crisis years of Wright.

Frank Lloyd Wright's Years of Crisis
Edgar Kaufmann, Jr.

Not only are decades artificial, but this decade of Frank Lloyd Wright's career is split down the middle by a famous event: his flight to Europe with his mistress, leaving his family behind him. In working over the material it seemed to me that it was quite possible to consider the whole flow of his career in terms of just this event. Just as one is used to thinking of the Prairie houses (or many of them) as being built around a nucleus from which space expands with an almost unbelievable lack of definition, so we might consider in this decade that Wright's career expands from his private problem and extends backward and forward in time without any very sharp breaks. In looking backward it seems that the most sensible point to make the break is not 1907 but 1906, because in 1906 the work on Unity Temple began.

The development of this quite important and very famous work of Wright marks the beginning of this portion of his career. It also marks the active beginning of Wright's use of cement and eventually reinforced cement, or concrete. As Henry-Russell Hitchcock has pointed out, Wright's interest in concrete extends farther back than that, to the early years of the century. It was in the early years of the century, too, that Wright claimed that his interest was first aroused in Japanese prints, another theme that runs through our decade here. In 1906 Wright had just returned from his first trip to Japan with his wife and his previous clients, the Willittses, and one cannot help supposing that some of the stresses and strains of his domestic arrangement were noticeable, since we know that he went off by himself, clad in Japanese kimonos, in search of more Japanese prints. Also, at the end of the time we are looking at, in 1917, after a much more tentative effort in 1907, Wright's collection of Japanese prints was exhibited in full splendor at the Arts Club in Chicago. The Japanese theme reached a crescendo during these years, as background music, perhaps, to a somewhat discordant foreground.

Wright's personal life began to unravel around 1905, and by 1907 his relationship with Mrs. Wright was indeed at a breaking point. He himself calls the year 1908 (extending over into the spring of 1909) the "miserable year of probation and demoralization," and it was during that miserable year that he was able to create two of his most famous monuments: the Avery Coonley House and the Robie House [figure 8].[1] Those years were also ones in which he was preoccupied with two of his most grandiose schemes that were not executed: the house for Edith Rockefeller McCormick and the putative ideas developed for Henry Ford. Then we come to 1909–11, the years abroad.

I have asked Mrs. Linn Cowles, a student in my seminar at Columbia last term, to tell you a little bit about the extraordinary material she was able to elicit from Lloyd Wright, the architect's son and an architect himself. This material includes—besides that which I wish to quote to you now, with her permission—some very valuable documentation in the form of photostats of an autographed letter sent by Wright from Japan in 1921, plus some passports from the U.S. government, all of which conclusively prove that, as Professor Hitchcock has maintained for so long, Wright was born in 1867 and not in

1869.[2] He himself admits it in the letter, and the government confirms it in the passports. I believe that this is the first time that there has been both personal evidence from Wright himself and objective evidence—not a matter of family record—that confirm Professor Hitchcock's acuity.

Then, too, we have to take a moment to think about a point that I've already raised by implication: the relationship between what Wright himself called "a worm's eye view of society" and what Professor Hitchcock long ago drew to our attention when, twice within a few pages in *In the Nature of Materials*, he used the phrase, "Wright was far from being without work" in reference to the years 1911 and 1914–5 specifically.[3] At the end of our period, of course, we find Wright embarked on two of his most extraordinary adventures—the Imperial Hotel and Olive Hill. But it is important to note the situation of Wright at the moment we're looking at, and at its beginning particularly. I'm drawing (more than usual, perhaps) not only on his autobiography but also on the book by his son, John Lloyd Wright, *My Father Who Is on Earth* (1946); another book by his sister, Maginel Wright Barney, *The Valley of the God-Almighty Joneses* (1965); and a somewhat distasteful but nevertheless useful book by Mr. Finis Farr called *Frank Lloyd Wright: A Biography* (1961).

The first thing that strikes one from a perusal of these useful texts is that it is necessary to understand the Lloyd-Jones family as part of Wright's background. This was, indeed, a clan: it was much more than a family. They were dedicated to the idea that whenever any member of the clan was in trouble, whether it was money trouble or private trouble, the clan drew in and supported him or her. This is particularly evident in the way they supported Wright's mother when she sent her husband out into the poor weather. It went further than mere support. There was a certain way of living among these people in which it was fairly evident that the difference between *meum* and *teum*, mine and yours, was not terribly acute. They shared things pretty readily and without much worry.

This was to have quite distinct repercussions in Wright's life. Thanks to the confirmation of his birth date, we now know that Wright's father and mother were not quite as old as we used to think they were when they got married; in fact, they were forty-two and twenty-eight, respectively, which is not so late to have children. The real question is, then, what was the effect on Wright of this peculiar and rather special marriage, the second marriage for his father? It's perfectly obvious that his mother, Anna Wright, was never willing to be separated from her son Frank. As soon as any separation occurred, it was patched up, and she was very soon by his side again. This continued until 1923, when she died at age eighty-three.

We should also remember Maginel Wright Barney's story of meeting her father by accident on the street after her parents had separated and his buying her a complete new outfit, after which she went home and had all the articles stuffed into the furnace. This indicates as well as anything Anna Wright's attitude toward her marriage after its breakup, and it helps us understand the peculiar and not entirely supportable statement that Wright makes in his autobiography when he says, "Is it a quality? Fatherhood? If so, I seemed born without it."[4] Yet there is plenty of evidence from his children, and even, indeed, from the autobiography itself, that he was a rather exceptionally reasonable father. He supported his children, they liked him, he liked them; there was scarcely anything that we can say about his not being a good father except what he himself felt.

I think we have to attribute this feeling to the pressure that Anna created. Anna was very close in her work as well as in her family ties to Frank Lloyd Wright's aunts, Nell and Jane Lloyd-Jones, who ran the Hillside Home School, later to become part of Taliesin, and it is important to trace the echoes of this school throughout this decade and even later in Wright's career. The whole practice of the Hillside Home School, which has been rather charmingly, if not very minutely, evoked in Mary Ellen Chase's *A Goodly Fellowship* (1939), had its own character, and this character was carried over not only quite distinctly into the Taliesin Fellowship but also into an intermediate event that hasn't received all the attention it might in terms of understanding Wright's career. Somewhere around 1894, if we're to trust Grant Carpenter Manson's *Frank Lloyd Wright to 1910: The First Golden Age* (1958), Wright added onto his small family house, which was located on a smallish lot that also included another house where Anna was installed. He added an extraordinarily large playroom with a barrel-vaulted ceiling and a very considerable floor area. It was much the biggest room around, and it functioned as a neighborhood kindergarten. Although we do not know for sure, I would like to raise the question of whether, considering the background that I've outlined, it isn't very much more likely that it was Anna who ran the kindergarten than his wife Catherine. Obviously, Anna was better equipped to do just this, being an experienced teacher, and at this date less pressured by having young children. When we turn to the men and women who worked for and with Wright in the Oak Park office in these same years, and their not infrequent complaints about money, pay, and the way they were treated generally, we may think a little bit about the ways of the Wright clan and their *meum-teum* attitude. Undoubtedly their complaints were justified, but I think there is also another side to the story; namely that these issues were not so important within the circle in which Wright grew up.

We ought to take a moment to consider in more detail the curious figure of Anna Wright. First, we know that she fainted at her son's wedding to Catherine. We also know that Wright himself wrote about her relationship to his mother-in-law, Catherine's mother Mrs. Tobin, "and the several grandmothers agreed none too often."[5] I suspect this may have been something of an understatement. Then, after the split-up of the original Wright family, there was Mamah Borthwick. It is perfectly obvious that Anna Wright and Mamah didn't get along extraordinarily well, yet there is one thing that must have helped their relationship to some degree. This was the Lloyd-Jones clan motto, "Truth against the World." In Anna Wright's mind there was truth in standing up to the fact that when you were through with your mate, you were through with him. She had done it, and I think she wasn't entirely displeased to see her son do the same with respect to Catherine.

Finally, we come to the lady who occupied the closing years of our period of interest in Wright's life—Miriam Noel. We know very well that when Wright became sick in Japan, Anna Wright came over to take care of him, and Miriam flounced out, as indeed one might expect: obviously, the two didn't get along. We can only say that one of the great, and by no means the only, good fortunes of Olgivanna Wright, the present widow, is that she happened to meet Frank Lloyd Wright after Anna died in 1923. Incidentally, Miriam Noel, an extremely exasperating lady, came from a district that has produced another lady well known for exasperating architects: Fox River, outside of Chicago.[6]

I would now like to counterbalance these somewhat acid remarks by briefly evoking the extremely noble and ethical spirit in which the breakup of the

Wright family took place. I am not going to recall the well-known passages from *An Autobiography*, but I do wish to quote briefly, and point out some sidelights, from Wright's first commercially produced book, *Love and Ethics*, by Ellen Key. This sixty-four-page book was translated by Wright together with Mamah Borthwick and issued by the Ralph Fletcher Seymour Company of Chicago for one dollar circa 1912. Ellen Key was Norwegian, by the way, but Mamah and Wright's authorized translation is taken from the German. In this book we find the following statement:

> Not the marriage service, but the will of two people to bear the responsibility of their children; not the 'legitimacy' of the children, but their quality; [these] be the standard of value for the morality of parenthood.... All these new princi- ples require an organic growth of duty together with happiness, an increase of responsibility together with right.... [E]rotic happiness becomes a vital social value.... Happiness is...in its deepest sense the enhancement of life through the vicissitudes of life. And in the deepest sense also does happiness become the sacred duty of one who sees the aim of life in life itself.... Life is no *made* thing, but a *becoming*, with unsuspecting possibilities.[7]

You get from this the holy reverberations in Wright and Borthwick's somewhat unholy situation. I wish not to dwell on this but to fish out of this quotation for you three particular ideas, besides the struggle for sexual emancipation, that show the wider range of values in this book, which both of them believed to be so important. The first idea is related to the phrase "enhancement of life." We're familiar with this principally from Bernard Berenson, but it was a general idea of the time. Next is the goal of "life in life itself." The notion of the *Ding an sich*, the work of art as a physical object first and a representation or record of feel- ings second, is here visible in another form. Finally, there is the idea of "no *made* thing, but a *becoming*." This emphasis on process rather than product is another testimony of the general level of forward thinking not only in Wright's art but in his values and his actions as a free and rebellious person.

I want now to read, with Mrs. Cowles's permission, from the letter that she received from Wright's son Lloyd, describing something we have never under- stood before so clearly. This is what really happened when the Wasmuth portfo- lio was being prepared, in his description:

> Then came the break-up of the Oak Park family life, with the advent of Mamah Borthwick, and the building of the first Taliesin in the Spring Green valley on the Wisconsin River. My brother John, and myself, were attending Wisconsin University in 1909, where I had gone to prepare myself to be an architect and landscape architect so that I could assist in my father's work. The rest of the chil- dren were with Mother in the Oak Park home.[8]

Notice this sequence: "the building of the first Taliesin," and "my brother John and myself were attending Wisconsin University in 1909." We're accustomed to thinking of Taliesin starting to be built in 1911, but this indicates that the first Taliesin was in use before Wright left for Europe in 1909, and indeed Wright on more than one occasion says that when it was burned in the spring of 1914 it was already five years old. To continue with Lloyd:

The House of Wasmuth had approached Frank Lloyd Wright about producing a monograph of his work.... Father had gone to Germany that fall [of 1909] with Mamah Borthwick to see what the project might entail and to escape the news hounds' rabble-feeding persecution. It was a difficult and crucial time for all of us. After some time, in Germany, Father wired funds for me to join him in Italy. A draughtsman who had been in his employ for several years, named [Taylor] Wooley, was already there. A sensitive draughtsman, a Mormon from Salt Lake City, and though lame, was active, helpful, and a hard worker....

Though this work in Italy would break into my college year of 1910, Father felt the experience would be worth it to me in more ways than one — it was indeed!...

I found Father already established in the little Villino 'Fortuna' just below the Piazzale Michelangelo and the David statue — in Florence.... Across the street was a walled nunnery with its tinkling bells and olive trees reaching over the wall. The *villino* was divided into two parts opening from a tiny inner court. A charming Russian couple who played chamber music with their friends had one apartment, and we enjoyed their cultured company. We had the street apartment overlooking the nunnery. There were no rugs on the stone floor and it was cold. The three of us set up our tables in the living-room and brought in braziers to warm the room and our freezing hands for it was the end of the winter season and we had to thaw out to do the essential and delicate work....

Father had had shipped to him all of the drawings from Taliesin and the Chicago office that he planned to include in the brochure on his work. It was a mixed lot of water colors by various Chicago men, line drawings by Marion Mahony and other draughtsmen in the office, and his own renderings and sketches which showed the influence of two very different sources — the Japanese prints and the pen drawings filled with sunlight, by [the Spanish illustrator Daniel] Vierge [Urrabieta]. These, together with Father's own typical expression, created a type of rendering unique to itself and its creator, Frank Lloyd Wright. It was ideally suited to convey a record of his work....

This work had to be done quickly and all correlated, reconstructed, and prepared for the Wasmuth edition. We worked long and continuously....

Father, Wooley, and I traced with crow quill pens on tracing paper all of the drawings and matters he wished to have published in the brochure. We worked at modifying, building up, correcting, simplifying, and converting all of the material into the totally coordinated plates that were reproduced for the *Ausgeführte Bauten und Entwürfe von Frank Lloyd Wright*, by Wasmuth in Germany.....

During the several months we were engaged in this work he returned several times for several days at a time to Germany to consult with the Wasmuth concern about the publication, and to see Mamah Borthwick, who had stayed behind in Germany. He told of seeing the composer Brahms, and his disappointment, for he thought that Brahms was not as great as he had imagined him to be.... He said nothing about lectures there.... This was Father's first trip to Europe; he wrote his English texts. He could not speak German, I do not know who made the German translation....

It took high concentration, time, and application of an intense order to turn out the work, under the circumstances.... After we completed the drawings of the plates, they were taken to Germany and the lithograph stones were there prepared from them....

The work done, Father gave Wooley and me a stake with which to "do" Italy to study the gardens, urban plans, and great art works of the country. We travelled third class.... I returned through France, where I met Father in Paris for a good visit....

Because of my interest in landscape architecture, we went to see the gardens of Versailles and several chalets. Then followed the Tuileries, seeing the treasures of the Louvre, and the Folies-Bergère, and the night life of Paris. Then we spent a day at the then growing airport of Le Bourget. I wanted to see what they were doing in France with aerodynamics....

Our work and traveling accomplished, Father then joined Mamah Borthwick in Fiesole, where they stayed for several months in a charming *villino* overlooking Firenze and enjoying the fruits of his labors and the beauty of that loveliest of cities before returning to Taliesin in Wisconsin.[9]

These excerpts give us quite a different picture of this important passage in Wright's life than we've had up to now. I would have liked to discuss with you [the impact of these biographical events on] Wright's work during this decade and have prepared a chart [comparing his commissions and executed buildings during this period to the one previous], but time is too short to look at it.

The Middle West
H. Allen Brooks

I shall preface my remarks by saying that I will be very interested in Mrs. Cowles's remarks tomorrow concerning the Wasmuth edition, because you've caught me in mid-stream with an article concerning the attribution of these drawings that will appear in the June issue of the *Art Bulletin*. The article is in galley proofs now so I don't think I can make any changes according to what is said tomorrow.[10]

The decade 1907–17, in actuality, is a very valid chronological unit for discussing modern architecture in the American Midwest. The period opens as the Prairie movement begins to flourish and concludes at precisely the moment of its unexpected collapse. From the very first years of the century one can discern the growing influence of Wright on his Chicago contemporaries. His designs of the 1890s as well as his more familiar Prairie houses, which evolved in the early 1900s, struck a responsive chord among his colleagues. But several years elapsed before a consistent trend was apparent and before any real alignment or allegiance was discernible within the group. By 1904 or 1905, however, architecture critics began to take note of Wright's influence in the Midwest and refer to his "school" of architects, whose residential work embraced common objectives and was expressed in forms of similar ancestry. In 1908 both Frank Lloyd Wright and Thomas Tallmadge wrote of the existence of the school among the residential architects, and each man coined for it a name. Wright called it the

"New School of the Middle West"; Tallmadge, the "Chicago School." Whereas Wright's title never enjoyed wide currency, Tallmadge's has, although its meaning has become perverted to the point where today it symbolizes skyscraper architecture of the 1890s rather than residential architecture of the early twentieth century. For this reason, I coined the term "Prairie School" when referring to early twentieth-century developments in Midwestern architecture — especially as these buildings are so distinct from the tall commercial buildings that, by 1907, already represented something from the past.

The year 1907, therefore, was one of great promise. A vigorous school of architects had come into existence and was rapidly expanding both in number and in the amount of executed work. The dictum of Louis Sullivan that the World's Columbian Exposition would set back the cause of architecture by fifty years seemed unnecessarily pessimistic in spite of the fact that an academic reaction was underway. In 1907 Wright was commissioned to design the Harold McCormick House, which suggested that social approval by families of great wealth and prestige was in the immediate offing. For families at the other end of the economic scale, Wright published, in 1907, his Fireproof House for $5,000 in the *Ladies' Home Journal*.[11] This design, a highly sophisticated refinement of the ubiquitous boxlike house so familiar in the Midwest, offered a feasible solution at inexpensive cost. Indeed, upon no other Wrightian theme were there to be played more variations.

But Wright was not alone, as a cross-section of the work done by his contemporaries during the years 1907–9 will attest. Robert Spencer, Jr., and his partner Horace Powers designed, in 1907, the Edward McCready House in Oak Park. The design is monumental and dignified, superbly detailed, and has a Palladian massing, in spite of the off-center doorway. It exhibits much of the clarity and classical order that are to be found in Wright's Winslow House. The McCready House is contiguous with Wright's George W. Furbeck House, and owing to the power of Spencer's design, this work is often mistaken for its Wright-designed neighbor.

In nearby River Forest, the John W. Broughton House of 1908 again attests to the caliber of Spencer and Powers as designers. Built of common rather than Roman brick, the L-shaped house stresses the horizontal line with its ribbon windows, stringcourse, and cornice line. The proportions of the building make no real concession to lowness, yet repose is admirably achieved. Neither Spencer nor Powers had worked for Wright and therefore their designs were freer from his influence than the work of architects who had spent several years in his studio. For example, William Drummond's First Congregational Church in Austin of approximately 1908 is obviously indebted to the Larkin Building, which Drummond, from his experience in Wright's studio, knew well. Likewise, Walter Burley Griffin's design for the Frederick Carter House in Evanston of 1911 shows firsthand knowledge of Wright's work, especially of the Beachy House in Oak Park. Yet within a few years, the work of these men developed into a more personal expression. Tallmadge and Watson's Easterbrook House of 1908, also in Oak Park, is closer to a bungalow with its one-story plan, while the Charles Purcell House by William Purcell of 1909, in River Forest, Illinois, was more upright in its massing. Its brick base contrasts with the smooth plaster above, and the design has some suggestion of a country cottage. Louis Sullivan, with the aid of George Elmslie, built the Henry Babson House, located in Riverside, Illinois, in 1907, the same year in which the National Farmers' Bank in Owatonna, Minnesota, commenced. Carl Schurz

High School in Chicago, by Dwight H. Perkins, of 1910 is another, much more expressionistic example from this period.

About 1910 a series of events occurred that profoundly affected the future. These were mostly related to Wright's departure for Europe in autumn 1909. Most notable were Wright's two Wasmuth publications. As for the Prairie School itself, Wright's departure had two direct, although opposite, consequences. First, it sent the last of his studio apprentices out to work for themselves, thus adding impetus to the movement. Also, Wright's departure led to the loss of vital commissions, which resulted in strained relations between Wright and his former colleagues. The bitterness that developed is expressed in Wright's article "In the Cause of Architecture" of 1914. Those who knew Wright well were unwilling to enter into a business relationship with him, so when he left for Europe in 1909 he found it necessary to leave his practice in the hands of Hermann von Holst, who was not sufficiently familiar with his work. The great tragedy was that Henry Ford had just commissioned Wright to design an estate in Dearborn, Michigan, and Wright, who had already lost the McCormick commission, left for Europe without, apparently, developing a project for Ford. A design was prepared, however, under the aegis of Von Holst and Fyfe, which was actually the design of Marion Mahony, formerly of Wright's office. It is sufficiently dissimilar to Wright's work to suggest that Wright played little or no part in its preparation. The long, open axis through the house lacks the typical juxtaposition of countering spaces that Wright would certainly have designed, and the thick-set proportions of masonry, window mullions, and so forth are quite distinct from Wright's work. The design, unfortunately, was not executed, and the commission was finally turned over to an architecture firm in the East.[12]

The Ford House was not the only major commission lost in the Detroit region. In 1910 William Drummond was asked to design an estate for Dexter Ferry in Grosse Pointe, Michigan, overlooking Lake St. Clair; this occurred thanks to Mrs. Avery Coonley, Ferry's sister. Wright's Avery Coonley House in Riverside is well known, yet Mrs. Coonley was also a client of William Drummond, who built for her a kindergarten in Brookfield, Illinois, in 1911. Drummond prepared two separate designs for Ferry in 1910. In what is probably the earlier scheme, the symmetrical yet decentralized massing gives indication of a highly imaginative plan, with great, open flowing spaces in the interior. The other project for Ferry was more conservative, not only in its exterior massing but particularly in its interior. There is no strong axis in the plan, and the spaces are compartmentalized. The plan was also more compact, with a smaller total area of floor space. It would undoubtedly have been more economical to build. Both projects were for large houses and included several outbuildings, landscaping, and extensive grounds. The important point here, however, is that two projects of prime importance were not built by the Prairie architects. Adding the McCormick House to this list means that three major commissions were lost, all in a very short period of time. Had they been built, immeasurable prestige would have been added to the Prairie School, and this would have given the movement impetus at a critical moment. As it was, the McCormicks, the Fords, and the Ferrys were all to have their homes built by conservative East Coast architecture firms.

In spite of such adversities, the Prairie School continued to expand and flourish, and between 1911 and 1914 it showed extraordinary vigor. Hundreds of buildings, mostly homes, were spread across the Midwest and, literally, from coast to coast, as well as in Canada. The establishment of the firm of Purcell and Elmslie in 1909 was of great importance, not only for the quality and variety of its work but because it executed more designs than any other architect, including Wright. Typical of Purcell and Elmslie's designs are the Bradley Bungalow at Woods Hole, Massachusetts, of 1911 [figure 17] and the Edison Shop in Chicago of 1912. By contrast, Walter Burley Griffin's designs were always more compact, massive, and solidly rooted to the ground—for example, his Hurd Comstock House in Evanston of 1912 and Stinson Memorial Library in Anna, Illinois, of 1913. The year 1913 was, in effect, when Griffin severed his connections with the Midwest, having won the international competition for the design of Canberra the preceding year. Henceforth his career was primarily to be an Australian one. In 1914 Barry Byrne, who had worked in Wright's studio from 1902 to 1907, returned from the Far West to Chicago. His J. F. Clarke House in Fairfield, Iowa, of 1915 indicates his predilection for elimination. From both Louis Sullivan and Irving Gill he had learned to respect simple, severe forms and basic geometric elements. John Van Bergen, who studied under Griffin and later Wright, executed numerous homes in the Midwest, including the Alfred Bersbach House in Wilmette, Illinois, of 1914 and three houses for Flori Blondeel in Oak Park, all of which very closely reflect the work of Wright.

I would like to present a brief case study of a single architect—an architect who is all but unknown (whose work I only saw for the first time this past weekend). His designs are unpublished, his name is obscure to the architectural historian, yet his houses are of the highest quality. Three things strike me about his work: its high intrinsic value, the rich variety among its different designs, and its imaginative conception of interior space. The architect I refer to is Percy Dwight Bentley. His hometown was La Crosse, Wisconsin, on the banks of the Mississippi River. Bentley studied architecture at Armour Institute (now Illinois Institute of Technology) and while in Chicago became fascinated with the work of Wright. He returned to La Crosse in 1911 and continued to practice there until shortly after the war, when he went to Arizona. Within a few years, Bentley and his followers did much to transform the architectural image of La Crosse, with the result that his local influence was almost equal to the impact that Wright had upon his hometown of Oak Park. The Henry Salzer House of 1912 is one of Bentley's earliest designs. Yet it is the work of a mature designer who has a fine sense of proportion. The Emil Mueller House of 1915 [figure 32] is more reminiscent of Wright, yet again one cannot help but be impressed by the quality of the design. The interior was originally entirely of quarter-sawn oak, and Bentley also designed handsome fittings like lamps. Unfortunately, the interiors of most of Bentley's houses have been extensively painted now, covering most of the fine oak woodwork and the fireplace brickwork. But in the M. L. Fugina House in Fountain City, Wisconsin, of 1916 the original owner still occupies the house, with the result that the interiors are in mint condition. The Edward C. Bartl House in La Crosse of 1910 results from Bentley's assimilation of the ubiquitous boxlike farmhouse typical of the Midwest combined with Wright's Fireproof House scheme for *Ladies' Home Journal* of 1907. It is interesting that the small central window over the porch in the latter, reflecting a bathroom, also appears in the massing of the Bentley scheme.

Bentley's work suffered the same consequence as most of the Prairie School. Increasingly the client demanded a Colonial or Tudor Gothic design, and the client usually had his way. The Salzer House is actually an example of this trend. Mr. Salzer wanted a Wrightian house, but his wife insisted upon a Colonial design. A compromise was finally reached when Bentley agreed to design a Prairie House exterior for Mr. Salzer and a Colonial plan interior. Thus one enters into a large central hall that divides the house and contains the stairwell; to the right is the living room and to the left, the dining room and kitchen. The next step in this conservative reaction is recorded in the Argyle Scott House of about 1917 — the terminal date of our study decade. In this design, also by Bentley, the plan is almost identical to that of the Salzer House across the street, but now the exterior has been made to conform stylistically with the interior.

If 1907 was the year of promise, 1917 was the year of rejection. When Tallmadge reviewed the Chicago Architectural Club exhibition of 1917 for *Western Architect* he noted with regret the absence of any representation of the Prairie School.[13] Indicative of the club's revised values were the new conditions imposed upon the winners of its traveling scholarships. These required "that the winner will spend two months in the East, primarily for the study of Colonial architecture."[14] Indeed, the conservative reaction had brought to a virtual standstill the work of the Prairie School. Only a few scattered examples of it were to be built in the years that followed the war.

If the years 1907–17 encompassed the flowering of the school and witnessed its sudden decline, it was also the decade when Europe became acutely aware of this development in the American Midwest. The English architect C. R. Ashbee visited the Midwest for the second time in 1908, and the Dutch architect Hendrik Petrus Berlage, on the encouragement of William Purcell, came in the autumn of 1911. Both returned home to spread the word of what they had seen. Griffin's successful bid for the Canberra competition focused attention once again on the Midwest. Of course, Wright was the brightest star, and no medium of communication with Europe was half so important as the 1910 and 1911 publications of his work by Ernst Wasmuth. Wasmuth in 1910 also published *Das amerikanische Haus* by F. R. Vogel, which somewhat more broadly represented this most vital phase of early twentieth-century American architecture.

The West Coast Architecture Scene
David Gebhard

Throughout the twentieth century, the architecture of the West Coast of the United States has experienced two rather distinct urges. In the first place, there has been a deep-seated desire to re-create that which was familiar, fashionable, and correct in the centers of the East and the Midwest. Thus much of the architecture of Los Angeles, San Francisco, and Seattle could loosely be labeled a type of provincialism. A second, though contrary, urge has been that of experimentation — as if the individual, no longer feeling the pressure to conform to his former environment, could now be as free as he wished. The interest in trying out new ideas has been accelerated by the mild year-round climate of the West Coast. This has meant that not only could rather bold experiments be made in relating indoor and outdoor space, using new materials and structural forms, but also — and I think that this is of prime importance — many people, even those who remained permanently, have viewed the area as a year-round vacationland. Thus their demands and their expectations of architecture were quite different from those that one would normally experience in the Midwest or on the East Coast.

In 1907–17 that architecture which directly emulated the modes and fashions of the Midwest and East — the classical revivalism of McKim, Mead & White and Daniel Burnham, the neo-Gothicism of Ralph Adams Cram, or the early domestic Colonial Revival — produced little in the way of really outstanding buildings. The work of John Galen Howard on the Berkeley campus of the University of California or the early neoclassical buildings of the San Francisco Civic Center may possibly inspire local nostalgia and pride, but when seen in the context of European and American architecture, these years are, at best, quite minor. It is certainly true that when classically inspired forms were loosely used — as they were by Bernard Maybeck, or by Louis Christian Mullgardt in his Court of the Ages at the San Francisco World's Fair of 1915 — they were often indeed refreshing and highly inventive. Still, the only important eclectic form that stimulated the architectural scene in a creative way was the Spanish baroque, or Mexican baroque revival, best seen in the buildings of the Panama-California Exposition in San Diego of 1915 by Bertram Goodhue and Carlton Winslow [figure 34].

The one major area where the neoclassical tradition did make a notable contribution on the West Coast was in landscape gardening. The California communities of Woodside, Burlingame, Montecito, and Pasadena contained innumerable formally laid-out gardens that surpass anything found elsewhere in the country. Time and time again, one finds that the owner of a large estate has lavished almost all of his care and almost all of his financial resources on the garden, almost completely neglecting the house itself.

While the neoclassical tradition forms a significant chapter in the history of the twentieth-century architecture of the West Coast, it is the experimental modes that constitute its major contribution. In contrast to the Prairie School of the Midwest, the Secessionist group of Vienna, or the group centered around Charles Voysey and Charles Rennie Mackintosh in England and Scotland, the avant-garde or experimental architects of the West Coast never presented anything approaching a unified point of view. Not only were there a variety of different approaches by individuals, but it was more normal than not to find a single architect using one, two, or perhaps even three of the experimental approaches simultaneously. The West Coast architecture that we label experimental expressed itself in a number of ways. First, there was a concern with the development of new form. Second, there was a use of new materials and structure, particularly of reinforced concrete and prefabricated steel and glass units. Third, there were new ideas about urban planning, as seen in the bungalow court, for example. Finally — and this had far-reaching significance — there was the establishment of extensive private development organizations that concentrated their attention on large-scale building production and marketing of individual houses.

The West Coast venture into new forms (labeled at the time, by the way, as Secessionist or art nouveau) was a highly mixed affair, both in its variety and in its quality. With the exception of a figure like Irving Gill, the average avant-garde West Coast architect tried his hand at a number of the newer modes rather than commit himself to one of them. But even though a great variety of forms were used during these years, two elements seemingly permeated all of these experiments. The first was the Craftsman aesthetic, prevalent between 1900 and 1910; the second, which was closely related, was the Mission

Revival, which saw its major examples created in the first two decades of the century. The Craftsman ideal is expressed in the Bent House of 1909 in Los Angeles by the firm of Hunt, Eager & Burns [*figure 6*], with its interest in an open, informal plan, intimacy of scale in both detail and space, and frank and expressive use of materials and structure, whether in furniture, buildings, or gardens. This became an underlying aesthetic premise for most West Coast designers. With its extreme simplicity of basic form and details, and with its historic references reduced to a minimum, the Mission Revival formed a natural link with the West Coast version of the Craftsman aesthetic. Even in an average and rather typical example of the Mission Revival such as the Riverside Public Library of 1903 by Burnham and Bliesner of Los Angeles, the architects were forced to concentrate their attention on the broader problems of proportion, scale, and volume rather than on historic detail.

In many ways, the West Coast designers were as aware of what the avant-garde was doing in Europe as they were alert to the innovations of the Prairie School in the Midwest. A case in point is the work accomplished between 1900 and 1917 by the little-known Bay Area architect John Hudson Thomas. The basic massing and high-pitched gabled roof of the Fleager House in Berkeley of 1912 obviously owes much to the work of Mackintosh, Voysey, and M. H. Baillie-Scott, designers whom Thomas very much admired. The same holds true for his more complex Wintermute House, built in Berkeley in 1913, only here there are many details that would certainly point to Vienna rather than to Glasgow or London. But like other Bay Area architects, such as Julia Morgan, John Galen Howard, and Willis Polk, Thomas could be quite free and informal in his designs. His Kelly House in Santa Barbara of 1915, with its open V-shaped plan, hovering low-pitched roof, and modular exterior wall, owes very little to European precedents. The same is true of much of the work of Bernard Maybeck, as in his Matheson House in Berkeley of 1919. But even Maybeck cast more than a side glance at what was happening in Europe. The low-hipped roof tower struts, the broad overhanging roof supported by diagonal struts, and other details of his Hearst Hall at the University of California at Berkeley, built in 1899, as well as the articulation of the tower on a project for a church of 1905, must have been inspired by the Viennese work of Otto Wagner and Josef Hoffmann. Perhaps the closest Maybeck ever came to the Viennese Secessionists was in his concrete Lawson House in Berkeley of 1901. His use of the arcade, freestanding piers, and surface patterns created by the incision of lines and tile is free and offers a rather loose variation on similar forms that were used in Vienna, Darmstadt, and elsewhere in Central Europe.

Direct reflections of Louis Sullivan and the Prairie School were also quite pronounced during the years 1900 to 1917. Houses designed by Douglas and Hartmann in Los Angeles, or some of the San Francisco houses of Glenn Allen, certainly are a direct reflection of Sullivan's work. The commercial designs of Sullivan were emulated in a number of buildings in San Francisco and Los Angeles as well. The most apt exponent of this mode was Charles Whittlesey, who operated in Los Angeles before going to San Francisco. He encrusted his Philharmonic Auditorium and Office Building of 1905 with ornament that is highly reminiscent of the designs of Sullivan and of George Elmslie. His Pacific Building, built in San Francisco in 1907 — perhaps his best work — came far closer to expressing a real understanding of what Sullivan was about. Whittlesey's domestic work was highly varied, ranging from the Mission style to a 1904 house built near Raphael Soriano's Lukens House in West Adams, Los Angeles. Buildings such as this one were probably inspired as much by the monumental work of the Chicagoan George Maher as by the classic designs of the Prairie School. Before the Barnsdall House of 1917, Wright had completed only one structure on the West Coast: the Stewart House, built in Montecito between 1909 and 1910. The only Prairie architect or architects who were in any way directly involved with the West Coast scene were Purcell and Elmslie. In fact, it could well be argued that many features of the Midwest work of this firm had as much to do with the architecture of the West Coast as it did with the architecture of the Prairie School itself. Their single West Coast residence, the Little House, built in Berkeley in 1913–4, therefore seems completely at home in the Bay Area. Their shop for the Edison Company in downtown San Francisco of 1914 was more obviously within the commercial tradition of Sullivan. In Seattle, Andrew Willatsen produced several residences that are pure Prairie in spirit. Other examples, such as the tightly organized design of a San Jose house by Wolf & Wolf of 1915 or a similar concept expressed in a Los Angeles house by Paul Needham of 1909, could be loosely grouped with the Prairie style. Of these, the southern California examples are probably the most original, if for no other reason than that the Mission Revival flavor entered very strongly and simplified their designs.

In its basic formal quality, the California bungalow of the years 1907 to 1917 represents an amalgamation of ideas derived from such diverse sources as the late-nineteenth-century Queen Anne Revival, the Shingle Style, vernacular board-and-batten buildings of the West Coast, California's single-story provincial adobe houses, the Japanese house, and very romanticized versions of the Swiss chalet. At this stage of our historical knowledge, it is really not possible to accept uncritically the assertion that the California bungalow was invented by any single architect. But there can be no doubt that the brothers Charles and Henry Greene were thought of as the major exponents of this mode in their own time. An analysis of their buildings indicates that much of their work had more to do with carrying on the late-nineteenth-century Shingle tradition than with what popularly became known as "California Bungalow." The Bandini House certainly falls within the classic California bungalow tradition, as do the Freeman Ford House and the Crow House. Their most widely known and admired works—the R. R. Blacker House of 1907 and the Gamble House of 1908, both in Pasadena—are in many ways late versions of the Shingle style. A more original work like the Culbertson House in Pasadena of 1911 [*figure 13*] was both Mission and Bungalow.

In the sense of establishing a close rapport between interior and exterior space, the work of a number of other California designers is of equal importance. For example, the Montecito architect Francis Underhill produced a remarkable U-shaped plan in his own house of 1904–5 that, through the use of extremely large plate-glass windows, created the feeling of an open, semi-enclosed series of pavilions. The Los Angeles firm of Walker and Vawter accomplished the same sense of openness in many of its houses through the use of sliding doors, folding doors, and such elements. In the Bay Area, Louis Christian Mullgardt, in a project for his own house in Piedmont of 1906, opened all of the bedrooms by means of glass doors onto a pergola—a sort of a semi-enclosed courtyard—and then on the opposite side he faced a glass-walled corridor onto the entrance area. But while the form and in some cases the structural contribution of these early California bungalows were indeed impressive, the major impact of the bungalow lay in the area of mass housing, a point that I shall touch upon later in this paper.

Of the architects who practiced on the West Coast during these years, unquestionably the most committed was Irving Gill, whose work is so often compared to that of Adolf Loos. Gill's position in California was both a tremendous asset and a decided disadvantage. It was a disadvantage because the West Coast was a provincial area, a center far removed from the mainstream of either American or European architecture. This not only meant that Gill's ideas had very little direct effect on what happened in Europe and America during the 1920s and 1930s, it also meant that he himself was deprived of immediate stimulation in his own environment. The distinct advantage that Gill enjoyed over Loos, or any European, was that the set of historical forms with which he began—the Mission Revival—already constituted a simple, rather direct architectural statement. Gill's "negation of the non-essential" and his "unequivocal faith in the architectural beauty of plain surfaces, simple curves, and straight lines," to use the words of a critic of 1912, were thus much easier to achieve than the experience of Loos and others.[15] By 1906, in the Lee House in San Diego, Gill had worked out his basic concern with the straightforward cubic box. By 1910, with houses such as the Miltimore in South Pasadena [figure 20], he had fully realized his ideal—a rectangular, smooth-surface cube that was related to its garden by extensive open terraces and pergolas. By 1911, in his Timken House in San Diego, he had become even more abstract in the way in which he related each of the rectangular volumes to one another. By 1919, in his Horatio West Court in Santa Monica, he came remarkably close to the spirit of the European International Style of the early 1920s; with the exception of the arches used in the entrance, there was little left to indicate that the heritage of these buildings was the turn-of-the-century Mission Revival style.

Gill's concern with the problem of form and detail was intrinsically connected to his experiments in concrete and other, newer materials. The history of the use of concrete on the West Coast still awaits a detailed study. It is known that it was used as early as the 1880s, in the San Francisco work of Ernest L. Ransome. Gill first began to use the material for walls, floors, and ceilings as early as 1905, and by 1910 he was using the tilt-slab method of construction and metal frames exclusively for doors and windows. Gill, of course, was not entirely alone in his use of concrete. Maybeck had used this material in the early years of the century. Concrete was also a favorite material of Whittlesey, who used it both in his large commercial buildings and, like others, in residential work. C. W. Buchanan, a Los Angeles architect, employed concrete and hollow tile in a number of his residences built around 1910, as did Wolf & Wolf in San Jose.

One further contribution was made by several designers. This was in the area of school planning. The mildness of climate encouraged the development of open-air schools, where exterior space was fully united with exterior porches, pergolas, and courtyards. In northern California, a number of such schools were built by Wolf & Wolf and by John J. Donovan. In the south, William Templeton Johnson, who later became one of the important figures of the Spanish Colonial Revival of the 1920s, built the Parker School in 1912 in San Diego, in which an entire wall of the classroom folded open.

The great period of twentieth-century city planning on the West Coast did not occur until the 1920s with the Spanish Colonial Revival, although there were several interesting redevelopments of older cities, such as that carried out in Ojai by the firm of Mead & Requa from 1916 to 1917. Gill worked with the Olmsted brothers on the layout of the city of Torrance in 1913, but few of his buildings were actually constructed and, regrettably, even fewer exist today. Probably the most inventive approach to West Coast planning during these years was Gill's project for Casa Grande, which was to have been built in the Santa Monica Mountains near Los Angeles in 1915. Undoubtedly the one unique urban planning idea of the decade 1907–17 was the bungalow court, and again, Gill stands in the forefront, with his Lewis Courts in Sierra Madre of 1910. Gill placed the buildings against the edge of the street, leaving the interior space to be divided into private and public gardens and terraces. Each of the dwellings retained its privacy, but at the same time the entire complex of buildings, walls, terraces, pergolas, and gardens assumed a simple but forceful repose. Gill's work at Lewis Courts reminds one rather closely of Tony Garnier's projected Industrial City of 1901 and of several projects by Adolf Loos. Gill continued his interest in the bungalow court in later works such as Echo Park Court in Los Angeles of 1912. Other architects also took up the idea, with the result that Pasadena and Hollywood eventually boasted a number of bungalow courts. The best of these were designed by the Pasadena architect Arthur Heineman, especially his Bowen Court of 1910, Los Robles Court of 1912, and Alexandria Court of 1916. Implicit in all of these was the view that a new relationship should be established among the residences themselves, the public street, and the common park-like space of the court.

The boom in California's population between 1900 and 1917 encouraged one other contribution: mass-production builders' houses. In Los Angeles, San Diego, and San Francisco, and also in Portland, Oregon, vast residential areas were laid out, not (as so often happened at this time in the Midwest or East) for upper-middle-class suburban housing but rather for housing for the middle and lower-middle classes. Many of these projects were large-scale business operations, demanding not only tremendous capital but extensive business organizations that could handle the problems associated with financing, surveying, laying out land, and constructing forty, fifty, or even several hundred houses. It was the work of these development companies that really established the urban character of many of our West Coast cities. The acres of wood bungalows and, later in the 1920s, of Spanish Colonial Revival houses was a direct result of this private profit-making approach, which has come to characterize not only the urban character of the West but that of other places in the United States as well.

By the mid-teens, a decided reaction had set in on the West Coast against the more avant-garde architectural forms. The Mission Revival slowly gave way to the more correct Pueblo Revival and to the classic Spanish Colonial Revival, best experienced in the work of the Santa Barbara architect George Washington Smith in his Brooks Frothingham House of 1922. The interest in the exotic, which had always been around and was exemplified in Sumner Hunt and Silas Burns's entrance to the Southwest Museum in Los Angeles of 1912ff, affected not only the course of historic-oriented eclecticism but also the West Coast work, certainly, of Lloyd Wright and many others, but also, to a certain degree, of Frank Lloyd Wright. Only in the work of R. M. Schindler and, later, Richard Neutra did the West Coast maintain any direct continuity with the modern movement.[16]

The Skyscraper
Winston Weisman

My assignment, as I understand it, is to discuss the state of the skyscraper during the years 1907–17 and to consider its relation to the development of modern architecture. This area of architectural history is more or less uncharted. No one to my knowledge has assembled and carefully studiedthe vast amount of material available to learn precisely what occurred and how events of this decade relate to what went on before and affect what happened later. Nevertheless, and with this in mind, I would like to address the topic at hand using a morphological, rather than a chronological, approach in the hope that it may clarify some issues and stimulate thought and further research.[17]

Let me begin by stating what is obvious but often obscured by emphasis on questions of style and geography: in the entire history of architecture, no type of building ever evolved at such a phenomenal rate as the skyscraper. Between 1870 and 1930 — a mere sixty years — office buildings skyrocketed from 60 to 1,250 feet, with an attendant increase in sheer bulk. The problems presented to architects from a technological and aesthetic point of view in this short span of time and with the momentum of the development were unprecedented. It must have been obvious that the method of building and designing a ten-story building would not work as well for one of twenty stories, and probably would not work at all for a thirty-story structure. By the same token, a satisfactory scheme for a thirty-story building would not do for one of fifty or sixty. By 1890 most of these construction problems had been solved. But for this very reason, the design problems multiplied. Each significant increase in height and bulk called for a change in form. This dynamic morphological process seems to have slowed down with the scheme for Rockefeller Center [figure 105], although variants of it are still making their appearance all around us today.

In order to isolate and evaluate what was going on between 1907 and 1917, it will be necessary to consider briefly what went on before and then after that period. As is well known, the first elevator building, the Equitable Life Assurance Building in New York of 1868, derived from the five-story commercial palaces of the 1850s and 1860s. Like them, the architectural features were horizontally disposed, but the increased height of the building to 130 feet apparently suggested to the designers, Gilman & Kendall and George B. Post, a monumental order of two stories instead of the usual one-story treatment. The advantage of such a scheme becomes clear when the Equitable is compared with the Bennett Building in New York of 1872–3, by Arthur Gilman. In this ten-story structure, the single-story windows are horizontally accented. The effect is one of dull monotony, which even the grouping of the floors into blocks fails to alleviate. Another difficulty, illustrated in the design by Griffith Thomas for the Domestic Sewing Machine Building in New York of the same years, is that unless the increased number of elements is organized carefully, the result will be chaotic. An additional problem that arises from the use of the Equitable mode may be seen in the Western Union Building in New York of 1873–5, by Post. The division of the elevation into two proportionally related parts resulted in a large mansard, which was economically unsound because it was costly to erect and maintain, and because the space underneath the roof was hard to rent. These handicaps foretold the disappearance of the mansard manner by the time of the economic depression of the late 1870s.

The 1870s and early 1880s witnessed a series of interesting experiments and two major solutions for the ten- to twelve-story elevator buildings that were being erected during these years. One was a stacking system in which several stories were grouped together on a proportional basis and then stacked one on top of the other. The second was to deal frankly with the office floors as individual elements beyond the base and cap them with a cornice. Contrary to the horizontal system used in the Bennett Building, in this scheme the windows are tied together vertically by projecting the columns and recessing the spandrels. The Morse Building by Silliman & Farnesworth in New York City of 1878-9 is transitional. It shows some affinity with the Bennett, but an attempt is made to achieve an interesting effect by accenting the columns, thus separating the windows into varying patterns and stacking groups of stories. Notable too is the absence of the mansard. We see the formula repeated, with some minor changes, by William Le Baron Jenney in the Home Life Insurance Building in Chicago of 1883-5. We have a Richardsonian version by Shepley, Rutan & Coolidge in the Ames Building in Boston of 1889, and a classic variant in the American Lithograph Building in New York City of 1895-7, by Richard Ferber. The inability of the stacking method to cope with the increasingly tall structures of the 1890s may be seen in the designs for Kimball & Thompson's eighteen-story Manhattan Life Insurance Company Building of 1893-5, which was 348 feet to the tip of its tower, and in R. H. Robertson's Park Row Building of 1896-9, which was 382 feet high, both in New York City. In each instance, the grouping of stories fails dismally in its effort to give a sense of scale to the mass or a proportion to the parts.

As was said earlier, this stacking formula played little part in the development of the skyscraper between 1907 and 1917. However, the second scheme — treating the office floors as individual elements above the base and capping them with a cornice — did. This involved vertically articulated buildings such as Adler & Sullivan's Wainwright Building in St. Louis of 1890, which can be traced back to compositions such as the Jayne Building in Philadelphia of 1849-51, by William Johnston, and Holabird & Roche's Marquette Building in Chicago of 1894, where we have the same breed of building as the Shillito Department Store in Cincinnati of 1877, by James W. McLaughlin. This formula was to become a favorite of Holabird & Roche, as seen in the Republic Building in Chicago of 1905 and the Brooks Building in Chicago of 1909-10 [figure 11]. In 1911-2 the firm composed the Monroe Building in Chicago, a gable-top version that recalls the Bayard Building in New York City by Adler & Sullivan of 1899. The Woods Theater Building in Chicago by Marshall & Fox of 1917 shows the theme still going strong.

But by 1915, in the Century Building in Chicago by Holabird & Roche, there is evidence of a tripartite composition, which indicates the influence of another concept. The tripartite or Aristotelian scheme was introduced about 1890 and remained popular to the end of the 1907-17 decade because of the many advantages it offered. It was well suited to the elevator building of ten or twelve stories and could be stretched to fit the skeleton-frame structure of twenty or even thirty stories by varying the number of stories within the so-called base, shaft, and capital. Whereas a ten-story building might consist of a two-story base, a six-story shaft, and a two-story capital, a twenty-story building would have essentially the same proportions with a 4 to 12 to 4 ratio.

Obviously there would come a time when the height of skyscrapers was such that the stretching process could no longer work satisfactorily. A comparison of D. H. Burnham & Company's Edison Building in Chicago of 1907 with Post's Havemeyer Building in New York of 1891–2 shows that these compositions are basically the same. The Chicago structure rests solidly on a row of colossal Corinthian columns raised on a plinth that masks the structural steel columns behind. The shaft is separated from the base by an entablature. This is halted by a transitional story that leads to the piers carrying the arches of the uppermost section. To keep the large number of openings in the shaft together, the edges of the elevation are treated more solidly so as to enframe the windows. What results is a composition that is clear in the relationship of parts.

This tripartite formula was borrowed from the Aristotelian notion that every good work of art should have a beginning, middle, and end, a principle reinforced by the classical tradition of the Greek column. It is generally believed that the tripartite system originated on the East Coast; Bruce Price's American Surety Building in New York of 1896 is often cited as an example. However, it should be noted that by 1892–3 Adler & Sullivan were using much the same compositional scheme in the Union Trust Building in St. Louis. Holabird & Roche used the same formula in 1894 in the Old Colony Building in Chicago. By 1899 Cass Gilbert, in the Broadway-Chambers Building in New York, used not only classical details but also color and texture to mark the three different stages of the composition. In 1908 Shepley, Rutan & Coolidge restated this solution in the Corn Exchange Building in Chicago, as did D. H. Burnham & Company in Chicago's Conway Building of 1913. The tripartite scheme was so commonplace by 1909 that it was used to mask a vast number of buildings.

The December 1910 issue of *Architectural Record* contains an interesting article by A. C. David on a group of loft buildings that were then being completed on Fourth Avenue in New York City.[18] These buildings were commercial not only in the sense that they served commerce but also that they were considered merchandise; the greatest amount of rentable space was made available at the lowest possible cost. These speculative buildings involved what became known as "cost and return planning," in which a minimum expense was set aside for aesthetic purposes. In almost every instance, lip service was paid to the Aristotelian method, while major attention was given to well-lighted and ventilated space through the employment of a grid of verticals and horizontals filled with glass. The Everett Building in New York by Starrett & Van Vleck of 1908 [*figure 4*] is a good case in point, as is Daniel Burnham's much more ornate Peoples Gas, Light & Coke Building in Chicago of 1909–11.

By 1914 it was apparent that this tripartite-type system also had its limitations. The thirty-four-story Adams Express Building in New York by Francis H. Kimball of 1912–6 illustrates the difficulties involved in maintaining a satisfactory proportional relationship between the three parts. The base and capital should both have been six to eight stories; this would have required columns and other architectural elements of colossal size in order to work aesthetically. However, in less tall buildings, such as the Lexington Gas and Electric Company Building in Baltimore by Parker, Thomas & Rice of 1915–6, the tripartite scheme continued to be employed.

By the beginning of the twentieth century, economic and social forces joined to push the skyscraper to new heights. In 1906 Ernest Flagg was already planning an addition to his Singer Building in New York, initially designed in 1902. The form chosen by the client and the architect was a forty-one-story, 612-foot tower. Such a form involved something more than the creation of a good shape. By this time experience had proved that it meant extremely high construction costs and relatively low revenue potential. For that reason towers were rarely undertaken by speculators or building loan associations. They were favored by great corporations and important individuals because of their value as status symbols. Historically the tower was associated with commercial buildings as early as the Middle Ages, when it was employed as a dominant feature in the Cloth Guild Hall in Ypres, Belgium. It was equally prominent in the design of the Royal Stock Exchange by Thomas Gresham in London of 1671. In the nineteenth century, it appears at the very beginning of skyscraper history in the New York Tribune Building of 1873–5 by Richard Morris Hunt, where it once again has a symbolic, not utilitarian, purpose.

In the years that immediately followed, the influence of practicality and rationalism was strong enough to discourage the use of the tower form. Proposals like Leroy Buffington's twenty-eight-story Romanesque-inspired tower of 1888 and Price's tower for the *New York Sun* of 1890 were not only not built but were scoffed at. However, by 1906 circumstances had altered. The status value of a very tall building was considered worth paying for, and the tower form was an obvious possibility when compared to the stacking or tripartite solutions. The Singer was followed by the Metropolitan Life Tower of 1909 by Napoleon Le Brun & Sons, which was modeled after the Campanile on Piazza San Marco in Venice and became so famous a landmark that when the original headquarters of 1890 (by the same architects) was demolished, it was decided to keep the tower intact. In 1912 Trowbridge & Livingston erected the Bankers Trust Building on Wall Street, which was a financial burden from its inception, but so powerful was the expressive element that the tower with its pyramidal top—which found many imitators in the 1920s—still stands. Baltimore had an example in Joseph Evans Sperry's Emerson Tower of 1910–1, and in that latter year one of the most famous towers of our decade—namely, the Woolworth Building [*figure 22*]—was erected by Cass Gilbert in New York as a monument to the man who founded the five-and-dime store and to his company. The size of the Woolworth, which is no longer a free-standing tower, of fifty-eight stories and 792 feet presented the now familiar problem of scaling and proportion in a new form. The solution was a base of approximately forty stories, with a tower in several stages culminating in a cone-shaped top. The base and tower are tied together by vertical shafts of differing thicknesses, the latter undoubtedly introduced to avoid monotony. The thrusting verticality was subdued somewhat by stringcourses at five-story intervals. On the whole the Woolworth is considered by many critics to be one of the most successful solutions to the extremely tall building problem, even to this day. One source for this solution may be found in Louis Sullivan's Fraternity Temple project of 1891 in Chicago, where the tower emerges from a complex base and is designed to provide maximum amounts of light and air.

That even the tower-with-base scheme had its limitations is indicated by Ralph Walker's Barclay-Vesey Building of 1926 and Shreve, Lamb & Harmon's Empire State Building of 1931. In both instances the extreme height of approximately one hundred stories and 1,250 feet required a site of considerable size if the base and tower were to have any artistic meaning. What was needed was an unencumbered area of some dimension surrounding the building in order to solve the problem of scale and proportion. It wasn't until Rockefeller Center in the 1930s that a successful solution to this new problem was found. By going beyond the traditional city-block limit into a three-block site, it was possible to build an extremely tall tower of slab proportions and yet maintain a satisfactory scale by surrounding the major feature with smaller, subservient structures. The Rockefeller Center model has been repeated often because it successfully solves not only the architectural and aesthetic problems but the economic and social difficulties as well.

The New York City zoning code of 1916 was to have a significant effect upon the skyscraper form in the years that followed. This code resulted from buildings like the Equitable by Ernest R. Graham of 1915, in which enormous quantities of space were developed in a single scheme. The building's H-shaped plan housed about a million and a half square feet of usable space. This unconscionable exploitation stems from the development of building and loan associations that came into being in the 1890s, intent more on profits than aesthetics or civic responsibility. Two of the earliest examples of the effect of the new zoning code, which required setbacks at given intervals depending upon the width of the street, can be seen in the Fisk Rubber Building of 1920–1 by Carrère & Hastings and the Standard Oil Building of 1922 by Carrère & Hastings and Shreve, Lamb, & Blake. On the whole these solutions were ungainly because the setbacks were predicated on the development of the utmost amount of space at the lowest cost rather than aesthetic considerations. This attitude produced some of the dreariest and ugliest skyscrapers ever erected, such as Rapp & Rapp's Paramount Theater Building of 1926. However, in some instances, such as the Daily News Building by Hood & Howells of 1930 [figure 80], we have an elegant and extremely successful solution.

Before concluding this portion of the review, it might be worth calling attention to the Hallidie Building by Willis Polk in San Francisco of 1917 [figure 38], which comes at the very end of our decade. Even though it may not be considered by some as a skyscraper because of its limited height, nevertheless its novel use of glass curtain-wall, in contradistinction to the systems used in the examples already discussed, points to a form that was to become commonplace in the post–World War II period. In practically all of the cases cited earlier, glass was not considered aesthetically. It was merely a means of introducing light. Generally speaking, greater amounts of glass appeared in loft buildings and warehouses because more light was required, whereas in office buildings it was considered more important to achieve an impressive effect through the use of stone or terra-cotta ornaments. In such office buildings, generally, the massing was thought of being volumetric, with the stone or terra-cotta exterior walls conceived as planes supported by the skeleton frame. In the Hallidie Building, the stone curtain-wall is replaced by glass. This tends to do away with all connection between the structure and its reflection on the outside, which was also the case in the 1880s, when cage construction required that the walls be sturdy enough to support themselves. Contrary to popular belief, the introduction of the skeleton frame did not encourage structurally expressive design, which was more logical in the cage system, but led to a volumetric approach, which was more natural with curtain-wall construction. In the Seagram Building by Ludwig Mies van der Rohe and Philip Johnson of 1957, we have an up-to-date version of the glass curtain-wall, except that the use of the welded I-beam on the exterior recalls the practices of the 1880s for much the same reason — namely, that it makes the wall palpable through the use of three-dimensional form, providing light and shade.

As for the relationship of the skyscraper to the development of modern architecture during 1907–17, there seems to be little direct connection. There is no doubt that the use of the skeleton frame, which was widespread throughout America by this time, had impressed itself upon the minds of European architects, so that men like Mies van der Rohe, Walter Gropius, and Le Corbusier were all influenced in varying degrees by this structural system. The Fagus Factory by Gropius and Adolf Meyer of 1911 is a case in point. While there was undoubtedly much thought expended on how to make use of pre-fabricated metal and brass units by individuals and organizations such as the Werkbund, these schemes never materialized as skyscrapers on European soil during this period. Mies's skyscraper projects of 1919 and shortly thereafter [figure 45] are too late for our period, as are Le Corbusier's cruciform towers in his project for the 1922 Ville Contemporaine. Nevertheless, they do prove that the skyscraper, as an architectural form with great potentialities, was being given serious consideration. Fitting more precisely into our decade would be Antonio Sant'Elia's skyscrapers included in his 1913–4 design for a futurist town. On the other hand, the features of what was to become the International Style had no impact upon the American skyscraper for years to come. It was not until the schemes of Gropius and other European competi-tors for the Chicago Tribune Tower were done in 1922 and given subsequent widespread publication that the effects became noticeable. Not until the 1930s, in such buildings as McGraw-Hill in New York and the Philadelphia Savings Fund Society Building, were the features of the International Style actually employed. The skyscraper in its modern architectural dress really came into being — both here and abroad — in the post–World War II era.

Scandinavian Architecture
Leonard K. Eaton

In Scandinavia during the period 1907–17, as elsewhere in the Western world, the architectural situation was confused, and several different currents can be seen. For the sake of convenience and not necessarily in order of importance, I have grouped these as Americanism, National Romanticism (a word or a coinage I wish I could get rid of because it is neither national nor romantic), Scandinavian Jugend, and Neoclassicism. These occur in three Scandinavian countries in varying ways. My purpose is to indicate the manner in which the major architects — Martin Nyrop and Anton Rosen in Denmark, Lars Sonck and Eliel Saarinen in Finland, and Carl Westman and Ragnar Östberg in Sweden — participated in them. The situation is particu-larly confused by the tendency to focus on a few important buildings, notably the Copenhagen and Stockholm town halls and the Helsinki Railroad Station. This tendency has led to the overlooking of many interesting and important men and structures. One of my primary purposes, therefore, is to go beyond those town halls and that railroad station. I also want to indicate the major relationships to the architecture on the Continent and in this country and to deal with one or two promising areas for historical research.[19]

Everybody knows the Copenhagen City Hall, which antedates our period slightly [figure 1]. It was done by Martin Nyrop between 1892 and 1905. The psychological significance of this building for the Danes was simply overwhelming. It made Nyrop the leading architect in the country, and it entrenched him in a position of authority at Denmark's sole architectural school, the Royal Academy of Fine Arts. He became the acknowledged leader of the Danish architectural profession.

Opposite of Nyrop, working in several different veins, was Anton Rosen. The younger architects in Copenhagen — people like Kay Fisker and Aage Rafn — admired Rosen's Palace Hotel of 1909 a good deal more at this date than they admired Nyrop's town hall. It is a building with strong German affiliations: a good deal of Richard Riemerschmid can be seen in it, and also a good deal of German Jugendstil, particularly in the entrance. Yet at the same time it is thoroughly Danish in its finishing (it is worthwhile noting that Rosen designed everything, down to the ashtrays and the uniforms of the personnel). Even more in the Jugendstil vein, with some overtones of Antoni Gaudí, is a curious structure by Rosen on the Strøget, the main shopping street of Copenhagen — a combination theater and shop known as Hector's Metropole Theatre, designed in 1912. This is a very powerful building, framed in concrete and extremely well expressed. Rosen was much more internationally minded than Nyrop. He traveled a good deal on the Continent and even went so far as Spain, and I've wondered, looking at this building and certain other of his works, if he got to Barcelona. His office attracted the most enterprising younger generation of Danish architects. Fisker worked there, as did Rafn, and so for a little while — probably from about 1912 to 1914 — did the Finn Lars Sonck. It seems probable to me that disordered conditions in Finland attendant on the agitation prior to World War I brought Sonck to Copenhagen. Nyrop, by way of contrast, did his best to recover Danish tradition. His Copenhagen City Hall, however, is really an Italianate building with a good deal of Danish brickwork. At the Royal Academy of Fine Arts he was so authoritarian that he even tried to forbid students from reading foreign periodicals. He was particularly bitter against Finnish magazines; he wanted desperately to be Danish. Rosen, on the other hand, was open to a variety of sources. His Savoy Hotel, also in downtown Copenhagen, of 1906 is pretty clearly influenced by American precedent. There is a Danish version of a Chicago window, and it is clad in bronze. The building section makes clear that he used a skeletal construction quite advanced for the time.

In 1912, however, a new (although fairly short-lived) neoclassical wave began when the architect Carl Petersen undertook a museum on the small island of Funen — the Faaborg Museum, devoted to the preservation of Danish art. Many people took an interest in this kind of design in Denmark. Hack Kampmann, who admired the Faaborg Museum, was influenced by it in his police headquarters in Copenhagen, a major building project that continued until 1924. It was actually undertaken by a consortium of architects, but Kampmann became the leader. It is a curious structure, with some resemblances to the High Renaissance-style palace of Emperor Charles V in Granada. It has a great circular interior court and is very severe and classical in its detail. After it was finished, incidentally, it provoked a good deal of protest from the citizens of Copenhagen. They had the feeling that this was a colossal, forbidding sort of structure, not an appropriate police headquarters for a democratic country like Denmark. It was, I believe, the last major structure that Kampmann did.

In Sweden there was somewhat the same situation with the Stockholm Town Hall, which is a sort of Italianate dream by the waters of the Baltic. Developed by Ragnar Östberg between 1909 and 1923, this was a very large building project that captured the imagination of the Swedes during these years and made Östberg the foremost architect of the country. Yet at the same time, an architect like George Nilsson, hitherto overlooked, could do a commercial building like the one of 1912 at Regeringsgatan 9 in downtown Stockholm, again, pretty clearly based on American precedent. In this case it seems to me to be less a study of Sullivan than of someone like Holabird & Roche. The building has a maximum area of glass and is very beautifully detailed with a rather elongated bay system. Nilsson did one or two other buildings of the same kind in Copenhagen but devoted himself largely to the reform of Swedish school design. He occupies in Sweden a position not unlike that of Dwight H. Perkins in the United States.

The great proponent of Swedish Jugend was Ferdinand Boberg. The Nordiska Kompaniet Department Store in Stockholm of 1915 was the last major building project that Boberg undertook. He had been through an extremely Richardsonian phase earlier — which I have dealt with elsewhere[20] — after which he moved into a Jugend phase that owes a certain amount to Alfred Messel's contemporary Wertheim Store of 1904 in Germany. Boberg however occupied a position analogous to that of Rosen in Denmark; that is, he was outside the architectural establishment. Rosen always wanted to teach at the Royal Academy; he couldn't because Nyrop and his school were entrenched there. Boberg, in a comparable way, ran into a great many problems with a building for the Nobel Foundation in 1912 and after 1915 devoted himself to making a historic record of old Swedish architecture. Traveling about the country in an ancient Volvo, he made about five or six thousand charcoal sketches of decrepit Swedish buildings, and these drawings are now preserved in various museums.

Probably the real heir to Östberg and the man who was to set the pattern for Swedish architecture during these years was Carl Westman. He worked in a much more sober manner. His Law Courts in Stockholm of 1912–5 are a good example. It is Westman who is probably the most Swedish architect of the period; Boberg and Östberg are more the exotics. Westman completed his Town Hall at Nyköping in 1910–1, with traditional Swedish brick detailing and form, and the Röhsska Museum for Design and Handicrafts at Göteborg in 1916. It is worth noting here several negatives, which are oftentimes as important in history as the positives. In neither Denmark nor Sweden was there a great deal of interest in Walter Gropius or the early Werkbund movement in Germany. In neither Denmark nor Sweden was there very much impact of Frank Lloyd Wright. (As a matter of fact, the only references I have been able to find are to a series of lectures on Wright given by Wilhelm Wanscher at the Royal Academy in Copenhagen in 1910 and a very minor publication on the Larkin Building in Buffalo in a Swedish book of 1917.)

It is probable that, in the long run, the most important development in Swedish architecture was the continuing purchase of land by the city of Stockholm, beginning about 1904 and extending throughout our decade of 1907–17. It was this municipal ownership that made possible the great Stockholm planning developments of the 1930s and 1940s and even later, to the present date. It is likewise notable that Gunnar Asplund, who was to be the true mover of Swedish architecture onto the international scene with his famous Stockholm Exhibition of 1930, had at this point not yet made much of an impact. He was occupied with teaching and with editing the Swedish periodical *Arkitektur*.

Concerning developments in Norway, I have not been able to find much of interest, other than one example of Scandinavian Jugend—the Forretningsbank in Trondheim by Johan Osness of 1907. I have not been able to discover much material on Osness so far. The building looks rather Finnish and may serve as an introduction to Finland, which was by far the liveliest country in the north at this period, as it is today. Once again, everybody focuses on the Helsinki Railway Station [*figure 29*], ignoring the buildings that surround it, lead up to it, and lead away from it. This was Eliel Saarinen's major work, undertaken between 1906 and 1914. It started out as a building by the Saarinen firm, Gesellius, Lindgren and Saarinen, and it finally became Saarinen's own building, becoming considerably simpler and more solid in the process. It is interesting to note that this is the first monumental construction in reinforced concrete in Finland, with the facades partly in granite and partly plastered. An extremely interesting development in Helsinki very Richardsonian in character led up to this structure. An example is the clubhouse for the students of Helsinki Polytechnic, designed by Lindahl & Thomé in 1903. For a variety of extremely interesting psychological reasons, I believe, the Finns were drawn to the rough Richardsonian textures; at the same time, they rejected H. H. Richardson's round arches and went in for pointed and truncated arches, as we shall see shortly with Lars Sonck. The Lindahl & Thomé building has a good deal of Jugend flavor in it, including a truly magnificent door handle—a huge thing, about ten or twelve inches, and one of the finest details in the entire building.

Sonck worked, as I just suggested, in what I call the Finnish Richardsonian mode, exemplified in his Telephone Building of 1905. A very vigorous, forceful, and sometimes rather cranky architect, Sonck uses a good deal of Nordic detail in this building, quite arbitrarily truncating the arches and preserving a roughness of texture that relates to a long Finnish history. It is important to emphasize that this is a manifestation of a true national architecture and of true National Romanticism, a movement that had a good deal more vigor in Finland than it did in Denmark or Sweden, precisely because Finland was engaged in finding itself as a nation. It is the same quest for identity to be found in the music of Jean Sibelius (recall all his tone poems based on the Kalevala legend).[21] The interior has a highly personal character, with the vault flattened out and unhappily marred by some quite dreadful murals (Scandinavians have a habit, in my observation, of making nice buildings and then messing them up with some really awful murals and mosaic work).

This Finnish Richardsonian manner began to decline, began to be flattened and smoothed out, in the project for the Helsinki National Museum by Gesellius, Lindgren and Saarinen of 1910 [*figure 10*]. This is a building with a curious agglomeration of textures, again partly Richardsonian, and on the whole having a rather startling resemblance to a Finnish medieval church. This is especially visible from the side elevations, where the front of the building appears a bit like a narthex, with a long nave stretching to a rather diminished apse at the building's eastern end. The whole has a disjointed quality to it and a rather arbitrary feeling, as in the round turrets. What you have in Finland as of about 1912 is a movement toward the flattening out of the surfaces, the loss of the Richardsonian texture, and the development of the mode that Saarinen ultimately brought to this country in 1924. Finally, Sonck's excellent Kallio Church in Helsinki of 1912 is perhaps the last building of the period where the extremely rough textures of the Finnish Richardsonian mode are preserved. The interior is one of the finest that Sonck did.

I hope I have suggested the complexity of the architectural scene in this part of the world and indicated some of the opportunities for research.[22]

Rudolf Steiner and the Emergence of Expressionism
Eugene Santomasso

On New Year's morning, 1923, in Dornach, Switzerland, in the Jura Mountains, a building lay in smoldering ruins. It had been the center of a movement of spiritual science — Anthroposophy — that in 1913 had been founded by its guiding force, Rudolf Steiner. Known as the Goetheanum, the building was the largest of several structures on the Dornach site and had been conceived as a central meeting hall and theater for the cult [figure 76]. As its name suggests, the Goetheanum had been erected in homage to Johann Wolfgang von Goethe, aspects of whose thought were embodied both in the building's form and in the system of Anthroposophy. In the Goetheanum, and in other related buildings at Dornach, Steiner abandoned past architectural styles and worked out an expressionism guided by Goethe's concepts of nature and organic law. Steiner's buildings became as controversial and misunderstood as the Anthroposophical movement itself, as is testified by the Goetheanum's wanton destruction by fire.

Anthroposophy, comprising the Greek words *anthropos* and *sofia* which taken together mean "wisdom of man," was for Steiner a way of knowing, explicitly guided by Goethean principles. He took from Goethe the theory that knowledge proceeds from the penetration of the human mind into the objective material world. From a contemplation of the material world, men gained insight into the greater spiritual reality that permeates all things. Man is thereby capable of moving from the sensible or material realm to the supersensible or spiritual realm by means of his intellect. For Goethe, nature is an entity within which is locked the mystery — namely, the spiritual laws — of the universe. Steiner accepted Goethe's metaphysical concept of the presence of spiritual laws in nature as well as his morphological principle by which these laws of nature determine the shape and metamorphosis of all things. In order to understand natural occurrences as material forms, one must penetrate their visible exterior to discern the organic laws manifest in them. The spiritual science of Anthroposophy teaches man the necessity of living "with and into" objects, or "things," as Steiner called them, if he is to understand the spiritual forces active in the world. Anthroposophy advocates a kind of pantheistic identification with material phenomena so that one may attain higher realms of understanding.

Steiner's earliest architectural designs date from our opening year of 1907, when he was general secretary of the German section of the Theosophical Society. In 1913 he broke with the Theosophical circles to found the Anthroposophical Society and its colony in Dornach. During these years he was evolving his designs for a wholly unique gathering place for the adherents of occult science. On the occasion of the eighteenth annual International Theosophical Congress, held in Munich in May 1907, Steiner felt it important that the assembly hall of his German section be distinguished with occult symbols and forms befitting the interests of the members. To this end he designed seven emblematic seals depicting the spiritual evolution of man according to the Apocalypse of Saint John and the interpretations of spiritual science.[23]

More important for our purposes were his seven columns, which represented the seven ancient planetary spheres. Occult literature tells us that history and the ages of man proceed in seven progressive stages that are controlled by the planets. Consequently, Steiner's columns, representing the canonical seven planets — Saturn, the sun, the moon, Mars, Mercury, Jupiter, and Venus — were conceived in an evolutionary series, with the capitals of each changing to convey this sense of development. The columns were free of pictorial symbols or allegories and expressive of what Steiner called the "cosmic" or spiritual forces that shaped them. The differences in the capitals were achieved by varying the motions of polar forces, the interaction among which created the appropriate shapes and patterns. Goethe's concept of spiritual force, which determined the shapes and metamorphosis of natural forms, was here demonstrated in plastic form. According to Steiner the cosmic forces expressed in the capitals were sounds of spiritual music and therefore demonstrated the notion of the musical harmonies of the heavenly spheres, with each planet signifying a different note. The capitals were, he said, a kind of "frozen music," a metaphor he borrowed from Friedrich Schlegel, which would reappear in his discussions of the forms of the first Goetheanum.

Early in 1908 Steiner proceeded to design bases for the columns, presumably so that they would appear as complete units with a correspondence between the bases and the changing capitals. By the summer of that year, he had conceived a total interior setting for the columns and had commissioned a large-scale model to be built according to his specifications. In 1909 a model in plaster and wood was finished. From it a hall for the Theosophical Society was to be erected in Malsch, Germany. Plans for this hall were abandoned, but the following year the idea was incorporated into the program for a new house for the Theosophical Society in Stuttgart. Steiner's columned hall was built entirely of stone and located in the building's cellar beneath a large auditorium. It was completed during the winter of 1911–2. The subterranean hall was a windowless elliptical space as in the original model for Malsch. The rows of sandstone columns supported a continuous arcade from which the central domed vault spread directly, with no entablature intervening. While the other walls were painted red, the vault had a blue field on which were painted signs of the zodiac and astral bodies. In the original conception, light was to enter through an oculus in this main vault so that at nine in the morning on the spring equinox the sun's rays would strike a certain spot on the interior. The same oculus was built into the subterranean hall, but it is not known what provisions, if any, were made for the transmission of natural light into this space.

Certain religious traditions of India and the Near East are suggested by the cosmological program of the hall. The elliptical space may refer to the Hindu image found in the popular writings of the Purana of the cosmic egg, or bubble, from which all reality is eternally created. Steiner described this very notion in his book *Occult Science: An Outline*, which was published in 1909 as an expansion of a lecture series he gave in 1906. One of the revelations of occult science, he writes, is the astral sheath, egg-shaped in form, that permanently surrounds man. The more overt cosmic symbolism in the Stuttgart hall relates to the astro-religious beliefs of the ancient Near East. The world is imagined as a system of parts that are spiritually controlled by the movements and configurations of heavenly bodies. Everything on earth is believed to be encompassed and guided by celestial forces. These ideas, which were inherent in the planetary columns at Munich, were more fully integrated in the Theosophical Society hall for Stuttgart, while the Goethean principles of organic law were superseded by Indian and Near Eastern concepts.

Anthroposophy, which is more Western and Christian in its philosophy, would initiate a new iconographic program at the Goetheanum. As the Stuttgart hall was nearing completion, Steiner was developing plans for an auditorium and theater that was to have been the center of the project in Munich. It is clear that the theater was to serve primarily for the presentation of Steiner's cycle of four mystery plays, which were being introduced in Munich, one each year, between 1909 and 1913. Sketches of the interior indicate that Steiner was continuing to evolve an architectural setting in which all forms — in particular, the columns — would exist in harmony with one another. The relatively static disposition of the forms and symbols at Stuttgart did not convey adequately the active forces in the universe. Those forces, which hitherto were embodied only in the changing forms of the columns' capitals and bases, were now spread to the arches of the colonnade and to the wall surfaces above them. Steiner was working out an architecture that would be totally responsive to nature's cosmic laws.

The Goetheanum, begun on September 20, 1913, was the outcome of these endeavors. It consisted of the interpenetration of two domed, cylindrical spaces of unequal size. The main space faced west; the smaller, apsidal space faced east, with transverse wings at the juncture of the two sections. The building was of timber and was raised on a concrete substructure whose periphery undulated in conformity with the perimeter of the inner wooden structure. Steiner considered such a design to be organic, and his description of the relationship between a nutshell and its kernel seems applicable here: "The nut has a shell. This nut is formed around the kernel, according to the same laws as those by which the kernel itself has grown, and you cannot imagine the shell being any different from what it is, once the kernel is as it is." [24] Correspondences in the plan between the exterior protrusions and the interior forms were in keeping with this organic analogy. "Natural laws," he said, "were to have created an organism no one part of which could be changed." The two interpenetrating domes were symbolic of Goethe's idea of the unity and interdependence of the two realms of knowledge — the sensible and the supersensible. Inside the Goetheanum one moved from a knowledge of the material world to a perception of a higher spiritual world.

The plan of the Goetheanum also suggested the cosmic harmonies experienced by initiates into an occult science. In his lectures on the building Steiner alluded to the arching curve of the human head as a reflection of the static vault of the universe. This kinship may be sensed in the anthropomorphic, somewhat skull-like aspect of the plan and in the domed vault, the two main features of the elevation. Here, replacing the cosmic egg of the hall at Stuttgart, is the circle, which for Goethe had been the pattern of the unending dance of nature. The Goetheanum expressed what, for Steiner, was the twofold purpose of architecture: a sheltering from outside cosmic forces and an opening movement into the cosmos. The result was an architecture of both enclosure and expansion, one that responded to the so-called formative forces of the universe, producing what he called a "dynamic mechanic" interaction of exterior and interior form. Walls, therefore, were not static, continuous planes but were converted into multiple levels so as to give the impression of "a living organism that allows elevations and depressions to grow out of itself." [25] Aiding these wall effects were palmetto motifs, symbolic of the enclosing forces of the earth and varied to express the different positions and shapes of wall openings; over windows the palmettos were cusped lobes in high relief, while over doors they were indented. This organic movement was carried beyond the walls to the boldly projecting, curved eaves of the entrance and transverse wings. The mobility of the lower portions of the Goetheanum's exterior contrasted with the static volumes of the dome.

One entered the building on the lower level, ascending by either of two curving stairways to a foyer on the main level and then proceeding into the auditorium under the organ loft and down the center aisle. In the changing sequence of levels and spaces there was a sense of ritual, which began at the entrance stairways. A pillar supporting each staircase was a freely modeled, zoomorphic form that seemed to exult in its performance, unlike the rigid piers nearby. Steiner compared the elliptical arches that framed the stairway to the semicircular canals of the ear and apparently derived them by intuiting the sensations of calm and balance that he wanted to evoke: "I said to myself, whoever goes up there must have the sensation 'there I will be secluded with my soul, there is peace for the soul, so it can receive the highest truths for which man can as yet have strived.'" [26]

In the auditorium, double rows of seven columns converged toward the proscenium arch, while corresponding rows of six columns each were repeated in the apsidal stage space. Orientation toward the apsidal stage, as if it were a sanctuary, created an interior that seemed to be both theater and temple. Since the ultimate experience was to be man's recognition of higher truths, one may well relate the series of seven columns to a passage in *Proverbs* 9:1: "Wisdom has built her house. She has set up her seven pillars." The respondent series of six columns in the apsidal stage must have embodied the ancient idea of perfection, which was symbolized by that number. The sense of changing shapes in the column capitals and bases was augmented by the metamorphosis of similar shapes along the arches and the entablature. Rising and falling movements gave active expression to the normally static principle of load and support. The columns and entablature were intended to be felt empathically as embodying the spiritual forces of good and evil, Lucifer and Ahriman. Levitating Luciferian forces were opposed to compressive Ahrimanic forces, and in the equilibrium between the two was to be sensed the presence of the divine spirit of Christ.

The guiding aesthetic principle of this interior was, once again, Schlegel's analogy of architecture as frozen music, which Steiner had used in 1907 to explain the columns in his Munich project. For the columns at the Goetheanum, Steiner carefully chose seven different-colored woods and compared them to the notes of the scale, which seems to indicate that besides referring to the musical harmony of the heavenly spheres the columns were now also thought of as polyphonic sequences of color. The subtle chromatic intervals between the columns modulated, in a sense, the flowing forms of the arches and entablature. The plastic movements were thought to be in resonance with the vibrations from the organ and with "the spoken music," as Steiner called the recitations and lectures. Forms were also to be attuned to the dialogue and movement of the mystery plays and eurhythmic dances that were to be, but were never, performed there due to the fire.

Steiner's Wagnerian mission at the Goetheanum was to create an interior that harmoniously united the formative and musical arts. As he stated in a lecture of 1915:

> Here lies the direction for the further development of art, from our time onward to the future. We shall have to learn to experience the *reconciliation of the arts.*... We have tried in our building to make a beginning in this direction, for it is our intention that its very form shall express this reconciliation of architecture with music.... Music will be more plastic than it has been in the past, and architecture and sculpture more musical.[27]

The Goetheanum manifested throughout a sculptural approach to architecture. As we have suggested, major surfaces on both the exterior and interior were activated with hollows and protrusions, creating a counterpoint of positive and negative shapes. In the auditorium, forms, colors, and sounds were drawn into resonant rhythms and fluctuations. The entablature and columns directed all movement from the west to the east. One progressed, as we have observed, from the sphere of the physical world toward the sphere of spiritual revelation: the apsidal stage. There, in a central niche, would have stood the sculpture group of Christ surrounded by Lucifer and Ahriman, the visual embodiment of those very forces whose presence was to have been sensed in the forms of the auditorium. What is perhaps the most programmatic expressionist architecture ever devised was produced here at the Goetheanum. Steiner's avowed intention was "to translate the static geometric structure of previous architecture into an organic-dynamic method of designing and shaping."[28] He believed the structure to express, and thereby embody, the antithetical forces of the cosmos, an idea conveyed by the correspondences between positive and negative surfaces and shapes and the consistent arrangement of forms in pairs.

Steiner, following Theodor Lipps, believed that one had to project himself completely into a form in order to perceive its significance. This reliance upon the empathy theory of Lipps is especially meaningful in Steiner's case; Lipps's theory of empathy belongs to a Romantic philosophical tradition leading back to Goethe. It is easy to imagine that Steiner, like so many others, was captivated by Wilhelm Worringer's *Abstraktion und Einfühlung* (*Abstraction and Empathy*), published in Munich in 1908. Unquestionably it was Worringer's chapter on ornament that strengthened Steiner's views on the formal and symbolic significance of the palmetto motif in art. Steiner's discussion of the acanthus and palmetto forms in a lecture of June 1914 essentially paraphrased Worringer. These connections proved to be consequential in the designing of the Goetheanum where, as we have seen, palmettos were the only exterior decoration, the shapes and clusters of which were varied to elicit different empathic responses.

Other buildings at Dornach completed while the construction of the Goetheanum was still in its early stages indicate a change in Steiner's work. The heating and electric plant of 1914 and Haus Duldeck of 1915, both of concrete, were successive steps in an evolution away from the heterogeneous forms and intricate symbolism of the Goetheanum toward a heightened interaction of abstract volumes and surfaces. These objectives culminated in the second and larger Goetheanum, which was begun in 1924. Goetheanum I and Goetheanum II represent contrasting "organic" solutions characteristic of expressionism: those of a predominantly flowing contour character, and those of a predominantly blocky, fragmented, or crystalline one. The overpowering cliff-like masses of Goetheanum II, prophetic of recent trends in modern architecture, tend to eclipse the Romantic programming of the earlier building. But as one looks out over the foothills of the Jura Mountains from the terrace of Goetheanum II, there still rises today the multi-horned chimney of the earlier power plant, emitting smoke, like some eruptive presence in the landscape.[29]

The Literature of the Decade, 1907–17
Adolf K. Placzek

This will be a very brief survey of the architectural literature of the decade. When speaking of 1907–17, one cannot really speak of a single unit of time but rather of two units, with a catastrophic break in the middle. That the curtain came down on much of Europe's old civilization in 1914 is such a paramount fact that we have to put it into the center of our symposium — much as the evil year 1933 was at the center of our 1964 discussion, whether we liked it or not. Thus, strictly speaking, we are dealing with what I might call a hexade ([sic] 1907–14) and a tetrade (1914–7) in all of Europe except Holland and the Scandinavian countries. The hexade 1907–14 was one of colossal strides toward the catastrophe but also toward the foundations of the very different postwar civilization.

In our symposium of 1962 it was emphasized by several participants that most of the architectural literature of 1918–28 was based on the insights, ideas, and projects achieved before 1914. This is indeed so, as a close look at the hexade will confirm. At the same time, the years before 1914 were years of spectacular buildings more than of spectacular books; in the decade 1918–28, the opposite, by and large, was true.

There are singular exceptions on both sides: on the one side, Frank Lloyd Wright's Wasmuth portfolio; on the other, Erich Mendelsohn's Einstein Tower, for example [figure 44]. But overall the observation can be maintained. There are several possible reasons for this relative paucity of architectural literature during the decade, and even during the hexade. The first reason — the most general one — can be found in the material reality of architectural progress. The building usually precedes the book, much in the way Jean-Paul Sartre says existence precedes essence. Much of the theory of architecture that was about to emerge is based on the actual designs of this hexade/decade. A second reason for the comparative thinness of literature as compared to building lies even more in material facts; specifically, in economics. The years 1907–14 were prosperous, indeed affluent, years, and for those who saw no handwriting on the wall, which obviously was the overwhelming majority of people, they were years of profound security. Thus, there was a great deal of building taking place: railroad stations, embassies, theaters, and above all factories. This was in sharp contrast to the years after 1918, when poverty, crisis, and inflation were the background to much sparser building and much more radical theoretical thinking and writing. All this applies specifically to architectural commentary.

In an area where the written work and the work of art, the design, are one—namely, in poetry—this was a hexade of conspicuous richness. Between 1908 and 1912, the following poets started publishing modern avant-garde poetry: Ezra Pound and William Carlos Williams in America; Saint-Jean Perse, Max Jacob, and Guillaume Apollinaire in France; Gottfried Benn and the Sturm and Aktion groups in Germany; Vladimir Mayakovsky and Boris Pasternak in Russia; Giuseppe Ungaretti and the futurists in Italy; and so on. It was a "design time" in literature, then, as it was in architecture. It was also the time of the cubist breakthrough in painting and the emergence of atonal composition in music, which started around 1908–9. This was also the time the psychoanalytic movement became known internationally in writing. Finally, the theory of relativity was taken seriously for the first time around 1911–2.

To return to architecture, and to the explanation for the elusiveness of architectural theories during this magnificent decade/hexade, there is a third reason lying in the historical—or what might be called "generational"—constellation. Art nouveau had already reached its climax and was beginning to recede into the quite aptly called "Style of 1900" (never the "Style of 1910"). The titans of the next phase had yet to grow to maturity. In 1907 Ludwig Mies van der Rohe was twenty-one years old; Mendelsohn, twenty; Walter Gropius, twenty-four; and Le Corbusier, twenty. Naturally, not much can be found in print about them—they were all just starting. These were the men born around 1886. Before them came the generation born around 1867: Joseph Maria Olbrich, in 1867; Peter Behrens and Charles Rennie Mackintosh, in 1868; Hans Poelzig and Tony Garnier, in 1869; Adolf Loos and Josef Hoffmann, in 1870; and Auguste Perret, in 1874. Hendrik Petrus Berlage and Louis Sullivan were born earlier, in 1856, as was Charles Voysey: a pretty rich year for architects-to-be. Victor Horta and Hermann Muthesius followed in 1861, and Henry van de Velde, in 1863. Otto Wagner was the earliest of the whole lot, born in 1841, and what a lot it obviously was. Not since the Renaissance has there been a shinier galaxy of great architects within a generation. To come back to my point, the older architects with whom we seem to be concerned the most—the men who were roughly forty in 1907—were not Mies, Gropius, Le Corbusier.

What then were the architectural books of the decade? We always run into conceptual difficulties when we ask this question because architectural literature consists of a variety of elements in its relationship to architecture itself. It is theory, it is program, it is manifesto, it is running commentary, it is a record and a description of buildings built, and it is, in a way, a *résumé* of achievements already reached. There are also many types of architectural literature: biography, collected works, the portfolio or album (the Wasmuth portfolio, for example, although it is not a typical one). The categories overlap.

Beginning with Austria, one of the crucial countries, Otto Wagner dominates the scene. At age sixty-six in 1907, he was a whole generation ahead of the decisive 1867–8 group and thus a pioneer in every respect. His great programmatic *Moderne Architektur* came out in 1896 but was repeatedly reprinted during the decade. The fourth edition came out in 1914 and had a very characteristic variation in the title: it was now called *Die Baukunst unserer Zeit*—not *Moderne Architektur* but "the architecture of our time." Wagner already had reached the illustrious status whereby he had a biography written about him, by Joseph August Lux, in 1914, and he also had an ongoing portfolio of collected works, which started in 1892 and continued seriatim up to 1922, called *Einige Skizzen, Projekte und ausgeführte Bauwerke*. (The simi-larity of his title with that of Wright's portfolio is quite interesting.) Olbrich had a sumptuous edition of collected works, too, simply called *Architektur*, published in 1901 on through 1913, right into our decade. Again, it was beau-tifully produced, visually stunning. Hoffmann and the Wiener Werkstätte, founded in 1903, received a good deal of publicity but almost entirely in periodicals. Hoffmann's great opponent, Loos, is an interesting case. He was highly articulate as both a writer and an architect. His famous "Ornament und Verbrechen" ("Ornament and Crime"), the arch-manifesto of architec-tural purism, was actually written and given as a lecture in 1908 but cannot be found in print anywhere until 1913, when it came out in French in *Cahiers d'aujourd'hui*. In German, quite incredibly, it was not available until 1929, and in English it is still rather elusive. Yet its impact was very great, if somehow underground, almost surreptitious.[30]

Turning to Germany, we find that the key figure was Behrens — the Otto Wagner of Germany, although much younger. He did not yet rate a collected works and never got one in the very different postwar period, but there is a fine book written about him pre-1914 by Fritz Hoeber.[31] A great, problematic event was the founding of the Deutscher Werkbund in 1907. The Werkbund *Jahrbücher* started only in 1912, but the first three volumes, which appeared before the war, were very important. Muthesius wrote a great deal during the decade; his *Kunstgewerbe und Architektur* came out in 1907. With regard to the periodicals, *Moderne Bauformen* started in 1901 but really got going in our decade. *Wasmuths Monatshefte für Baukunst* began in 1914 and was probably the most important periodical of the time.

Wright's Wasmuth portfolio should rightly be put under Germany rather than America because its influence was much stronger in Europe than in the United States. For those who are not completely versed, its full title is *Ausgeführte Bauten und Entwürfe* and it came out in 1910. A smaller volume, minus the *Entwürfe* (projects) — just the *Bauten* (buildings) — came out in 1911. The 1910 portfolio was almost certainly seen and read by Gropius, Mies, Behrens, and Poelzig, and, in fact, by everybody who was anybody. It was the great book of the decade and can be put in the category of collected works — but then again, not quite, because Wright was still under forty and had yet to reach greater heights. In that sense it was a pioneering and revo-lutionary statement, a coherent program of philosophy, and also the most up-to-date record of the running commentary type.

We now turn to Holland, the third key country during this decade. We must first say that there is no "hexade" or "tetrade" but rather a definitive decade. This is because the Dutch never got into World War I, and they kept on publishing, conspicuously detached from the European disaster. There were fine architecture books coming out in 1915, 1916, and 1917 — in fact, *De Stijl* started in 1917, and *Wendingen*, in 1918 (of all years), when almost every-one else was completely silent. Van de Velde's theoretical writings, some-what like Otto Wagner's, actually predate the decade, except for his fine volume of essays that came out in 1910.[32] The most prolific Dutch writer of the decade was Berlage. His wonderfully interesting American travel book, *Amerikaansche Reisherinneringen*, dates from 1913. What he chose to write about is noteworthy. (He certainly saw Sullivan on his trip, but this is another story.) His theoretical book *Grundlagen und Entwicklung der Architektur* came out in 1908, and his *Studies over bouwkunst*, written in Dutch rather than

German, in 1911.[33] By this point he had already built a great deal — the Stock Exchange in Amsterdam was ten years old — so again, the book follows the building rather than the other way around.

France is notable for having the most conspicuous lack of theoretical writing. It was the painters and poets who did all of the sounding-off. Auguste Perret was always a rather silent man; we know very little about him. There are two periodicals that appear rather at the tail end of art nouveau: one is *L'Architecture du vingtième siecle*.[34] Among the rarest of bibliographic rarities (I've never seen it; it's not in Avery Library) is a very early book by Le Corbusier, *Étude sur le mouvement d'art décoratif en Allemagne*, of 1911. Therefore it can safely be said that it was not a terribly influential book. Garnier's *Cité Industrielle* was written in stages from 1901 on and came out during the war in 1917. This was an enormously important statement in every respect: urbanistically, as a utopia, and also in terms of design. It ushered in the decade of *Vers une architecture* and *L'Esprit Nouveau*.

Turning next to England, one finds a preponderance of social and moral writing over the aesthetic, in typically English fashion. The Arts and Crafts movement was past its peak but still very active and producing quite a bit of literature. The prolific Charles Robert Ashbee must be mentioned. He pops up in very odd places, including the American context. His two remarkable books, *Where the Great City Stands: A Study in New Civics* (1917) and the earlier *Craftsmanship in Competitive Industry* (1908), exemplify the social slant. (Incidentally, Ashbee also wrote the introduction to Wright's second, smaller portfolio, of 1911.) Voysey had fairly good publicity in journals, but there is nothing about him in book form. Mackintosh was largely ignored; his work was mainly an aesthetic phenomenon. This was also a time of great urbanistic advances in England. A high point is Raymond Unwin's book of 1909, *Town Planning in Practice*, which comes in the wake of Ebenezer Howard's garden city movement, which belongs to the preceding decade.

Finally, we turn to the United States, and here the story is a rather complex one. I think we found out this morning how complex it really was. What I found (and I will probably be crucified at tomorrow morning's open discussion for saying this) is that there was a lack of any real impact of the Chicago School or the Prairie School in print, at least in the East. The literature seems to be almost totally dominated by the eclectics and, in the East, by the Beaux-Arts group. This was the golden age of the architectural monograph, of collected works, one after the other. There is the great McKim, Mead & White set, started in 1915. Bertram Goodhue got his monograph in 1914; he got another one later. Even Charles Platt had a beautiful monograph by 1913. For Sullivan, on the other hand, it was a dark decade. The *Kindergarten Chats* (1901) had been published; the *Autobiography* (1924) was yet to come; and *Democracy: A Man-Search* was being written but was not to be published until 1962. There was Wright's famous article in the March 1908 *Architectural Record*, "In the Cause of Architecture," which was then followed by several others of the same name. But that is my point. If you really want to look into the story of the modern movement in the United States, it is the periodicals that carry it most conspicuously. There were more architectural periodicals in the decade 1907–17 than there are now, which is rather interesting, and they were infinitely richer. The list includes *American Architect, Architectural Record, Brickbuilder* (later *Architectural Forum*), *Architects and Builders* (*Architecture and Building* after February 1911), and *Western Architect*, as well as the publications by the Chicago Architectural Club of its exhibitions and by the T-Square Club of its competitions. It is a very rich periodical literature, and in it you get something of the emerging story of the decline and downfall of Chicago architecture and the Prairie School.

Vienna
Eduard F. Sekler

I am happy that Dolf Placzek read his splendid paper previous to mine. It will enable me to be somewhat shorter, as I had planned to point out the great importance of the literature of the period. Having had an opportunity to work in some of the libraries these Viennese artists had used, I was impressed with the regularity with which recent publications, whether it was *Dekorative Kunst* or *The Studio,* must have arrived. I have one interesting little addendum which may not be known to all of you. There is an old tradition, at least among people who still are linked to Otto Wagner's school, that when Wagner first saw the great Wasmuth portfolio, he had it brought to school and into the studio and, with his students around him, looked through it. Then he said, "Meine Herren, hier ist einer der kann mehr als ich" (gentlemen, here is someone who can do more than I). This is something he would not normally say about any other architect. On the other hand, Frank Lloyd Wright did speak of "Professor Wagner, the great architect" as one of the few Austrians whom he valued highly.

A good way to come to the heart of the matter of what is most relevant in our decade in Vienna is to try to put oneself in the position of the young man in architecture. What was relevant to him in 1907? What would he find? Where would he turn? Where would he sense the really important developments taking place? What he would find in buildings was, no doubt, directly related to the people who designed them and who were his potential teachers. It is very important to realize that architecture was a profession taught in only a few schools, and that the developments in this decade and the following one are to be understood in terms of the professors who taught ten years earlier. One example is Friedrich Ohmann, who had just completed his monumental complex on the Wienfluss — the river that gives Vienna its name — in 1906–7. Ohmann had become Wagner's colleague at the Academy of Fine Arts, and stayed on after Wagner left, having reached retirement age, in 1911. Wagner was still permitted to teach those students who had enrolled earlier, but otherwise Ohmann, and Wagner's former pupil, Leopold Bauer, were the important teachers. Bauer went from being a very strong Wagnerian to designing the heavily neoclassical National Bank (1911–9) in our decade. We could call Ohmann's work a baroque version of art nouveau — he was somebody who knows the Secession, who knows how to handle that style, but whose sympathies were really with the past. This isn't surprising; Ohmann had become the court architect, commissioned to finish the Imperial Castle.

Wagner's Schützenhaus (sluice-gate building), on the other hand, put up in 1906–8, is a severely technical building, constructed during a great period of technical and urbanistic improvement in a vigorously growing city. If Vienna in 1890 had a population of 1,342,000, in 1910 it had more than two million — more inhabitants than today. This makes it understandable why you find great schemes everywhere, and the kind of concern that Wagner writes about in *Die Großstadt*, the study he published in 1911. But his kind of advanced thought, his manner of handling architecture, certainly was not one that fit the prevailing mood of the ruling circles. There is a famous anecdote about how, at the dedication of the church at the Steinhof in 1908, just at the beginning of our period, Archduke Franz Ferdinand supposedly said at the end of his speech, "but the nicest style of all is that of Maria Theresia." When Wagner pointed out to him that the cannons continued to be decorated and today we make them plain, the archduke turned away in icy silence; he persecuted the architect for the rest of his life, which was, of course, traumatically cut short at Sarajevo. Allegedly Wagner later remarked caustically that murder removed the single most important obstacle to the advancement of modern architecture in Austria.

There was a vigorously pulsating life in Vienna, capital of a great empire, one that was beset by the problem of the different nationalities who lived together there. The prevailing mood was described very well by Franz Servaes in 1908; Austrian statesmanship, on the whole, perpetuated a well-organized and smoothly oiled system of bureaucratic hindrances. The Austrian *Hofräte* and *Sektionschefs* were virtuosos in the art of preventing anything from happening. What did happen were rather small things at first, like Loos's little "American Bar" near the Kärntnerstrasse [*figure 2*], or a little cabaret by Josef Hoffmann (not so well known and no longer existing) called the Fledermaus, both designed in 1907. The comparison is instructive, both for what they have in common and for how they differ. There is a strong feeling for tectonic effects in the work of Loos — for example, the coffering of the ceiling, the way the supporting members are exposed. With Hoffmann, we have a treatment of plane surfaces with a very colorful, abstract mosaic done in ceramics or in white and dark gray. The ways of the two architects clearly have parted already.

I discuss these two places to remind you of the kind of clientele served by the most advanced designers — for example, the society ladies Klimt portrays in his paintings. The chic thing at that moment was to live *à l'anglaise*, out in a garden suburb like the Hohe Warte, where a house by Hoffmann (although it no longer exists) very clearly recalls English prototypes. It was, in fact, first published with a big quotation from William Morris right on top.[35]

Hoffmann showed just such an English-influenced interior in an exhibition that was a very significant event in the Viennese art world at the time. This was the *Wiener Kunstschau* of 1908, a show put up under Klimt's direction by a group that had seceded from the Secession. By 1905 the Secession was definitively dead as an avant-garde organization; the most advanced artists had left it and informally organized around Klimt. Hoffmann designed the exhibition pavilion for the *Kunstschau* in the vocabulary he had perfected during the four or five years prior to 1908. But this would be about the last time he would make such completely straightforward, unimpeded use of unbroken planes — a very atectonic handling, an almost Egyptian mastaba-type stepping back of the planes, as if they were ready to slide past each other, with the sculpture perfectly in keeping with this approach.

Hoffmann also executed several other designs for the *Kunstschau*, and in these you find echoes of his great building going up at this time, the Stoclet Palace in Brussels, to which I shall return in a moment [*figure 14*]. This pavilion that Hoffman designed celebrated sixty years of the emperor's reign. One of the young men in architecture who had come to Vienna in

1907 recalls visiting Hoffmann and finding him preparing some kind of big fête for the imperial court. This was young Mr. Jeanneret, who at the time was traveling through Europe, visiting, interestingly enough, the Vienna Kunstgewerbeschule, the painter Alfred Roller, and Hoffmann, who on the strength of his drawings invited him to work in his office. But Jeanneret decided to leave for Paris.

At the same time, the great activity of Hoffmann's old master, Otto Wagner, continued. He worked on a project through the whole decade and beyond but, to his great frustration, was unable to carry through — it was the museum on the Karlsplatz, again tied into a greater urbanistic scheme. When Wagner's protector, Karl Lueger, died, nothing ever came of it. The same happened to the Kriegsministerium design by Adolf Loos that dates from 1908, and this, of course, is of particular interest when compared to Hoffmann's *Kunstschau* of the same date.

Two years later Mr. Loos began building his house on the Michaelerplatz, about which Emperor Franz Josef is supposed to have said, "If that goes up I will move out of the Hofburg." What is not so well known is that in one of his earlier versions of the design, Loos had striations with a meander pattern in the marble of the facade, in spite of the plainness of the design. The ground floor is, of course, a trabeated design with a colonnade. Still I don't need to remind you that the outcry in Vienna against this building supposedly was sufficient to give Loos his famous stomach ulcer. Yet he continued in an undaunted fashion to pursue his search for very direct, straightforward, clear expression.

In the total picture of the man, however, it is also important to emphasize other components. Because of his earlier stay in the United States, he must have known what went on architecturally in Chicago. His project for a department store in Alexandria, Egypt, of 1910, has a certain classical discipline. But it also has what I would call American elements, something you find in many of his designs. You also see the Anglo-Saxon influence in the way he typically handles the stair and fireplace in some of his houses. At the same time, he believed that every architect should have learned from the Romans. In a 1909 statement he says of Schinkel, "May the light of this important and outstanding figure be cast above the coming generation of architects!"[36] In a design of 1916–7 for the Horticultural Association Grounds in Vienna, an important urbanistic complex, you see both these components. You see the skyscrapers in the back, and you see the classical colonnades in the front.

A severe classicism can also be seen in Josef Plecnik's Heilig Geist Kirche in Vienna, of 1910–3. By this time Hoffmann too had changed his vocabulary — turning strongly classical, following the general trend, and making it difficult to believe that the Stoclet Palace was only finished in 1911, an event considered extremely momentous at the time. At the Werkbund meeting in 1911, when everybody was very excited because the Italo-Turkish War had just started, Karl Ernst Osthaus called the meeting to order, saying that for members of the Werkbund it was more important to realize that the Stoclet Palace had finally been finished and that there had not been "a work of such maturity and artistic grandeur...in Europe since the days of Baroque." I have spoken at length about this building on other occasions.[37] What I want to remind you of is the way surfaces are handled as independent planes coming together at joints, as if they had been slid into place. This kind of passive dematerialization can be found in the interior too. There is not an active liberating of space, as you find in the oeuvre of Wright — a real exploding of the planes. With Hoffmann it is just at the edge that the planes slide past each other and open. We have the same attitude in Klimt's paintings, where figures slide and float past each other passively, as if everything were gliding and sliding. In a way, Hoffmann's style described his own period. As Hugo von Hofmannsthal characterized it, "[T]he essence of our epoch is ambiguity and uncertainty. It can only rest on that which is gliding and it is aware that gliding is what other generations believed firm."[38] Yet when we compare the stylization of the Stoclet with a stucco relief that Hoffmann did in 1902 for one of the Secession exhibitions, we realize that that the bold asymmetrical handling of planar elements was not coincidental, that it came from here. An even earlier example of this handling — a component that Hoffmann leaves behind in our decade — may be found in a student drawing he made in 1896 on a trip to southern Italy to study "anonymous" architecture, as we would call it.

A similar case of going back to sources — if not Mediterranean sources — in the decade we are considering is Hoffmann's Primavesi House of 1913, which uses Slavonic folk motifs, by this date part of a very prevalent movement in architecture. Of course nationalism was rampant at this time, not just in the work of architects. It was an attempt to return to a moment when there was a sound tradition. To return to Hoffmann's exhibition pavilion interior, if you look at the settee on which Mimi Marlow is sitting, in a photograph of her wearing a Wiener Werkstätte dress, you see a very strong Empire form. Echoes of the same may be found in a flat designed by Hoffmann and his collaborators at the Wiener Werkstätte. There is a kind of lighthearted playfulness that marks what is to follow: a spirit that allows a motif, once it has been invented, to be used on a piece of furniture — the top of a table, say — or the top of the Austrian Pavilion at the 1914 Werkbund exhibition [figure 28]. The atectonic attitude remains. To take tectonic forms like pilasters and then put a very thin slab on top is a very deliberate negation of the play between load and force. Yet, on the inside there was an extremely dignified noble entrance hall (which people who knew it tell me was one of the finest spaces in the whole exhibition), recalling the discipline that Hoffmann comes from, namely that of his great master, Otto Wagner, who, in 1913, designed the Lupus Hospital, pulling together once more his whole achievement in terms of a planar, slab-like handling and a direct expression of the carrying parts.

Let us return to the inside of the Werkbund pavilion, where we now find a new generation coming up that takes us to the end of our period. For the first time, Oskar Strnad comes to the fore. Hoffmann welcomed Strnad to the Kunstgewerbeschule when Strnad was a young man, although Strnad's approach would be quite different from the older architect's. A 1914 design by Strnad, Josef Frank, and Oskar Wlach for a house on the outskirts of Vienna with an almost aggressive ugliness shows that these people are trying to break away from routine. Although they were still working in a somewhat classical vocabulary quite deliberately, they were also posing new questions. Strnad, for example, was a great teacher. He had a great interest in the theater — something typical of our decade. I mentioned Roller, the great stage designer. Those were the designers who designed the first sets for Richard Strauss including *Der Rosenkavalier* and *Electra*. Strnad himself designed for Max Reinhardt, and Strnad's proposal of 1915–7 for a "total theater" for Reinhardt looks forward to the 1920s. He worked on it over the years, perfecting the ring-shaped stage, moving the audience to the center (thus engaging them as part of the form), and ultimately creating a new concept in theater design.

With this we come to the end of our decade, which in practice ends in the miseries of World War I. In 1917, food had already been rationed in the monarchy, and practically speaking building came to an end. It is indicative of this period that one of the last great projects by Otto Wagner was an unrealized church, the Friedenskirche (church of peace), of 1917–8, and that Hoffman designed an ideal project, the House of World Peace, in 1917. In 1918 Klimt died, as did Wagner, Kolo Moser, and Egon Schiele, to be followed in 1919 by Pieter Eichenberg, who, like Hermann Bahr, had so vigorously written about them. Loos had been in the army; when he came back he was the only one who, with those like Strnad, Frank, and Wlach, could take up the movement that had been interrupted — that cut short the Jugendstil impetus, that cut short what seemed about to come to fruition just after the Stoclet Palace but never did. These architects now took up this thread in the new context of a small country after the end of the Austro-Hungarian Empire. In 1921 Loos became chief architect of the Siedlungsamt (housing) department of the Commune of Vienna but quit after three years in disgust. The problems of social housing that Vienna then faced made the years 1907–17 truly appear as the world of yesterday.

Holland
Theodore M. Brown

The period under discussion was not a vintage decade in the history of Dutch architecture. Yet it was an important time as a source of work and ideas that flowered during the following ten years. Precise connections, however, have not yet been established between these periods, and herein lies the historiographical problem in Holland of 1907–17. Far more concrete information is needed to chart the relationship to subsequent historical events.

Few of the works of the period are nationally or internationally significant. Ideas are plentiful but their relevance is not always apparent. The standard story, homegrown in Holland, emphasizes the seminal influence of Hendrik Petrus Berlage in the development of the next chapter. He was an international giant in Dutch opinion, was behind such diverse figures as Michel de Klerk and Gerrit Rietveld. Everybody claims Berlage as "poppa," but it is not clear how this essentially nineteenth-century rationalist with mystical overtones could stand behind both the rampant personal excesses of the Amsterdam School and the astringent Puritanism of de Stijl. Furthermore, I believe that his work and ideas have been greatly overrated. The Berlage myth in Holland can be accounted for by perhaps two factors. One is that, simply, he was there, and apparently the only figure on the scene large enough to have done the job. Another reason for the Dutch emphasis on Berlage is that he was a well-known European figure — the Dutch are immensely impressed by authority. Berlage certainly was an impressive authority, but he was not necessarily the progenitor of the creative Dutch work of 1907 through, say, the early 1930s.

Whether or not Berlage was as influential as is assumed, clearly he was the single most conspicuous Dutch figure of the decade. By 1907 his Bourse in

Amsterdam was four years old and, aside from his design for Holland House in 1914 [*figure 25*], one of his most successful works, Berlage's architecture was not particularly distinguished. For example, bracketing our decade are his unexecuted designs for the Peace Palace, of 1907, and his St. Hubertus Hunting Lodge at Hoenderloo (now on the Kröller-Müller estate), designed and built in 1917–8. Perhaps there is general agreement that the Peace Palace does not provide much basis for the Amsterdam School, nor does the Hunting Lodge launch us into De Stijl. Neither is historically pregnant when compared with advanced German, Austrian, French, or American work of the same period. Of far more significance were his well-known plans for the expansion of Amsterdam South and West, of 1915, and for The Hague, of 1908 — urban molds within which generally banal architecture was poured.

Berlage's ideas were published in a number of books and pamphlets beginning about 1908. Focused on art and society, the history and theory of architecture and furniture, beauty and society, and so forth, they resembled the writings of William Morris in subject matter and treatment. Conscious of social and technical circumstances as background, Berlage articulated his notions of architectural fundamentals: space, unbroken massive walls as space definers, and a priori proportional systems as a kind of musical score in the articulation of forms and spaces. One might see in these element seeds of De Stijl, but one is frustrated in attempting to twist Berlage's notions into the architectural convulsions of the Amsterdam School. The connections with De Stijl are also dubious. In 1925, for example, seven years after the beginning of De Stijl, Berlage published an essay on the development of modern Dutch architecture in Holland.[39] His text and illustrations scarcely acknowledged the existence of De Stijl form. To my knowledge, Rietveld's work, which is surely definitive of De Stijl architectural principles, was never mentioned in any of Berlage's writings. Indeed, Rietveld related verbally that Berlage had told him that he [Rietveld] had broken down everything that he [Berlage] had built up. So, if the older man had fathered the dominant Dutch movement of the 1920s, he was not very anxious to acknowledge the paternity.[40]

Of the facts about Berlage's career that are indisputably relevant, however, his trip to the United States and published views of it must be ranked as internationally significant. He traveled in the U.S. in 1911, where be examined the work of H. H. Richardson, Louis Sullivan, and Frank Lloyd Wright. The Dutch architect spoke of the trip in a lecture in Zurich in 1912, which was also published in the same year in Switzerland. More important, he published his impressions in 1913 in a well-illustrated book that expressed the European sense of discovery of a new world, the architectural and cultural wave of the future. With Whitmanesque exuberance, Berlage began his book with the following statement by Ralph Waldo Emerson:

> This mendicant America, this curious, peering, itinerant, imitative America, studious of Greece and Rome, of England and Germany, will take off its dusty shoes, will take off its glazed traveller's-cap and sit at home with repose and deep joy on its face. The world has no such landscape, the aeons of history no such hour, the future no equal second opportunity. Now let poets sing! Now let arts unfold![41]

Berlage excitedly recounted his impressions of America, his discovery of the architectural promised land, and of the messiah in the figure of Frank Lloyd Wright, whom he described as "a master whose equal is yet to be found in Europe." [42]

Shifting from Berlage to the work around him, the Scheepvaarthuis in Amsterdam of 1913–5, designed by Johan Melchior van der May and detailed by Michel de Klerk and Piet Kramer, is surely a major architectural event of the decade. Detail swallows form in this crusty amalgam of frantic corbelling, tortured masonry, and exotic figural carving—a dizzying stage set appropriate to *The Cabinet of Dr. Caligari* (1919). Housing of the period in Amsterdam South and West also exhibits the same breathless manipulation of forms, detail, materials, textures, and colors. De Klerk's architecture of our decade seems the work of a man convinced that his building would be a failure if it did not incorporate every architectural element known to man. Paradoxically, this architectural nervous breakdown was described by J. P. Mieras, a contemporary of De Klerk, in *Wendingen* as having the appearance of "the kiss of peace." The inclusion of a vast variety of elements, the forcing together of disparate parts, the tendency to include everything, was a dominant posture of the Amsterdam School during this and the next decade, and indeed has continued to be symptomatic of a Dutch aesthetic.

Also worth noting during these years are the small garden-city housing projects, such as Tuindorp Vreewijk in Rotterdam by Jan Granpré Molière, of 1916 [*figure 36*]. The return to the good old days of Dutch village life—canals, bridges, rustic pitched-roof row houses grouped around ponds, parks, and play spaces—established a suburban pattern repeated throughout the country down to the present day. Berlage also took a sentimental journey in similar housing developments in Amsterdam in 1919.

In opposition to the architectural gourmet's approach of the Amsterdam school and the bucolic sentiments of Granpré Molière was the lean and hungry look that foreshadowed this style. Very small in number during this decade (in fact, just one), the single great monument is Robert van 't Hoff's ferroconcrete Huis ter Heide near Utrecht, of 1915–6 [*figure 37*], a few miles from Rietveld's Schroeder House, of eight years later [*figure 60*]. Again, Wright enters the picture as a significant figure: Van 't Hoff traveled in the U.S. and had worked with Wright. On the exterior, the Dutch translation of Wright has the authority of an accomplished work; its interior leaves much to be desired, however. Tight, cramped, obsessively symmetrical, it lacks the grace of the interlocking volumes and the dramatic interplay of light and shadow of Wright's Prairie interiors.

The painters Piet Mondrian and Bart van der Leck must also be mentioned as belonging to the puritanical strand of Dutch thought and practice, as they were creating restrained metaphors of geometric purity during these years. This was a decisive time for Mondrian, starting with his *Woods near Oele*, of 1908—described by Robert Welsh recently as "Mondrian's *Les Demoiselles d'Avignon*"—and ending with the planar compositions of 1916 and '17, on the brink of his mature formulation. [43] [*Inaudible*]

Theo van Doesburg's essays, beginning in 1912, still remain a subject for close study. In his monograph on De Stijl, Hans L. C. Jaffé relied primarily on Van Doesburg's later writings, executed after De Stijl's position had been safely established. One suspects that if Van Doesburg's ideas before 1917 were to be more thoroughly analyzed, it would become apparent that, unlike

Mondrian, Van Doesburg was not sure of his position until fairly late in the game.

More relevant are the works of the philosopher M. H. J. Schoenmaekers, who in 1915 published *The New World Image* and in 1916, the principles of what he called "plastic mathematics." [44] Through a kind of mystical mathematics, Schoenmaekers projected a Platonic world of absolutes structured by numbers and beyond the chaos of specifics. Mondrian was close to the philosopher during 1915 and 1916 and undoubtedly absorbed Schoenmaekers's mystic [inaudible] as reinforcement of his own.

The decade ends (or the next begins) in Holland with both architectural and literary events rather unpromising for those who know how the plot develops. J. J. P. Oud designed an unexecuted bathhouse in 1915 — not very prophetic of the following decade. His military pill-box composition of the Villa Allegonda in Katwijk and his project for the blocky Seaside Housing project, both of 1917, are not much more prophetic of De Stijl's rich spatial composition. A totally unknown craftsman, Rietveld, was designing and building some weird chairs around 1917 and 1918, but these do not become public property until around 1920.

The literary events of the time provide a clue to the future, but not necessarily to the future that we know. The periodical *De Stijl* began at the end of 1917, and *Wendigen* in 1919. A third series is also worth noting: *Jaarboek Nederlandsche Ambacts-en Nijverheidkunst* began publication in 1919 and ran through 1931, through the years of *Wendingen* and *De Stijl*. This annual did a good job of covering the crafts, furniture design, and typography of the 1920s. *Wendingen* assumed the open-armed policy of accepting anything new and exotic in all and general inconsistent juxtaposition: primitive masks, oriental pottery, American skyscrapers, Dutch farmhouses, and Rietveld interiors can be found cheek by jowl in its pages. *De Stijl* operated from a position of aesthetic economy, admitting only those elements that conform to its astringent notion of art. In other words, *Wendingen* was inclusive while *De Stijl* was exclusive. The craft yearbook gave a voice to both sides, but clearly it was dominated by *Wendingen* thinking through the early 1920s, and it was not until 1929–30 and 1931 that it exhibited the purifying influence of De Stijl.

To generalize, Dutch architectural thought and practice of 1910–7, and indeed throughout the century, falls into two categories: the personal and the universal. The personal tends to be artistically promiscuous, at times rustic, expressionist: that is the Amsterdam School, Granpré Molière, and *Wendingen*. The universal tends toward the abstract, the classical, the absolute, the pure: this is De Stijl. Yet as different as these positions seem to be, they have much in common when compared with the practical and reasonable quality of, say, German and French style. Extending from a Hegelian sense of predestination, both Dutch strands were mystical, moralistic, spiritual, idealistic, a priori. Neither tends toward the reasonable and functional. Both are detached from the harsh facts of construction and planning. Both camps form a kind of architectural religion. The conflict of the two at the end of the 1910s and throughout the 1920s was a religious war within Dutch society. My thesis is that although *De Stijl* won a minor skirmish, *Wendingen* won the war in Holland.

If one considers the two choices available to the Dutch in 1917, the situation becomes very puzzling. The personal choice had behind it the available models of P. J. H. Cuijpers, Berlage, De Klerk, Karel de Bazel, Granpré Molière, and many others. Of the other choice—the universal—what was available in 1917 but one lonely work by Robert van 't Hoff? Hardly a tradition, and hardly a dominant trend in Dutch practice of the past century or more. Mondrian's pictorial constructions were perhaps the only other support for Van 't Hoff's position. Knowing what happens in the next historical chapter, we have tended to assume a divine inevitability in the development of Dutch architecture. Yet the probability was overwhelmingly high that De Stijl would have died in the bud and that the architectural issue of the next decade would not have been *De Stijl* versus *Wendingen* but rather the personal approach of the modern Amsterdam School versus the personal approach of the rustic Granpré Molière school. Even if one examines the bud of the style in 1917, the prospects of flowering are not very promising. The first issues of *De Stijl* were prayers for a new puritan aesthetic, but they were not guides for that aesthetic. An index of the architectural situation was published conveniently in 1917, in a book called *Het Moderne Landhuis in Nederland* by J. H. W. Leliman and Karl Sluyterman. Of the more than two hundred modern houses illustrated, none even vaguely hint at the universal trend; all fall within either a still vigorous nineteenth-century historicism, a Granpré Molière rusticism, or the modernism of the Amsterdam School. If one scans the twenty-volume *Moderne Baukunst in Nederland*, published in 1932 and 1935 after the De Stijl fireworks had subsided, one sees an almost equal mining of the two strands but with emphasis on the personal (except for such industrial works as the Van Nelle Factory by Brinkman & Van der Vlugt, with Mart Stam, of 1927–9 [*figure 63*], which would have been difficult to render with a thatched roof).

It is also important to consider some later developments with respect to the 1917 situation. Granpré Molière became a professor at Delft in 1924, at the high point of De Stijl influence and productivity, and led a popular reaction against the purists until well after World War II. The reaction against De Stijl built up vigorously at the end of the 1920s, and its momentum carried through the 1950s, as exemplified by such grotesqueries as the conspicuous provincial center in Arnhem, of 1955, so aptly described by G. E. Kidder-Smith as one of the outstanding recent continental horrors.[45] One should also remember the shaggy elements in Willem Dudok's middle-of-the-road work, even during the height of De Stijl influence in 1926, the year that his Hilversum Town Hall was being built.[46] In addition we should not forget Oud's Shell Building in the late 1930s.

Finally, one has only to be reminded of the present everyday Dutch notion regarding design of houses, interiors, and furniture to realize that De Stijl has not penetrated very deeply into Dutch culture. By contrast, Frank Lloyd Wright's early work was in part a response to an indigenous American aesthetic. As a result, his work has been homogenized into American vernacular architecture, at least to a certain extent. But aside from [*inaudible*]. Having done so, it should not have been in the aesthetic form that it took but rather in some variety of Amsterdam school. Like the Swedes and Finns, the Dutch might have entered the century around 1930, or like the Norwegians, they could have sat out the century entirely. Thus, the central question for 1907–17 in Dutch architectural history is why did the Dutch produce a De Stijl architecture in the 1920s?

The German Werkbund: Antecedents and Interpretations
Sibyl Moholy-Nagy

In his book *The Architecture of Humanism*, in the chapter on biological
fallacy, Geoffrey Scott says that, "The object of evolutionary criticism is...not
to appreciate but to explain. To account for the facts, not to estimate them, is
its function. And the light which it brings comes from one great principle: that
things are intelligible through a knowledge of their antecedents." [47] The evolutionary method, then, is the exact opposite of the analytical method of criticism, which derives from observation and inference value judgments about
the whole. It seems that some guardian angel, therapeutically concerned with
my egocentric balance, assigns me now and then an architectural research job
that forces me from my accustomed and beloved analytical criticism, even to a
disinterested deductive approach, where the ultimate historical evaluation is
already given, and all I am supposed to do is to produce evidence that led to
this already fixed place in history. In the particular theme that is under consideration here, I feel that the exceedingly strong influence on twentieth-century
architecture between 1920 and 1950 of the Germans can be understood only
through an insight into the Werkbund movement. This is because the
Werkbund movement—which, in the very peculiar way it worked in Germany,
includes art nouveau on one end of the historical spectrum and the Bauhaus
program on the other—was the only actual original style that the Germans
developed throughout their thousand years of building history. They did
not participate in Byzantine, their Romanesque was a Lombard import, and
their Gothic was a French one. The scant manifestations of the Renaissance in
Germany are predominantly Plateresque, Italianesque; and German baroque is
a very talented Franco-Italian paraphrasing. The historicism of the nineteenth
century fell on the country like the proverbial second shoe, and there never was,
in Germany, a cast-iron revolution. But if one looks at some building by a good
architect from, say, 1912, one knows immediately that it can be only German.

The cause was the ever recurrent syndrome of the so-called *Spätstil*, a term
that Wölfflin virtually invented, whereby the tiny states of the multitude of
German princes lived in sycophantic dependence on the leading world powers, especially on France and England. In a tradition that is as ancient as tribal
over-lordship, royalty and aristocracy were, in Germany, alone *den Ton ange-
ben* (to set the fashion). They were, until well into the century, the absolute
arbiters of cultural, artistic, and social standards. In general, their taste was
gross, and German was, for many centuries, synonymous with bad taste, as
Frederick the Great once scornfully remarked.

The unprecedented fact that a trained architect, Hermann Muthesius, was
assigned as cultural attaché to the most important embassy that Germany
maintained—namely, the one in London—in 1896 showed that things would
be different culturally under the young Kaiser Wilhelm II. His mother was an
English princess, and his grandfather, Victoria's consort Albert, whose serious interest in art and industry had culminated in the Crystal Palace exhibition of 1851. Wilhelm, in his praise often called "the industrious Kaiser,"
dispatched Muthesius personally to England with a very special assignment,
and Muthesius, in William Richard Lethaby's words, "became the historian
of the English free architecture." All architects who at the time did any building were investigated, sorted, tabulated, and, I must admit, understood.
The object of his study was the new Arts and Crafts style that had come to

dominate English design since the 1800s, when the influence of William Morris broke through in a new generation of architects. Musthesius spent seven years in England and published the results of his findings in three stages: *English Building Arts of the Present*, in 1900; *Recent Ecclesiastic Building Arts in England*, in 1902; and finally, a monumental three-volume study in 1904 called *The English House*. The last study was an instantaneous success. This young architect, who had participated only half-heartedly in French art nouveau (which somehow always remained alien and quite unassimilable to the German temperament).... *[Inaudible]*

This patron of the new German generation of architects worked in the German tradition of the princely influence. Grand-Duke Ernest of Hesse-Darmstadt and the Rhine, who had his residence in Darmstadt, had commissioned the Viennese architect Joseph Olbrich to build a cultural center on the Mathildenhohe, starting in 1899. Olbrich, Peter Behrens, Paul Schmitthenner, and other young architects were invited to build villas there in the first years of the twentieth century. Their work there shows the struggle between the art nouveau and an irrepressible classical heritage. *[Inaudible]* The English sources opened up by Muthesius confirmed, rather than created, a German fin-de-siècle trend that had searched for liberation from the "neo" styles.

There was, of course, Alfred Messel's exceptional and very remarkable ferroconcrete emporium in Berlin,[48] and the astylar interior of Theodor Fischer's Garrison Church in Ulm, of 1905. My architect father did build a house for himself in Luschwitz outside Dresden, in 1896, which shows a clear affinity to Mackintosh's Glasgow School of Art *[figure 7]*, although the Kunstler Haus, in which I grew up, was designed three years earlier than the building in Glasgow. There was, nevertheless, a strong eclectic current in the domestic architecture of the German reform movement that swept the country after the publication of Muthesius's studies.

After his return to Germany, Muthesius was awarded an influential position as high counselor in the Ministry for Labor and Industry, which gave him a decisive voice in production and trade education. Since part of his special domain was the building of new workers' housing, there appeared all over the country faithful pastiches of English garden cities ranging from Letchworth to Port Sunlight. Wealthy manufacturers and inventors, eager to follow the official trend toward Anglicization, carefully selected architects who would build local versions of English country estates, for instance, the Hohenhof at Hagen by Henry van de Velde, which owes a great deal to Norman Shaw. Muthesius's own contributions are very typical, showing few derivations from his mentors on the exterior, and which are nicely balanced by British understatement in the interior design.

The next development toward what was to become the first German departure from established aesthetics, materials, and methods made its tentative appearance at the Third German Art and Crafts Exhibition (*Dritte deutsche Kunstgewerbe Ausstellung*) in Dresden in 1906. Under the purely programmatic slogan "from couch pillow to city plan," Muthesius had rallied artists, product designers, craftsmen, and architects to create work for companies that would mass-produce them. This is a very important point because it is here particularly that Muthesius went beyond the English model. It was he who contacted, or created the contact with, the German industrialists who would produce the individually designed prototypes. One can only speculate on how much pressure was exerted through the official power wielded by Muthesius's ministerial position, although it must not be overlooked that the majority of designers and manufacturers in the exhibition came from Saxony, which was an independent federal state. Under the new generic name *Kunstgewerbe*, literally "art-craft," the exhibition showed staggeringly rich, totally designed interiors — from official reception halls to cozy domestic living rooms — and included stoves, lamps, textiles (rayon, the absolutely new artificial fiber), furniture, and linoleum.

It is very difficult for us today to understand what storms of acclaim and protest this show of 1906 aroused. The issues raised came to a head when Muthesius delivered in the spring of 1907 an address at the Berlin Trade School titled "The Significance of Kunstgewerbe," which celebrated the just-closed Dresden exhibition as a victory over all and any application of historical style and elements. [Inaudible] Relying ideologically on John Ruskin's *Seven Lamps of Architecture*, and the rational demands of Gottfried Semper for utility and quality, he established the maxim that function, material, and craftsmanship are, and must be, the only directives followed by the artist, the craftsman, and the manufacturer. This made the building, actually the house — and this is very important when considering the later Bauhaus — the center to which all designs, from the largest to the smallest, must relate. He castigated popular architecture and furnishings, preserved by what he labeled "our tell-me aristocracy," as shoddy and dishonest. His main fury was reserved for manufacturers who adulterated their customers' taste by flooding the market with unserviceable, badly made, and aesthetically repulsive objects. With rather unconcealed promises and threats, he held out official support to those manufacturers who had joined the new movement, prognosticating decline and doom to the unregenerate. For the first time there appeared what was to become the chief goal of the ensuing Werkbund policy: an emphatic official bid for industrial support, and for the world market.

The implications of all that Muthesius did were clearly political. The majority of German manufacturers, tightly organized, saw in Muthesius's denunciation of their products a personal threat. The kaiser demanded, but did not enforce, the ouster of his former protégé from his ministerial post. It is very characteristic how Muthesius reacted to this. When this was published he withdrew from participation in the next Werkbund assembly, of 1909, but sent a deputy and kept on working behind the scenes. The designers, craftsmen, and manufacturers who had shown in the Dresden exhibition left the established professional organizations and founded a new group, which first met clandestinely at a hotel in Munich and then, when they — surprisingly — found support, moved to Berlin.

It was Muthesius, who, while he did not participate in the founding assembly, suggested the name *Werkbund*. Among the group's founding members were Peter Behrens, Theodor Fischer, Josef Hoffman, Joseph Olbrich, Bruno Paul, Richard Riemerschmid, Bruno Taut, and Henry van de Velde. The rather lengthy mandate can be pinpointed in the following passage:

> The purpose of the Werkbund is the ennoblement of production through the cooperation of art, industry, and crafts. Through education, propaganda, and group solidarity in all relevant questions. In the coordination of the highest

creative and executive intelligence does the Werkbund see its highest goal, the guarantee of the German culture.[49]

Members were to fall into four categories: artists, producers, experts, and patrons. It might be news to our generation that the Bauhaus program directed by Walter Gropius twelve years later adhered almost precisely to the wording of these Werkbund principles. More surprising is the discovery that twenty years later, Gropius's book *The New Architecture and the Bauhaus* (1935), published in England, paraphrases Muthesius's guidelines and his lecture "Werkbund Activities and the Future," which he delivered at the opening of the *First Comprehensive Werkbund Exposition* in Cologne in 1914.

The seven years that had elapsed between the founding of the Werkbund in 1907 and the *Werkbund Exposition* of 1914 had brought a tremendous success to the Werkbund movement. They had also resulted, perhaps as a consequence of this success, in a unique development, on which I have based my earlier claim that Werkbund style — if there is such a thing — is an original expression in the history of architecture. While residential designs stagnated and the production of furniture and luxury goods never got beyond a slightly improved *Heimatstil*, the Werkbund architects designed their first industrial and commercial architecture — for example, the large gasworks in Dresden and two railroad stations. There is no time here to quote the ideological considerations of Taut, Poelzig, Behrens, and others on the influence of the new design on industrial buildings. The gist is (and this is perhaps what is important for the later decades) the novel concept that the real commitment of architecture toward an ideal environment — a totally designed environment, a designed *Gesamtkunstwerk* — must now move from the purely domestic and private into the public realm of the impersonal building in industry and administration.

The results of this new aim are quite extraordinary in every aspect. Aesthetically these architects achieved a coordination of form and expressed function that created new building prototypes, which recall and at the same time refute the pronouncements of that reform patron saint of arts and crafts, Ruskin. Among this group were the first German architects to experiment with new materials and new aesthetic systems, not on paper, not as theory, but in reality. Poelzig's large waterworks of 1911 [*figure 16*] was monumental, heavy, the factory in the original meaning of the juggernaut, indifferent to human proportion, a commanding presence, an indifferent housing of their functions. In particular, it is Poelzig's Jahrhunderthalle (Centennial Hall) of 1913 that challenges Pier Luigi Nervi's aircraft hangers at Orvieto of 1935 in every respect as a most daring and the greatest structurally defined interior of the new age.[50] It is a space that could swallow Hans Scharoun's Philharmonic Hall in a single bite.

The most gifted figure of the Werkbund, and also the most influential as a teacher, Bruno Taut single-handedly saved German low-cost housing from the detached-unit garden-city blight and reestablished the continuous street elevation as a designed architectural element. No two of his scores (and there are literally scores) of developments are alike, however all adhere to a designed expression of visual continuity that would create community by the fact that a community is judged by its streets. He discovered the architectural potential of glass — beyond the merely expanded window panes of the Shoe-Last Factory. [*Inaudible*] His greatest work lies beyond our chronological limit of 1917: the first comprehensive and analytical city plan for Neu Magdenberg, of 1920, for instance; his experiments with color and architecture; the superb theater exhibition of 1925; and the enormous volume of his educational and poetic writings. Work for industry and government and commerce—starting, perhaps awkwardly enough, around 1910 but creating a new power image for both the architect and the patron—would bear its richest fruit in the 1920s in the further work of both the Tauts (Bruno and Max) and Poelzig and Mendelsohn. [Inaudible] It is a very sad testimony to the camarilla around the Bauhaus and CIAM that Bruno Taut is hardly mentioned in Sigfried Giedeon's *Space, Time and Architecture* and that neither the Werkbund nor the revered Taut exist in the thick monograph by our chairman on nineteenth- and twentieth-century architecture.

Compared to the originality and the scope of talent that I have shown you here, the immortality bestowed on Peter Behrens, which fell like an heirloom on his pupil Gropius, looks, to me at least, rather absurd. In 1914 the Werkbund combined its convention in Cologne with an elaborately prepared exhibition that today is mainly remembered for its entrance building by Gropius and its theater by Van de Velde. The survival of these two buildings in architectural history is symbolic of the ideological importance of the 1914 convention. In a speech "Werkbund Production and the Future," which he supplemented with printed guidelines, Muthesius—again in full, obvious command of the Werkbund, which had been justified by its success—characterized the word *Werkbund* as "an association of artists, merchants, producers, and craftsmen," in that order. This shifted the emphasis from the original association of art, craft, and industry toward the designer as, quoting Muthesius, "an element in national economy," an important instrument for the incipient German *Weltmacht* (world power). The word *Weltmacht* appears four times in Muthesius's 1914 speech: this, less than a month before the outbreak of World War I. The most necessary step to this international acceptance, according to Muthesius, was *Typisierung* (type-casting)—the unification of forms and production standards that would eliminate "the individual peculiarities of individualistic architects."[51] One is reminded here of Gropius's relentless war against the prima-donna architect: "Only with standardization, *Typisierung*, as the result of a healthy concentration, can an again generally accepted solid taste develop."[52]

The reaction of a large section of the membership to this course was explosive. Van de Velde led the opposition, with the opening sentence, "As long as there are still artists in the Werkbund, and as long as they have any word in its fate, shall we protest against any suggestion of a canon of type-casting."[53] He condemned the national obsession with export as a curse haunting German industry and made the observation that any preestablished standard necessarily destroys the result by sterilizing imagination and process. After passionate debates, the individualists left the Werkbund to form an association of free spirits who were all but crushed by the subsequent victory of the anti-individualists.

There remain two interesting questions to be asked: Why did the adherence of standards and type-casting prevail over the believers in architecture as subjective creation? [Inaudible] Why did the German descendants of the Muthesius wing of the Werkbund—Gropius, Mies, Breuer—and not his opponents—Mendelsohn, Taut, Poelzig, Scharoun—become the tutors and the form-givers of American architecture?

Behrens and Berlin
Stanford Anderson

In 1907, Peter Behrens left his academic post in Düsseldorf to become the artistic consultant for a large electrical industry in Berlin, the Allgemeine Elektrizitäts Gesellschaft (AEG). One of its directors, Walter Rathenau, was in these very years formulating his criticism and reconstruction of man and culture in an industrial society. In contact with such thought, and involved in industry, Behrens came to conceive of progress toward a utopian society as involving the use of technology under the control of human will. Behrens saw the control of the human will as shaped by traditional culture, resulting in a tension between the acceptance of new technology and an older set of cultural values. He saw this tension, however, as being open to resolution through a richer and more inclusive understanding of Western culture, an idea that he adopted from such nineteenth-century architects, philosophers, and art historians as Friedrich Gilly, Friedrich Nietzsche, and Alois Riegl. Such an interpretation lends coherence to the seeming contradictions in Behrens's work in Berlin — his involvement with new technology, his re-exploration of traditional forms, and his return to a harsh classicism along with an apparent proto-Expressionism.[54]

When Behrens participated in the Artists' Colony in Darmstadt, he was one of a number of artists confronting a more general problem of the day. These artists were concerned that the arts had become a matter of the salon, the gallery, and the museum. Art no longer had a functional role in society; it was merely parasitic. The importance in the late nineteenth century of the small, detached easel painting that conveyed only fleeting impressions of sensory experience was taken as evidence of the low state of the arts. Since the state of the arts was the reflection of an unhealthy social situation, it would not be sufficient merely to transform society in the image of the current arts, or vice versa. Rather, there had to be a reformation of both society and the arts to the end of achieving a satisfactory union. It was this union of social and aesthetic ends that encouraged the ambitious utopias of late-nineteenth-century artists like William Morris. The Darmstadt Artists' Colony was an attempt to establish a model of a new society in which art once again played a functional role. It failed because the envisaged utopia was almost totally unrelated to the conditions out of which it had to develop. The failure of the Darmstadt colony in the first years of the twentieth century was a great disappointment to all those who had lent their enthusiasm to it, including Behrens.

From 1903 to 1907, Behrens served as the director of the Kunstgewerbeschule — the School of Arts and Crafts — in Düsseldorf, during which time he was concerned with coming to terms with artistic tradition. Through the art historian Wilhelm Niemeyer, Behrens developed an interest in August Schmarsow's theory of space and architecture and in Riegl's liberating concept of classical antiquity.[55] The impact of these ideas on Behrens's work only began to become clear in 1907; consequently, I had thought to deal here with one or the other of these problems: Behrens's emerging conception of space, or his inclusive understanding of classicism. However, I have come to feel that these are both aspects of a more general problem that I shall consider instead — a problem that is moreover peculiar to Behrens's arrival in Berlin in 1907.

Behrens left Düsseldorf in 1907 to become the general artistic director of the AEG in Berlin. It was in this position that he won renown for his revolutionary work in what came to be known as "industrial design" and for his design of factories, which led him to an architecture that was increasingly monumental and classicizing. I would like to suggest that this work for the AEG represented the renewal of Behrens's interest in achieving a functional relationship between art and society—on what he hoped would be a more realistic basis than had been present at Darmstadt. This hope was still based on a utopian image, but an image that *did* enter into critical discourse with existing economic political and social conditions. The question as to the appropriate relations among art, industry, and society was hardly a new one, but Behrens's arrival in Berlin put him in a key position in a major modern industry, and in a firm directed by the Rathenau family. It is not mere coincidence that Walter Rathenau was one of the last great utopists of the twentieth century, as well as an industrialist and politician. His close connection with the art world of Berlin is a matter of common knowledge and his personal acquaintance with Behrens is documented in various ways, including a set of volumes by Rathenau inscribed to his "dear friend Peter Behrens."

Although Rathenau was making his own mark as a powerful industrialist in such peculiarly modern fields as electricity, automobiles, and electrochemistry, he nevertheless analyzed the distress and misery of modern man as being due to an unchecked capitalism, which inevitably led to the mechanization of man and of culture. In 1913, he wrote the book *Zur Mechanik des Geistes* (On the Mechanics of the Spirit). Despite this mechanization of the spirit resulting from industrialization, Rathenau was emphatic in his belief that the ills of society could not be removed by abolishing industry or by nineteenth-century dreams of a return to an agrarian and handicraft society. As he wrote, the "garden city idylls of the average architect and art-craftsman" were not only impossible but would condemn great parts of the increased population to death through inefficient production and distribution. Rathenau did not believe in an inevitable evolutionary progress toward a better world, but he argued that one could not rescind the effects of knowledge, technology, and industry. Human will must enter into the historical process, guiding the way to a better world through the use of technology. "Only mechanization itself can lead us beyond mechanization," he asserted, to "a kingdom of the soul" characterized by social consciousness and by solidarity, love, and creative responsibility.[56]

Once one accepted and entered into the historical process, then, it was clear that what was required was a reconstruction of the spiritual world, not of the intellectual and mechanical one. Rathenau said that the purpose of his book *Von kommenden Dingen* (*In Days to Come,* as the title has been translated), was to show how "the permeation of the mechanistic order with spirit" could "transform the blind play of forces into a fully conscious and free cosmos, into a cosmos worthy of mankind."[57] But Rathenau did not mean his call for spiritualization to be a retreat from life or a "historical romance." This would be "sterility":

It is incapacity to imagine, still less to shape the yet unknown.... Fearing the ugly present and the anxious future, the romantic takes refuge with the dear, good, dead people, and spins out further what he has learned from them. But every big man was a shaper of his own time, a respecter of antiquity and conscious of his inheritance as a grown and capable man may be; not a youth in sheltered tutelage, but a master of the living world, and a herald of the future. "Modernity" is foolish, but antiquarianism is rubbish. Life in its vigor is neither new nor antique, but young.[58]

As Rathenau conceived of the "big man" engaging the world in order to achieve a true and young culture, Peter Behrens, in his position in the Rathenau firm, and some of his contemporaries were working out the same challenge in the arts. In an article of 1908 about Behrens's work for the AEG published in the *Kunstgewerbeblatt*, the author recognized the close relationship between the means of production and artistic form. He specifically criticized the attempt by William Morris and his circle to restore an earlier cultural balance on the grounds that such an endeavor could not cope with the basis of modern production, which was the machine. New and appropriate forms were to be arrived at only by the acceptance of the machine and all its implications.[59]

Yet despite the apparent acceptance of the modern situation by Rathenau and Behrens, there remained a traditional, perhaps even conservative aspect to the modern utopia that they envisioned. Both men believed that there had been a peculiarly healthy relationship between the methods of production and the social and cultural conditions of certain earlier times—especially those of classical antiquity, the Middle Ages, and the Germany of around 1800. Those had been times of admirable cultural solidarity; it was clear that the present situation had to be coped with in a manner paralleling the orderly, if not monolithic image of these earlier epochs.

Rathenau characterized the "big man" as being not only a shaper of his own time but also "a respecter of antiquity and conscious of his inheritance." This historical consciousness is clearly revealed in Behrens's publications of the Berlin years, which repeatedly addressed themes of monumental art and of art and technology. According to Behrens the natural expression of modern life was technology; perfection of technique, however, was a purely material matter, contributing to the progress of civilization but not to the advancement of spiritual values, which found their embodiment in art and culture. Citing Riegl's theory that the artistic will of a time must be fulfilled even if this should require opposition to the material givens, Behrens insisted on the theoretical independence of art from technique. However, since technique *was* so central to the will of the present time, modern art and technology must indeed be unified. Behrens felt he was accomplishing this in his AEG Turbine Factory (1908–9) [*figure 5*], designed in collaboration with the engineer Karl Bernhard. Behrens concluded one of his major addresses on art and technology with the sentence, "German art and technology will thus work toward a single goal, toward the strength of the German land, which will be recognized by the fact that a rich material life has been ennobled by a spiritually refined form."[60] (You can see the similarity of this to the proposals that Mrs. Moholy-Nagy discussed.)

It is this emphasis on the strength or power of the German land achieved through the union of a strong material and spiritual life that accounts for the monumentality of a building like the Turbine Factory. For Behrens had claimed that monumental art naturally comes to expression in places in which people have realized their highest achievement and by which they are both moved and motivated. Behrens's buildings and writings both reveal that he aimed to give monumental form to the places of modern technology and that he felt this could not be achieved by attending only to the engineer's material considerations. Since artistic form must be considered independent of technique, it was in the realm of artistic form that Behrens sought to make a contribution that was at once new and traditional.

We learn more of Behrens's thoughts concerning artistic form from a man who probably helped to shape those thoughts, the art historian Wilhelm Niemeyer, who also taught at Behrens's school in Düsseldorf. At the time of Behrens's departure for Berlin and the AEG, Niemeyer wrote a laudatory article on his spatial aesthetic. He argued that Behrens possessed a sympathy for the art of classical antiquity, which however was a peculiarly modern sympathy. It was apparent in the work of Heinrich Schliemann, Jakob Burckhardt, and Friedrich Nietzsche, who he claimed had given color and vitality to the modern conception of antiquity, superseding the earlier, bloodless classicistic conception. New experiences had sharpened their appreciation of neglected aspects of ancient art; for example, knowledge of Japanese woodcuts opened their eyes to Greek vase painting. Studies by Riegl, the Viennese art historian Josef Strzygowski, and others brought both awareness and sympathy to an enlarged realm of ancient art, from late Roman to Coptic and Byzantine art, the works of the Cosmati, and so on. As Karl Friedrich Schinkel was the architectonic fulfillment of the Wincklemannian tradition, so Niemeyer argued, "Behrens is the architectural embodiment of the more inclusive, richer, modern understanding of antiquity." [61]

At the time this was written, just before Behrens's arrival in Berlin, Behrens's buildings were especially influenced by the Romanesque style of Tuscany, as in the crematorium in Hagen, which is at once medieval and classical. His graphics show direct borrowing from late antique metalwork, as discussed and illustrated by Riegl—again combining medieval and classical characteristics. Finally, in moving to Berlin, Behrens came to the city of Schinkel and Gilly as well as to a region of impressive late-medieval architectural monuments constructed of severe brick. Friedrich Gilly, active about 1800, was the favorite architect of the AEG's Rathenau. He was also the subject of the current researches of Niemeyer, who saw in Gilly a bold classicist of outstanding inventiveness, one who had first come to public attention through his moving drawings (later engraved) of the great medieval buildings of Marienburg. Both the Marienburg drawings and Gilly's classical designs combined a strong and direct sense of materials with an equally strong and dominant expression of abstract form.

In summary, Behrens's own interest in a unified culture, together with his new position in industry and his acquaintance with Rathenau, led him to the attempt to achieve an artistic and architectural form commensurate with modern conditions. Convinced that artistic form could not be achieved by attention to material considerations alone, he became a student of abstract concepts of form. At least partly through Niemeyer's influence, he accepted Schmarsow's concept that architecture should be conceived according to an abstract definition of space, while sculpture should be more concerned with material volume. Behrens's 1907 exhibition hall in Mannheim (as well as his correspondence about it) reflects how he had come to this new conclusion about the way architecture should be used to define planes and, by this means, space; sculpture, on the other hand, should be of an especially solid and plastic form and have its essence in the actual occupation of space. He was therefore adamant about having a work by Aristide Maillol in the exhibition even though he had to settle for a cast. This conception of the contrast between architecture and sculpture would continue in the work of an architect like Mies van der Rohe, in whose designs we find it again and again.

So this was one of the concepts of abstract form that Behrens was pursuing during these years. Receiving commissions for large industrial buildings, he conceived of these works as monumental, not only for their sheer magnitude but also for both their real and symbolic role in modern industrial society. Behrens found an adequately broad and flexible precedent for monumental form in his inclusive understanding of antiquity; he also found an earlier interpretation of this understanding in the vision of an architect like Gilly. This may be seen in the Egyptoid and yet classical forms of his Turbine Factory, as also in the bold forms and brilliant brickwork of his Gasworks in Frankfurt-Osthafen of 1910–2, which recall Gilly's beloved medieval Marienburg. If you compare Behrens's drawings for the Gasworks with Gilly's drawings of ports on the French coast or his classicist drawing of a medieval fortress, you can see a common conviction about the expressiveness of form. Behrens's Small Motors Factory for the AEG of 1910–1 likewise gives evidence of both the sturdy brickwork and sheer planes of late-medieval north German work and the blunt but expressive classicism of Berlin around 1800.

Given the role Behrens sought to play in the unification of modern and industrial society and the formal ideas briefly presented in this paper, one can see more easily how the same man could at the very same time build that harsh temple of state, the German Embassy in St. Petersburg of 1911–2 [*figure 19*], and such impressive monuments of enterprise as the Frankfurt Gasworks. Just as a new and powerful state had to be created that could ensure that modern technology would in fact advance the well-being of mankind, so this political act was to be symbolized and even aided by forms attuned to the machine but serving the objective of cultural solidarity.

Walter Gropius, 1907–17
James Marston Fitch

My task has been made considerably easier by the two speakers who have just preceded me, because it seems to me that they have succeeded very effectively in establishing a kind of reference frame, or *the* reference frame, in which the earlier Gropius — the adult Gropius — appeared and matured. Of course there is one liability, and that is, I may be suspected of belonging to a camarilla, and all I can say is that the field of art history and criticism seems to be characterized by the presence of many camarillae. I cannot pretend to have a completely disinterested position vis-à-vis Gropius, either then or now. He has had a profound effect on my development and the development of my whole generation in America.[62]

It seems to me that there have always been several Gropiuses, that he played quite distinct roles at three different levels: as a designer of artifacts and buildings, as a teacher, and as an ideologue-theoretician. We can see the beginnings of all three levels of this activity in this very earliest period of 1907–17. The decade doesn't fit him too conveniently. It's true that he stopped his formal education in 1907, but I think we'd have to carry him through the early months of 1919, when he succeeded in establishing the Bauhaus, in order to get any kind of a functional decade. He had been at the Technischen Hochschule of Charlottenburg in Berlin, and at the Technischen Hochschule in Munich for four years, when in 1907, exasperated with the inadequacy of the curriculum and the teaching, he decided to end his formal education. He had meanwhile done a year's military service for the Fifteenth Hussars out of Hamburg (1904–5), and in 1908 he inherited a thousand marks, which enabled him to make his first extended journey out of Germany. However, already in 1906 he had visited his aunt and uncle in Essen. His uncle was the president of the Prussian railway system, and as a result of being the nephew of a person this important Gropius had an opportunity to take conducted tours through the Krupps plant and also through the housing projects for the company's mid-level employees, of which Krupps was very proud. He remembers being struck by discrepancies between the ways in which fabrication was carried on inside the great Krupps armament and industrial factories and the hand-crafted Romantic cottages that were simultaneously being built for the workers. He remembers himself as even then being struck by this contrast and, even more, by the potentialities of modern industrial production and the implications it might have for housing. The possibilities for the application of mass production to the production of houses has been a thread running through Gropius's career and the speculation about him.

In the summer of 1907 Gropius took his thousand marks and went to Spain. When asked why to Spain, he said that it was because it was as far away from Germany as a thousand marks would take him and hopefully get him back. It struck him, in other words, as being the most exotic landscape that he could go to. He stayed there for a year, and during this year he had the opportunity to observe two things that played a very important role through-out the rest of his life. One was the very high level of craftsmanship that was obtained throughout Spain, and the other was the contradiction between this level of craftsmanship — the integrity of the artifacts that were pro-duced — and the poverty and low status of the Spanish workman.

Gropius went to Barcelona. He visited the church of the Sagrada Familia. He remembers very clearly having tried to meet Gaudí, who was very much talked about, but being an anonymous young German student Gropius never had the opportunity to interview the great man. He went to the work-shops on the cathedral site, however, and was enormously impressed by the now-famous scale models that Gaudí had made of the proposed structure. Gropius was fascinated, he said, with the virtuosity and skill not only of Gaudí but also of the magnificent family of craftsmen that he had organized around him, not only on the cathedral but in the apartment houses and other projects going on. But at the same time, he was dismayed and repelled by what struck him as the subjective, idiosyncratic aspects of Gaudí's designs, so it seems that he already confronted one of the paradoxes around which his whole life pivoted.

He traveled south from Barcelona with a young man with the improbable name of Pepe Weisberger, a Czech who sold insurance in Madrid. Gropius is not at all clear how he met this remarkable young man, but Weisberger was quite a connoisseur of art and apparently had a number of connections which enabled them to see more than Gropius would have seen otherwise. He was so intrigued by the craftsmanship of the Spaniards that he worked for a month in a Spanish majolica factory as a craftsman, where he fabricated a large mural out of this material and saw it fired and produced.

At the end of this year, Gropius went back to Berlin prepared to enter a profession. In 1908 he had already met the banker Ernst Osthaus, who was one of the founding members of the Darmstadt community, and through him he became acquainted with Henry van de Velde and the circle of men that [*inaudible*] already considered one of the most attractive opportunities that a young designer could have, and he went to work for Behrens at the end of that year. He stayed in the office for more than two years, until the end of 1910, ultimately becoming one of Behrens's principal associates. Gropius went with Behrens to London during this period as his assistant, to [try and secure] a job for the Behrens office. In this office he had the opportunity to observe first-hand one of the possible solutions to the paradox between the Arts and Crafts approach to production on the one hand and industrial production on the other, because — as we've just seen — the Behrens office was confronted with commissions for the design of a whole range of artifacts.

Gropius actually seems to have been very much involved in this subject even before he finished college. He remembers, for example, that his mother gave him a German translation of John Ruskin's *Seven Lamps of Architecture* — he thinks in 1903 or 1904 — which he read with great interest. Like most of his circle, he was thoroughly familiar with the Arts and Crafts movement in England, with William Morris and the doctrines of the group. He was attracted by the defense that these men made of the integrity of both craft and craftsman. This was the aspect of Morris's and Ruskin's work that appealed to him, but he was dismayed by their insistence that handicraft production was the only means of protecting this integrity. So at the very beginning, he confronts this contradiction, this paradox. Apparently this decade represents his oscillation between these two extremes, with his gradual decision that an industrial method of production was inevitable. Behrens — his "great teacher," as Gropius called him then and *still* calls him — enabled him to focus his whole attention on the work in the office on this problem of design in the period of industrialism. It was during this period that he met Hermann Muthesius, whose position in this field has also been quite adequately documented, and it was at this juncture that he joined the Werkbund. In 1911-2 Gropius first contributed to the Werkbund yearbook, which he subsequently edited: his involvement with this whole problem moved to the very center of activity and controversy.

Gropius left Behrens's office in 1910, nominally, as he said, because Behrens refused to pay him what he considered an adequate salary but actually because Gropius himself had matured and felt that he was prepared to now launch his own career. It was in that same year that Gropius's mother gave him a second book — the Wasmuth edition of Frank Lloyd Wright, which we have heard described. He says that this created an enormous impression in the Behrens office. He remembers very clearly the discussions that went on around the book. The buildings that most impressed him at the time were the office building for the Larkin Soap Company and the Robie House [*figure 8*]. At the time, a great exhibition of Wright's work was being held in Berlin at the Academy of Arts on Pariser Platz and Gropius recalls that every young architect in Berlin was milling in front of these remarkable buildings, greatly moved by the images that they saw there.

When he left the Behrens office, Gropius took Adolf Meyer with him. Meyer would be Gropius's associate until his premature death in the early 1920s, when he drowned in Holland. Apparently Gropius had made a number of contacts while in Behrens's office — with Walter Rathenau, for example, who asked him for a memorandum with his ideas on housing. This document was published by Nikolaus Pevsner a couple of years ago in *Architectural Review* and is one to which Gropius can point with real pride.[63] In this memorandum he advocates not only the prefabrication of whole houses but also of pre-fabricated elements that can be assembled into a wide range of house types and thereby (he hoped) avoid the very danger to which Mrs. Moholy-Nagy has so correctly pointed. This, of course, is exactly the program that he and Konrad Wachsmann attempted some forty years later with the General Panel Corporation. But for reasons that really had nothing to do with the design of the system, this failed in the early 1940s, as it had failed in 1910.

Gropius's first big independent job was the factory for the Fagus Shoe–Last Company of 1911, which is a remarkably prescient building, even though if analyzed in detail it is not at all remarkable, either structurally or spatially. It was during this period also that he read his first paper on "Monumental Art and Industrial Building." It had been just at this stage that be had begun to see the photographs of the great central grain houses in the American Midwest and in the Argentine, and these had all of a sudden confronted him with a possibility that he hadn't been aware of in European industrial archi-tecture. The thesis of this first paper was that implicit in the solution of industrial building problems was the opportunity for an authentically mon-umental architecture. These are the photographs that he subsequently pub-lished in the yearbook of 1913 and that created, by all accounts, an authentic sensation for people who saw them and that, I think, Muthesius later circu-lated as having been his own discovery. In any case this is one of the critical points in Gropius's career. As a result of his experience in Behrens's office on the one hand and his connections on the other, he was during this period able to design a sleeping car for the Prussian railway system and also a self-propelled diesel passenger car, both of which are extraordinary when seen today after the lapse of half a century.

The conflict within the Werkbund that Mrs. Moholy-Nagy has quite accu-rately outlined was actually the conflict between the two sides of the problem that had concerned Gropius. In correspondence published a couple of years ago, again in *Architectural Review,* about the attitude that Gropius took toward that famous debate between Van de Velde and Muthesius, Gropius has tried to establish the point that programmatically he thought that Muthesius was correct but that personally he thought that Muthesius had been unforgivably rude to Van de Velde; his defense of Van de Velde at that stage was a personal intervention and not a programmatic one. He says that Muthesius was "a most difficult man." [64]

Gropius had designed the Werkbund exposition building, which again has some very prescient elements. Obviously this didn't spring completely full-blown out of Gropius's brain, but nevertheless it has certain elements that seem to be authentically Gropius. World War I broke out within weeks of the opening of the exposition, and since Gropius was an officer in the cavalry he was immediately called up. This put an effective terminus on his career. He was very seriously wounded in the first few months of the war. After his convalescence he returned to the front as a communications officer. All in all he seems to have had several years that, while safe, were excruciatingly bor-ing. He apparently made some contributions to the communications set-up, which led to his being called back from the front for a conference in the office of General Erich Ludendorff. At just this juncture there was talk about the

American entry into the war, and Gropius, remembering the signs of industrial power that he had seen as a civilian, said he became disturbed about this possibility. He remembers having overheard a conversation in which one of Ludendorff's commanding generals raised the possibility of the Americans entering the war and Ludendorff replied, "the Americans — Barnum and Bailey stuff." Gropius, in contrast, began to lose confidence in the German cause — that is, the chance of a German victory.

In 1915 the Grand Duke of Saxony had communicated with him, at Van de Velde's request. Again Gropius was called back from the front and offered the opportunity, when the war ended, to take over the directorship of the two academies of the applied arts and the Academy of Art, in Weimar. Gropius went back to the western front and remained there until a few months before the armistice, when, because of his expertise in communications, he was sent to the Italian front on a special mission, just at the time of the collapse of the Italian front, as it turned out. He was in Vienna with his wife, the future Mrs. Mahler, when the armistice was declared. Still in uniform, he went back to a defeated Berlin. All of a sudden he realized that his uniform, far from being protection or a mark of status, was a symbol of the fact that the world had completely and permanently changed. It was at that juncture that he decided that he, too, would have to change, and he went to Weimar and began the creation of the Bauhaus.

Some Observations on the Villa Schwob
Colin Rowe

This talk will probably have the characteristics of a footnote and, like a footnote, I suspect it might quite possibly be brief. I had originally thought that it might conceivably be called, "Even the Villa Schwob." This is because when I received an invitation to attend this symposium, I was painfully embarrassed. I know nothing about the history of ideas in the later nineteenth century, and I am somewhat at a loss as to know how one establishes the meaning of forms in the early twentieth century, unless one knows something about the precedent history of ideas. That I found embarrassing. I would also be a little embarrassed, as I was, by the terminal date, which to me spelled the Russian Revolution and the entry of the United States into World War I. The first date implied to me a brilliant constellation of revolutionary manifestations that occurred at the beginning of the century. My dilemma was resolved when I received a letter from the chairman of this symposium who said to me, "You have always been fascinated by Le Corbusier, and I know that you find even the Villa Schwob more interesting than most of us do." I was astonished in fact by his clairvoyance. He was correct in his assumption that the manifestos of the period held no interest for me, and that I was intellectually under-equipped in any case to deal with them. (He did not say that, but I felt like that anyway.)

He was correct in his assumption that I was more interested in those things that had been left unsaid, rather than those that were over-publicly advertised. Frankly, I find the things that were publicly advertised to be, for the most part, a little embarrassing. One meditates, for instance, on the affiliations, say, or the possible affiliations, of fascism to futurism, and of Mussolini to Marinetti, and one doesn't necessarily wish to expatiate upon these themes. Instead, one wishes to confine one's remarks to something which interests oneself and which one believes to be of a genuine importance. Discovering that, I found the Villa Schwob [figure 35] interesting, I went on to believe—and I am now convinced—that it is quite the most interesting executed building of the decade.

One begins, I suppose, with the confrontation of the Maison Dom-Ino project [figure 33], or diagram, or generalization, of 1914 and the Maison Citrohan project of 1920–2 [figure 48]. Both of these are obviously among Le Corbusier's latest statements. Of the two, quite clearly Dom-Ino is the more polemical; Citrohan is the more specific, the more possibly actual, the less generalized, the less abstract. But both of them are major statements, and, if we are looking for a major subversive statement in the years preceding the great revolution that took place in the 1920s, perhaps that is Maison Dom-Ino. It establishes a proposition about space as something that travels in horizontal layers and that is in counter-distinction to the later proposition of Citrohan, which establishes a thesis about space as something that travels in open-ended tunnels. Both Dom-Ino and Citrohan are obviously architectural theses of outstanding clearness, but if either of them were to be pushed to its logical conclusion, it would necessarily contradict the other. The basic idea involved in Dom-Ino is that the ultimate datum for the reading of the building is the floor; and the basic datum involved in Citrohan as the manifestation of ultimate value for the reading of the building is the wall. Midway between these two things, then, lies the Villa Schwob, which is apparently scarcely a logical sequel of Dom-Ino. In fact, it seems to have nothing whatsoever to do with it, except for an incipient piloti that appears somewhere between the two front doors. Nor seemingly is the Villa Schwob anything that anticipates the Citrohan project. It is quite clearly a highly problematical building, and while earlier houses by Le Corbusier—those somewhat art nouveau and rather dreary chalets, the villas Fallet, Stotzer, and Jacquemet of 1906–8—seem to engage the attention of historians, and while the very Viennese and Hoffmannesque Jeanneret house and the Favre-Jacot House of 1912 also seemed to please, the Villa Schwob remains an object that Le Corbusier's admirers often seemed to wish away, including Le Corbusier himself, perhaps. He saw fit to publish his house in *Towards a New Architecture*, but he also saw fit to exclude it from the much more canonical collection of the *Oeuvre complète*. Yet I think that if any of Le Corbusier's early buildings from the decade 1906–16 were to be used to illustrate not a German or an Austrian allegiance on his part but a French one, or perhaps at least a Latin one, it would be surely the Villa Schwob.

Obviously, there is some indebtedness to Vienna. The indebtedness to such architects as Charles Garnier and Auguste Perret is also obvious and need not be stressed. There is a neoclassical flavor that may or may not be repulsive, but apart from this there remains the question of the Villa Schwob's mannerist content, which is overt, and it is probably in this area that the building really fails to ingratiate. The layering of the wall—the panels, for instance—might be suggestive of the sort of traits in which a mid-sixteenth-century architect like Bartolomeo Ammannati might indulge. The perversity of the equal and competing entrances is interesting. The ellipses in their carefully framed panels, which flank the central panel, and above all the carefully framed blankness of the center of the predominant motif, which both engages attention and fails to retain it: all this, which is so patently polemical in its intention, obviously can only be related with difficulty to the picture of Le Corbusier that one is predisposed to receive.

Yet, if we turn to the Villa Stein at Garches, which is surely one of the most eminently canonical of all Le Corbusier's houses, many of the ingredients of the Schwob House do seem to be recapitulated here. The two front doors of Schwob persist in Stein, although they have been desymmetrized. Both houses involve a somewhat obsessive concern with frontality (although I do not find it obsessive). Both of these elevations eminently have the quality of a frontispiece. Each developed a carefully framed episode. In the Schwob House, the episode is the blank panel, which has the qualities of a cyclorama and therefore, of an inferred deep space. In the Stein House, the framed episode is way up top and exists in actual space. Schwob deploys two vertical panels — the panels which bank the central motif. Stein deploys two anti-gravitational cuts, which might be seen as the two vertical panels of Schwob turned over sideways. Behind the Villa Schwob lies the Maison Dom-Ino, of which it is, we have noticed, not exactly a logical sequel. Anterior to Garches lies not only Dom-Ino but also Citrohan, and Garches doesn't really seem to be literally a logical sequence of either. One would not, for instance, suspect behind the facade of Garches a structure very like that of the Maison Dom-Ino. One would not expect, behind this facade, to find a cantilever tradition. Nor would one expect to find the flanking walls associated with the Maison Citrohan. But though it is not literally a logical sequel to the arguments involved in Citrohan and Dom-Ino, it does not actually contradict them either. The anti-gravitational cuts in the facade of Garches in some sense conform to the condition of the Dom-Ino scheme, though they do not literally issue from it.

At this stage, since these are simply observations, I wish to go off on an attack. Having related Schwob to Stein, one might be disposed to inquire as to the possible origins of Schwob. Very, very tentatively, one might intuit Frank Lloyd Wright's Hardy House at Racine, Wisconsin, as possible source material. Conceivably, a parallel of this kind is too little, but both houses do present a highly symmetrical *parti*, an extension of the building through subsidiary walls that screen the gardens from the streets, a two-story living volume, and a slot (clearer in the reading of the Racine House than in the Chaux-de-Fonds) that to some extent separates, at least in plan, the entrance from the body of the building which lies behind it. The slot is occupied in Le Corbusier's case by the staircase; it is occupied in Wright's case by a sort of entrance hall; but this sort of disengagement is apparent in both cases.

Obviously dissimilarities scarcely need to be stressed. The staircase and fireplace locations have been altered. We have already noticed the greater clarity of Wright's disengagements; one notices the greater complexity of Le Corbusier's space. And yet, for instance, in the lower plan of the Racine House, the projection of a terrace in front of the dining room might be seen as something that parallels Le Corbusier's elaborations, which are in place on a far less precipitous terrain. Conceivably, Corbu could have known this drawing from the Wasmuth portfolio. There is no reason, I suppose, why he should not have, and, allowing perhaps for his somewhat mannerist bias and temperament, it would seem probable that the Hardy House is the one Wright building that he could most easily tolerate. As to whether this conjunction of exteriors is really plausible or not, I am unable to say. One wonders whether a French-speaking Swiss would subject Wright's drawing to this particular sort of rendition. Reasonably, I think he could. But I am more amused in this case by what Wasmuth chose not to publish. Wasmuth published no drawing or illustration of the entrance front of the Racine House. If we imagine Corbu influenced by Wright's project (which I don't particularly wish to do), when it comes to the entrance front he is left on his own.

It is interesting, this reversion — or not necessarily reversion, but this playing with sixteenth-century precedents or prototypes. Both involved the idea of a cruciform elaboration of space. Both are three stories. Both involve the dilemma of two entrances. I am almost disposed to make a value judgment, but at this stage I will merely confine myself to suggesting how much more assertive Le Corbusier's statement of the vertical plane is than is Wright's. This assertion of the vertical plane is obviously in direct conflict with the logical conclusion of Maison Dom-Ino. It is a statement of the wall, which the Maison Dom-Ino diagram would seem, theoretically at least, to preclude. One notices something much more savage about Le Corbusier's building, and something much more comparatively benign about Wright's. There is perhaps in Le Corbusier's building a collision between the arrangements of the back and the frontispiece, which from some points of view partly conceals them. The frontispiece is elaborately rectilinear; the arrangements of the back are much more curvilinear. They are somehow in a state of rather violent conflict with each other, in a way that is quite clearly different from what one assumes to be the intention of Wright.

This collision between systems, again, leads me, through a chain of associations, to a parallel of this sort. At the risk of appearing somewhat facetious, I am about to suggest that one of the sources of the Villa Schwob might be Michelangelo's St. Peter's. The idea at first seems absolutely grotesque, but one has to remember Le Corbusier's great eulogium on Michelangelo in *Towards a New Architecture* (1923). One has to recollect that he seems to in some way have identified himself with Michelangelo and his preoccupation with big hands and big feet and all that stuff: Corbu had something of that same "fetishism," whatever it might mean. When he talks about St. Peter's, he says that Michelangelo was the man of the last thousand years, as Phidias was the man of the previous thousand years, and he leaves a convenient slot open as to who is to occupy the present thousand years. He also speaks of Michelangelo's moldings, of his modeling of the building at the rear of St. Peter's, and he speaks of these moldings as entirely new sections, revolutionary in appearance, as something harsh and pathetic. And one could conceive that this framing seen at La Chaux-de-Fonds is intended to be something harsh and pathetic, like the harshness and pathos of the rear of St. Peter's.

The drawing here [a plan of St. Peter's after Michelangelo] obviously derives from the fresco of, I believe, 1584, somewhere in the Vatican, and it is just casually interesting to notice some parts of Le Corbusier's elisions. He misses out, for instance, on the Vignola domes, but the most interesting elision of all, I think, we get if we look at the little plan — highly abstracted, very abbreviated, this little sketch — and compare it with the source that has presumably dictated it. One has to notice the way in which Le Corbusier elides a whole passage of the plan of St. Peter's. Now this might be simply an inattentiveness on his part, or it might somehow be the graphic equivalent of a Freudian lapse, the illustration of the propensity of a temperament. But one is interested in the way in which he misses out on the whole office area from here, so that this frontispiece business is rolled up against this particular wall here. I take that as being really something very symptomatic of his approach. He makes something more violent, more the collision between a frontispiece and a building behind out of Michelangelo's St. Peter's than its architect had initially intended.

One wishes to make, then, simply this parallel, and again it may seem absurd, but it is just possible that people do see this kind of stimulus and do act in this kind of way, and that some sort of modified simulacrum of Michelangelo's St. Peter's was intended in the Villa Schwob. I would wish to suggest this point rather than belabor it; I personally think that it is true.

But perhaps one is more interested not in the causes of a house like Schwob but rather in its effects. In this diagonal view of the Villa Schwob, shown alongside the plan of the Villa Stein, I wish to emphasize the very severe disengagement of the rectilinear elements of Schwob's frontispiece from the elaborations, again, which it may often conceal. There is no doubt at this point that some kind of disengagement is intended between this curvilinear element and the rectilinear element that is pressuring it and, in turn, being pressured by it. Similarly in plan here, one gets the intimately more elegant slot that separates the frontispiece of Garches from the body of the building that lies behind it. A profound community of intention underlines both of these facades, neither of which, as I said before, respond directly to either the Maison Dom-Ino or the Maison Citrohan.

I also wish to suggest that, like so many other Corbusian elements, these two facades are obedient to the exigencies of the eye rather than to those simply of the work itself. But they are obedient to the needs of the conceiving subject rather than the needs of the conceived object. Both exist very largely as a stimulant of heightened sensation; their basic reason for existence is optical. They are in some way the surface on which one measures the specific gravity of the block that lies behind it, on which the density of a three-dimensional substance is registered and inscribed.

If further argument is necessary to establish the legacy of Villa Schwob to a general discussion of Le Corbusier, one can produce it certainly in the plan of La Tourette, where the side wall of the church presents itself as the frontispiece of the monastery. But where a disengagement similar to that of Garches and of La Chaux-de-Fonds ensues, at La Tourette the pinwheeling, U-shaped block of cells is emphatically the body of the building. [Inaudible] One obviously must use the simple frontality of Villa Schwob and the obvious compounding of frontal and three-quarter views at La Tourette to distinguish these buildings one from the other. But what must be insisted upon, perhaps, in each case is a self-contained and self-conscious wall erected in front of the body of the building, which, I suspect, is a device that we would find occurring again and again in Le Corbusier's buildings and which, if we could recognize it to be a principle of his practice (perhaps first making its appearance here at La Chaux-de-Fonds), would enable us to envisage this house not as an item extrinsic to his major endeavor but as something at least as essential to it as were the projects for the Dom-Ino and Citrohan houses, and perhaps even as something that might be seen as mediating between the inferences of Dom-Ino and Citrohan. Obviously, any important study of Corbusier will inevitably necessarily concern itself with Maison Dom-Ino and Citrohan. What I am simply trying to establish is that, at present, it seems unlikely that anybody is going to concern themselves with Maison Schwob. Nobody would apparently wish to dilate upon its importance. I simply wish to suggest that the complexity, the hybrid nature, of Le Corbusier's style can perhaps be best ascertained by examining buildings such as this and not simply regarding them as anomalous.

···

The City-Planning Scene
George R. Collins

I would like to suggest that the development of city planning between 1907 and 1917 is fully as important—or even more important—then any other development of the period. The idea of designing on a large scale created a watershed in truly modern architecture. It precipitated a move away from the scale of the Arts and Crafts and of interior design, which had occupied so many of the leading architects of the late nineteenth century.

Although actually an age-old calling, town planning became a new profession during the 1910s. The term itself had come into English usage only just before our decade opened and, largely over the course of this decade, professional city planning developed the independent character, range of particular interests, and international outlook that were to contribute so greatly to the tenets and aspirations of the succeeding generation. The first professional periodical devoted to planning, *Der Stadtbau*, appeared in 1904, followed by *American City Magazine* in 1909, *The Town Planning Review* in 1910, and *The Journal of the Town Planning Institute* in 1914. The international meetings of city planners, held almost annually by the Garden City Association, began to supplant in significance the international meetings of architects.[65] Almost every year from 1910 to the outbreak of World War I, an important international meeting of planners took place. The year 1910 was of special importance, for it saw both the great town-planning exhibition in Berlin, in connection with the competition for the expansion of Greater Berlin, and the conference on planning sponsored by the Royal Institute of British Architects (RIBA) in London, at which the Canberra competition was announced. Of similar importance was the *International Congress and Comparative Exhibition of Cities* in Ghent of 1913.

The period of 1907 to 1917 was also marked by the appearance of books that were to serve as basic texts for some considerable time to come. These included, among others, updated editions of both Josef Stübben's 1890 *Der Städtebau* (Urban Development, 1907) and Camillo Sitte's 1889 classic *Der Städte-Bau nach seinen künstlerischen Grundsätzen* (City Planning According to Artistic Principles, 1909), as well as new works such as H. Inigo Triggs's *Town Planning, Past, Present and Possible* (1909), Raymond Unwin's *Town Planning in Practice* (1909), Thomas Mawson's *Civic Art* (1911), Otto Wagner's *Die Grossstadt* (The Big City, 1911), and Patrick Geddes's *Cities in Evolution* (1915).

With respect to the historical studies of cities, we have the papers of the Berlin-Charlottenburg seminar every year and the early works of A. E. Brinckmann. In general it can be said that as our decade opened the architectural and preservationist aspects of planning dominated. The "Sitte-esque" ruled on the continent, but a neo-baroque movement was developing that would receive Daniel Burnham's work with great enthusiasm. The search was for amenities that, like garden-city theories and the parks movement of England and America, might bring to the middle classes a sense of relief from the intense urban expansion and congestion. But the social problems of

housing betterment and so on that were to so inflame the writers and designers of European architecture after World War I began to reveal themselves
at the end of our decade. A clear instance of the widening perspectives, and
of the extra-European interest developing among planners, is the move of
Geddes to India in 1914.

Public transport and traffic problems began to receive increasing attention
and occasionally gave rise to architectural fantasies, extrapolated from the
remarkable accomplishments of urban engineers. If we take the mechanistic
technological "plug-in" manifestations of futurism to be among the original
contributions of our decade, we can find certain of its origins in the schemes
and publications of city planners. On the one hand, planners showed an
open-mouthed admiration for the accomplishments of engineers. New York's
Church Street subway station and London's Hudson Tube Building, both skyscrapers with multilevel terminals in their basements, were famous products
of our decade. France's Eugene Henard, at a session of the 1910 RIBA conference devoted to the City of the Future, argued for multilevel streets; buildings
raised on pilotis; flat, usable roofs; and conveyor belts and vehicular bridges,
with airplanes buzzing in and out. Edgar Chandler's Road Town suggested
the infinitely expandable , with its own, built-in rapid transportation system.
In short, not only did city-planning practice and theory undergo radical
transformation in our decade, but the very directions in which it moved were
indicative of the programs and manifestos that leading architects of the 1920s
were to take on as their own.[66]

Action History in Spain
David Mackay

As a practicing architect, not an historian, what interests me is what I call
"action history," that is, history that conscientiously participates in a creative
act of architecture. I'm not referring to the mere transplanting of historical
forms, which some architects do, but the reevaluation of historical problems
and their solutions. One of the roles of architectural historians, as I see it, is
to discover and throw out these problems and solutions, and to encourage a
conscious incorporation into the current vocabulary of architecture. This is
what we could call a "live history." True, history floats in the waters of interpretation, which may well suggest different ideas to different architects, but
it still remains as an essential instrument in the creative process of architecture. The interpretation of architecture involves the study of the tides and
turns and consequences, the ideals and works, that constitute the historical
process of creation — of people and times and places, with all their political,
economic, geographic, and historical commitments and influences. History
must be opened up, prepared for dialogue with the present, but above all it
must be soundly based on a wide font of archaeological evidence. In other
words, it has to be founded on a whole mass of detailed observation and completely freed from hasty interpretations. It is only then, when all the evidence
is available, that interpretations can be made. Too often, hasty conclusions
are attached to the first discoveries, which may be intuitively right but often
are very misleading.

If we wish to use history, it can be divided into three chapters. First there
is broad research based on archaeological evidence — gathering all the minute

details together, a sort of micro-history of the question in hand. Second comes interpretation and synthesis of the evidence — an open history that can contribute actively to the final, third chapter. This third chapter is the actual use of history in the creation of contemporary architecture. I believe, too, that there is room for feedback from practicing architects to enlighten historians on the various syntheses and interpretations of primary historical evidence that they have before them.

A classic example of confused history is provided by the story of Antoni Gaudí. Apart from one early exception, a deluge of interpretation has lasted for more than forty years before detailed archaeological research has been undertaken. I suggest that the period under review suffers from polemical interpretations that are founded too often on the sands of intuition. We've been hoodwinked by genius. Both those histories that are limited to the study of the early masters alone and those histories that involve a narrow, formal evolutionary study are too closed and dogmatic. It is frivolous to explain Frank Lloyd Wright only by his family background and the early influence of Sullivan when, as Allen Brooks suggested yesterday, Wright was the brilliant product of the design environment he was part of. The same could be said about Gaudí, who without the Catalan Renaissance merely appears irrational. Geniuses are original but they are not to be explained by irrationality.

A typical example of a Barcelona block has a house by the architect Luis Domènech i Montaner, the Casa Lleó Morera, which displays the discipline of an ordered composition together with a systematic application of decoration based on historical research; farther along, the Casa Ametller by Josep Puig i Cadalfalch, with a sort of Dutch gable and the spirit of disciplined Gothic details, which include humorous monkeys taking photographs; and right next to it, the Casa Batlló of 1905-7, by Gaudí, which involved the total reformation of an existing building, with the facade inspired from the story of St. George and the Dragon — the former being the patron saint of Catalonia. All were built about the same time.

Gaudí's Parque Güell of 1900–14 was an attempt to establish a small neighborhood — a garden city on a very small scale — but it failed because all the money was spent on the access roads and bridges necessitated by the landscape. Gaudí built the curving bench-balustrade (which is extremely comfortable to sit on) with the help of Josep Maria Jujol, his assistant architect, who was a master with tiles and mosaics.

As I suggested, Gaudí was not the only genius within this movement. A great deal of credit is due to the rational approach of Domènech i Montaner. His Palau de la Música Catalana of 1905–8 featured the first steel frame in Europe with glass curtain walls. Behind the double row of columns on the front facade is a complete two-story glass pavilion. The whole building gives the sensation of being a tremendous transparent space. The purity of the structure is not immediately apparent — you really have to study the plans — and was considered less important than the tremendous sculptural decoration, which is very much in the vocabulary of the Catalan Modernisme movement.

Returning to Gaudí, we have the Casa Milà, with its curtain wall of stone flowing with horizontal bands around the cut-off corner of the Cerdá grid-plan. Gaudí is always deeply symbolic, but here he produces an introduction to expressionist architecture. The apartment house offers a prophetic vision of the use of the steel frame and of free planning, anticipating the history of the modern movement. At the Colonia Güell, a very simple village of about six hundred people just outside Barcelona, with workers' housing by Gaudí's assistants, including Francesc Berenguer, the plan consists of a small rectangular grid. The modest two-story houses, built before 1910, were constructed very cheaply, using all the techniques of the period. With respect to Gaudí's chapel, whose crypt was started in 1898 and completed in 1916, one of the most interesting aspects is the siting off the axis of the village plan. The structural relationship of the spaces responds to his observation of human behavior: the gathering of people around the altar and a generous porch that merges with the pine trees for the social gathering after the service.

There were many other architects participating in the Catalan Renaissance, which was very widespread. Rafael Masó (1880–1935) worked in Girona just north of Barcelona and was influenced by Charles Rennie Mackintosh as well as by the Catalan expressionists. Lluís Monconill (1868–1931) was very important as an expressionist architect and used large spans in Catalan vaults (for example, at the Aymerich i Amat factory in Terrassa of 1907), which is another subject about which an important study should be made. What I want to emphasize is that while there are plenty of general studies on this period, there is much to be done based on primary material to be gathered with fieldwork.

Another point I wish to make is that both Gaudí and Domènech worked with teams. They weren't each just one architect with assistants. Gaudí had two other architects working with him, along with four or five assistants, and he counted on sculptors, artists, and all sorts of workmen to interpret his ideas. Otherwise, this architecture would have been absolutely impossible. Domènech, too, in the design of the Hospital of San Pau, had I think five architects working with him. It was a complete act of teamwork in the architects' offices.

It is worth mentioning that both the architect Puig i Cadafalch and Doménech went to work in Vienna, and they brought back the influence of Joseph Olbrich and the Viennese school. There was at this time very extensive information in Barcelona about the work of the Viennese architects, as is quite obvious from some of the details in the buildings of the Catalan architects. Puig himself, it's interesting to note, was visited by Gropius in the first decade of the new century, and Puig showed Gropius how the Catalans were designing and manufacturing ceramic tiles. It was in Spain in 1903 or 1906 that Gropius learned about industrial design. As Gropius told me when he visited Barcelona three or four years ago, it was actually in Barcelona that he "found his calling." It is worth remembering that in 1910 there was an exhibition of Gaudí's work in Paris.

Finally, later in our period, we can see in a house of interlocking cylinders by Jujol outside Barcelona in Sant Joan Despí, the Torre de la Creu of 1913–6, further indication of the richness of Catalan architecture at this time.

I would like to conclude this talk just a little bit more generally and situate the context of this period. Politically it opens with the consolidation of the Catalonian identity—inspired by the rediscovery of the Catalonian heritage in the middle of the nineteenth century—which came after two centuries of centralist suppression. This cultural rebirth coincided with an economic boom prompted by exploitation of the Cuban market, which launched and financed the Catalan industrial revolution, giving Catalonia a wealth that enabled it to embark on its art nouveau adventure. Turning their eyes toward

Europe—away from Madrid—the Catalans adopted their own particular form of art nouveau, which they named Modernisme. It was the cultural expression of their patriotism. This is what gave it a force, not found anywhere else, so much so that Catalonia has been called—and I don't think it's an exaggeration—"the Athens of art nouveau." But the Catalans were not entirely sure of themselves and continued to watch events in Europe to ensure their own progressiveness.

At the beginning of the twentieth century, when the artistic expression of Modernisme reached full maturity, the seeds of reaction were sown by the young art critic Eugeni d'Ors. His daily column in the newspaper *El Poble Català* finally turned the intellectual current to follow the new classical reaction taking place in the rest of Europe, which, after about 1902, entered a new period in art, literature, and architecture that came to be called Noucentisme. The freedom that founded Modernisme was replaced by discipline and order. Meanwhile, the epoch was active with anarchists, with their bombs, assassinations, and executions, culminating in 1909 in what was called the *Semana trágica*.[67] The period ended with the triumph of the separatists in the elections of 1917, and the first solidarity of the various workers' groups. This political situation would finally lead Catalonia to socialism in the 1930s, with its architectural expression in the Grupo de Artistas y Técnicos Españoles Para la Arquitectura Contemporánea.

Anarchism, dictatorship, and civil war, the military occupation, censorship, ostracism, and, lately, an anti-intellectual political policy have combined to camouflage the essentially rich contribution of the Catalans to the history of modern architecture. There has been no way of communicating this period to the world. All that I ask is that more research be done, so that one day Catalan architecture will get the recognition it deserves.

The Problem of Mackintosh
Thomas Howarth

The second section of Charles Rennie Mackintosh's Glasgow School of Art [*figure 7*] was redesigned in 1906 and built between 1907 and 1909. It contains the library, which is undoubtedly his most striking and most important contribution to interior space. It is difficult to point to any other single example of his work that better expresses his control of space and his interest in the use of materials—in this case, wood, glass, and metal. After completing this project, Mackintosh's contribution dwindled considerably. He concentrated on watercolors and did a good deal of interior design and furniture. The latter section of the Ingram Street Tea Room was completed in 1911.[68]

One of the most difficult things those of us interested in international affairs have found is to ascertain the extent to which Mackintosh influenced others in Europe at this time. I don't believe Mackintosh had any significant influence after about 1905–6, when the Willow Tea Rooms and the Glasgow work was widely publicized on the continent. H. Allen Brooks has done a great deal of work on the topic. Eduard Sekler was a great help to me personally in the early days in assessing Mackintosh's contribution in Vienna, and together we came to conclusions about this that, I think, subsequent work by other historians has borne out.

When the war came in 1914 it cut right across this development. Not until the 1930s did our friend Nikolaus Pevsner revive interest in him.

Futurism
Sibyl Moholy-Nagy

I must say that I spent a very sleepless night after yesterday. I left the very nice party very unhappy, because I felt we had spent so much time on all these totally irrelevant little villas, little churches, little this and little that. It was a bit of rustication here, a bit of new material there. All this so totally defeated my personal idea of architectural history that I think Mr. Mackay beautifully formulated, paraphrasing Francis Bacon: History is a computation backward from our own time. If this is so, then I think it is our duty to find out what it actually was in the past that created our current concept of architecture, or at least our current problems of architecture.

No matter from which side you slice it, it is futurism and the idea of both the highly rational, as far as structure is concerned, and the totally irrational, as far as concept is concerned, which is the contradiction of man in modern society that actually has created, or is creating, the current character of our architecture. I find again and again that the pronouncements of Antonio Sant'Elia are actually the anticipation of what besets us today, and then, if you look at the visual material, it is Charles Garnier's vistas (not of the little, individual cast-concrete block houses but of his total vistas) that are actually what have made our problems for the first time relevant in history. We are always speaking about Sant'Elia's 1914 *Manifesto dell'Architetto Futurista*, which supplemented the first appearance of some of what were later 250 drawings made between 1906 and 1915, of the new city. But the statement by Sant'Elia that is much more important is the preface to the catalogue of the first futurist exhibition, called *Nuova Tendenza* and held at the Familia Artistica in Milan in May and June of 1914. Sant'Elia wrote a *messaggio* for this catalogue, of which I will quote a few passages, because they are really what met us in that era:

> The problem of modern architecture is not a problem of rearranging its lines, not a question of finding new moldings, new architraves for doors and windows. Nor of replacing columns, pillars, those corbels, those caryatids, hornets, or funny frogs, not a question of leaving a facade bare, leaving it of brick or facing it with stone or plaster. In a word, architecture has nothing to do with defining formalistic differences between the new buildings and the old ones. But to raise a new built structure on a same plan, gleaning every benefit of science and technology, settling nobly every demand of our habits and our spirits, rejecting all that is heavy, grotesque, unsympathetic to us: tradition, style, aesthetics, proportion. Establishing new forms, new lines, new reasons for existence, solely out of the special conditions of modern living and its projection as aesthetic value in our sensibilities. Calculations of the resistance of the materials, the use of reinforced concrete and iron, exclude architecture "as understood in the traditional sense." Modern structural materials and our scientific concepts absolutely do not lend themselves to the disciplines of historical styles, and are the chief cause of the grotesque aspect of so-called nouveau mode-ish construction where we see

the ripeness and the proud slenderness of girders, the slightness of reinforced concrete, bend to the heavy curves of the arch, aping solidity, in either marble or plaster. We must invent and rebuild ex-novo our modern city, like an immense and tumultuous shipyard; active, mobile, everywhere dynamic, and the modern building like a gigantic machine. Lifts must no longer hide away like solitary worms in the stairwells, but the stairs, now useless, must be abolished, and the lifts must swarm up the facades like serpents of glass and iron. The house of cement, iron, and glass, without cloth or painted ornament, rich only in the inherent beauty of its lights. Extraordinarily brutish in its mechanical simplicity, as big as need dictates, and not merely as zoning rules permitted, it must rise from the brink of a tumultuous abyss—the street—which itself will no longer lie like a doormat at the level of the thresholds, but plunge stories deep into the earth, gathering up the traffic of the metropolis, connected for necessary transfers to metal catwalks and high-speed conveyor belts. And I conclude in this favor of mode-ish architecture, of every style and of every notion. Classically sullen architecture, hieratic, theatrical, decorative, old or new, monumental, graceful or pleasing, preservation, reconstruction, reproduction, perpendicular and horizontal lines, cubic and pyramid forms, static, great, oppressive, absolutely foreign to our new sensibilities. Use of materials that are massive, bulky, durable, and expensive. All opposed to the complexity of modern culture and modern experience. And I affirm that the new architecture is the architecture of cold calculation, of timorous boldness, and of utter simplicity. The architecture of reinforced concrete, iron, glass, textile-fibers, and all those replacements for wood, stone, and brick that make for the attainment in maximum of elasticity, lightness, and motion.[69]

I feel very strongly that we have totally neglected, in all that we have looked at—which Mr. George Collins now, to a certain extent, I think rectified—the idea that there is a city that comes into being as a new environment, and not the individual house, or church, and not the individual interpretation of lines. For me, almost everything we saw yesterday is a conclusion and not a new beginning. The old military prison by Schinkel and the Ubrig House by Mies van der Rohe makes perfectly clear that this is the conclusion of something that had started with the Renaissance, had gone through its various transformations, and came to an end. [Inaudible] In Paul Bonatz's Railway Station in Stuttgart, started in 1911 but only finished after World War I, you see quite clearly that this is a terminating classicism. [Inaudible]

And this is, of course, that excessive machine romanticism that desperately tries to make out of the machine a part of that lovely art nouveau environment, full of elegance, full of nice lines, and full of a romantic reintegration of the machine into a harmonious design environment, which I think comes out of Henry van de Velde's idea very well. On the right side [points to the projection screen] is an engine room that he designed, which has, of course, a beautiful art nouveau skylight that is, so to speak, to shed its blessing on the machines underneath. By contrast, Sant'Elia dared to face the machine: he saw the age of the machine as something absurd, ugly, oppressive, but nevertheless completely new environment-making.

In conclusion, I would like to say that I feel that all the movements we spoke about yesterday, including the Werkbund, are actually paraphrasings of John Ruskin's *The Seven Lamps of Architecture* of 1849. They are all still a desperate search for sacrifice, truth, power, beauty, light, obedience, and memory in the romantic transcription of idealism. Idealism is always connected with the Germans, but this was particularly the case with the Bauhaus and its insistence on morality in architecture — of architecture as moral and social tendencies. I feel very desperately that if we are going to have more of the symposia, what is needed is a new evaluation of technology and space and form and architecture as it has developed historically, not as it is today.

For instance, the first reinforced-concrete bridge from 1890 makes Robert Maillart look rather pale, because you suddenly see that certain great aesthetic forms developed from new needs and new technologies that far antecede our textbook heroes: it was these needs and technologies that were the great history-determining aspects. The same goes for the mushroom columns of 1910, which did not start with Wright's Racine factory but are so much older.

To my horror, Auguste Perret was totally omitted from our considerations yesterday. It is absolutely unbelievable to me that a man like Perret, who made a new concept of the interior, who created a completely new interior space out of structural elements that never had been there before, could be passed over. With Charles Garnier also, and his slaughterhouse in Lyon of 1909, we see what we miss out on people who did not believe in the *Seven Lamps of Architecture* but rather in the "Seven New Structural Materials and Methods" and from these created the expression of our own time, or at least created the problems.

What we usually see of Garnier's are very lovely drawings of his houses, because they look so much like the early Le Corbusier Dom-Ino house [*figure 33*]. Actually, I think the key to the whole Garnier problem is two drawings of [*inaudible*]. You might recall the separation of zones into industrial and residential in plan: here you see something completely different, something that is extremely related to what we now call "infra-cities," on which we still chew. They are at present the comic strips of our architectural magazines, but I hope they will one day lose their comic-strip character and become the reality of our new cities. Think back to something like the Montreal propositions for 1967, their idea of prefabs, of building up units in an urban sense, and you get something like Garnier's design, something that takes your breath away; and this, from 1900 to 1903.

Tony Garnier's railroad station for his Cité Industrielle, published in 1917, features a magnificent cantilever and the first electric transportation system that was ever evolved (his buses were to be powered electrically). Compare this to the 1912 plan by Walter Burley Griffin for the city of Canberra, and to a 1785 plan of the Canadian town of Sydney, which was proposed by a French colonel or high military man named Joseph Frederick Wallet DesBarres, who became a governor of the province of Quebec. I desperately searched the Avery Library the other day because I wanted to knew whether Griffin was by any chance Canadian, because to me the relationship between these two plans is absolutely *incredible*. It is not that they are so similar to each other but that both of them are futuristic in character: both of them are pure communication schemes. That with the terrible lag in cultural understanding Canberra has become a great disaster as far as city life is concerned doesn't change the fact that the original concept of Griffin was one of utter mobility. Unfortunately, I have found very little on DesBarres' plan for Sydney, which was to be a completely *new* town.

In closing, I want to emphasize that historical emphasis must be placed on those concepts that — like the plans of Sant'Elia, Garnier, and DesBarres — emphasize the idea of mobility that came with the industrial revolution and completely changed the notion of the static individual house, in contrast to the static plaza. These are the realms of our investigation.

Adolf K. Placzek: In defense of some of yesterday's proceedings, I would like to speak up for things which constitute history per se or history *an sich* (as a thing in itself) — things which have no direct application to what we are doing now but which are interesting as historical phenomena, in Ranke's words, "as it actually happened." As for [Francis] Bacon's "computation backward," I think architectural students whom we are trying to fill with a little bit of knowledge of historical forms, historical shapes, historical phenomena, will always be glassy-eyed as soon as they think what they are learning cannot be applied to Harrison and Abramovitz.

Moholy-Nagy: [*Inaudible*] a misunderstanding.

Placzek: I am not saying that you are doing it, because you have put into these students more historical understanding than most other people. I think there might arise a slight misunderstanding here as to our objective. Do we really only want to see history applied? Or do we want history per se?

Moholy-Nagy: It is not applied when it speaks of concepts: that's the important point.

Placzek: Concepts per se rather than concepts that can be "computed backward" — and I am just giving this whole question of methodology to the assembled group.

Collins: I'd tried to suggest this morning that we'd missed some of the major groundswells in our effort. I'd be curious to know what others think about this, because one of the things we were going to precipitate today were suggestions for [the symposium to be held in] 1968.

Henry-Russell Hitchcock: May I read part of a sentence from my, so-to-say, editorial?

> The purpose of these gatherings has never been to arrive at conclusions, even tentative, but rather to revive historical and critical interest in topics that have long been taken too much for granted — to revive interest and to throw light on half-forgotten divergences in theory and in form that have often proved to be almost as lively matters for discussion today as they were in the periods reviewed.[70]

Behind that is another thought. The early histories of modern architecture were inevitably works of propaganda, whether they were written by architects or by critics. At some point (it is hard to say exactly when) we suddenly realized that this propaganda had produced myth, and we began to desire to investigate what lay behind these myths and to dissolve them. In other words I do think that it is curious and a fact of real cultural interest that these controversies revive, but I think that we are no longer merely concerned with what were thought at he beginning to have been the few constituent elements. It is very hard for us to say now what is constituent until we have the broader type of examination that we have tried to carry through here. Fortunately, Mrs. Moholy-Nagy has well made up for Peter [Reyner] Banham's absence. But whether there is anyone who can make up for the absence of Peter Collins I don't know, because not only has Perret been neglected but so has the history of concrete construction on both sides of the Atlantic, including the Kahn factories, for example. Furthermore, until this brief presentation, we have almost totally neglected a country that many of us were brought up to believe was the only country in which art and architecture were important: France. For, of course, Le Corbusier in the period we are dealing with was not a Frenchman, he was a Swiss, and he had not built in France. I don't know whether we can repair that. I would, however, like to call on Mrs. Sekler, who has something to add on Corbusier in this early period.

Le Corbusier and the Maison du Diable at Le Locle
Patricia May Sekler

In 1912, when Charles-Edouard Jeanneret was building the villa for his parents in La Chaux-de-Fonds, he was also working on a villa in La Locle, which is some ten kilometers distant (and the town from which his family, the Jeanneret-Gris branch of the Jeannerets, originates). This was the Villa Favre-Jacot, which also became known as La Forêt. Its location was quite similar to that of his earlier villas in La Chaux-de-Fonds: on an elevation, overlooking the town, with a southeastern exposure. He had to cope with a very narrow site, cut into the hillside of the Billodes, and also to incorporate two existing retaining walls as well as stables. Now as Mr. Rowe pointed out to us yesterday, this villa in Le Locle and the villa for Jeanneret's parents mark a turning point in his career: he was turning away from the earlier concept of architecture as something that had a very specific, direct connection with the decorative arts. However, it is with another project in La Locle that we see this more clearly, and that is what I want to talk about. It relates to something that came up very often in our symposium yesterday: the interest in folk architecture. We saw it in Josef Hoffmann's drawings in the late nineteenth century. We also saw it in Mission architecture.

The man for whom the Le Locle villa was designed, Georges Favre-Jacot, owned other property in the same town, on the opposite side. One of the buildings that he possessed in the area — known as Le Molière — was an old farmhouse, reported to be one of the very oldest buildings in the region. It was thought to have been built in the early fifteenth century on the foundations of a structure built three centuries earlier. In local parlance it has the marvelous name of La Maison du Diable, "the Devil's House," having gained this epithet in the late nineteenth century for an historical event that happened at the time. The farmhouse had very massive walls, and its exterior reflects a very complicated interior arrangement. The south-facing facade of the building had a doorway opening onto a corridor giving access on the left to a large chamber — the kitchen — and on the right to a vaulted cellar. On the eastern facade, a door gave access to the *première étage*, which included a separate apartment reflected on the facade by many small windows grouped together. On the northern facade were the stables, a door into a third apartment, plus a barn and a loft that one approached by a ramp.

About the time that Jeanneret designed the villa for Favre-Jacot (the dates on the plans for that villa range roughly from 30 March to 1 June 1912), the local newspapers reported that this old farmhouse was about to be demolished because its upper portions were threatening to fall down. Demolition did take place, but the lower portions were retained. Whether it was at the inspiration of Favre-Jacot or whether it was Jeanneret's own idea, I do not know, but there survives a sketch that bears the inscription in Jeanneret's own hand: "*adaptation de la Maison du Diable.*" Jeanneret was clearly interested in this house that Favre-Jacot possessed. It seems likely that he saw it at the point of demolition after the roof had been removed and that this image of a massive masonry structure with a horizontal emphasis on the upper portion affected his design. Jeanneret's adaptation of La Maison du Diable included an arcade above the eastern facade with an abutting exterior stair, and above the southern facade, an extensive pergola. One has the feeling that this was to be a roof garden overlooking the entire valley.

On seeing the character of this adaptation, one is reminded of Jeanneret's early travel sketches, particularly those from the Near East. But, as Jeanneret's early writings tell us, he did not have to go very far afield in order to see such elements. His sensitivity to vernacular forms is made clear in his 1914 article "La Maison Suisse," written as a dialogue between "Pierre" and "Juste," in which the speakers verbally peruse the highways and byways of Switzerland, attempting to pinpoint the specific characteristics of the national style. At one point Jeanneret, noting the similarities between the domestic architecture of Romania and Switzerland, says of the Romanian forms, "It's the back turned to Gothic forms, the preeminence of large stone surfaces, the disappearance of detail, the tendency towards a unique and sober silhouette." [71] Included with the illustrations was a Swiss example — buildings on a street in Schulz — with thick exterior masonry walls not unlike those of La Maison du Diable.

The period of Jeanneret's life between 1907 and 1917 presented him with problems somewhat similar to those Walter Gropius had to face. He had to reconcile his early interest in the applied arts with new impulses: impulses that would allow him to make the jump from here to 1917, to his later work in Paris. During this time — a period of immense activity — he was not only teaching in La Chaux-de-Fonds but also traveling very widely. Writing in the mid-1920s on the decorative arts, he reflected on this period in his life very philosophically, saying in *L'Art Décoratif d'Aujourd'hui*:

Return.
Digestion.
A conviction: one has to begin again at zero.
One has to pose the problem.
The whirlpool of life. It is not only a question of aesthetics. Between 20 and 30, it is then that one rounds the Cape of the Tempests. It is then that a being's deepest drives are active and a life finds its course. One makes the choice for one's life without being aware of it, without being able to pretend: here or there. A tiller is in your depths that becomes fixed, that takes a form and orients itself on a bearing. At thirty years one finds oneself in a certain place, having or not having passed the Cape of the Tempests.[72]

The year 1917 found Jeanneret, age thirty, in Paris, where he took up residence in the Latin Quarter, met Amédée Ozenfant for the first time, and within three years adopted the name Le Corbusier. But I have a feeling that, having survived the Tempests, he took stock of the cargo that had survived this long journey and that one important item was La Maison du Diable. It survived practically unscathed in a little sketch in a letter to Paul Poiret, a prospective client, concerning a proposed villa. The forms in the sketch, I feel, are quite similar to those for the adaptation of Favre-Jacot's old farmhouse. Unfortunately, the date of this project for Poiret is not clear. The *Oeuvre complète* places it at approximately 1916. Two of the more developed sketches, along with the plan, were published again in *Creation is a Patient Search*, where the first contact with Poiret is given as 1921.[73] He writes concerning his illustrated letter to Poiret that "architectural themes were submitted to him, rupturing aesthetic traditions and proposing the elements of a style of reinforced concrete, of new dispositions, new liberties, and a thoroughly new attitude."[74]

When one considers the sources of inspiration for the Maison Citrohan of 1920-2 [*figure 48*], one can again consider La Maison du Diable; the similarities in concept are totally clear. In discussing the sources of Citrohan himself, Le Corbusier mentions only his interest in rational planning, stimulated in particular by his discovery one day of a practically organized restaurant in Paris frequented by coach drivers, as well as by the abundant and well-propotioned fenestration of factories.[75] But I am inclined to think that perhaps he could have mentioned the Favre-Jacot farmhouse as well. Indeed, he may have had it in mind in his statement about Citrohan, where he writes, "With that house, one turns one's back on architectural conceptions of the academicizing school, as well as the *modernes*."[76]

The Purpose of Symposia in the History of Architecture
Rudolf Wittkower

I suppose you want me to speak about the little controversy that has arisen here between Mrs. Moholy-Nagy and Mr. Placzek. I'm always delighted to listen to Mrs. Moholy because she brings a fresh approach, and she has the real makings of a prophet, a propagandist, a great critic. And when she talks it all sounds very convincing, but my own feeling, if I may just say a word about my reaction to what happened yesterday, is that I felt it was a very profitable day. Not only did I learn a lot, but it was the kind of historical, objective approach we like. It was a kind of critical game that one enjoys.

One feels a lot of things have not been said; for instance, when I came home, I thought it very strange that Auguste Perret hasn't been mentioned, and I pulled out the book on Perret that I had and found that the garage, which you all know, is probably more important to the Villa Schwob [*figure 35*] than a number of things that have been said here in the extremely stimulating talk that we had last night. And this is the kind of thing, I feel, we indulge in and that we as historians have to discuss and possibly rectify. We have to find our way through a great deal of evidence and try to get an objective picture of the past. It is relatively easy to have hindsight and say we only want to concern ourselves with what has turned out to be important, but this is never the way history works. If we approach history on a broad basis, in a sense we get nowhere, and we would have to eliminate a great deal of historical evidence that is very important to us and that we as historians like to deal with — not only *like* to deal with but *have* to deal with. If I think back for a moment and try to consider the fifteenth, sixteenth, seventeenth, and eighteenth centuries in the same way, and only lift out what is interesting and important for the future, I strip history of a great deal of very interesting evidence. If I may mention here a particular friend of mine, who is probably known to some of you, who comes at the end the eighteenth century and is a completely dead hen. If we apply Mrs. Moholy's critical approach to such a man, we would have to cut him out entirely, because he is a dead hen. But if we cut him out entirely we lose a great deal, because this man was fantastic: he had original ideas, always on old stuff, and as I say, they didn't lead up to anything, but they're extremely important to us because they enrich the picture of the whole period.

In the same sentence, I think we are bound to point out within the decades we're choosing for consideration the entire panorama of what happened. I personally, for instance, am not terribly interested in all the little houses in the western United States, but I think they belong to the panorama. We have to discuss them. We have to find out what's going on here and there. What is the basis of the realms that influence architects in various areas? Where do they get their information, their stimulation? So I feel very distinctly, if I may also speak for the future of these symposia, that we should carry on, plow on, in a proper historical fashion. We should discuss all the evidence and bring it to bear upon the whole area, the broad panorama, with which we are concerned — to try to re-create, as Dolf Placzek has said, the entire picture of the past, meanwhile never forgetting what is important for the present situation.

General Discussion
Led by Henry-Russell Hitchcock

Hitchcock: I think the time has come to throw this open to a wider discussion of shorter remarks. We've been almost as formal so far this morning as yesterday. First, however, I want to mention what I should have remembered and what has been called to my attention. The building in which we are sitting was built in 1911. We now know that Vince Scully was misquoted. Buildings don't speak to him, and therefore I cannot call on a representative of the period, in the person of this building, to address us. But I know that there are others who have spoken before who will want to contribute to the particular topic that Mr. Wittkower has been talking about. One of them, I noticed, is Mr. Sekler.

Eduard F. Sekler: I just want to add details that seem pertinent. I don't feel so badly about having had Professor Erwin Panofsky recently start a lecture by quoting Aby Warburg, who used to say, "*Le bon dieu est dans le détail.*" (We used to hear a similar statement in architectural school about God living in the detail.)

The detail I'd like to add has to do with Sant'Elia and futurism. It is something that has been said before and is known, that he was influenced by Otto Wagner's teaching. The Wagnerschule is a curious historic phenomenon.[77]

Between 1900 and 1907, perhaps, a number of simply incredible student projects were produced that anticipated a great deal. There you find suspended structures. You find the sky cities. You find modern technological means used in the most utopian fashion. These projects were never built, and it's rather sad to see how many of these students, in their later life, did not live up to their promise. It makes you think that Wagner must have inspired them. How did he inspire them? When you read very carefully his programmatic statement *Moderne Architektur*, at one point he tries to define what is coming in the future, as far as he can. This must have come not easily to a man who had started completely in the historicist tradition.

I was struck again, hearing you read Sant'Elia's manifesto here, how much of that comes straight from Otto Wagner. When Wagner speaks about the new technology, the new means of society, the better democratic society, we get the seeds of Sant'Elia twenty years earlier. A historical phenomenon of great interest to me is how did Wagner's thinking reach Italy? Why did Sant'Elia take it up?

A final note on some of these pictures of Wagner, which would bring in the countries that haven't been mentioned at all: the old monarchies — Czechoslovakia, Hungary, and what is Yugoslavia today. People like Jan Copera and Josef Plecnik went out, became professors, and built some of the most remarkable buildings that are now being rediscovered.

Hitchcock: Lately some remarkable stuff in Bohemia has been published. Dr. Rosenau, I think you have something to contribute to this.

Helen Rosenau: I'm wondering whether in your future deliberations you would perhaps devote some time to words that have been frequently but very loosely used, especially the word "utopia," which I noticed had been used in five different ways. Even if we couldn't agree on, let us say, a philosophical definition, we might perhaps at least agree on a working definition. The same seems to me true of the word "expressionism," which has been used even more widely than the word "utopia." Now the word we have used most is the word "influence." I would like to suggest that we use it in two basic manners. One is the influence of one artist on another, where the artist acknowledges the influence and the influence is in fact documented. But there is a second influence that is much more difficult to assess, which is the one that works unconsciously through the artist who uses it. I was particularly interested in what Mrs. Sekler said about the early influences in Le Corbusier. What you have is an unconscious penetration of the environment, as it were, into the work of the artist. It is this, the second manner of influence — the unconscious one — that I think poses the greatest problem.

To make matters more complicated, there is also convergence. You have, in fact, historical situations that are, let's say, revolutionary in their social sense, without wanting to define revolution. I'm sorry I have to come back to the late eighteenth century, into the period of Boullée and Ledoux, but the Gropius that you showed us, and the Taut that you showed us, they honestly look as if they were influenced by certain of the *grand prix* designs. Now this may not have been a conscious influence: I quite admit it. But I think the knowledge of what architecture and design was in France at the end of the nineteenth century was a factor that penetrated enormously into the consciousness, certainly of Perret and quite definitely of Le Corbusier, to whom I wrote a letter and who replied saying, yes, indeed, he was quite conscious that there was a tradition there in which he was working still.

This is all perhaps that I wanted to say, except that it seems to me we shouldn't start with *[inaudible]*; we should really start with the sources. We should start with the material which is there. I would implore the Le Corbusier specialist (which I am not) to find out where Le Corbusier visited when he was a child, because the Saline de Chaux and the theater of Besançon are very near to where Le Corbusier grew up. And, of course, the barriers of Paris are still there for all to see.

So I would make a plea: if you do look for influences, do look for the two types — the conscious and the unconscious. And also, be quite happy to admit that what first appears to be influence might actually be convergence.

Stanford Anderson: I think most of what Mrs. Moholy-Nagy said I would happily underline, but the very clean-cut distinction that seemed to grow out of her comments, between futurism and what had gone before (including the Werkbund) is something that I would like to try to hedge just a bit. As you know from what you read, there was this complete rejection of tradition in the futurist statements. Take, for example, the kind of enthusiasm they expressed about the automobile: the business of rushing out of the house, throwing yourself across the hot breast of the automobile, leaping into the car, racing about, driving it into the ditch, climbing out of the sludge, and embracing the car again in an enthusiasm for the machine. There is a romance about the machine.

In contrast to that, a whole decade earlier a very important man whom no one has heard of — the author Otto Julius Bierbaum, a minor lyric poet from southern Germany — undertook to drive a car for someone down to Italy, and all the way down he wrote all kinds of charming notes about lovely things like the transparency of the alabaster windows in medieval churches and how glorious the past was in Italy. When he returned to Germany, he wrote a little book called *Eine empfindsame Reise im Automobil: Von Berlin nach Sorrent und zurück an den Rhein* (A Sentimental Journey by Automobile: From Berlin to Sorrento and Back to the Rhine), which sounds very romantic too. What he says is that someday we'll realize that the automobile is not a thing that is important for its ability to be raced, but it is important because it provides individual mobility for everyone. The later times, I think, have shown that this vision of everyone having an automobile, of everyone having mobility, has much more to do with architecture and planning as it evolved, and perhaps will still evolve in the future, than the image of us throwing ourselves across the hot breast of the machine. So I feel that I'm not really trying to contradict what you were saying, because I sympathize with so much of it, but only trying to say that there still is a great deal in the somewhat more prosaic thought of the Werkbund that may have more importance than the very powerful imagery of futurism.

Moholy-Nagy: First, one word of clarification to Professor Wittkower. As in every field of the sciences and every field of *geisteswissenshaften* (the humanities or social sciences), there are two approaches: pure research and applied research. And where would we be, the applied researchers, without you, the pure researchers? I have not only no objections to but an enormous admiration for pure research, which I personally am not capable of doing. (I just get bored stiff, so I can't do it.) But I have enormous admiration for those of you who give us the enormous field of knowledge from which we then can take our bearings to provide an explanation of what we are doing today. I refuse to believe that pure research in the highest sense in which you have done it in your book on the baroque has not the greatest value, but I feel that if we need to speak about the modern, and modern architectural symposia, it is the model that makes the difference. We are speaking about our own century, and applied research is what I felt was excluded to a certain extent, given the totally uncritical redundancy of some of the material. If we are speaking about the sources of the century or about architecture of the past, I would perfectly agree. But who was speaking about a modern architecture symposium?

The reason I showed the two plans by Garnier and Griffin was that I feel that out of the enormous dramatization of Sant'Elia's highly romantic and at the same time highly futuristic (in the literal sense of the word) formulations came this very clear, applicable integration with life as we had it. These plans are based exactly on the automobile as motion and not as the "hot breast" of the automobile that ends in a ditch. I only wanted to say that if we speak in concepts, which is all that interests me in architectural history, the idea is that the concept of futurism then permeated modern architecture of this century. By the way, I find Bierbaum fantastic: I never knew him from that side, so that is a very interesting thing. But I wanted merely to point out in my reference to futurism that, in contrast to the classical school, its concepts actually led to an actual force that reshaped our architectural environment.

Eckhard Siepmann: I think we could convincingly argue that the dates on this should be changed, that the dates should be 1907 to 1914. I have been quite surprised, indeed, that the historians would elide over the convulsive and mortal phenomenon of World War I and assume that architects were doing nothing during that time. There has been only one mention of Mr. Gropius's experience with the Hussars and then with the Signal Corps. I think it would be extremely important to the development of architecture in the 1920s to know how many architects, how many engineers, were working for example on the design of zeppelins—these light, delicately trussed fabrics of aircraft—and their hangars. For the first time in the history of the world, the architects were brought into the technological production of machinery in the factories, and we've completely avoided this problem. We haven't looked at it in the slightest degree, and yet it's quite evident that after the war this single and violent change occurred. It may well have been because of the fact that they were cut free from the quirks and flourishes of their little houses.

Hitchcock: It is, of course, curious that no one has mentioned the wartime sketches of Erich Mendelsohn: we mentioned them when we were talking about the 1920s, but it's just one of those things that got lost, like a problem that interests me, which is the distribution of the American factory style through the international operations of Kahn's firm. But the whole problem of concrete tended to get neglected.

Joseph M. Shelley: In view of Professor Wittkower's remarks that we should look at others as well, that we should look at what actually happened rather than what we prefer, I would like to suggest that there was a great deal of building that went on in this period that was completely unfashionable, like the Woolworth Building, for example. Quite eminent architects tried to keep the old Pennsylvania Station [*figure 15*] from being pulled down, so evidently it had some value for us today. If we're going to be completely objective, should we confine ourselves to pioneers of the modern movement, or should we observe all of these things that we regard as aberrations now? I can easily conceive of the horror with which a graduate school would proffer a student who proposed investigating, say, the Woolworth Building. I'm sure that he would be discouraged from doing it.

Moholy-Nagy: No, not at all, not at all. I have been assigning it to students for years. I think that it's very important.

Shelley: Well, good for you. One thing that has impressed me at this symposium is that we talk about exactly the same people over and over again. We may not like these other phases, they may have been a dead end, but they were there, and this is something I think we might bear in mind.

Hitchcock: I know that Mr. Kaiser has something brief to add about the Werkbund.

Kenneth H. Kaiser: I would like to challenge the traditional interpretation of Hermann Muthesius's notion of *Typisierung* (type-casting) at the 1914 Werkbund meeting. We often credit Muthesius with believing in 1914 that architecture should aim at standardization or typology, emanating from forms and techniques of the industrial world. We traditionally present as a realization of this theory Gropius's factory at the 1914 exhibition, and the two together are now a vested interest of most historiographical schemes of modern architecture.

In order to hold this view, I believe that we would have somehow to explain away Muthesius's own two buildings at the exhibition and disregard major pavilions there which were, of course, done under his direction. The interior of the Hamburg-America Line by Muthesius is about what we would expect, since we expect nothing revolutionary from him. The exterior of this building, however, challenges our notion of Muthesius's theory. I suggest that at an architectural scale he meant by *Typisierung* a uniform national architectural vocabulary, a formulated style—and one quite different from Gropius's. This facade connects faultlessly at the left with this street of shops by [*inaudible*], who Muthesius had apparently [*inaudible*]. The major building of the exhibition—the culmination of the cross axes—is by Theodore Fischer and also uses these canonical forms, as does Peter Behrens's Festival Hall. A further problem with our traditional view of the exhibition is the rustic village, called "Neues Niederrheinisches Dorf," which was included under the direction of Georg Metzendorf and was received very well in the journals by the Werkbund. If we insist on placing Werkbund architecture as here shown into an evolutionary picture, it would come out as a precursor not of modernism of the 1920s but rather of the double-pronged style, formal and folksy, that Germany used so effectively in the later 1930s.

I suggest, on the contrary, that evolutionary pictures have and may again prevent us from understanding the works at the exhibition. For example, do we yet know what the young Gropius was up to with his grillwork in the courtyard at his factory? That grill did not look inspired by the Machine Age to me.

Or do we know what he was doing with the cabinet he also designed for the 1914 exhibition?

Hitchcock: On the question of Muthesius and the degree of his sympathy for the style that was about to emerge, Julius Posener pointed out to me that when Muthesius died in 1927, his last action was a condemnatory criticism of the *Werkbund Ausstellung* at the Weissenhofsiedlung in Stuttgart [*figure 72*]. This parallels the reaction of one of his own English heroes, Charles Voysey, who likewise was very much shocked when he was told in the 1930s that he was a father of modern architecture. He disowned the child very vigorously. I think that we can easily confuse what sound to us like highly pregnant state-ments — and perhaps as processes of thought *were* pregnant — with the actual production, especially in this period.

There is one name that turns up here that we heard a lot about in the first of these symposia; a man who belongs to this period, which is Paul Scheerbart. Mr. Plazcek, you have the Scheerbart book out on display. I wonder if you would care to say anything about how Scheerbart fits in, or doesn't fit in, during these years.

Plazcek: I'm not especially familiar, actually. The book, called *Glasarchitektur*, is terribly exciting. It goes through the use of glass as walls, on decorative ele-ments.... George [Collins], do you have more?

Moholy-Nagy: I think the publication fits in much more with the area of the futurists than it does the Werkbund. It was a lot of the absurd; a lot of the surreal. The motto of [Bruno Taut's 1920–2] *Frühlicht* book is sort of like a new version of François Rabelais — "laughter is the essence of mankind." And the whole thing exudes an absolutely wild protest against the stuffy professors, the Baurade, the Geheinrade. Just as in Sant'Elia, it suggests a love of the infinite possibility given by glass, given by light, given by the purpose that is not yet specified, that is still totally in flux: this is the whole idea.

Plazcek: *Glasarchitektur* is more sober, really. It is more...well, I won't use "expressionistic"....

Moholy-Nagy: Yes, but you really cannot think about this without thinking about August Macke and Franz Marc and painters like these.

Christian F. Otto: In considering people like Scheerbart and the influence of the expressionist architects, I'm wondering if you don't have to take into seri-ous consideration the caesura that suddenly emerged about the time of the sta-bilization of the mark, because what is published by Taut in his various books and what he actually does later on in the 1920s are two completely different stories. One wonders what is actually going on and what these fantasies mean in relation to his later work.

Collins: Well, we have some students here who might like to contribute a word, if they're not too shy to do so. Mr. Wiedenhoff has been working with Scheerbart's material. Would you care to say something?

[First name unknown] **Wiedenhoff:** Well, I would just comment that in the period we are considering "expressionism" is an important word, because Scheerbart's *Glasarchitektur* was published by Der Sturm, which is the organization under Herwarth Walden in Berlin that was not only exhibited expressionist artists but was also very much in contact with the futurists. Nell Roslund Walden, his divorced wife, has written a book in which she traces the influence of this circle of Der Sturm, this expressionist movement, on architecture.[78]

Hitchcock: Yesterday, about a third of our time was given up to American topics. Today, except for a few brief words about Wright, we have missed this country almost entirely. I wonder if Mr. Jordy has anything to say with regard to America in these years. Even in America, [although] we heard about skyscrapers in the East, and houses in the West, but vast areas of American architecture were left untouched.

William H. Jordy: I don't really have any comments to make specifically on the American developments, but as I thought over the many observations made yesterday and some of the implications of the arguments raised today it seemed to me that an overarching theme of this period is the broad transformation, psychically and intellectually, toward a group aesthetic, toward solidarity, toward an increased social awareness, which makes it possible for the aesthetic of McKim, Mead & White to develop, on one hand, and the aesthetic of Gropius, of the Werkbund, of Behrens's neoclassicism, to develop on the other hand. It seems to me that one of the ironies of the development of modern architecture is that, just as the profession was beginning to produce architects as original in terms of individualism, naturalism, and even revealed structures as their nineteenth-century predecessors, a subtle shift in the intellectual climate deprived them of full realization of their careers: this whole generation of architects who appeared around 1900 led truncated careers. We can think of Sullivan, of the entire California School of architects, of Horta and Mackintosh and Gaudí (except for the fact that he had managed to build a specific project over a long period of time); it seems to me that all of these architects, who worked within the nineteenth-century tradition of modernity were somehow frustrated in this very decade by a profound shift in the intellectual climate.

Hitchcock: Mr. Wittkower implied, although he didn't develop it, the fact that historically, negatives are of significance. When history doesn't move as fast as we think it ought to, or when history stops in its tracks — as in certain respects the more inventive American architecture stopped in its tracks roughly in 1917 — the answer is obviously not to be found in visual documentation....

Wittkower: You mentioned historical negatives just now, and that is a very important problem. We never know when historical negatives become historical positives. We have seen this in our own time all too often. When I grew up in the 1920s, we wanted to do away with the art nouveau. It was not only so disgusting to us when we were young that we felt it should all be destroyed, but we also felt that it was absolutely senseless to do scholarly work on it. I was a student then: now that forty years have gone by, my judgment has settled down and I tend to be more objective. And times have changed, and the historical negative — or many historical negatives — in the period with which we are concerned appear to us now as historical positives. That is, of course, one of the reasons why it would be a mistake to limit ourselves only to ideas which seem to us important at this particular moment. Thirty years from now we may have another symposium, and some of us may be here, and we may have the minutes of this symposium before us. I wonder to what extent the values will have changed.

Moholy-Nagy: I have only one additional remark to Mr. Eckard's very relevant remark that the war did so much. I once made a study of the architects of the Chicago School who had been involved in the Civil War, and it is quite extraordinary how people like William Le Baron Jenney, through their experience in the engineer corps, really shaped the Chicago School and its influence. [*Inaudible*]

Hitchcock: A very curious sidelight of the Civil War is that the work on the cast-iron dome of the U.S. Capitol building was continued on President Lincoln's specific order because he thought it would be good for morale. The thought of using all that metal in the middle of the war for a symbol strikes us in the twentieth century as very curious.

But I think that it is probably also true that there is a negative reaction from war. I have always felt some of the fantasy of the 1919–20 period in Germany was a reaction against World War I. Of course, there was very little building at that point: when building began again, it tended to take a quite different direction. But it seems to me that the flight into the world of fantasy is the negative reaction to the war, whereas Mendelsohn's sketches and—in a certain, more remote sense—Sant'Elia are more positive responses to the war experience.

Paul F. Norton: After this discussion on the importance of the war, I suggest that the thing to do—although rather gloomy—might be to take up for the next symposium the effects of World War I. I've been bothered in my own research recently, on Robert Maillart, by this war interlude because I found out that one of his earliest and most beautiful bridges, done in 1905 or 1906, was not repeated in that quality. There was an intervening period of perhaps almost two decades in which something happened to his aesthetic, and it wasn't until the 1930s that he produced, in my opinion at least, bridges of equal quality in terms of their sheer beauty or their use of concrete. Maybe this war interlude is of very considerable importance and we should study it next.

Placzek: On the possible next topic, I think what George Collins implied in his opening statement, and what was underlined in some other statements, is the importance of problems that go beyond the individual piece of architecture. Everybody is well aware of that. Whether it is the garden city movement or the various cottages and small things put up in groups around cities, or the big urbanistic schemes, or the social housing that comes up in many cities after the war: all this is a group that seems to be well worth considering.

Hitchcock: It's quite obvious that there are broad and major themes that have gotten lost by the fragmentation of our programs. One of these, it seems to me, is city planning. Another one I think that we certainly were not able to do as much as I hoped we might with in this session is the structural and material developments of the period. [*Mr. Hitchcock cites various examples in steel and concrete.*] But whether it would work to give up the idea of a period frame—I mean, even if we did deal with materials, we'd have to have some frame or we'd never get beyond 1850. What do you think, George?

[*Collins suggested repeating the exercise of selecting ten important buildings within a designated period, as Robert A. M. Stern and Philip C. Johnson had done as part of the present symposium. Hitchcock offered some brief reflections on the selections made by Stern and Johnson and then asked Mr. Collins to close the proceedings.*]

Collins: I want to close off just by reading a couple of things into the record; namely, our appreciation as a group here for the financial support of the graduate faculties of Columbia, the School of Architecture, Philip Johnson, and in particular our own department, which took on all the secretarial work (Mrs. Colmeyer, who typed up all those things by which you have been deluged and which you have in your briefcases), and also Mr. Placzek's wife and my own for putting on the parties, along with all the members of the Avery staff. And to Mr. Otto, who has functioned as assistant to Professor Hitchcock, and to all the rest of us for getting through the weekend....

[*Collins extended his thanks to various individuals for their assistance in organizing the symposium.*]

And finally, of course, I want to say thanks again to our indomitable chairman, to whose ruthless and exacting handling of both time and fact and to whose jolly disposition I think we can truly say we owe the success of this symposium.

Dolf, do you want to say anything?

Placzek: Really only one thing: we are terribly flattered, as it has turned out that there is already a great deal of talk about the next symposium, because all of us—our wives, our staff, etc.—were devoutly hoping the last few days that this would be the last one. This now seems to be in doubt too, among other things. Still it's very exhilarating for us that you feel that way, and we are terribly happy to have had you and the symposium here. Thank you.

The meeting is adjourned, sir.

Notes

1. Frank Lloyd Wright, *An Autobiography* (New York: Duell, Sloan and Pierce, 1943), 164.

2. See Henry-Russell Hitchcock, "Frank Lloyd Wright, 1867(?)–1959," *Art News* 58 (May 1959): 25.

3. Henry-Russell Hitchcock, *In the Nature of Materials, 1887–1941: The Buildings of Frank Lloyd Wright* (New York: Duell, Sloan and Pearce, 1942), 61, 67.

4. Wright, *Autobiography*, 113.

5. This phrase also appears in ibid., 109. —Ed.

6. Kaufmann is referring to Edith Farnsworth and her relationship to Mies van der Rohe. —Ed.

7. Ellen Key, *Love and Ethics*, tr. Mamah Bouton Borthwick and Frank Lloyd Wright (Chicago: Ralph Fletcher Seymour Co., 1912), 22, 51, 58, and 13.

8. Lloyd Wright to Linn Cowles, 2 Feb. 1966. Frank Lloyd Wright Collection, Department of Drawings and Archives, Avery Architectural and Fine Arts Library, Columbia University, New York, New York.

9. Ibid. A more complete version of this letter appears in Edgar Kaufmann, "Crisis and Creativity: Frank Lloyd Wright, 1904–1914," *Journal of the Society of Architectural Historians* 25, no. 4 (Dec. 1966): 294–5, a revised and expanded version of Kaufmann's Columbia presentation. —Ed.

10. See H. Allen Brooks, "Frank Lloyd Wright and the Wasmuth Drawings," *Art Bulletin* 48, no. 2 (Jun. 1966): 193–202. Brooks also published "'Chicago School': Metamorphosis of a Term," *Journal of the Society of Architectural Historians* 25, no. 2 (May 1966): 115–8; and, a year earlier, "La Prairie School," *Edilizia moderna* 86 (1965): 65–82. His contribution to the history of modern architecture in the Midwest also includes "Chicago Architecture: Its Debt to the Arts and Crafts," *Journal of the Society of Architectural Historians* 30, no. 4 (Dec. 1971): 312–7; *The Prairie School: Frank Lloyd Wright and His Midwest Contemporaries* (Toronto: University of Toronto Press, 1972); and "The Prairie School in the History of Architecture," *Rassegna* 20, no. 74 (1998): 16–31. —Ed.

11. See Frank Lloyd Wright, "A Fireproof House for $5000; Estimated to Cost that Amount in Chicago, and Designed Especially for *The Journal*," *The Ladies' Home Journal* 20, no. 2 (Jan. 1903): 24. —Ed.

12. For a recounting of the complicated history of Mahony Griffin's design, see David Van Zanten, "The Early Work of Marion Mahony Griffin," *Prairie School Review* 3, no. 2 (1966): 1–2, 5–23, 27. —Ed.

13. See Thomas E. Tallmadge, "The Thirtieth Annual Architectural Exhibit in Chicago," *Western Architect* 25, no. 4 (Apr. 1917): 27.

14. This phrase is taken from the Chicago Architectural Club's description of its Traveling Scholarship; see its *Book of the Annual Exhibition of the Chicago Architectural Club* (Chicago: The Club, 1917). —Ed.

15. The critic was Berta H. Smith. See her "Creating an American Style: Mr. Gill's Distinctive Concrete Houses—The Gospel of Simplicity and Straight Lines," *House and Garden* 26, no. 1 (July 1914): 18. —Ed.

16. Gebhard's 1964 essay "The Bay Tradition in Architecture" (*Art in America* 52 [June 1964]: 60–3) laid the groundwork for much of the discussion of northern California presented here. See also Gebhard's "The Spanish Colonial Revival in Southern California, 1895–1930," *Journal of the Society of Architectural Historians* 26, no. 2 (May 1967): 131–47. —Ed.

17. In introducing the speaker, Henry-Russell Hitchcock made the following comments: "There has been a certain irony to me in sitting here in New York and looking at these houses in the Midwest and on the West Coast. In 1917 I was twelve years old, and I was already sufficiently interested in architecture so that I had developed an admiration for Edwin Lutyens. But, I certainly already knew something—or thought I did—about American architecture, and I would have said firmly that the two great triumphs of American architecture were in New York City. One of these Mr. Stern has recognized: Grand Central Station. The other was, of course, the Woolworth Building. We're now going to hear about what *at the time* impressed the whole world, far more than the buildings that we've been seeing, which interest *us* more. Mr. Weisman will tell us about what happened to the American skyscraper in this particular period of years."

Weisman had completed his dissertation on Rockefeller Center and authored numerous articles on the skyscraper by 1966, including his "New York and the Problem of the First Skyscraper," *Journal of the Society of Architectural Historians* 12, no. 1 (Mar. 1953): 13–21. In the 1970s he would expand the scope of his contribution to skyscraper history: see his "The Chicago School of Architecture: Symposium," *Prairie School Review* 9, nos. 1–2 (1972): [entire issue]; and "A New View of Skyscraper History," in *The Rise of an American Architecture*, ed. Edgar Kaufmann (New York: Praeger, 1970). —Ed.

18. A. C. David, "The New Architecture," *Architectural Record* 28, no. 6 (Dec. 1910): 389–403.

19. In his introduction to the speaker's talk, Henry-Russell Hitchcock remarked, "I…think that this is the first time at one of these sessions that we have had as many as four American papers. However, it is one of the interesting aspects of the period under discussion that American architecture began seriously to influence the outside world. We've remarked on Wright's move to Tokyo and Griffin's move to Australia; now we are going to shift to a European topic, but one that shows some evidence of the influence of American architecture abroad."

Eaton's earlier contributions to the discussion of Scandinavian modern architecture include his 1964 article "Finnish Architecture: Traditions and Development," *Progressive Architecture* 45 (Apr. 1964): 154–[61]. —Ed.

20. See Leonard K. Eaton, "Richardson and Sullivan in Scandinavia," *Progressive Architecture* 47, no. 3 (Mar. 1966): 168–71.

21. Professor Hitchcock has dealt with this building in his article, "Aalto versus Aalto: The Other Finland," *Perspecta* 9/10 (1965): 131–66.

22. Mr. Hitchcock made the following observation, following Eaton's presentation: "The Scandinavian countries, which created a good deal of excitement in the 1920s, are now being looked at from a rather different point of view. One of the surprises, which Mr. Eaton has been documenting, is the definite American influence. I perhaps wouldn't use 'Richardsonian' quite as freely, yet I must say that Sonck's Lutheran Cathedral in Tampere and Telephone Building have a strongly Richardsonian flavor. However, in the Kallio Church, as Mr. Eaton pointed out, while there are rough-faced surfaces, the Richardsonian feeling is fading. Interestingly, it is as if the Scandinavian countries went through phases rather hurriedly in the first decade or so of the twentieth century that in England and America were gone through in the last quarter of the nineteenth century. This is surprising because in the past twenty years, of course, Finland has been a leader rather than a follower. But the vitality of the Finns is evident, especially in contrast to the relatively lesser vitality of the Swedes." See the original transcription of the MAS 1966 proceedings. —Ed.

23. For more on Steiner generally, see Santomasso's dissertation, "Origins and Aims of German Expressionist Architecture: An Essay into the Expressionist Frame of Mind in Germany, Especially as Typified in the Work of Rudolf Steiner," Columbia University, 1973; and his article on Steiner in the *Macmillan Encyclopedia of Architects*, vol. 4, ed. Adolf Placzek (New York: Free

Press, 1982), 123–7. —Ed.

24. Rudolf Steiner, *Der Baugedanke des Goetheanum; Einleitender Vortrag mit Erklärungen zu den Lichtbildern des Goetheanum-Baues, Gehalten in Bern am 29. Juni 1921* (1938, rpt. Stuttgart: Verlag Freies Geistesleben, 1958), 22. For Engl. translation, see Rudolf Steiner, *The Architectural Conception of the Goetheanum: A Lecture given at Berne on 29th June 1921* (New York: Anthroposophic Press, 1938).

25. Rudolf Steiner, *Ways to a New Style in Architecture: Five Lectures by Rudolf Steiner Given during the Building of the First Goetheanum, 1914* (London: Anthroposophical Publishing Company, 1927), 21.

26. Steiner, *Der Baugedanke*, 52.

27. From Steiner's lecture "Art as Seen in the Light of Mystery Wisdom, Lecture Six: Working with Sculptural Architecture I," Dornach, 2 Jan. 1915. See also Rudolf Steiner, *Das Moralische Erleben der Farben und Tonwelt, Plastisch-Architektonisches Bilden* (Dornach: Philosophisch-Anthroposophischer Verlag, 1935).

28. For a similar statement of Steiner's intentions, see Steiner, *The Architectural Conception*, 8. —Ed.

29. Subject matter discussed in this presentation is referenced in Santomasso's subsequent writings, "The Austrian Connection," *Skyline* 1, no. 6 (Mar. 1979): 3; and "Josef Hoffmann's Reliefs at the Beethoven Exhibition of the Vienna Sezession, 1902: Beginnings of Abstraction," *Structurist* 21/22 (1981–2): 25–32. —Ed.

30. The first English translation of Loos's essay appeared in 1966, in Ludwig Münz and Gustav Künstler, *Adolf Loos: Pioneer of Modern Architecture*, tr. Harold Meek (New York: Frederick A. Praeger), 226–31.

31. Fritz Hoeber, *Peter Behrens* (Munich: G. Müller und E. Rentsch, 1913).

32. Henry van de Velde, *Essays* (Leipzig: Insel-Verlag, 1910).

33. H. P. Berlage, *Amerikaansche Reisherinneringen* (Rotterdam: W. L. & J. Brusse, 1913); *Grundlagen & Entwicklung der Architektur: vier Vorträge gehalten im Kunstgewerbe Museum zu Zürich* (Berlin: J. Bard, 1908); and *Beschouwingen over bouwkunst en hare ontwikkeling* (Rotterdam: Brusse, 1911).

34. Although not mentioned during the presentation, the other may have been *L'Architecture Usuelle*, which also appeared in 1908. —Ed.

35. See *Hohe Warte* (Wien: Hohe Warte, 1905–6), vol. 2, 133ff. Sekler wrote on the British influence on Vienna in his article "Mackintosh and Vienna," *Architectural Review* 145 (Dec. 1969): 455–6. Also related to the subject matter of this presentation is Sekler's "Art Nouveau," *Architectural*

Review 149 (Feb. 1971): 75–6.

36. "Möge das licht dieser überragenden gestalt auf unsere kommende baukünstlergeneration fallen!" Adolf Loos, "Architektur" (1909), rpt. in *Trotzdem* (Innsbruck: Brenner Verlag, 1931), 111.

37. See Eduard Sekler, "The Stoclet House by Josef Hoffmann," in *Essays in the History of Architecture, Presented to Rudolf Wittkower*, ed. Douglas Fraser, Howard Hibbard, and Milton J. Lewine (London: Phaidon, 1967), 228–44. —Ed.

38. Quoted by Carl Schorske, in "Schnitzler and Hofmannsthal," *Wort und Wahrheit* XVII (May 1962): 378.

39. H. P. Berlage, *De ontwikkeling der moderne bouwkunst in Holland* (Amsterdam: Maatschappij voor Goede en Goedkoope, 1925).

40. Brown wrote extensively on Rietveld. In addition to his full-length monograph, *The Work of G. Rietveld, Architect* (Utrecht: A. W. Bruna, 1958), he also contributed "Rietveld's Egocentric Vision," *Journal of the Society of Architectural Historians* 24, no. 4 (Dec. 1965): 292–6; and "The Life and Work of Gerrit Thomas Rietveld, 1888–1964." *Bauen und Wohnen* 19 (Nov. 1965): [entire issue]. —Ed.

41. Ralph Waldo Emerson, *The Complete Works of Ralph Waldo Emerson*, vol. 7, *Society and Solitude* (Boston, New York: Houghton Mifflin, 1903–4), ch. VII, "Works and Days," 180. Berlage quotes this in English in *Amerikaansche Reisherinneringen*, 5.

42. After visiting the Larkin building, Berlage writes: "Ik ging te minste vandaar in de overtuiging een echt modern werk te hebben gezien, met achting voor den meester, die iets maakte, dat voor zoover mij bekend, in Europa zijns gelijke zoekt." H. P. Berlage, *Amerikaansche Reisherinneringen*, 44. —Ed.

43. "More than any other work, it represents in his career what *Les Demoiselles d'Avignon* represents for Picasso." Robert Welsh, *Piet Mondrian: 1872–1944* (Toronto: Art Gallery of Toronto, 1966), 106.

44. M. H. J. Schoenmaekers, *Het nieuwe wereldbeeld* (Bussim: C. A. J. van Dishoeck, 1915), and M. H. J. Schoenmaekers, *Beginselen der beeldende wiskunde* (Bussim: C. A. J. van Dishoeck, 1916).

45. G. E. Kidder-Smith, *The New Architecture of Europe* (Cleveland: World Pub. Co., 1961), 25.

46. Dudok was involved in the town hall project beginning in 1915, with the bulk of the final design happening between 1922 and 1924. Construction took place from 1928 to 1931. See Herman van Bergeijk, *Town Hall Hilversum: W. M. Dudok* (Inmerc: V+K Publishing, 1995). —Ed.

47. Geoffrey Scott, *The Architecture of Humanism: A Study in the History of Taste*

(New York: Charles Scribner's Sons, 1924), 168–90.

48. Alfred Messel, Wertheim Department Store of 1896.

49. See Hermann Muthesius, "Die Veredelung der gewerblichen Arbeit im Zusammenwirken von Kunst, Industrie und Handwerk," quoted in *Hermann Muthesius im Werkbund-Archive*, ed. Eckhard Siepmann (Berlin: Werkbund-Archiv, 1990); as partially cited in John Maciuika, *Before the Bauhaus* (Cambridge: Cambridge University Press, 2005), 168. —Ed.

50. The Jahrhunderthalle in Breslau was in fact designed by Max Berg; Poelzig was involved in designing ancillary structures as well as exhibits at Breslau for the centennial of Napoleon's 1893 defeat. See Kathleen James-Chakraborty, *German Architecture for a Mass Audience* (New York: Routledge, 2000), 21–31. —Ed.

51. "[I]ndividualistischen Verschiedenheiten der Einzelwerte." Hermann Muthesius, "Die Werkbundarbeit der Zukunst," in *Die Werkbund: Arbeit der Zukunst* (Jena: Verlegt bei E. Diederichs, 1914), 42.

52. "Nur mit der Typisierung die als das Ergebnis einer heilsamen Konzentration aufzufassen ist, kann wieder ein allgemein geltender, sicherer Geschmack Eingang finden." Hermann Muthesius, "Leitsäbe zum Vortrag von Hermann Muthesius," in *Die Werkbund*, 32.

53. "Solange es noch Künstler im Werkbunde geben wird und solange diese noch einen Einfluß auf dessen Geschicke haben werden, werden sie gegen jeden Vorschlag eines Kanons oder einer Typisierung protestieren." Henry van de Velde, "Gegenleitsäbe," in *Die Werkbund*, 49.

54. This lecture was based on a part of the author's Columbia University dissertation, completed in 1968. Anderson continued to research and publish actively on Behrens throughout his career, culminating in the book *Peter Behrens and a New Architecture for the Twentieth Century* (Cambridge, Mass.: MIT Press, 2000). For material directly related to the subject matter of his 1966 MAS presentation, see Anderson's "Behrens' Changing Concept," *Architectural Design* 39, no. 2 (Feb. 1969): 72–8; "Modern Architecture and Industry: Peter Behrens and the Cultural Policy of Historical Determinism," *Oppositions* 11 (Winter 1977): 52–71; "Modern Architecture and Industry: Peter Behrens, the AEG, and Industrial Design," *Oppositions* 21 (Summer 1980): 78–97; and "Modern Architecture and Industry: Peter Behrens and the AEG Factories," *Oppositions* 23 (Winter 1981): 52–83. —Ed.

55. See August Schmarsow, *Das Wesen*

der architektonischen Schöpfung (Leipzig: Hiersemann, 1894); and Alois Riegl, Stilfragen: Grundlegungen zu einer Geschichte der Ornamentik (Berlin: Georg Siemens, 1893), and Spätrömische Kunstindustrie (1901, rpt. Darmstadt: Wissenschaftliche Buchgesellschaft, 1973).

56. Quoted in Harry Graf Kessler, Walther Rathenau (Berlin: Klemm, 1928), 107.

57. Walther Rathenau, In Days to Come (New York: Knopf, 1921), 44.

58. Ibid.

59. Carl Widmer, "Handwerk und Maschinenarbeit," Kunstgewerbeblatt, n.s. 20 (Dec. 1908): 49–51.

60. Peter Behrens, "Kunst und Technik," Elektrotechnische Zeitschrift 31, no. 22 (2 June 1910), 555.

61. Wilhelm Niemeyer, "Peter Behrens und die Raumästhetik seiner Kunst," Dekorative Kunst 10, no. 4 (Jan. 1907): 141ff.

62. By 1966 Fitch had published extensively on Gropius: see his monograph Walter Gropius (New York: Braziller, 1960), and the contemporaneous essay "Three Levers of Walter Gropius," Architectural Forum 112 (May 1960): 128–33. A year after the symposia, Fitch's essay "Utopia Revisited: The Bauhaus at Dessau Forty Years On" appeared in the Architectural Review 141 (Feb. 1967): 97–9. —Ed.

63. Walter Gropius, "Gropius at Twenty-Six," Architectural Review 130 (July 1961): 49–51.

64. Nikolaus Pevsner, "Gropius and Van de Velde," Architectural Review 133 (Mar. 1963): 165–8.

65. The Garden City Association later became the Garden Cities and Town Planning Association and is currently known as the Town and Country Planning Association. —Ed.

66. George Collins published a number of items on modern city planning a year prior to this MAS appearance: Camillo Sitte and the Birth of Modern City Planning (London: Phaidon, 1965); "The Humanistic City of Camillo Sitte," Architects' Yearbook 11 (1965): 99–103; and "The Linear City," Architects' Yearbook 11 (1965): 204–17. His essay "Linear Planning" appeared in the journal Forum XX, no. 5 (1968). —Ed.

67. This "tragic week," from July 25 to August 2, 1909, was marked by a series of bloody confrontations between the army and the working classes of Barcelona and other Catalan cities, caused by the prime minister's calling up of reserve troops to be sent as reinforcements for Spain's colonial activities in Morocco. The violence was largely incited by anarchists, communists, and republicans who opposed the government's militaristic and colonialist policies. The revolt was finally crushed by government troops

with much brutality. —Ed.

68. Thomas Howarth was not scheduled to present a paper but was asked to speak by Mr. Hitchcock. At the conclusion of David Mackay's talk, he remarked: "Another country that was totally neglected, except for references to its influence elsewhere, was Great Britain. But also included in the exhibition upstairs was the later end wing of the Glasgow School of Art. By a happy coincidence, while Mr. Mackay was speaking, there came into the room the most perfect person to speak to us briefly on the interesting problem of Mackintosh in these—for him, I fear, fallow—years 1907–17." Howarth would publish Charles Rennie Mackintosh and the Modern Movement (London: Routledge Kegan & Paul) in 1977. —Ed.

69. For a full although different translation of Sant'Elia's "Messagio," see Esther da Costa Meyer, The Work of Antonio Sant'Elia: Retreat into the Future (New Haven: Yale University Press, 1995), 211–2. Moholy-Nagy's source may have been Giovanni Bernasconi's "Il messaggio di Antonio Sant'Elia del 20 maggio 1914," Revista Tecnica della Svizzera Italiana (July 1956), 145–52, which da Costa Meyer notes was the first republication of the "Messagio," as distinguished from the more commonly cited "Manifesto of Futurist Architecture," a point also made by Moholy-Nagy. —Ed.

70. See Hitchcock's "Chairman's Memorandum," MAS 1966, 229.

71. "La Maison suisse," Etrennes Helvétiques, Almanach Illustré (Dijon, La Chaux-de-Fonds, and Paris: n.p., 1914), 33–9.

72. For a more recent English translation, see Le Corbusier, The Decorative Art of Today, tr. James I. Dunnett (London: The Architectural Press, 1987), 213. —Ed.

73. Le Corbusier, Creation is a Patient Search, tr. James Palmes (New York: Praeger, 1960), 45.

74. "Dans une lettre illustrée de croquis, des themes architecturaux lui ètaient soumis, en rupture des traditions esthètiques et proposant des éléments d'un style de béton armé, de nouvelles dispositions, des libertés nouvelles et une attitude foncièrement neuve." Le Corbusier and Pierre Jeanneret, Oeuvre complète de 1910-1929, third ed. (Zurich: Editions Dr. H. Girsberger, 1943), 27.

75. Ibid., 31.

76. "Par cette maison, on tournait le dos aux conceptions architecturales des écoles académisantes comme aussi des 'modernes.'" Ibid.

77. See Otto Antonia Graf, Otto Wagner: Das Werk des Architekten, 1841-1918 (Vienna: Historisches Museum, 1963).

78. Nell Walden and Lothar Schreyer,

Der Sturm: Ein Erinnerungsbuch an Herwarth Walden und die Künstler aus dem Sturmkreis (Baden-Baden: Woldemar Klein Verlag, 1954).

Index

Contributors

Rosemarie Haag Bletter

An expert on twentieth-century architecture, Rosemarie Haag Bletter is well known for her work on German expressionism, art deco, and the modern skyscraper typology. Professor Emerita at the Graduate Center of the City University of New York, the architectural historian and critic has also taught at Yale, Columbia, and the Institute of Fine Arts at New York University. She has also curated numerous exhibitions and created, with Martin Filler, a series of documentary films on contemporary architects. As a doctoral student at Columbia she attended the 1966 MAS; like that event, her scholarship has pushed canonical boundaries to create a more inclusive, nuanced understanding of modern architecture. Among her publications are "The Interpretation of the Glass Dream: Expressionist Architecture and the History of the Crystal Metaphor," *Journal of the Society of Architectural Historians* (1981); "Transformations of the American Vernacular," in *Venturi, Rauch & Scott Brown: A Generation of Architecture* (1984); and *Adolf Behne: The Modern Functional Building* (1996).

Joan Ockman

The architectural historian and educator Joan Ockman was a member of the faculty of the Columbia University Graduate School of Architecture, Planning and Preservation for more than two decades, serving as director of the university's Temple Hoyne Buell Center for the Study of American Architecture from 1994 to 2008. Currently a distinguished senior fellow at the University of Pennsylvania School of Design, she has also taught at Harvard, Yale, Cornell, Cooper Union, and the Berlage Institute in the Netherlands. Ockman began her career at the Institute for Architecture and Urban Studies, where she was associate editor of the journal *Oppositions* and responsible for the Oppositions Books series. A prolific writer, her many essays and edited volumes critically assess the disciplinary and institutional constructs that influence architecture and its historiography. Her publications include the seminal *Architecture Culture: 1943–1968* (1993) and, most recently, *Architecture School: Three Centuries of Educating Architects in North America* (2012).

Nancy Eklund Later

Trained as an architectural historian at the University of Virginia, Nancy Eklund Later is an editor specializing in books on architecture and the built environment. She has assisted in the creation of more than one hundred volumes. She lives with her husband and daughter in New York City.